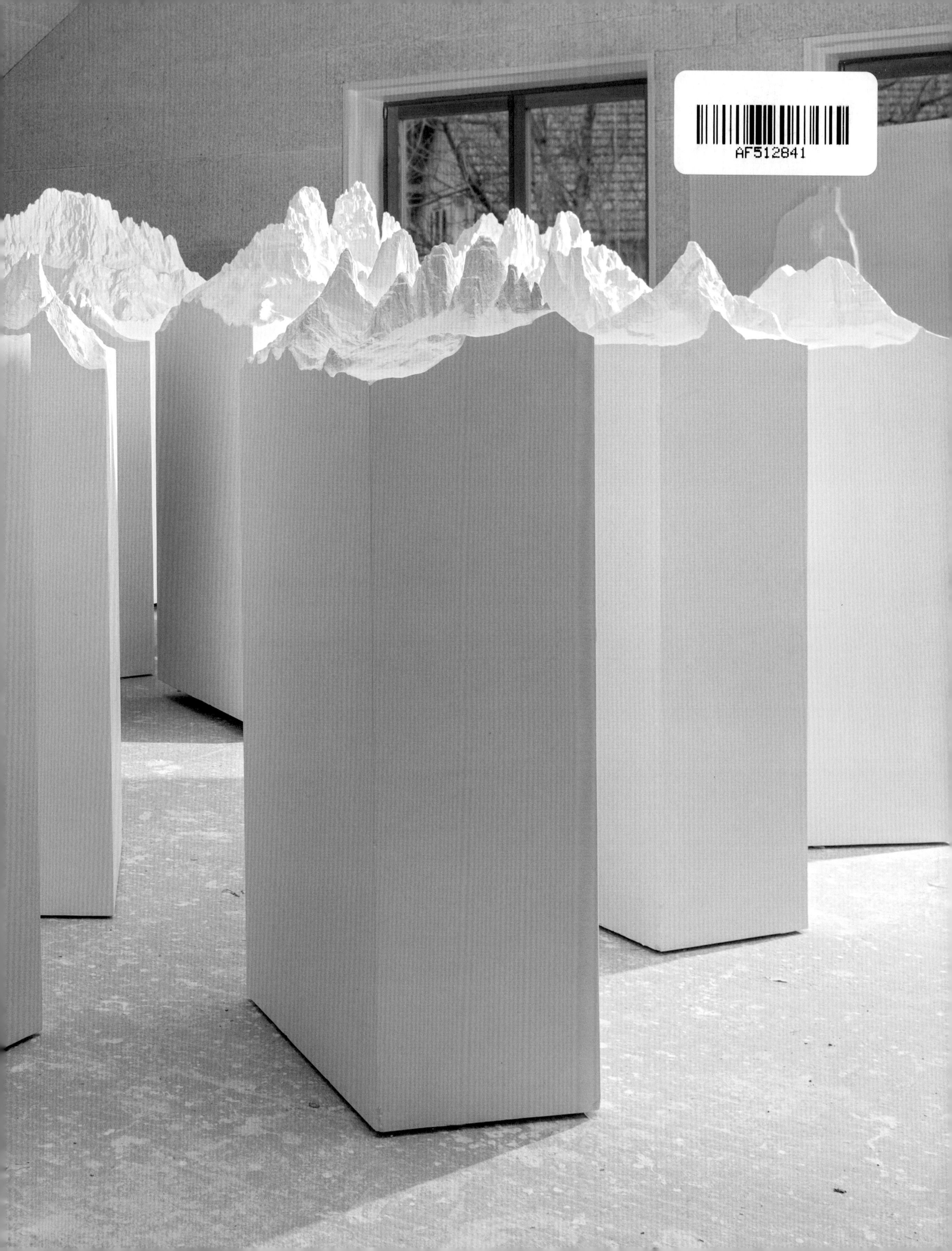

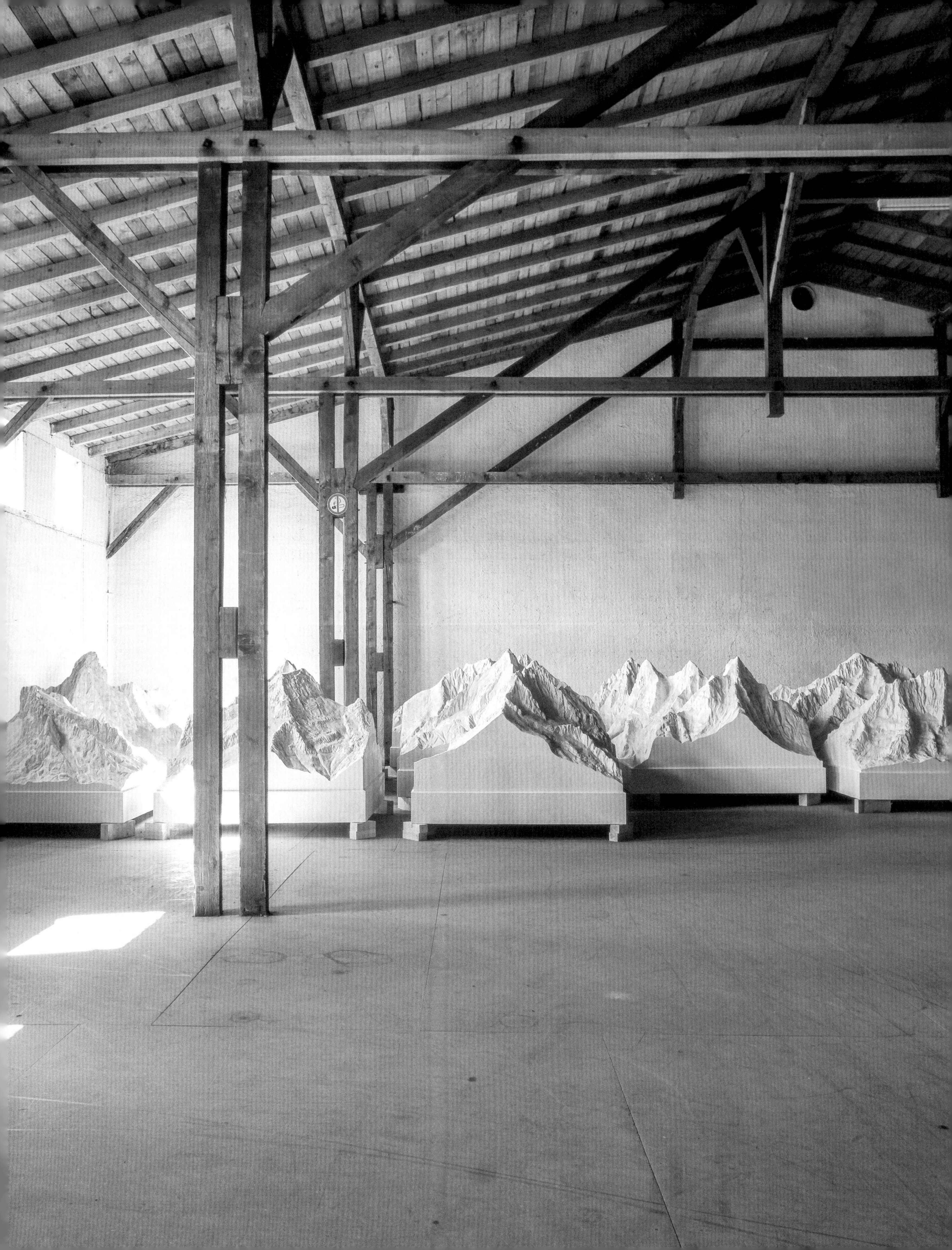

Stephan Huber Gran Paradiso

Herausgegeben von
Edited by
Petra Giloy-Hirtz

HIRMER

Poetik der Berge The Poetics of Mountains

Petra Giloy-Hirtz

Inmitten der Stadt mit einem Berg von Stephan Huber zu leben, wie ist das? Mit einem Berg, der weiß aus der weiß getünchten Wand der Wohnung ragt: das Modell als Fragment eines wirklichen Berges, ein Kranz, zerklüftet, nicht Abguss oder Scan, sondern geformt von der Hand des Künstlers. Bei allem Artifiziellen holt er die Erinnerung an den anderen Ort hervor, an das wirkliche Gebirge, weckt er Sehnsucht und die Lust nach draußen. Seine Betrachtung löst eine eigentümliche Stimmung aus, eine Träumerei im Alltag, die den Träumer hinaus in eine andere Welt versetzt, die das Merkmal einer Unendlichkeit trägt, wie Gaston Bachelard es in seiner *Poetik des Raumes* (1957) beschreibt. Fern von den Unermesslichkeiten „können wir durch die einfache Erinnerung, meditierend, in uns die Nachklänge dieser Kontemplation der Größe erneuern".

Der Berg, für Stephan Huber die „unhinterfragbare, perfekte, ideale Skulptur", erhebt sich dominant im gesamten Œuvre des Künstlers in einer Fülle seiner Erscheinungsformen, einer Vielzahl von Medien und Materialien. Von der Postkarte zum Buch, dem frühen *Roten Bergbuch* (1979) oder dem *Kletterbuch* (1980), von kleinen Objekten zu raumfüllenden Installationen; als Siebdruck auf Marmor, Siebdruck auf Glas, als Leuchtkasten oder die Konturen der Gipfel in Neonlinien auf die Wand gebracht. Passwege, Bergkränze, Zeichnungen auf Landkarten (ab 1998) und Spiel mit historischen Fotografien legendärer Expeditionen. Berge in jedweder Form und Dimension, erfunden oder in idealisierter Weise der topografischen Realität nachgeformt, verschmolzen mit dem Sockel, gekippt im Raum oder vertikal an der Wand, an Seilen von der Decke hängend. Stephan Huber hat die Berge aus den Alpen in den öffentlichen Raum des Flachlandes versetzt. Er hat sie riesig ins Regal gestellt, sechsstöckig, in den künstlichen See vor der Messe München (*Grand Paradiso*, 1997), und über Stockwerke ihr Schmelzwasser von den Gipfeln hinabstürzen lassen (*Die Alpen*, 1992, am Flughafen München). Er holt sie ins Haus wie Einbauten (*Saussures Herz*, 2001) oder formt sie als Landschaft wie ein Bühnenbild (*Shining*, 2001).

What is it like to live in the middle of the city with a mountain by Stephan Huber? With a mountain that rises in white from a wall painted in white: the model of a fragment of a real mountain, a crown, jagged, not a cast or a scan, but formed by the artist's own hands? In spite of its artificiality, he evokes the memory of another place, of the real mountain, arouses desire and the longing to go outside. Looking at it triggers a strange mood, causes a daydream that transports the dreamer to another world, one characterised by infinity, such as Gaston Bachelard describes in his *Poetics of Space (La poétique de l'espace*, 1957). Far from the immensities, 'merely through memory, we can recapture, by means of meditation, the resonances of this contemplation of grandeur.'

The mountain, for Stephan Huber the 'indisputable, perfect, ideal sculpture', emerges dominantly from the artist's entire oeuvre in an abundance of forms and in a variety of media and materials. From the postcard to the book, the early *Rotes Bergbuch* (Red Mountain Book, 1979) or the *Kletterbuch* (Climbing Book, 1980); from small object to room-filling installation; from silkscreen on marble, on glass, as a lightbox, to the outline of the summits inscribed in neon lines on the wall. Mountain passes, ridges, drawings on maps (from 1998 on), and the play with historical photographs of legendary expeditions. Mountains in every form and dimension, invented or modelled on topographical reality in idealised appearance, fused with the pedestal, tilted in the space or vertical on the wall, or hung by ropes from the ceiling. Stephan Huber has transported the mountains from the Alps to the public space of the lowlands. He has placed them, a giant six storeys high, on shelves; set them in the artificial lake in front of the Munich Trade Fair complex (*Gran Paradiso*, 1997); and let the snowmelt cascade from the peaks over storeys (*Die Alpen*, The Alps, 1992, at Munich airport). He has built them into the house (*Saussures Herz*, Saussure's Heart, 2001) or shaped them into a landscape as stage scenery (*Shining*, 2001). He presents them in blazing white light or dramatically in darkness, whether in elegant secular rooms or in a sacred space, in cool

Er inszeniert sie in gleißend hellem Licht oder dramatisch im Dunkel, ob in elegant profanen Sälen oder im sakralen Raum, in kühler Perfektion oder Unordnung und Chaos der Umgebung wie im Arsenale in Venedig.

Eine solche Obsession, die immer neue und aufregende Formen gebiert, sie hat ihre Wurzel offenkundig in Kindheitserfahrungen. Aufwachsen im Westallgäu, „immer die Wand vor dir", 150 Kilometer Berge, Weiß von Ende Oktober bis Ende April, wie eine „stumme Decke" über alles. Eine Welle aus Schnee, die alle Geräusche verstummen lässt; die Welt im Winter: Gefangenschaft. Und dennoch, lieber die Berge als Begrenzung im Süden als im Norden die Öde. Die Mutter nimmt den Jungen mit, auf Fellen unterwegs schon im Alter von fünf Jahren, er wird eingeweiht in die Schneewelt, die da womöglich ein wenig von ihrer Monotonie und Langeweile verliert. Eine Gegenwelt aber tut sich dem Kind auf in der Literatur des Großvaters. Die ganze Welt war hier Sommer, bunt: Stiche vom Amazonas, Walt Disneys *Die Wüste lebt*, der Atlas, topografische Karten ... Sein Elternhaus hat Stephan Huber in späteren Arbeiten in die Schneewelt versetzt, offenkundig als einer Metapher der Kälte (*Family Affairs*, 2016). Er selbst wird vom „Allgäuer Schneemenschen" mit 18 Jahren zum Städter, geht nach New York, nach Paris, wird zum urbanen Menschen und feiert dies als Befreiung. Wenn man ihn heute besucht, dann findet man Stephan Huber im Allgäu wieder, zumindest sein Studio, eine alte Mühle. Ein Ort von unfassbarer Schönheit und Faszination. Nichts scheint sich da zwischen Haus und Bergketten zu schieben, kein Wald, kein Dorf: eine weite Ebene – und dann ...

Stephan Huber stellt in vielen seiner Arbeiten die Welt auf den Kopf, indem er Maßstäbe verändert, Miniatur und Monumentales verschränkt, oben und unten vertauscht und so Gesetzmäßigkeiten außer Kraft setzt. Der alltäglichen Lebenswelt entliehene Objekte wie Hut, Werkzeugkasten oder Schubkarre enthebt er zum Staunen der Betrachtenden – durchaus auch mit Witz

perfection or in the disorder and chaos of the surroundings, as in the Arsenale in Venice.

Such an obsession, constantly generating new and exciting forms, apparently has its roots in childhood experiences. Raised in the West Allgäu region of Bavaria, 'always with the wall in front of you', 150 kilometres of mountains, white from the end of October to the end of April, covering everything like a 'mute blanket'. A wave of snow that silenced all noise; the world in winter: imprisonment. Yet, better the mountains as a barrier to the south than the barrenness to the north. When he was only five years old, his mother took him on fur-covered skis, initiating him into the world of snow, which perhaps lost a little of its monotony and boredom there. An alternative world, however, opened up for the child in his grandfather's books. The entire world here was summer, filled with colour: prints of the Amazon, Walt Disney's *The Living Desert*, the atlas, topographical maps... Stephan Huber moved his parents' house to the world of snow in later works, apparently a metaphor for coldness (*Family Affairs*, 2016). He himself turned from being an 'Allgäuer snowman' into a city person when he was eighteen, moved to New York, to Paris, became an urbanite and celebrated this as a liberation. When you visit him today, you will find Stephan Huber in the Allgäu once more, at least his studio in a former mill. A place of incredible beauty and fascination. Nothing seems to exist between the house and the mountain range, no forest, no village: a broad plain – and then...

In many of his works, Stephan Huber turns the world upside down, by altering dimensions, interweaving the miniature and the monumental, switching up and down, thus annulling regularities. Objects taken from an everyday lifeworld such as a hat, a toolbox, or a wheelbarrow are stripped – often with wit and humour – of their banality and familiarity in foreign contexts, amazing observers. Oak floorboards on the ceiling, a chandelier on the floor, hanging walls, stars that plunge from the sky. These surreal inventions in a

und Humor – in fremden Kontexten ihrer Banalität und Vertrautheit: Eichenparkett an der Decke, Kronleuchter am Boden, hängende Wände, vom Firmament stürzende Gestirne. Es sind surreale Interventionen in eine vermeintliche Normalität, die Kunst in das soziale Ganze einbinden will – im utopischen Vertrauen in deren Wirkungsmöglichkeiten.

Und doch zeigt sich nichts mit solch barocker Wucht in seinem Werk wie der Berg, für Stephan Huber der „Archetyp von Pathosform". Zentrum der Erde, Weltachse, *imago mundi*, Schnittstelle zwischen Himmel und Erde, Pforte der Götter, Symbol des Aufstiegs und des Übergangs, so lehrt es die Symbolforschung: Das Gebirge ist Zeichen der Wiedervereinigung, das erste und heiligste Heiligtum, der Archetypus aller Tempel. Deshalb sind frühe Tempel als zentraler, mehrstufiger Berg gebaut wie die asiatische Stupa, der Tempel ist dem Berg gleichgestellt. Wie viele Kirchen sind auf dem Berg erbaut, um dem Himmel näher zu sein! Bei Stephan Huber ziehen die Berge in den Tempel ein. Naturform wird hier zur Kunstform ohne große Abstraktion: *Weisshorn, Civetta, Sassolungo*. Nur um das „Modell" des Weltenschöpfers an Pathos und Dramatik zu übertreffen, ist die Vertikale verdeutlicht und die Proportion nach oben zum Gipfel hin überhöht. Vier Berge hintereinander – der vierte ist ein Fantasiestück, frei aus der Erinnerung nach dem Film *Unheimliche Begegnung der dritten Art* (1977) von Steven Spielberg –, sie bilden ein spektakuläres Kraftzentrum im Mittelschiff der Kirche Heilig-Geist in Landshut im Kontext der Ausstellung *Schöpfung* (1999). Eine Augenweide und emotionale Erfahrung: Kirche und Berg, Heilig-Geist und Alpen, nach oben strebende Pfeiler, dramatisierte Gipfel und darüber das hohe Netzgewölbe wie ein Himmelszelt – die Installation zeigt Stephan Hubers ganze Lust an effektvollem Schauspiel und Hintergründigkeit.

Gott als Berg denken, welch ein Titel!

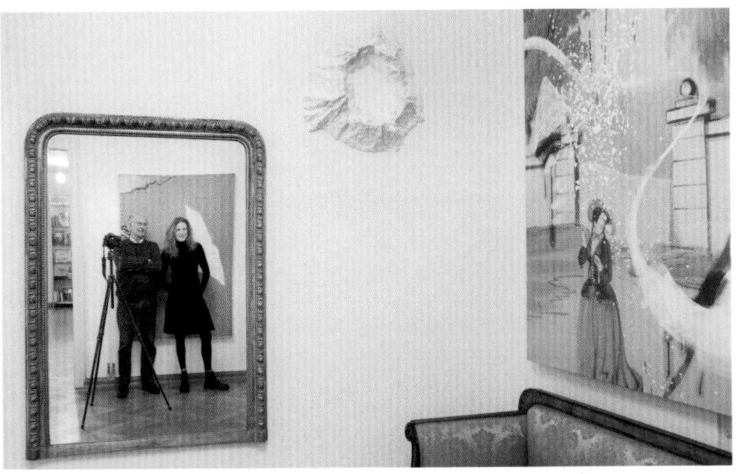

Blick auf die Wand mit *SL1*;
im Spiegel: Petra Giloy-Hirtz
und Stephan Huber
View of the wall with *SL 1*;
in the mirror: Petra Giloy-Hirtz
and Stephan Huber

supposed normality aim to integrate art in the social totality... in the utopian trust in their capacities of impact.

Yet nothing else appears with such Baroque fury in his work as the mountain, for Stephan Huber the 'archetype of the pathos form'. Centre of the earth, axis of the world, *imago mundi*, interface between sky and earth, gate of the gods, symbol of ascension and transition, as the lore of symbols teaches us: mountains are the sign of reunification, the first and holiest of holies, the archetype of all temples. For this reason, early temples were constructed as central, multi-stepped mountains, such as the Asian *stupa*; the temple is equated with the mountain. So many churches have been erected on top of a mountain – to be closer to heaven! Stephan Huber moves the mountains into the temple. Natural form becomes an art form, without great abstraction: Weißhorn, Civetta, Sassolungo. The vertical aspect is emphasised and the proportions towards the peak exaggerated, only to surpass the 'model' of the Creator of the world in pathos and drama. Four mountains behind one another – the fourth a fantasy mountain, created from memory from Steven Spielberg's film *Close Encounters of the Third Kind* (1977). They formed a spectacular centre of power in the nave of the Heilig-Geist-Kirche in Landshut during the exhibition *Schöpfung* (Creation, 1999). A feast for the eyes and an emotional experience: church and mountain, holy spirit and Alps, pillars that strive upwards, dramatic peaks, and above them the ribbed vaulting like the firmament – the installation displays Stephan Huber's pleasure in striking theatrics and subtleness.

Think of God as a Mountain, what a title!

Die Alpen
1992
Flughafen München / Munich Airport

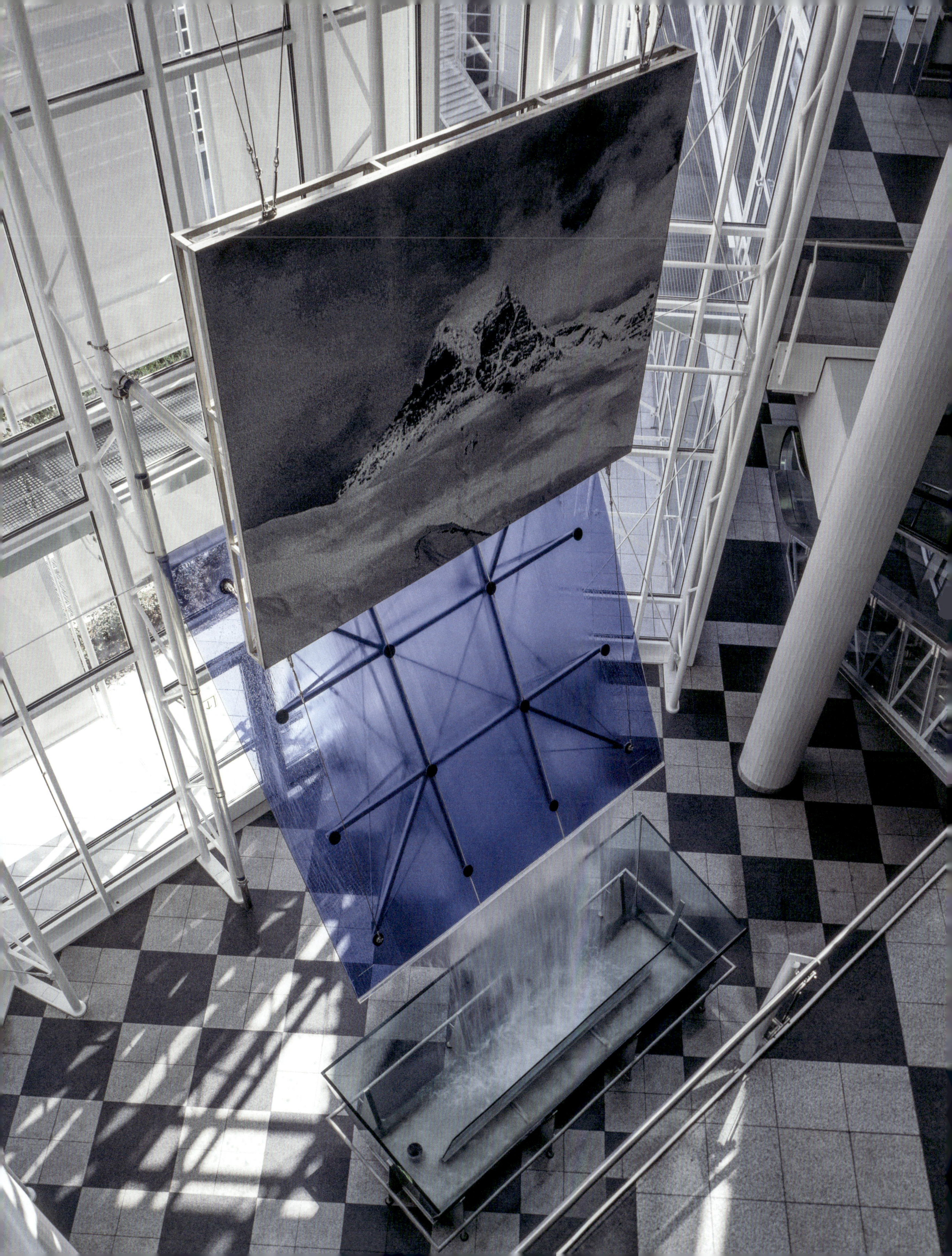

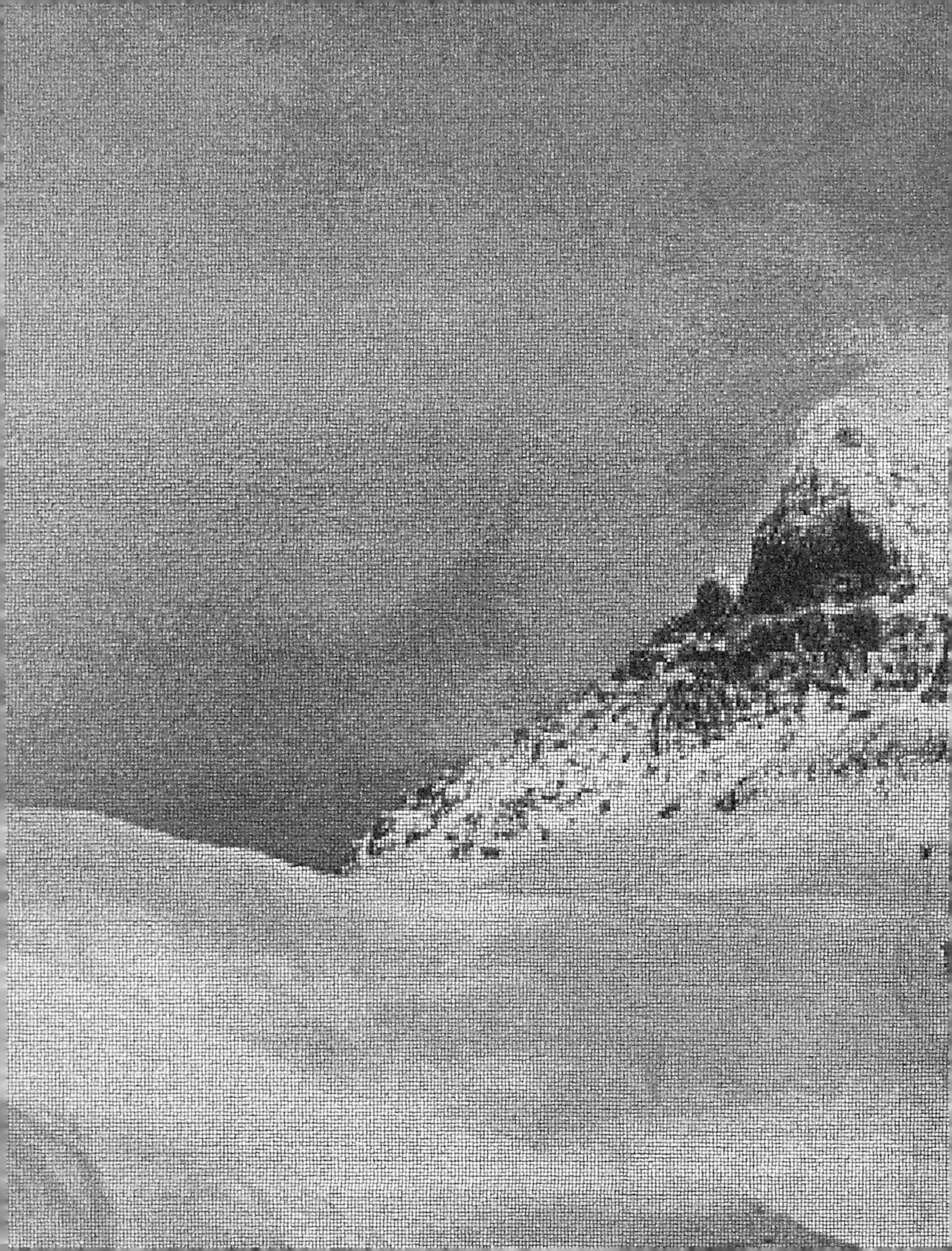

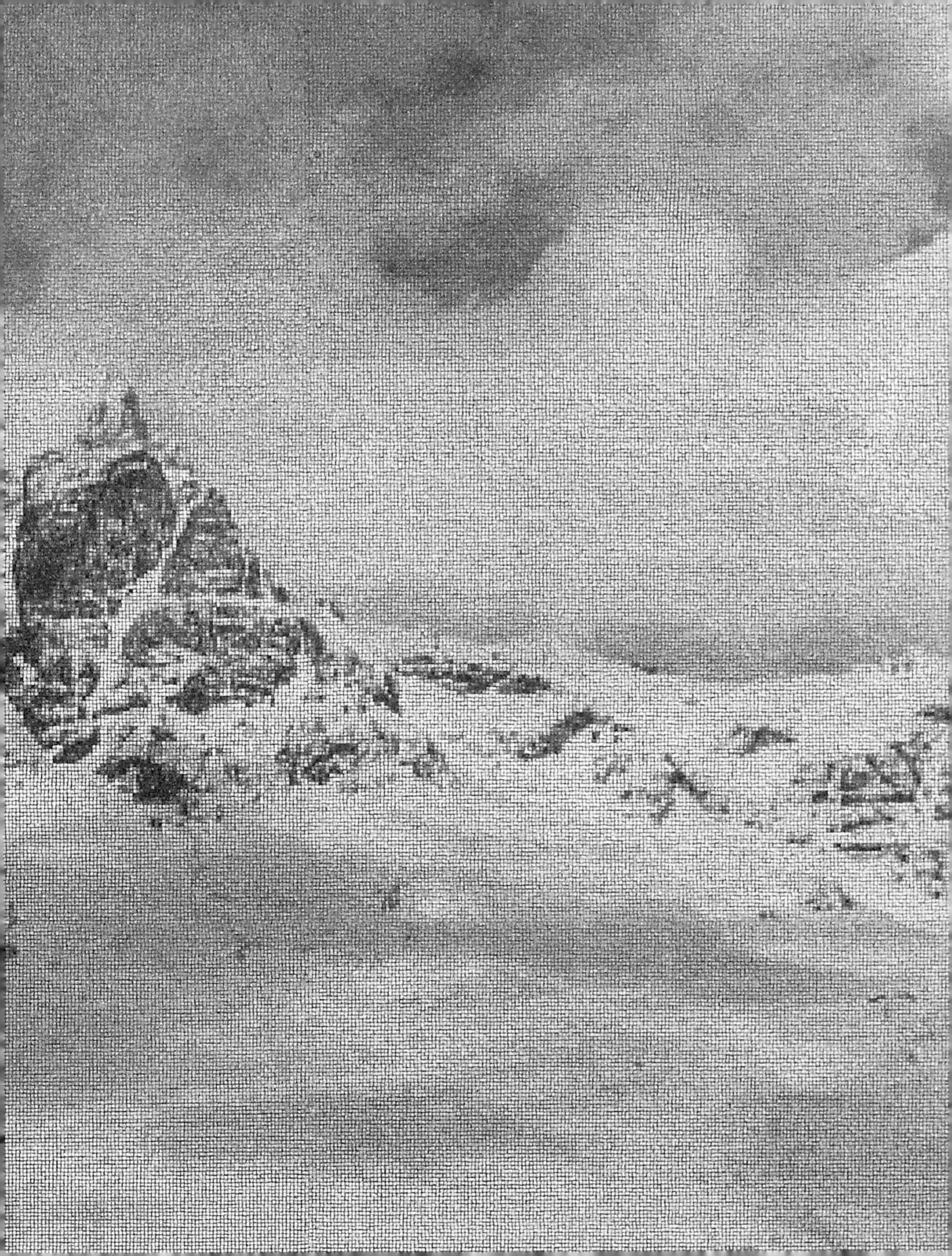

Die Wahrheit bin ich
1994
Haus der Kunst, München / Munich

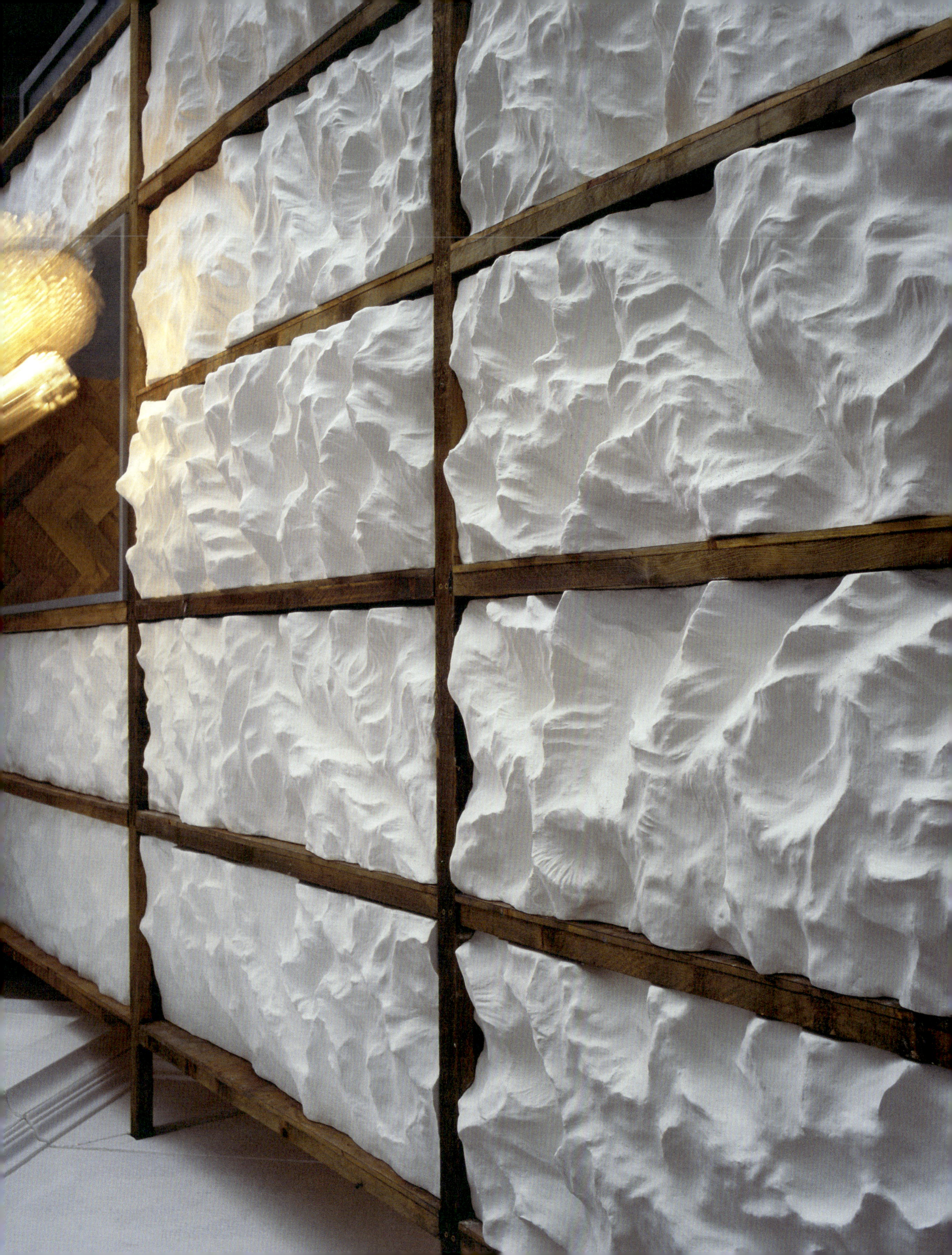

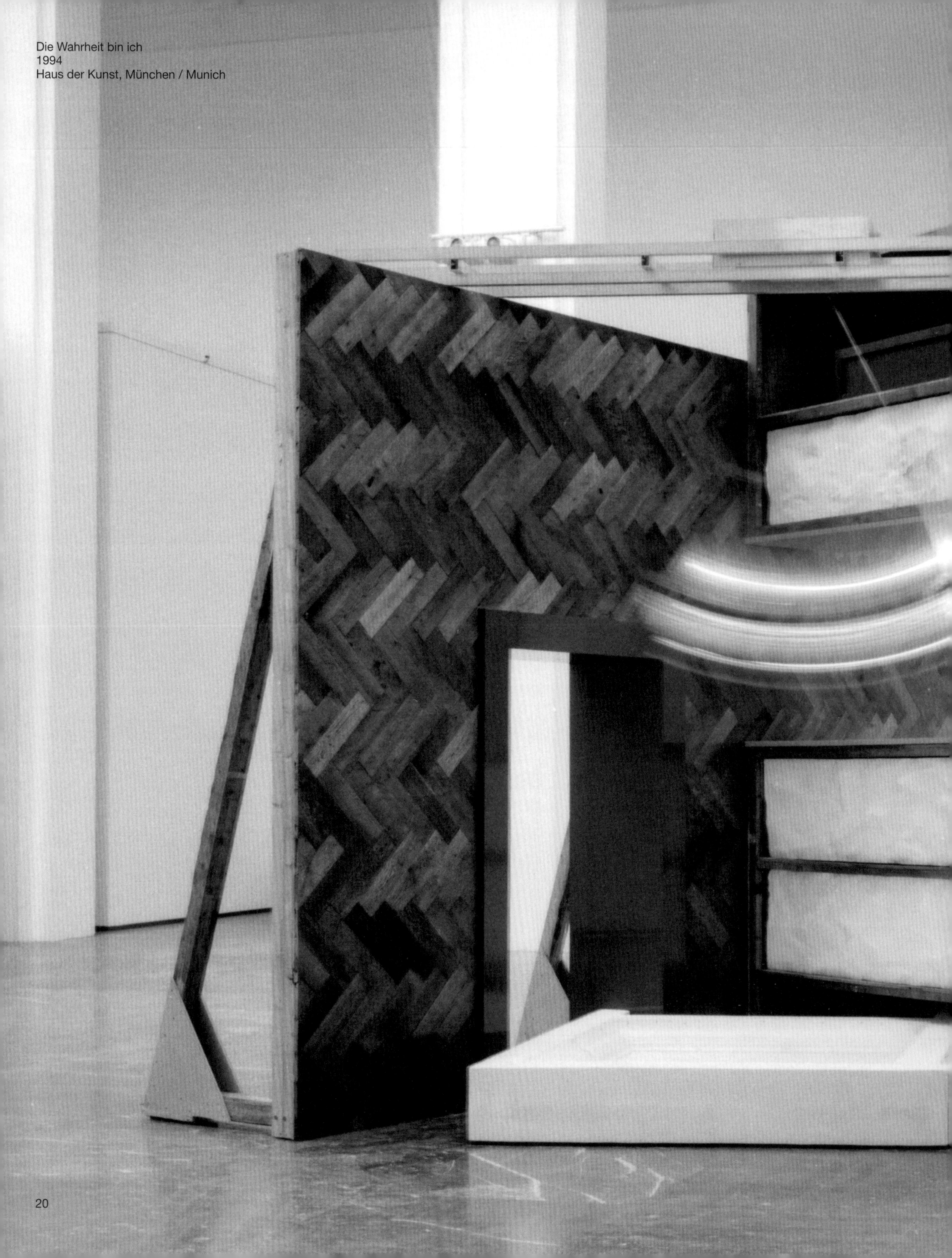

Die Wahrheit bin ich
1994
Haus der Kunst, München / Munich

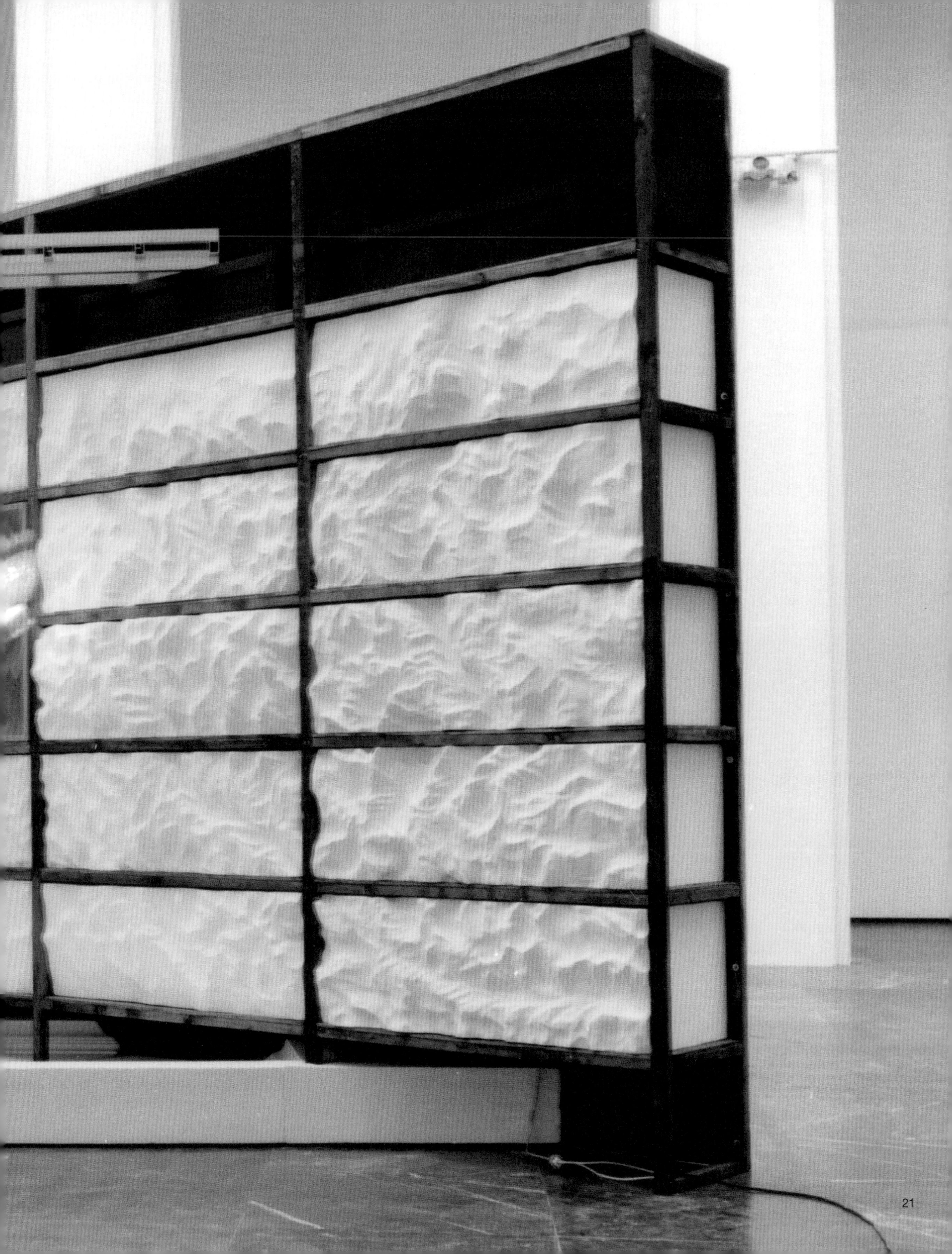

Die Wahrheit bin ich
1994
Haus der Kunst, München / Munich

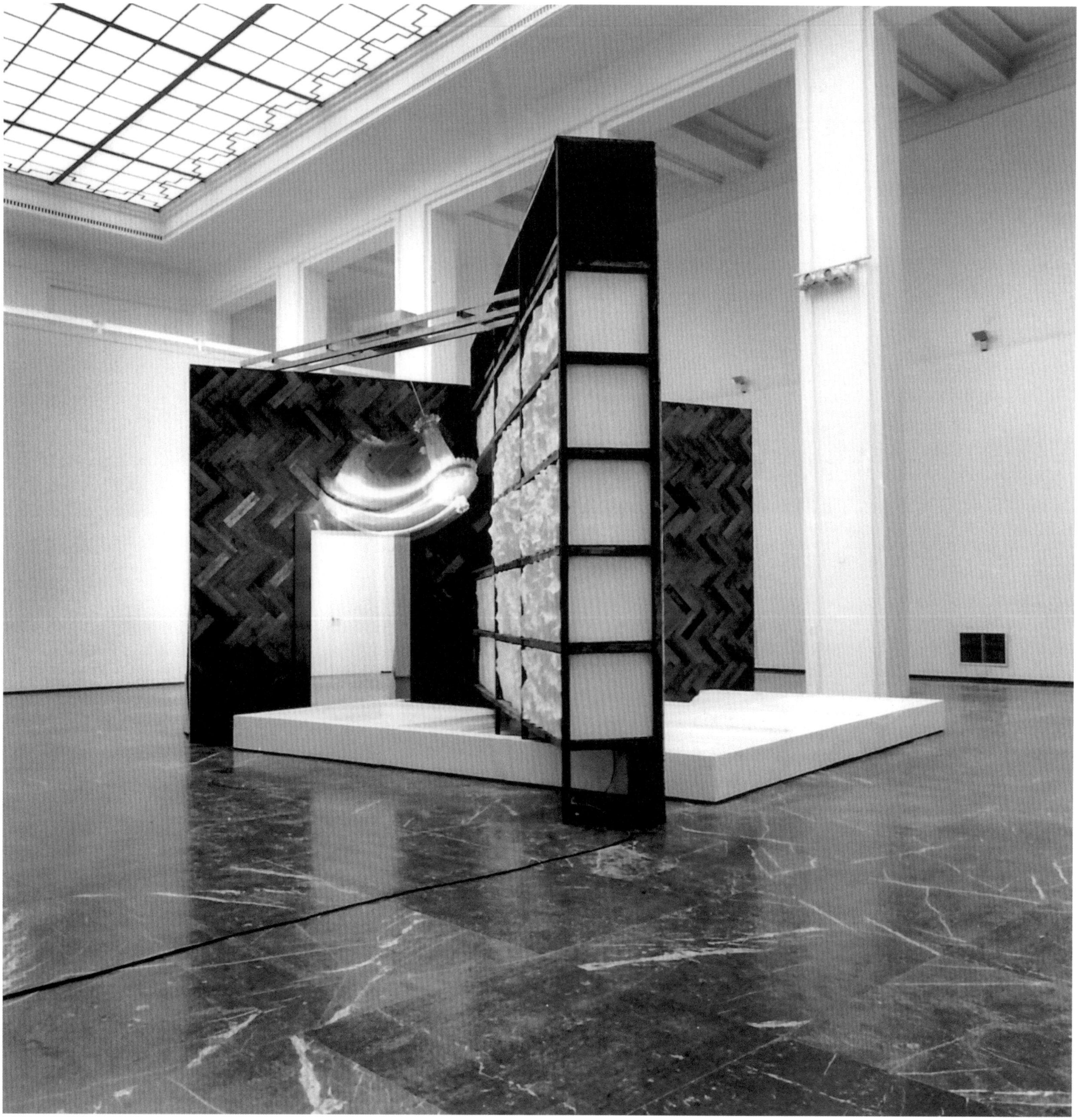

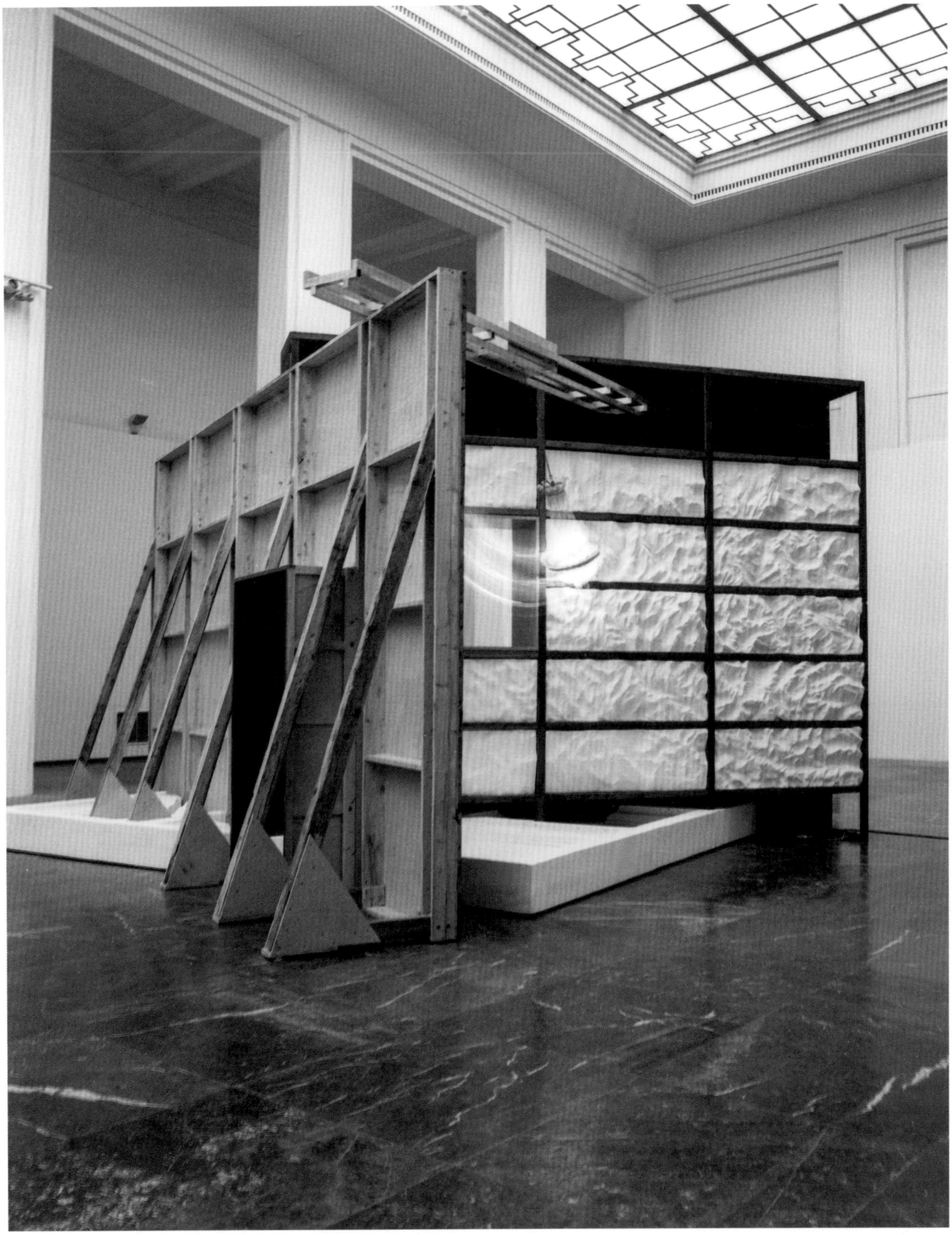

Das rote Bergbuch
1979

Berg und Steinbuch
1980

Das Kletterbuch
1980

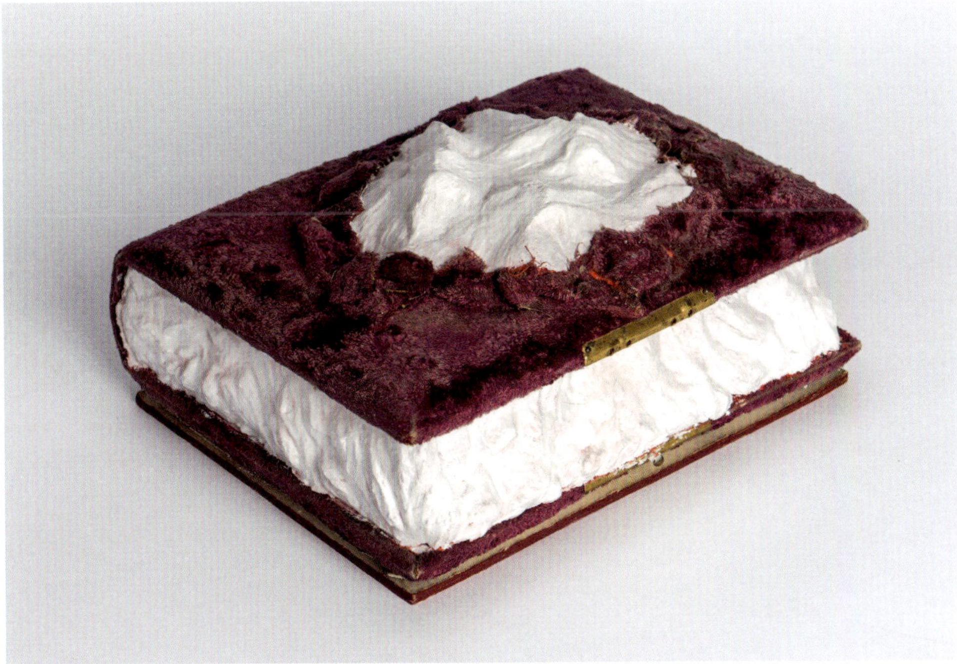

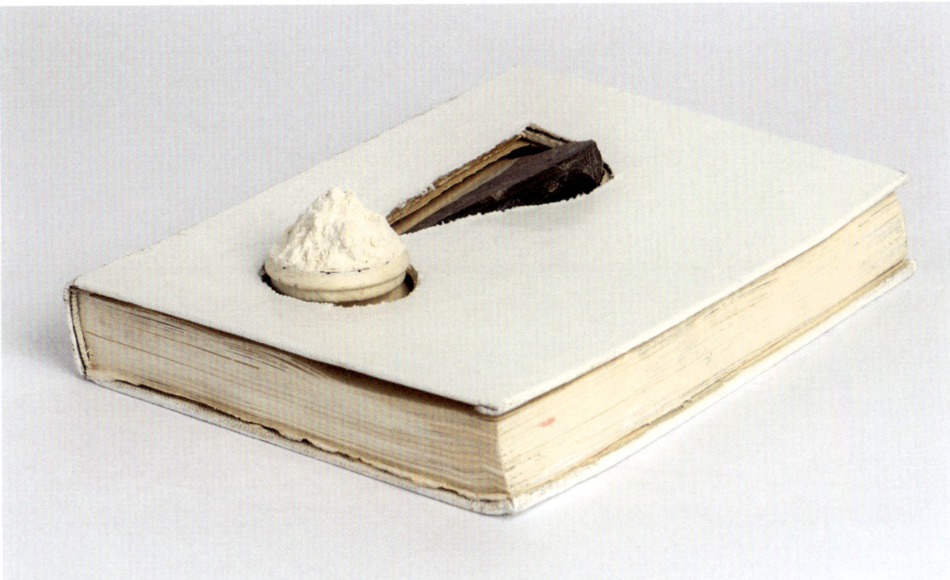

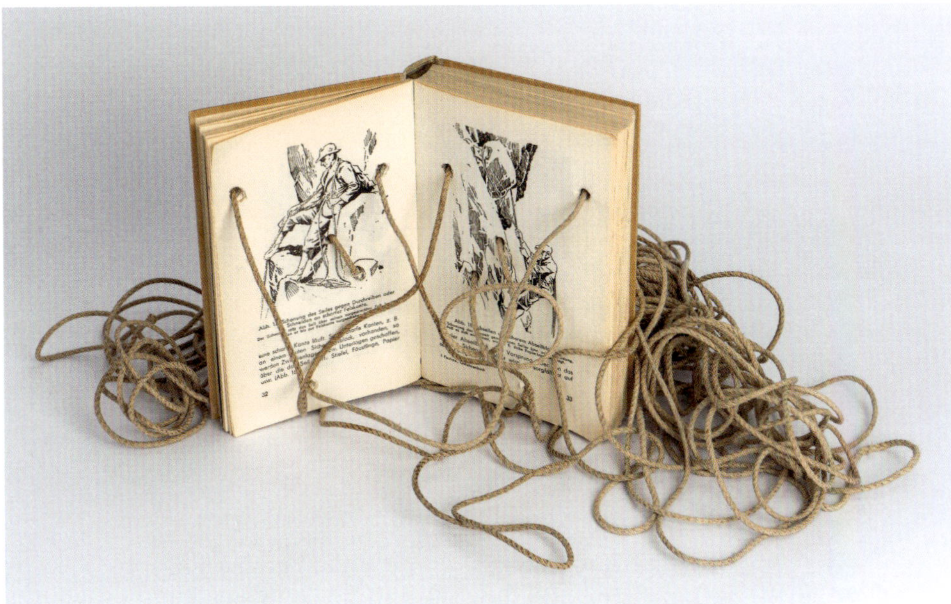

Heimat
1993

Odessa
Eismeer
Die Alpen
Petrograd
Südkreuz
Leuchtfeuer
Sunrise
Houston - Riad - Bangkok
Trichter der Vernunft
Block B
Blaue Himmel
Idylle
Rote Sonnen
Sebastopol
Kraftwerk
Bauhütte / XX. Jahrhundert
Melancholie
Nordwand
Altar / Cree
Rote Insel
Palermo

Gotthard
1993

Tautologisches Konstrukt
1993

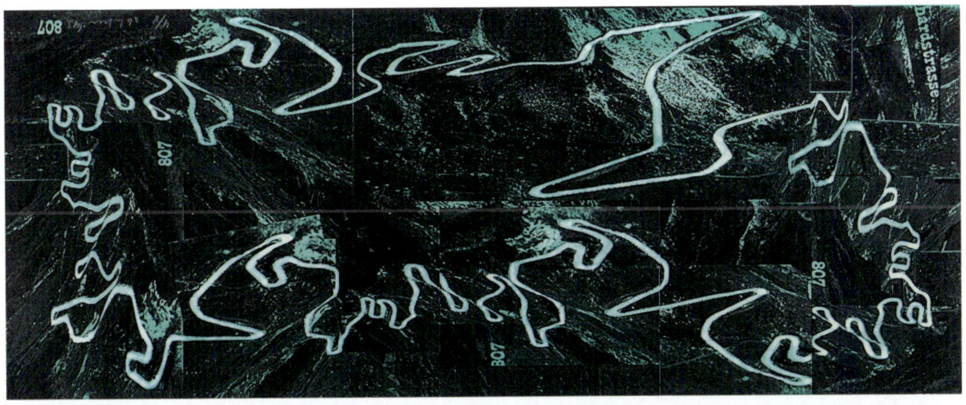

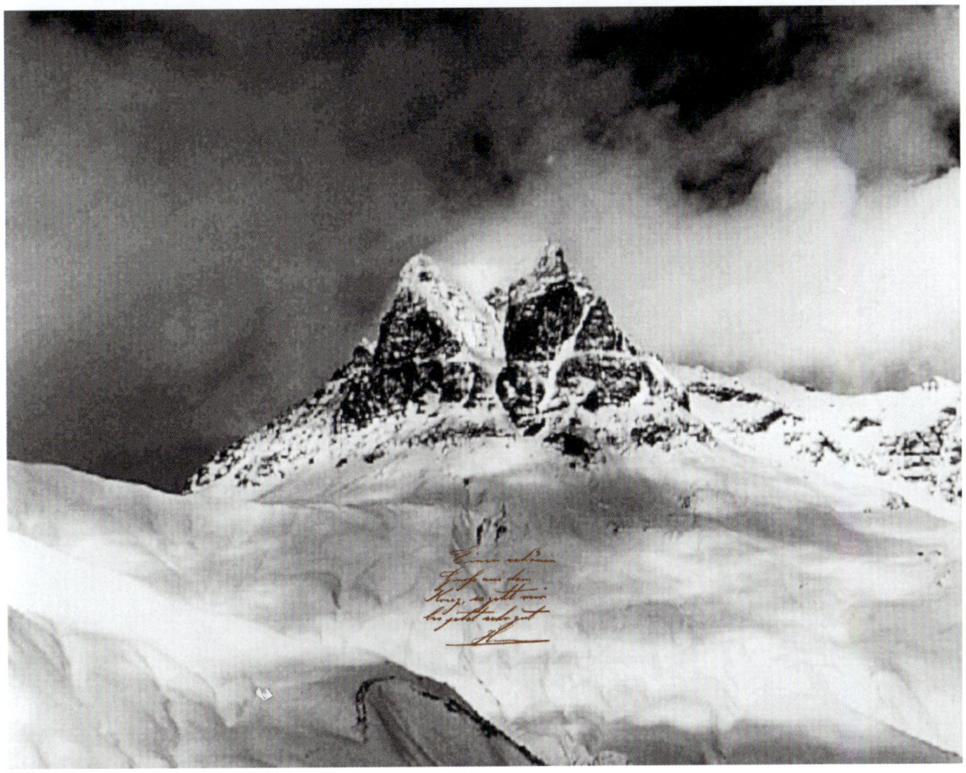

Wasser & Stein
1992
Privatsammlung / Private collection

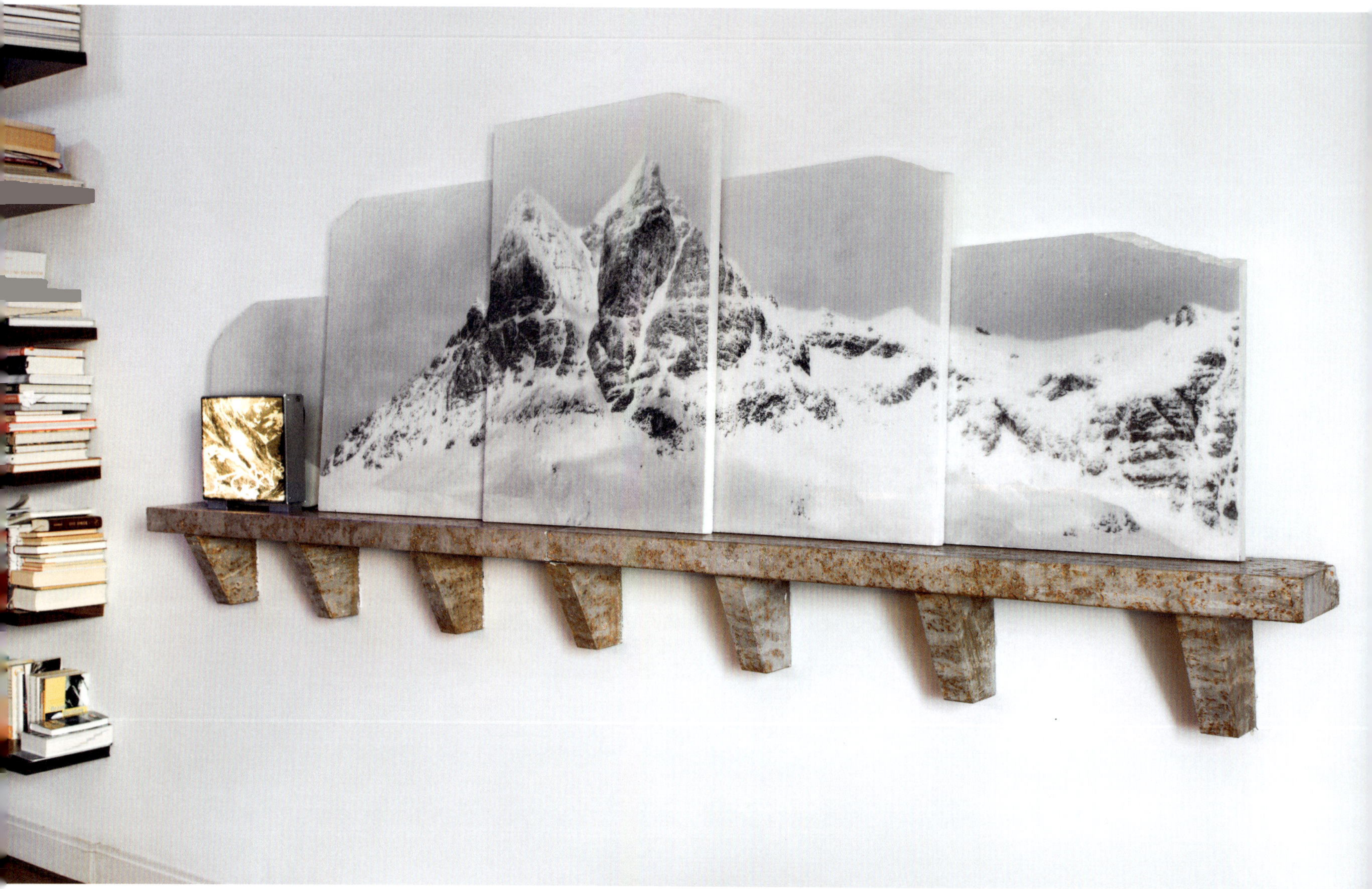

Wasser & Stein
1992
Privatsammlung / Private collection

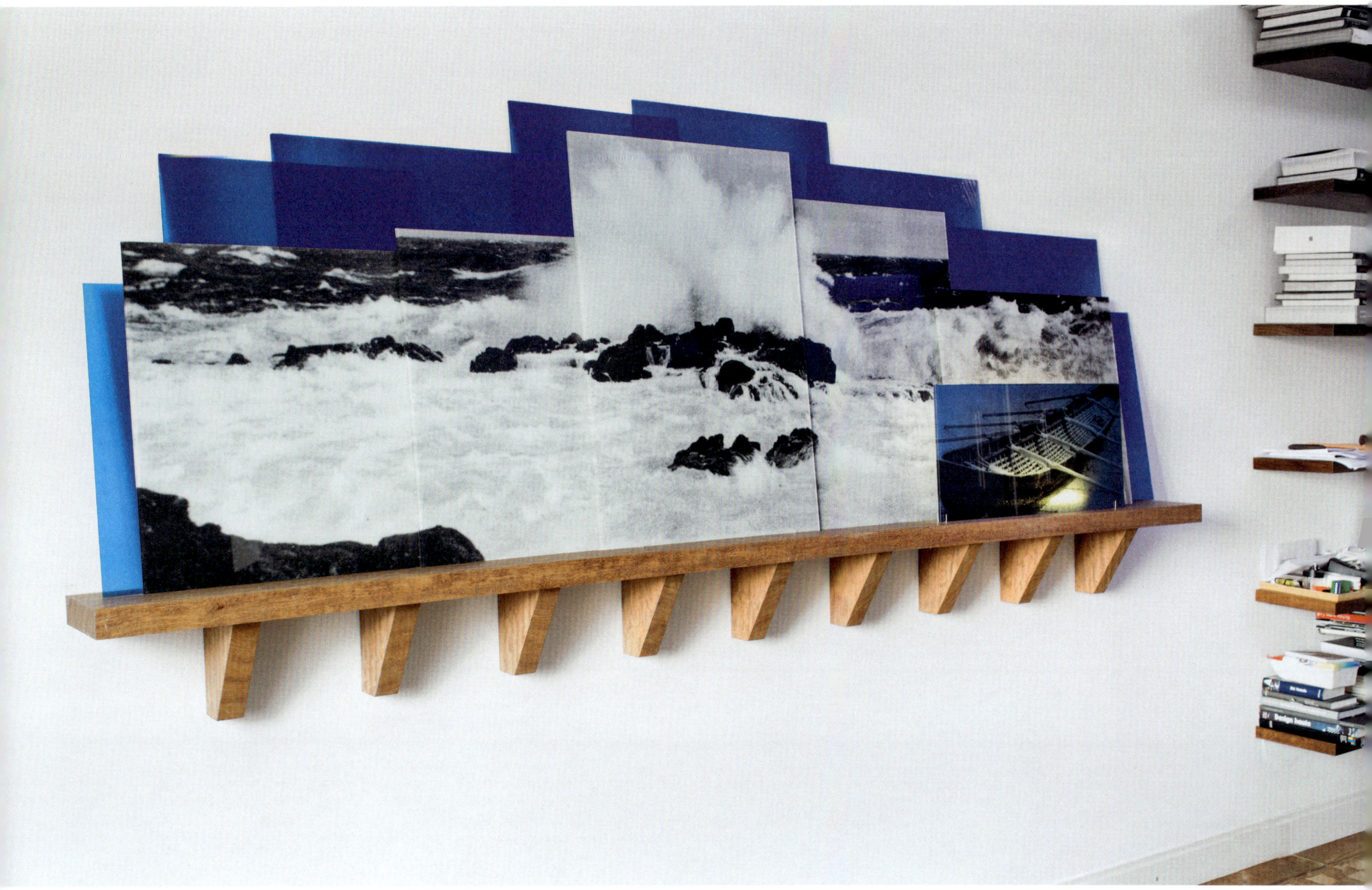

Südkreuz
1995

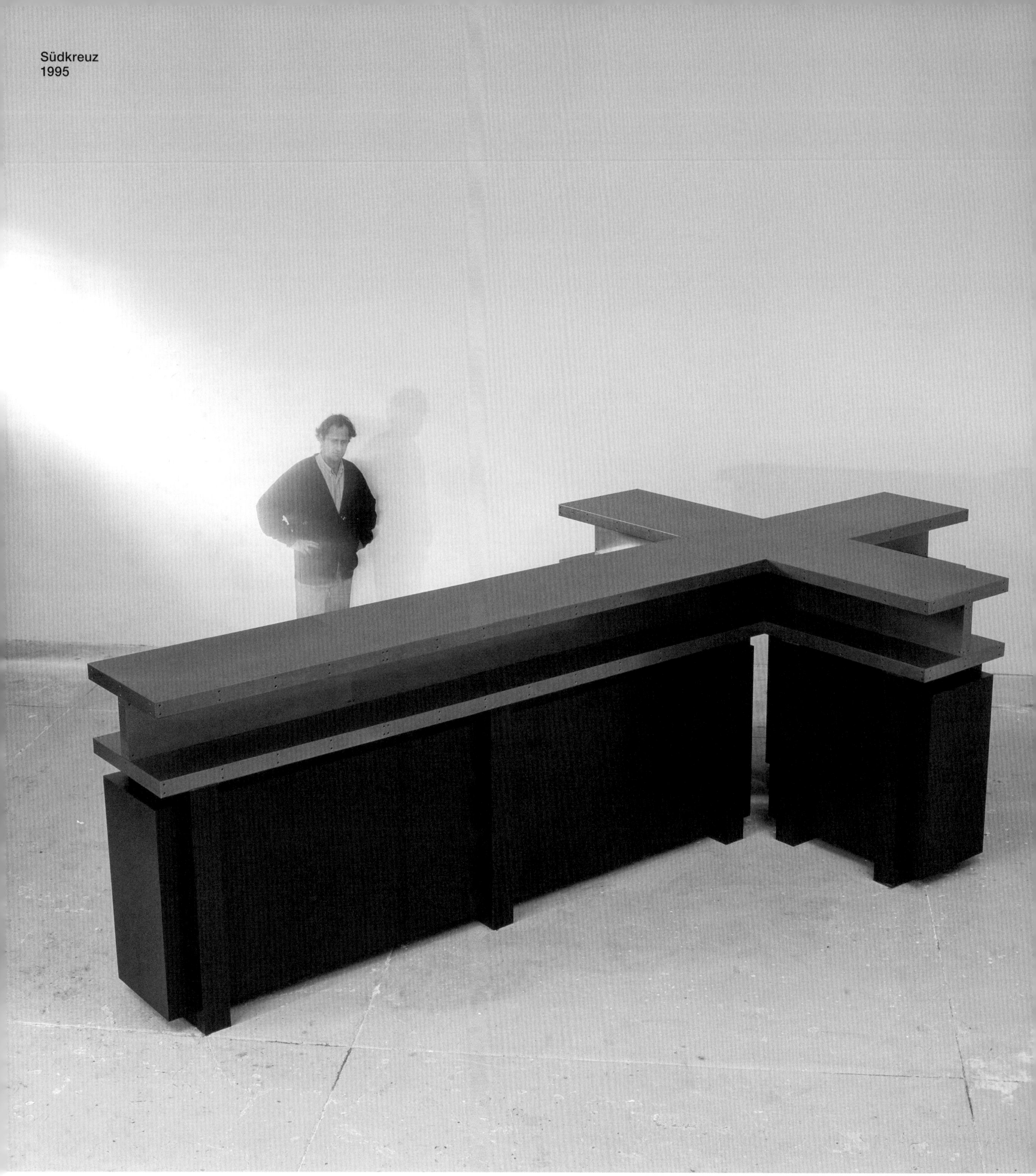

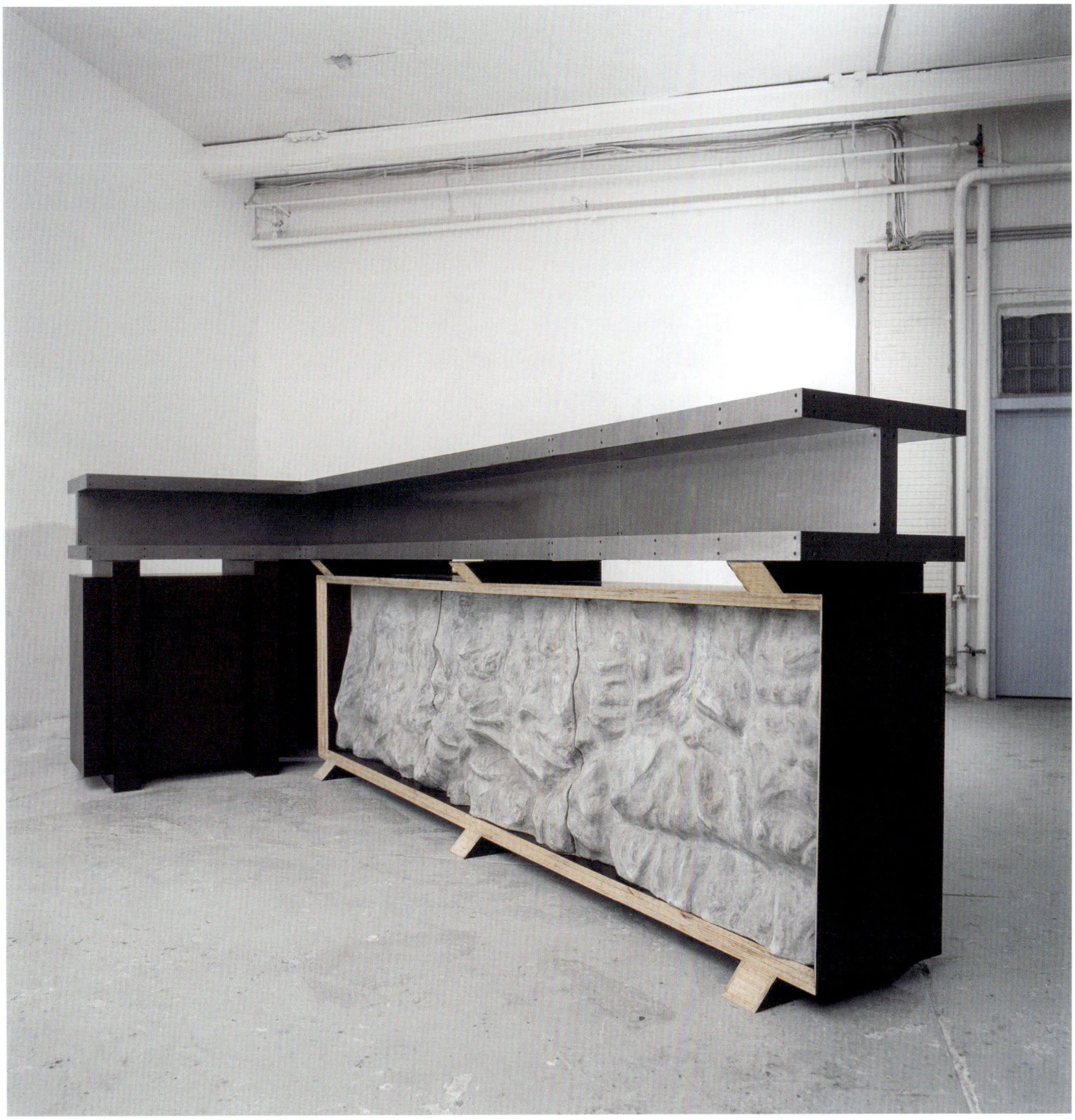

Nobile
1997

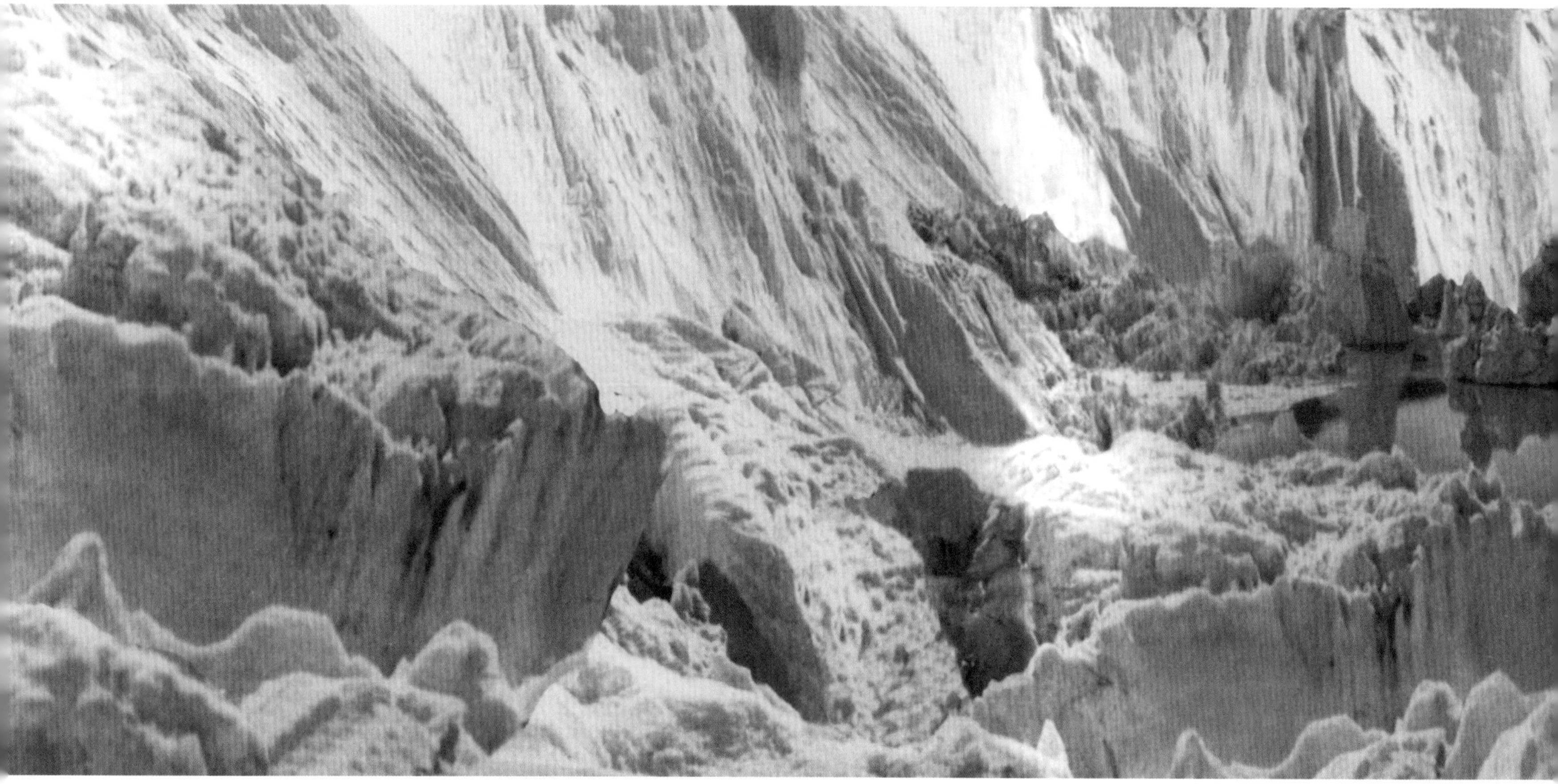

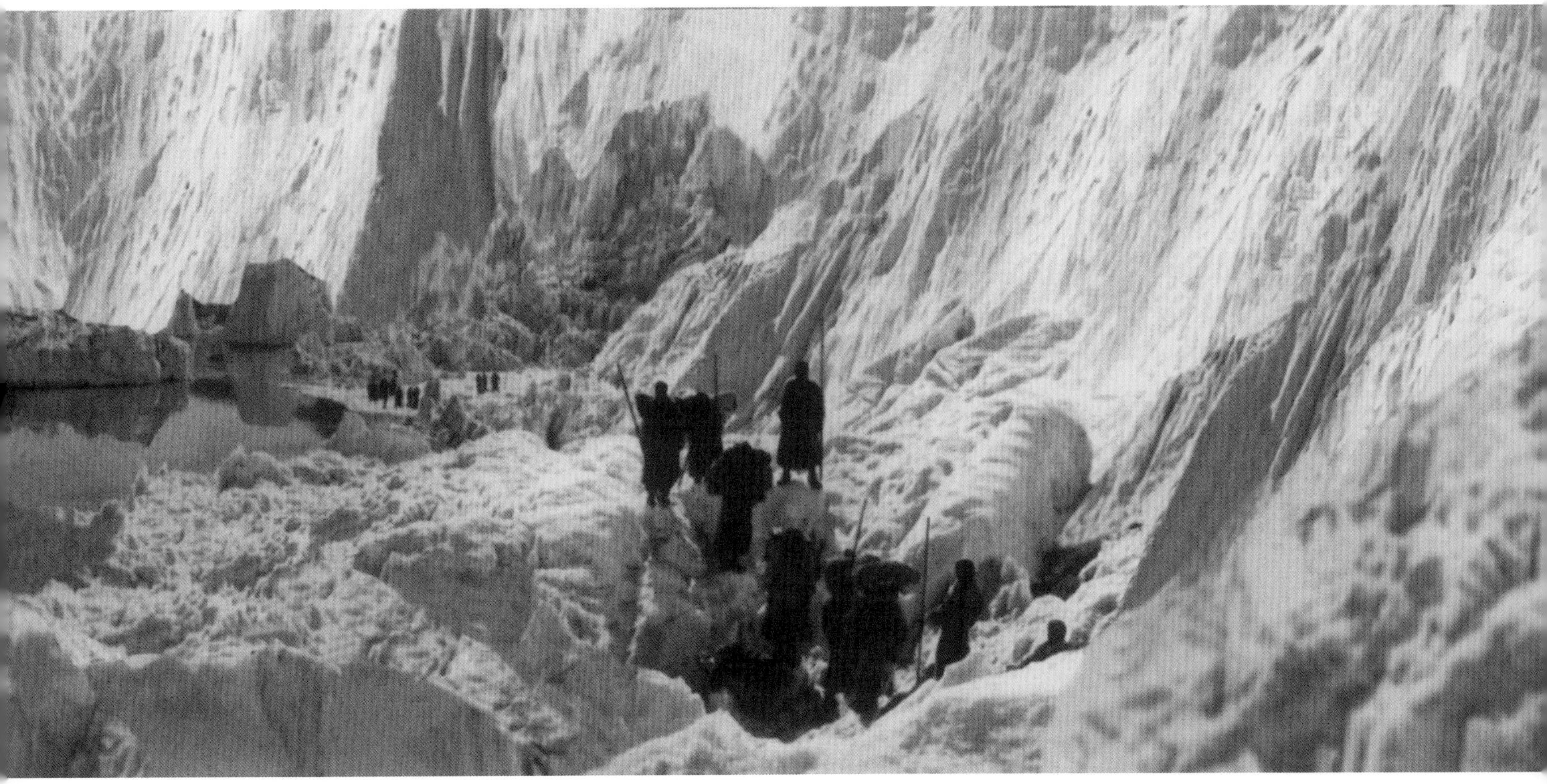

Nobile
1997

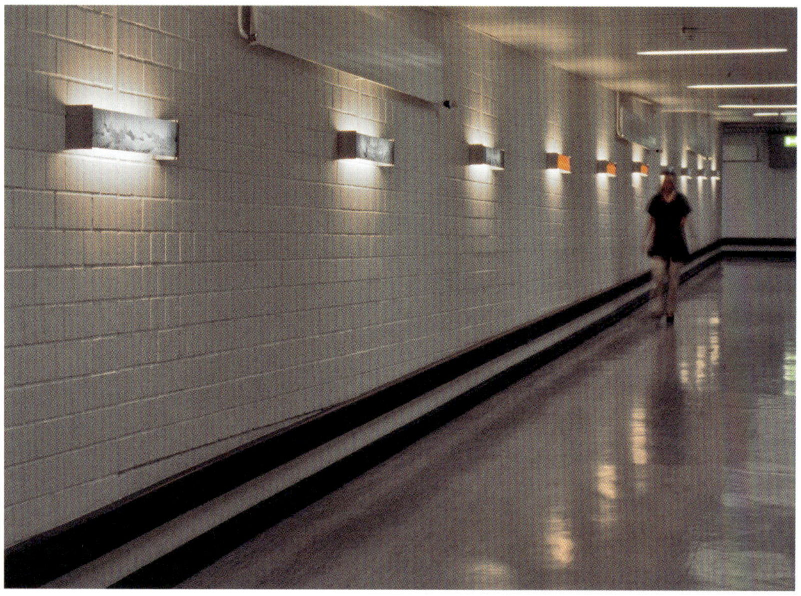

Landesbank Baden-Württemberg, Stuttgart

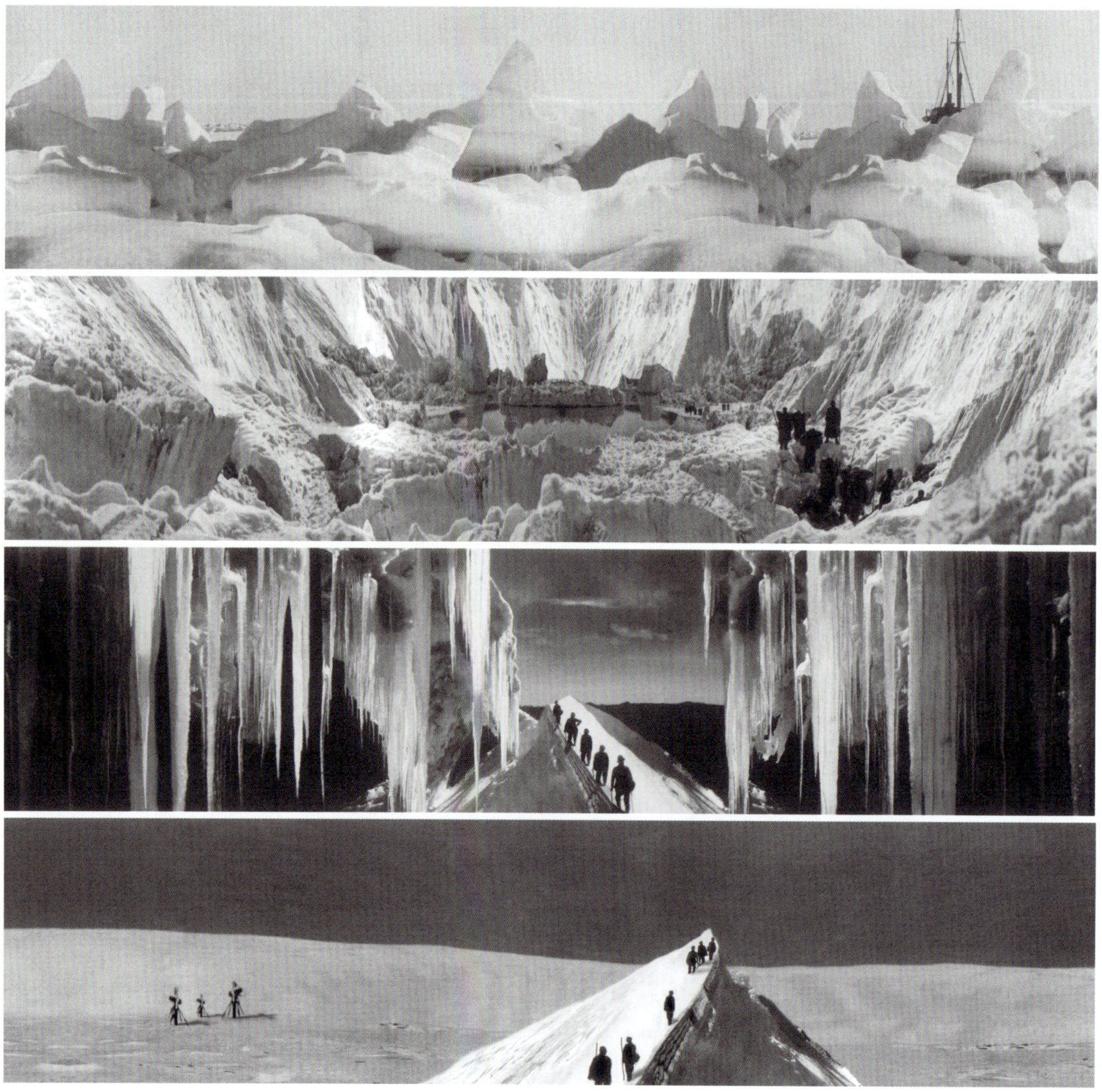

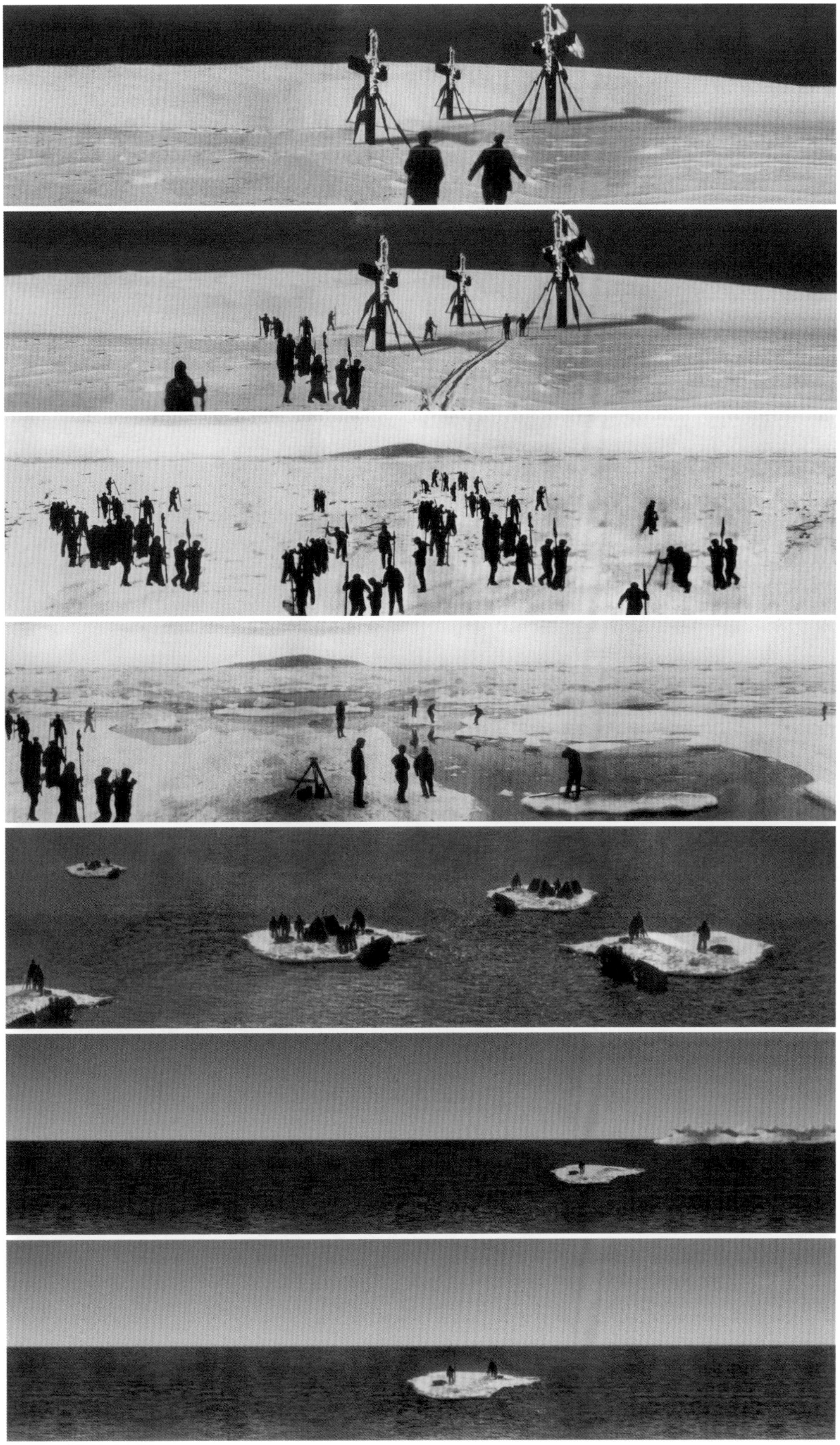

Gran Paradiso
1997
Neue Messe München

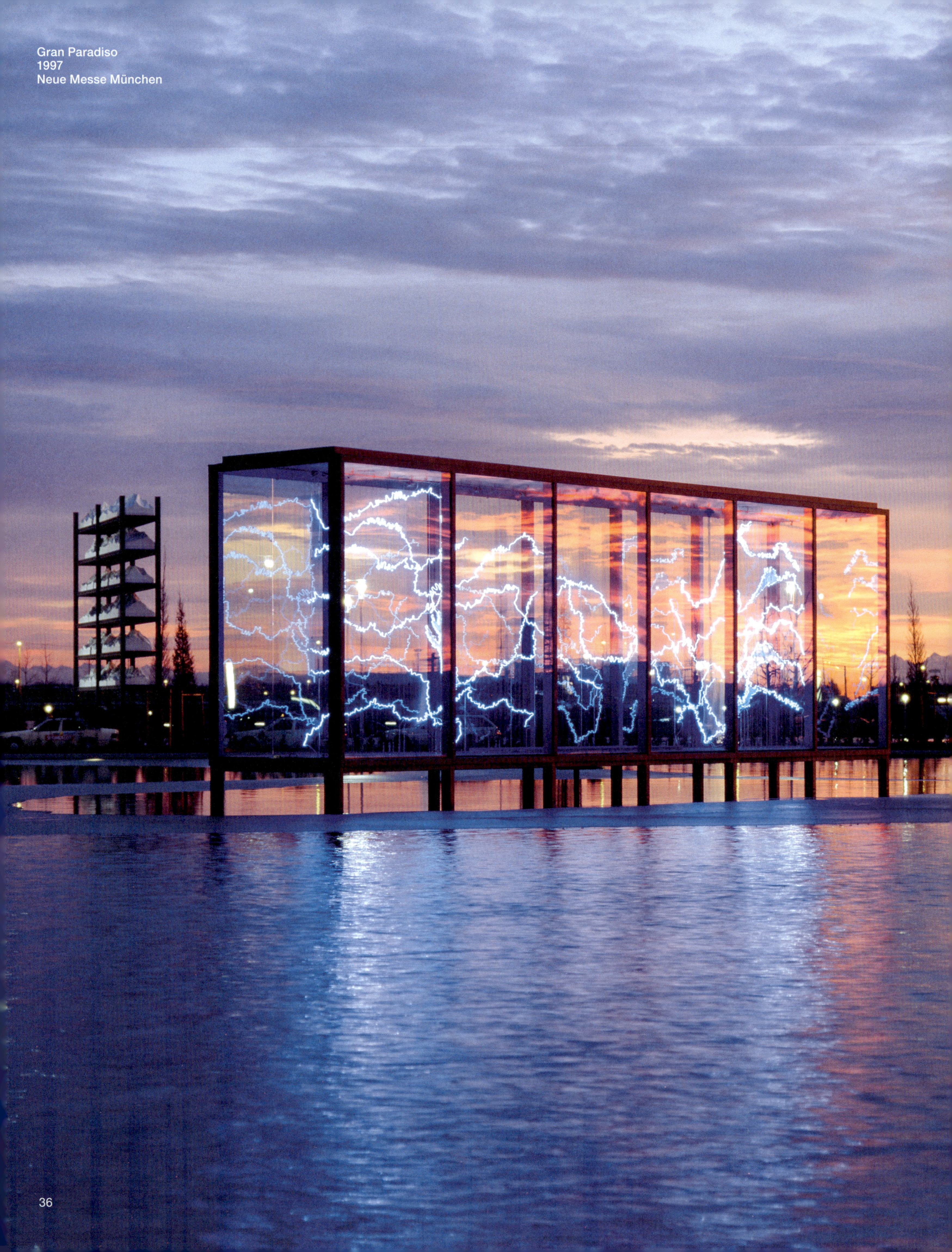

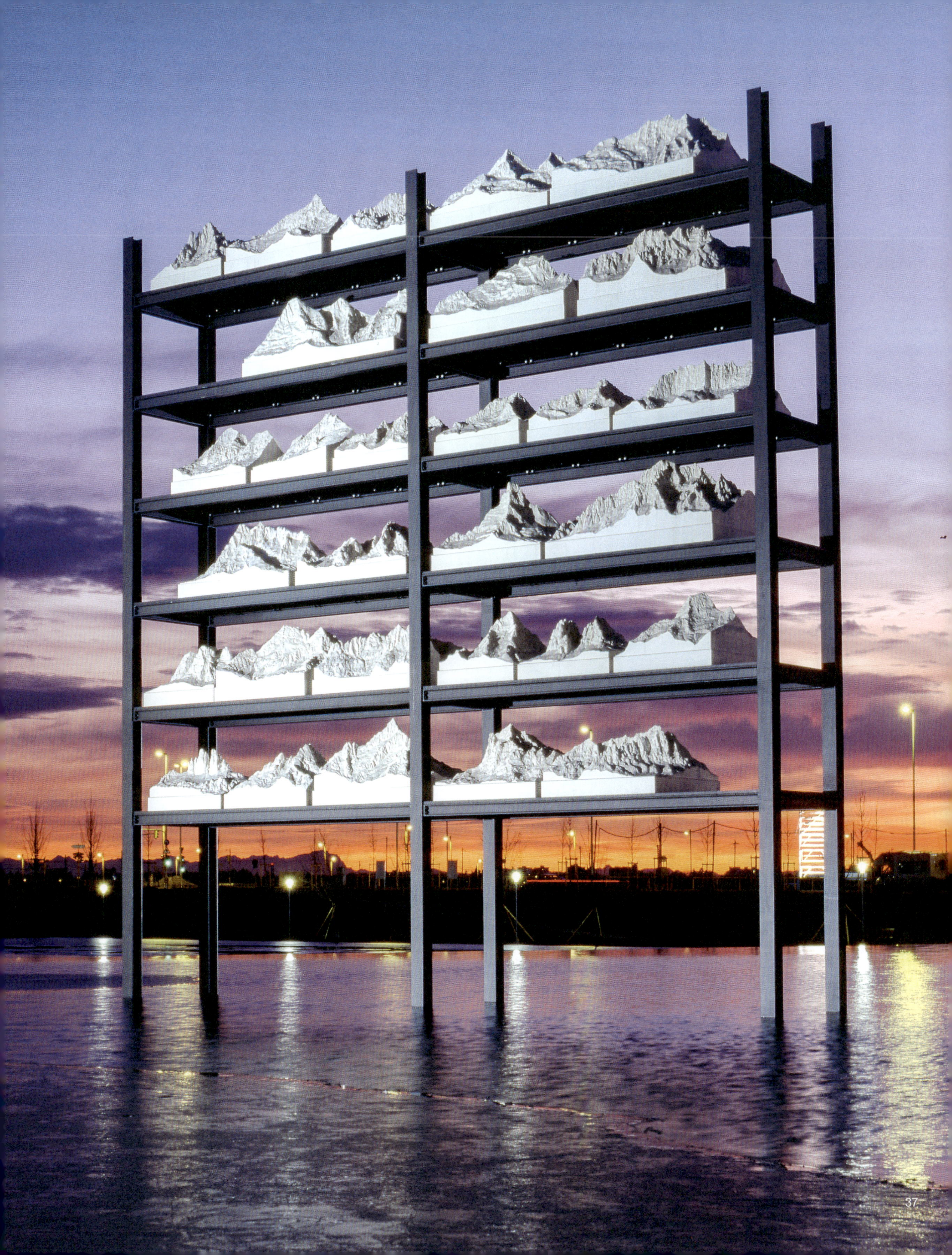

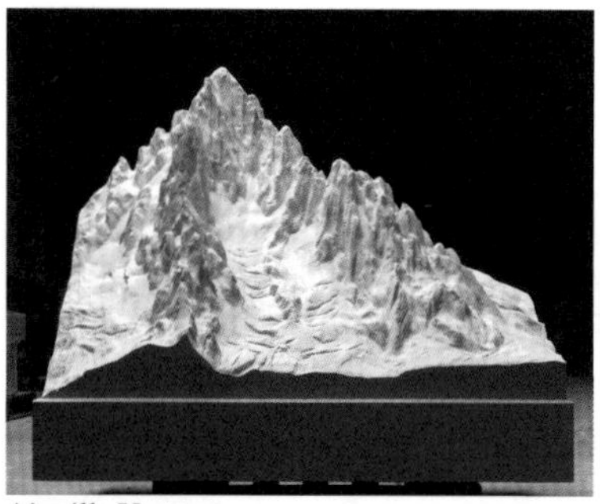
Aiguille Verte

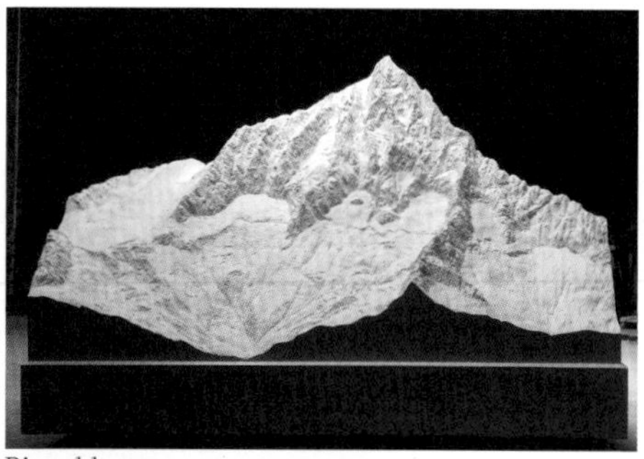
Bietschhorn

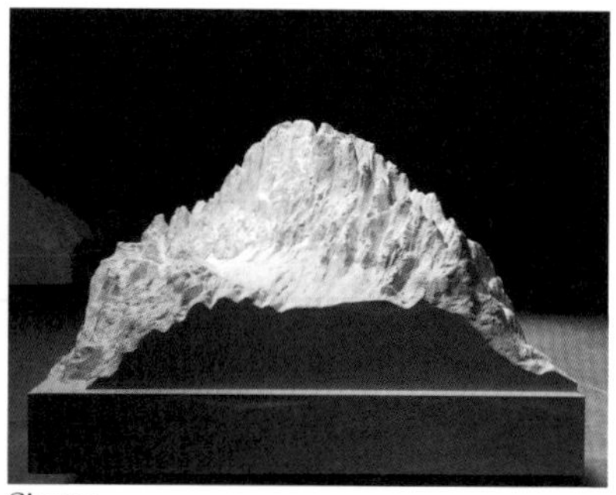
Civetta

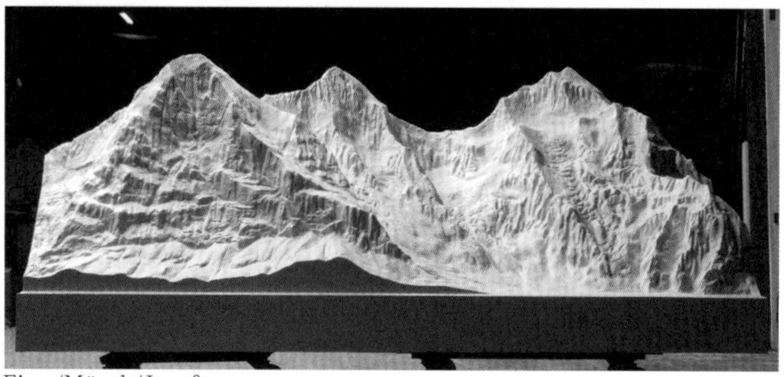
Eiger/Mönch/Jungfrau

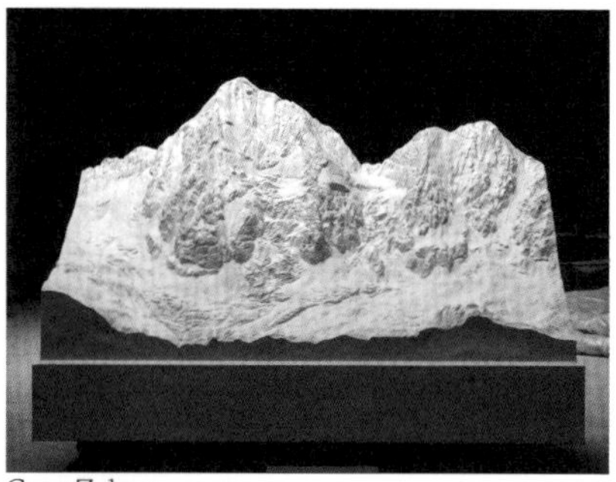
Gran Zebru

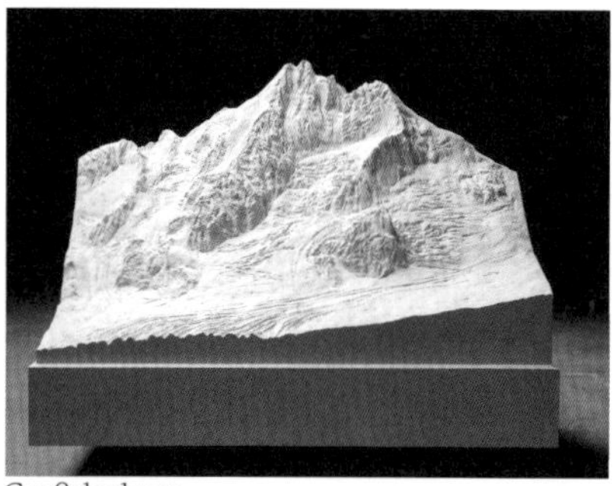
Großglockner

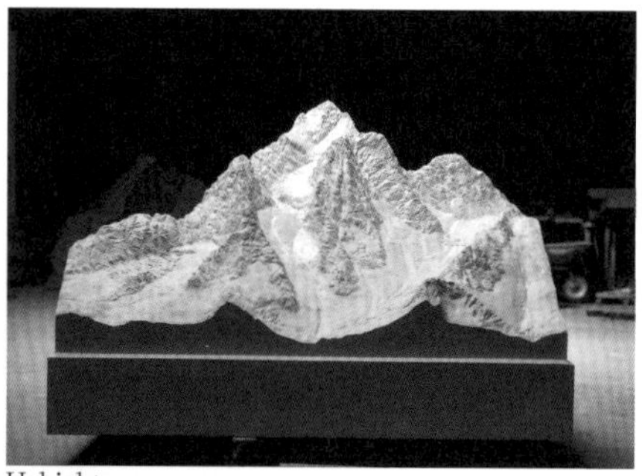
Habicht

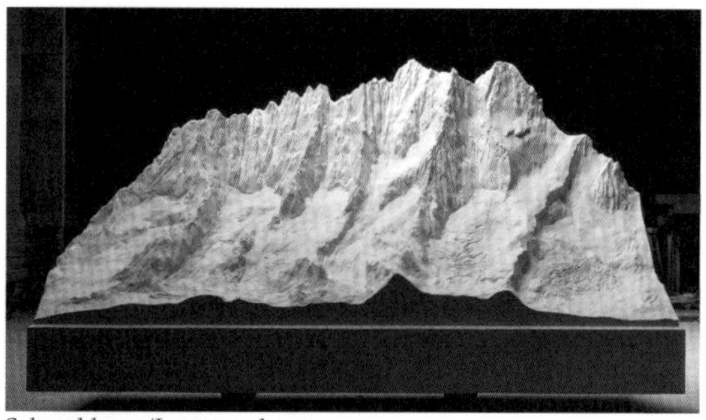
Schreckhorn/Lauteraarhorn

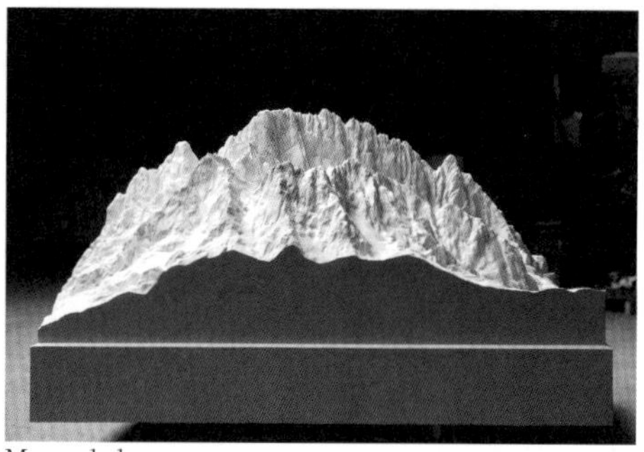
Marmolada

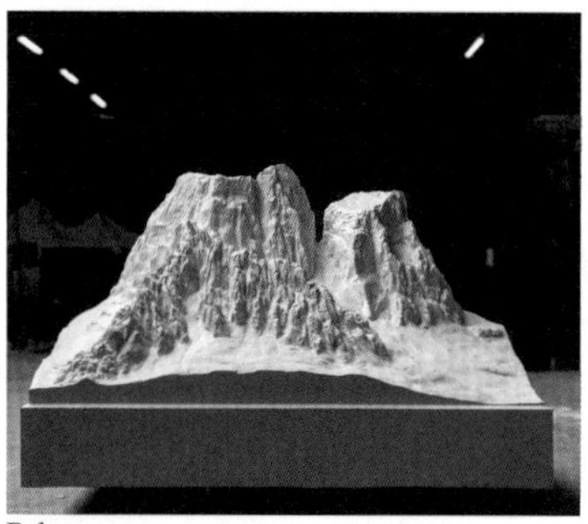
Pelmo

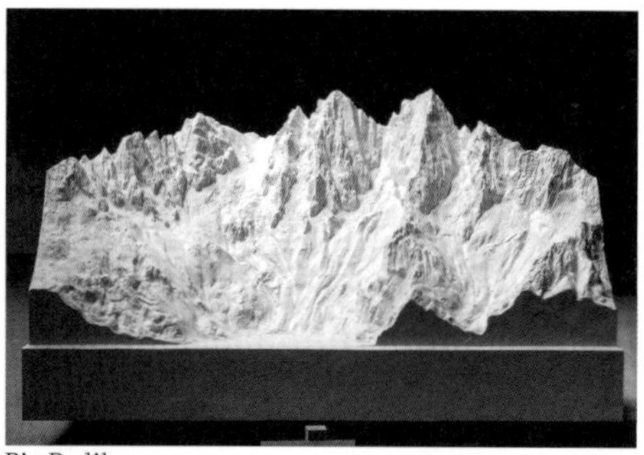
Piz Badile

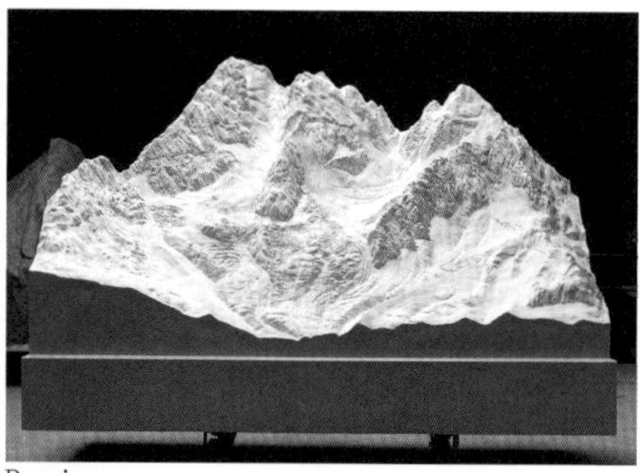
Bernina

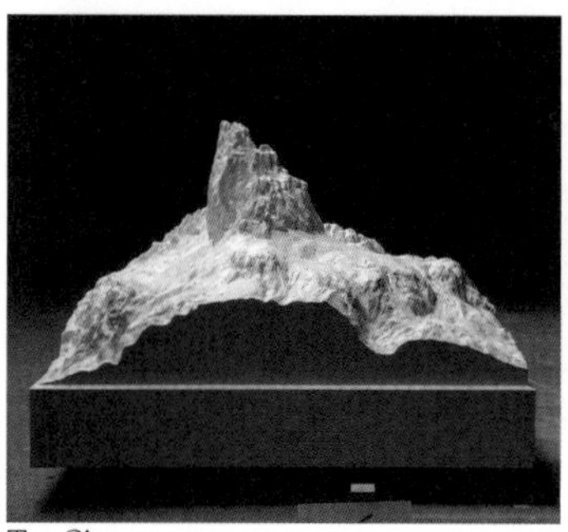
Tre Cime

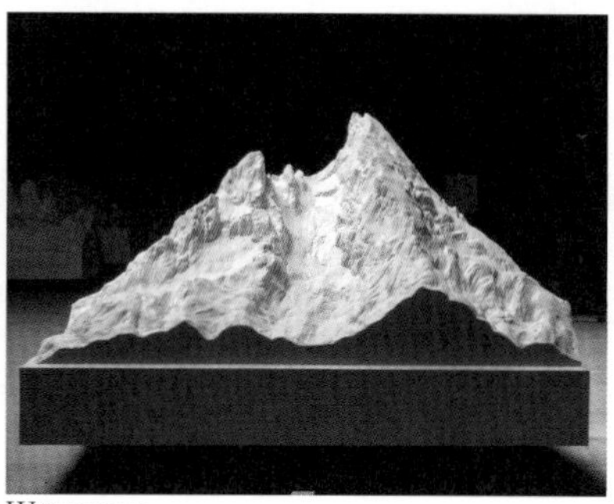
Watzmann

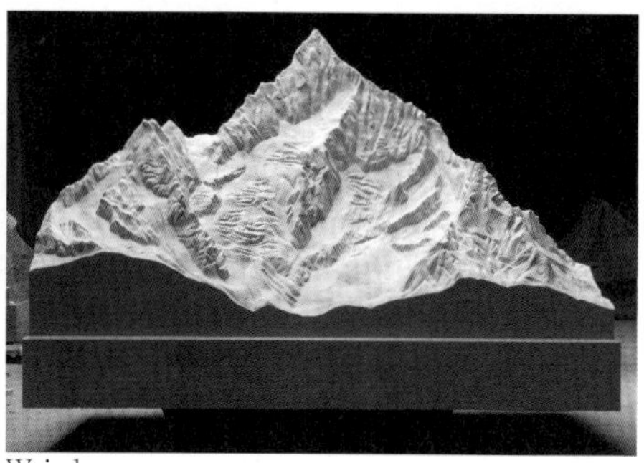
Weisshorn

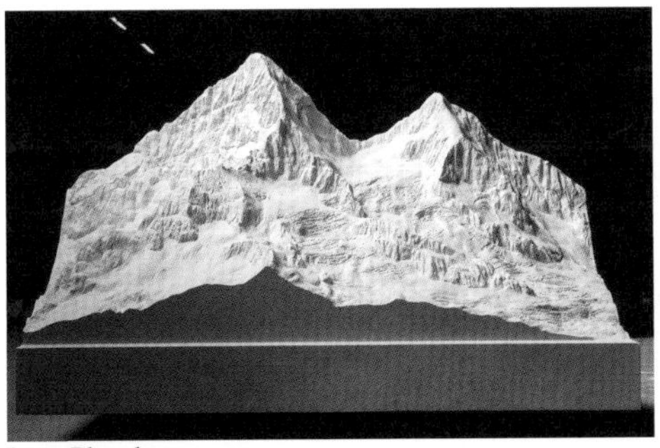
Dent Blanche

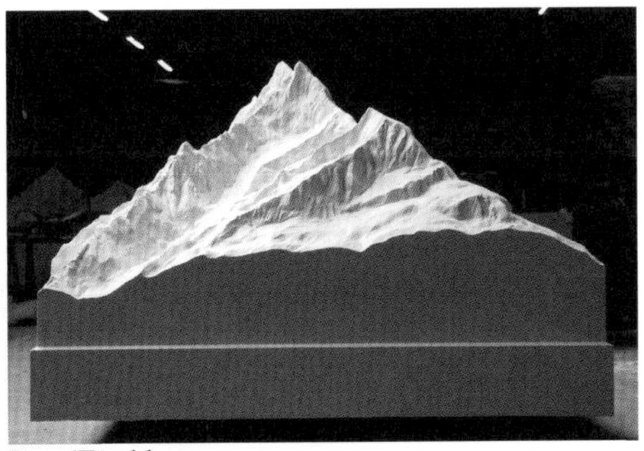
Dom/Täschhorn

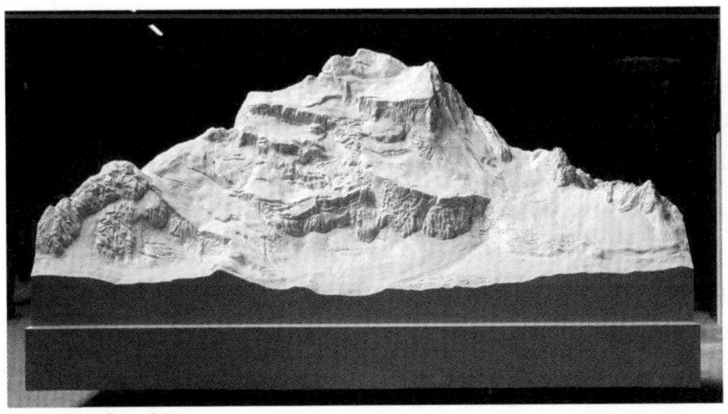
Grandes Combin

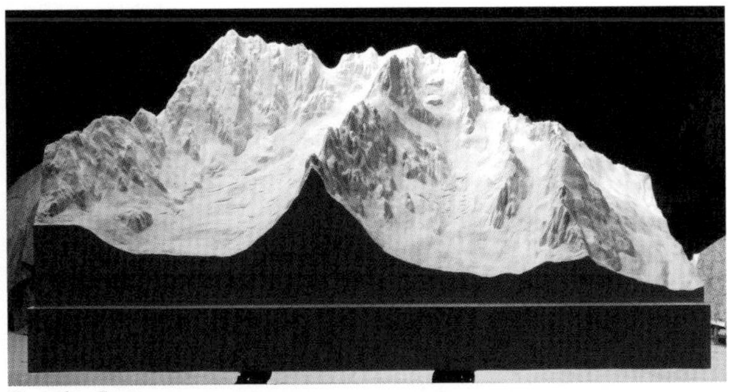
Grandes Jorasses

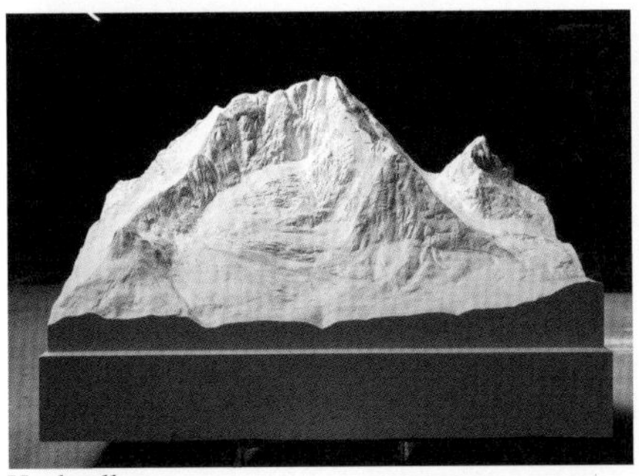
Hochgall

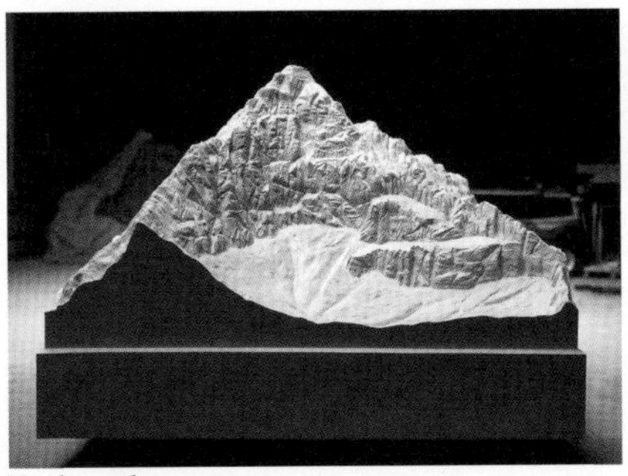
Hochvogel

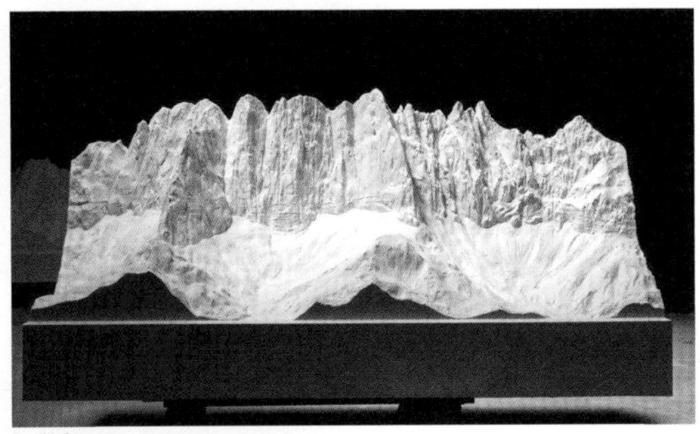
Laliderer

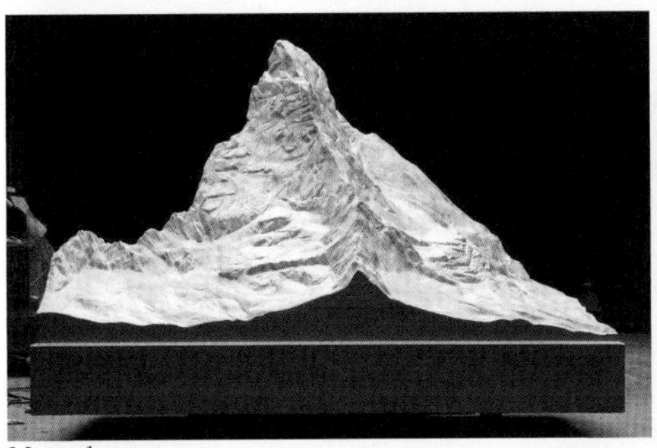
Matterhorn

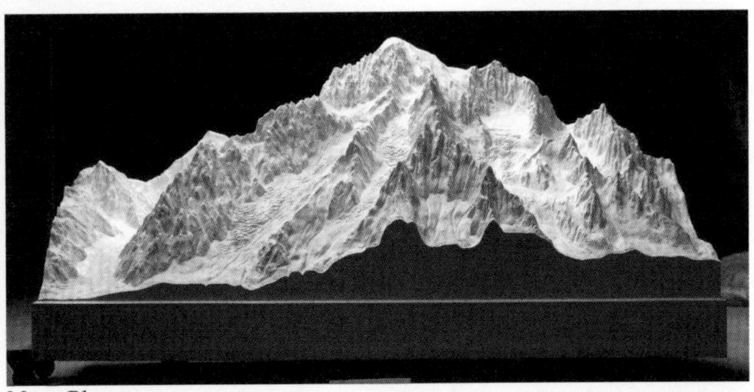
Mont Blanc

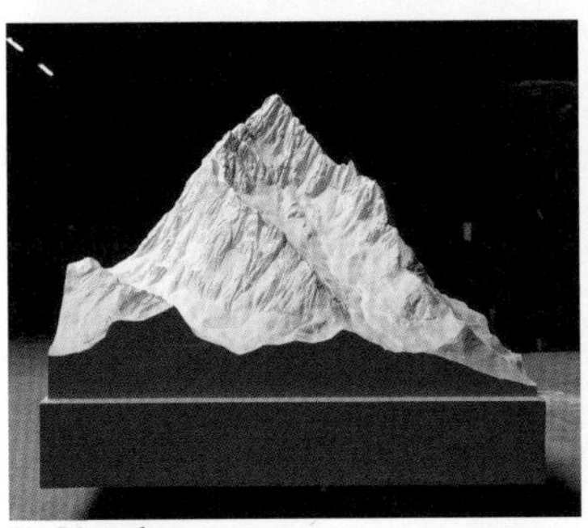
Piz Linard

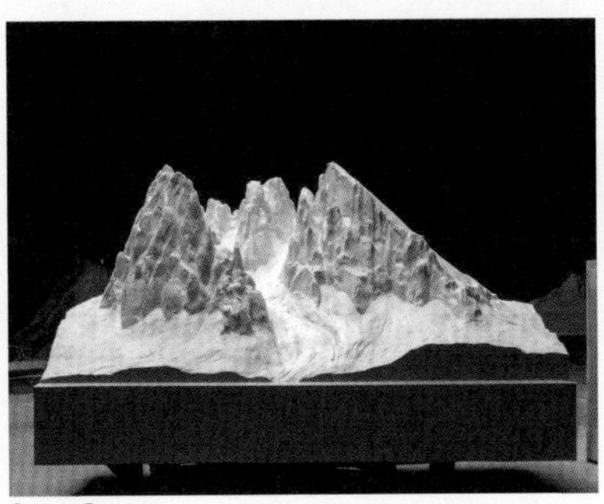
Sasso Lungo

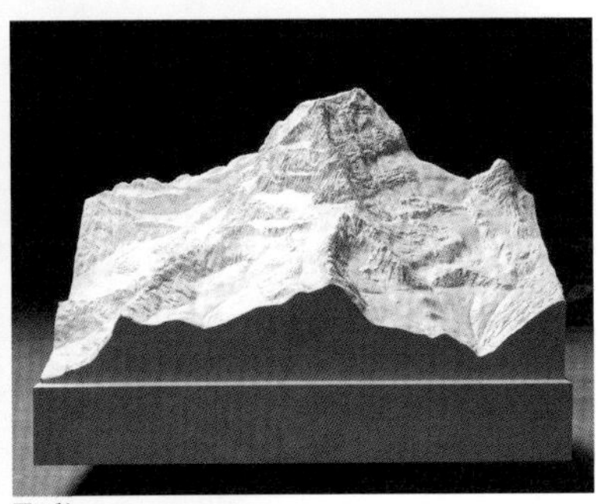
Tödi

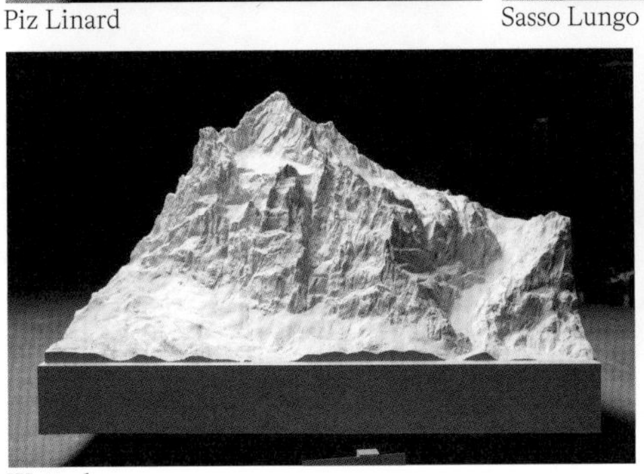
Wetterhorn

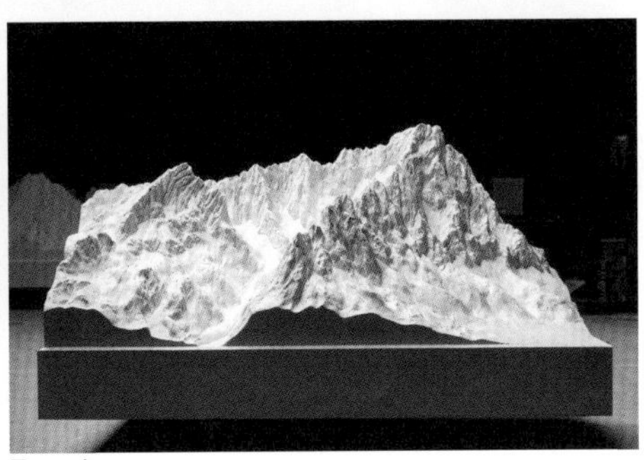
Zugspitze

Rauminstallation
Room installation
1998
Galerie Six Friedrich Lisa Ungar,
München / Munich

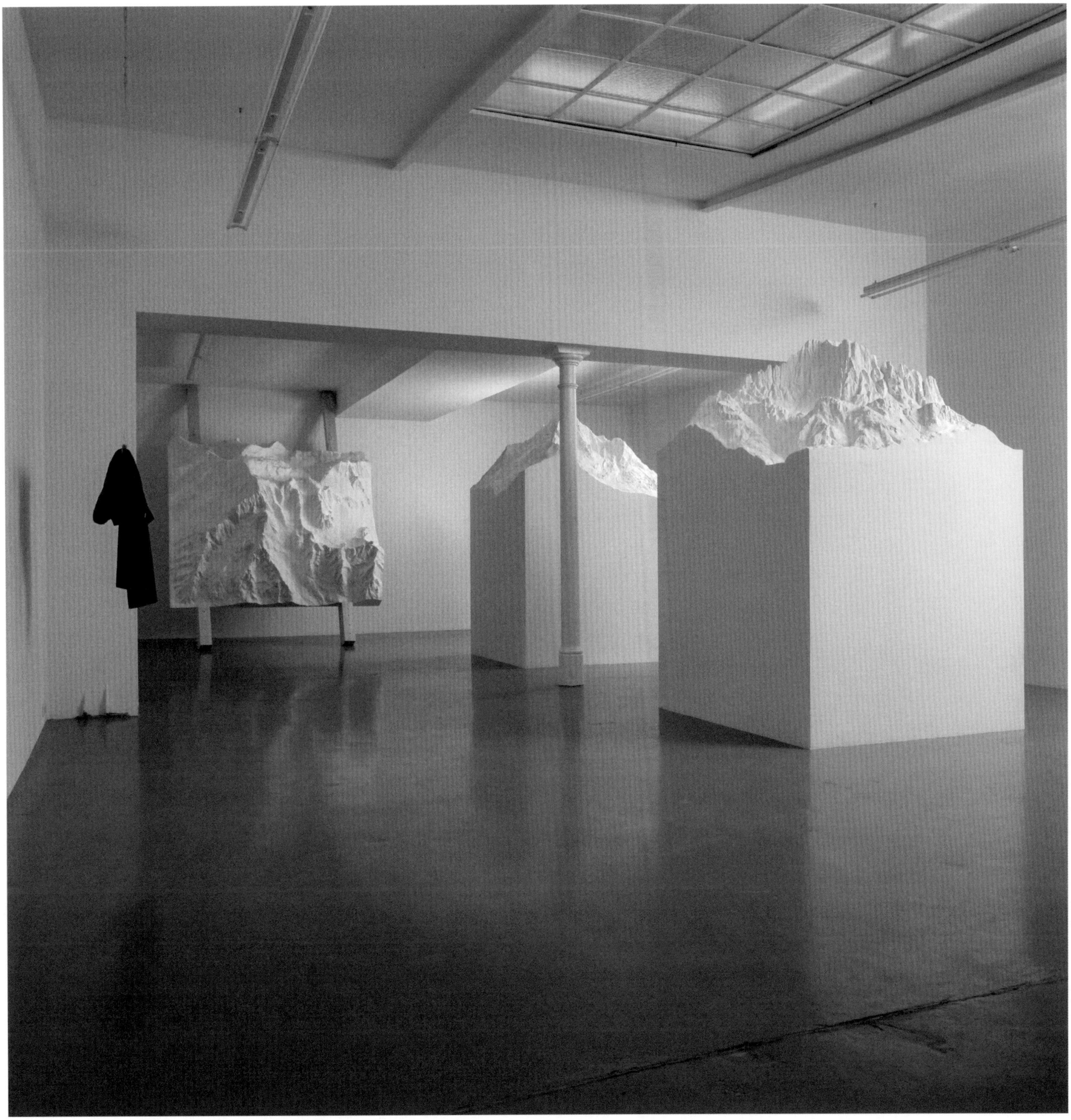

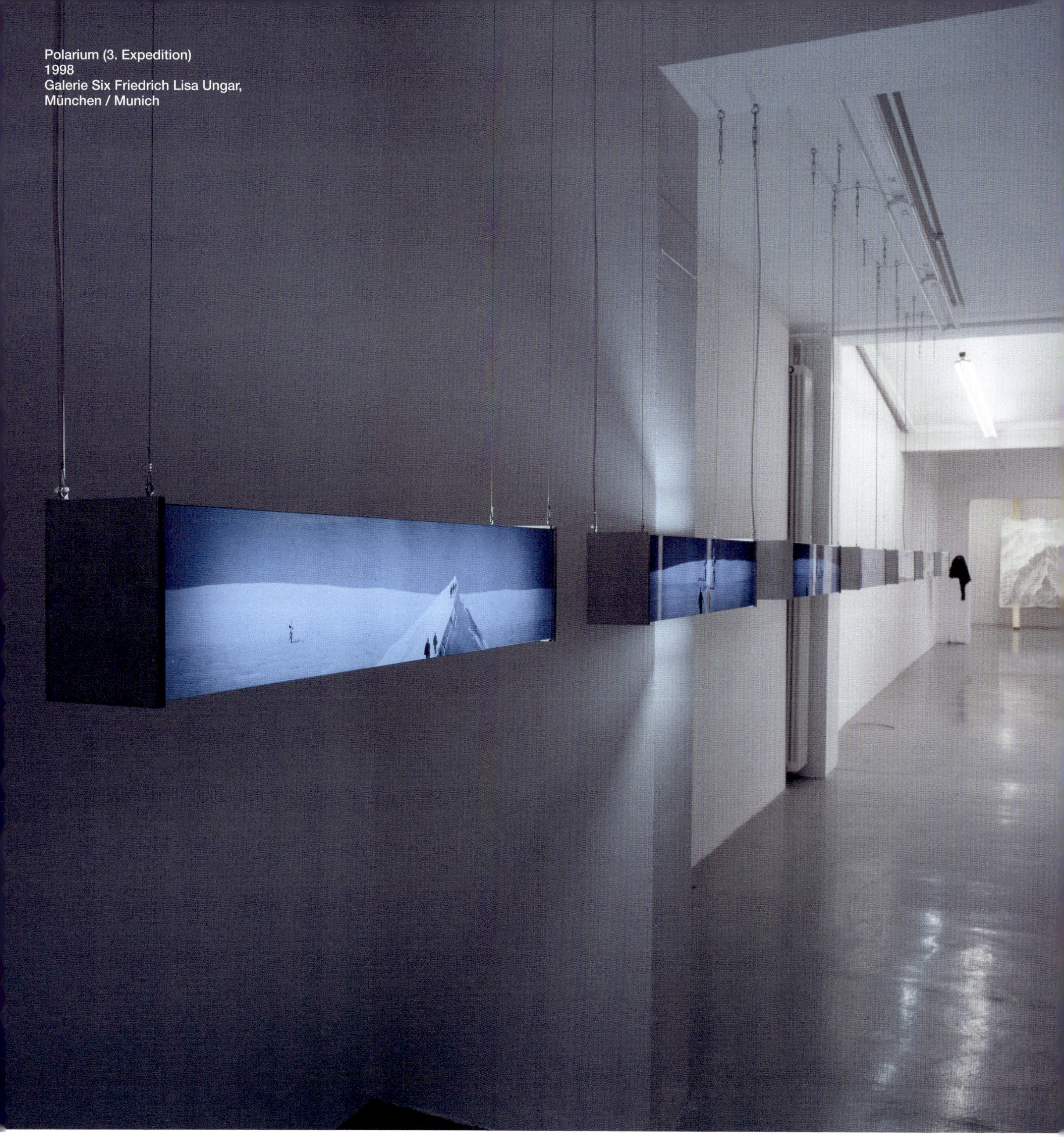

Polarium (3. Expedition)
1998
Galerie Six Friedrich Lisa Ungar,
München / Munich

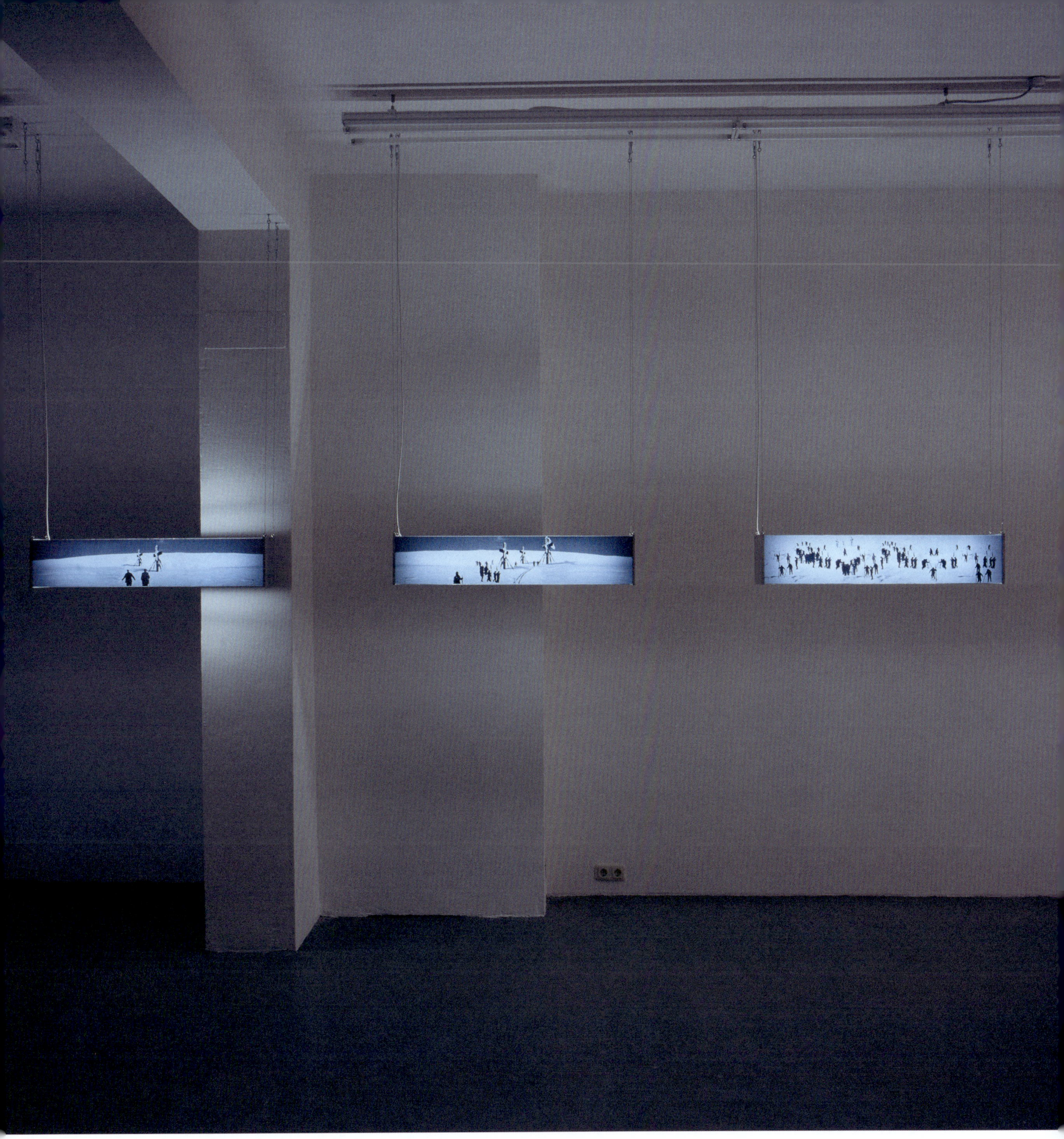

Polarium (3. Expedition)
1998

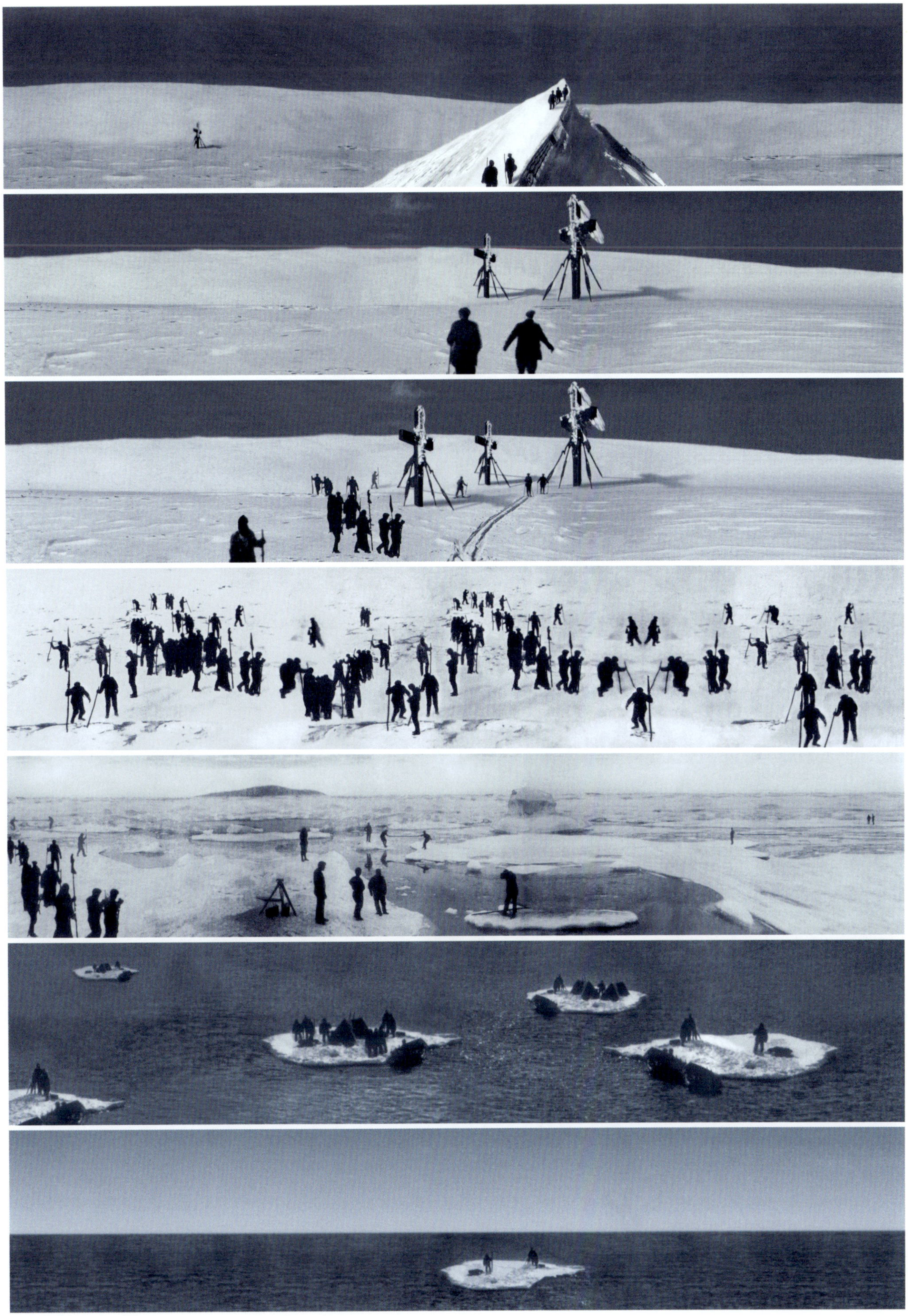

Trägerstaffel
1998

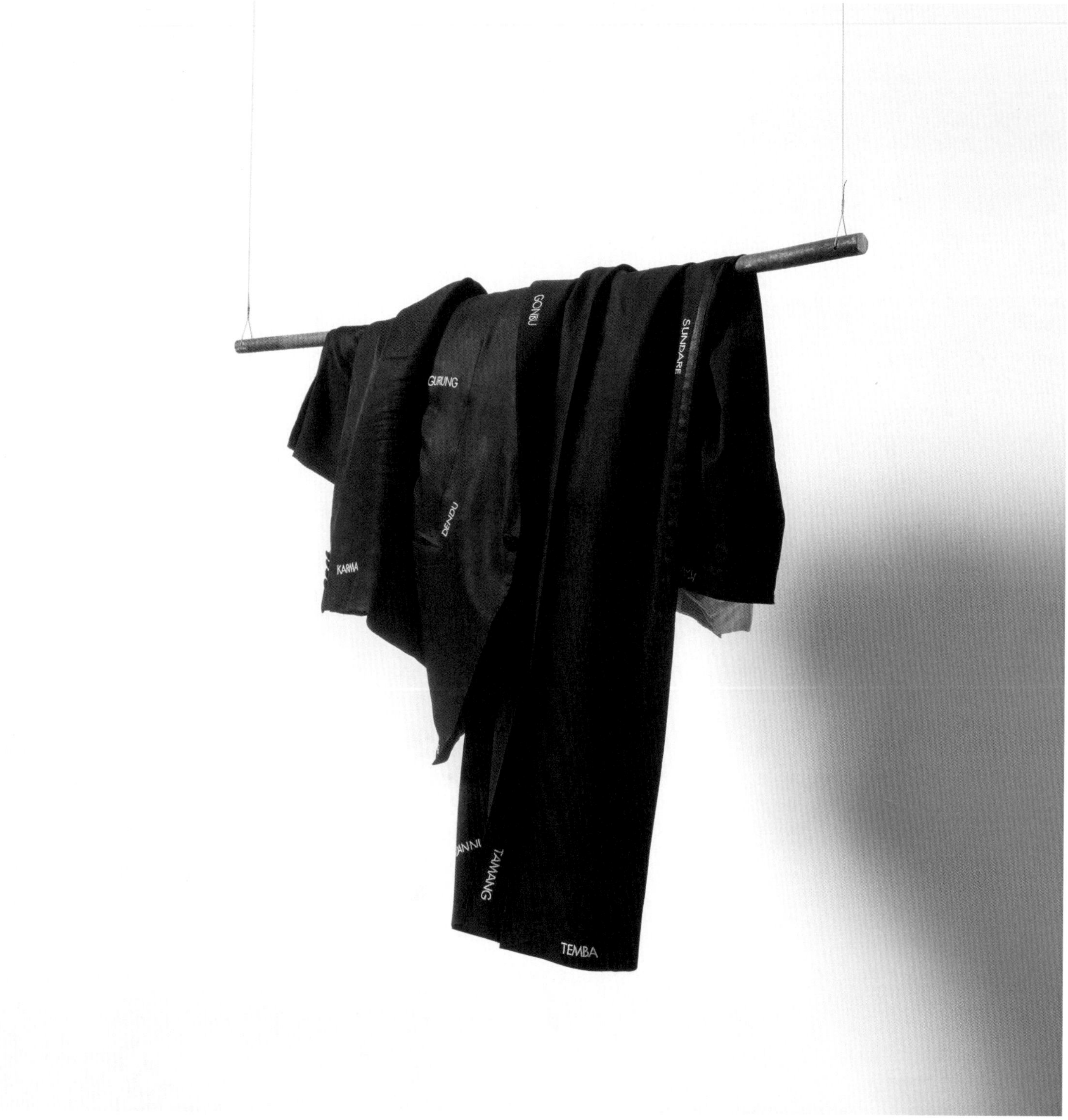

Civetta
Weisshorn
1998
Galleria La Nuova Pesa, Rom / Rome

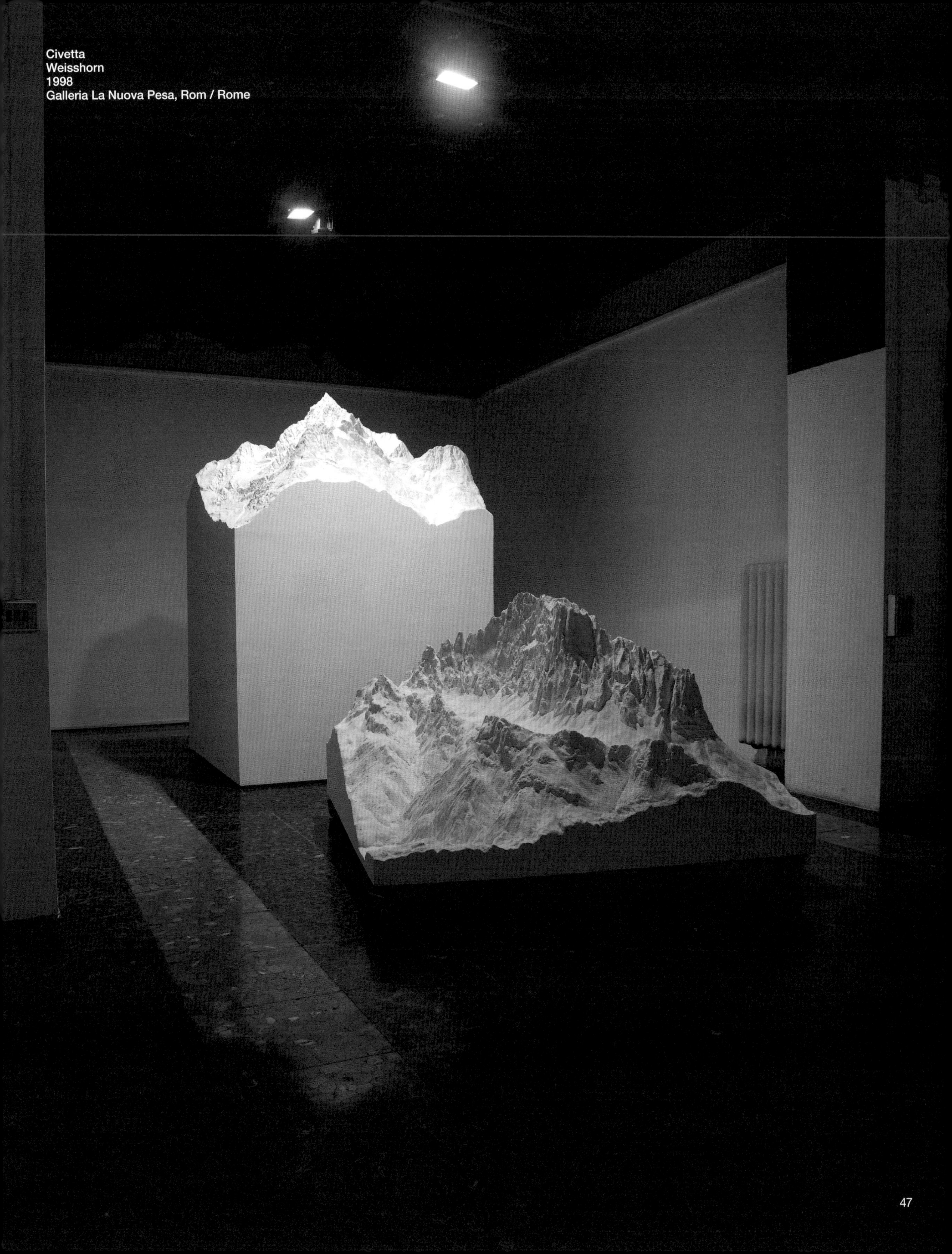

Weisshorn
1998
Villa Comunale, Neapel / Naples

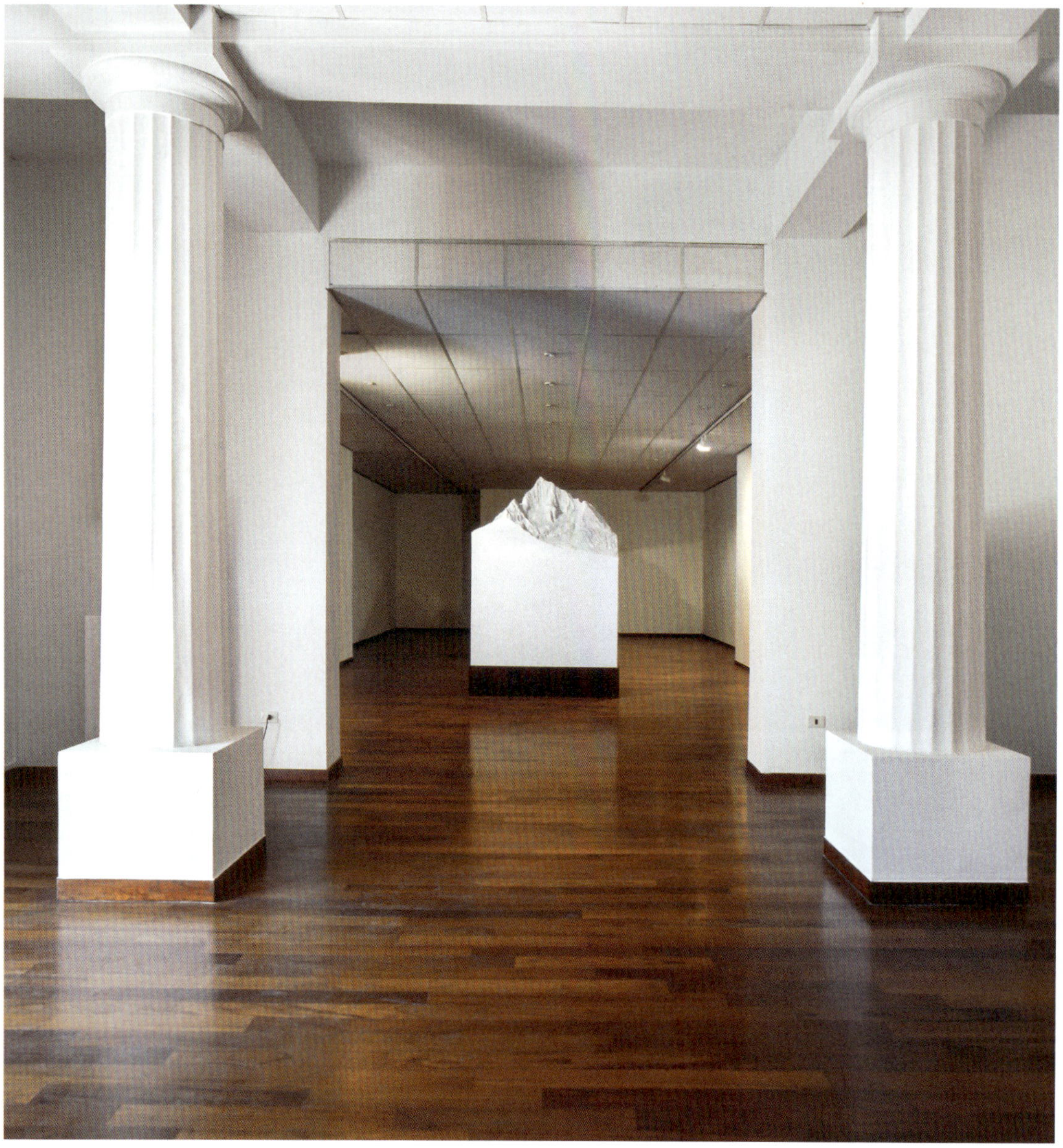

Gott als Berg denken
1999
Heilig-Geist-Kirche, Landshut

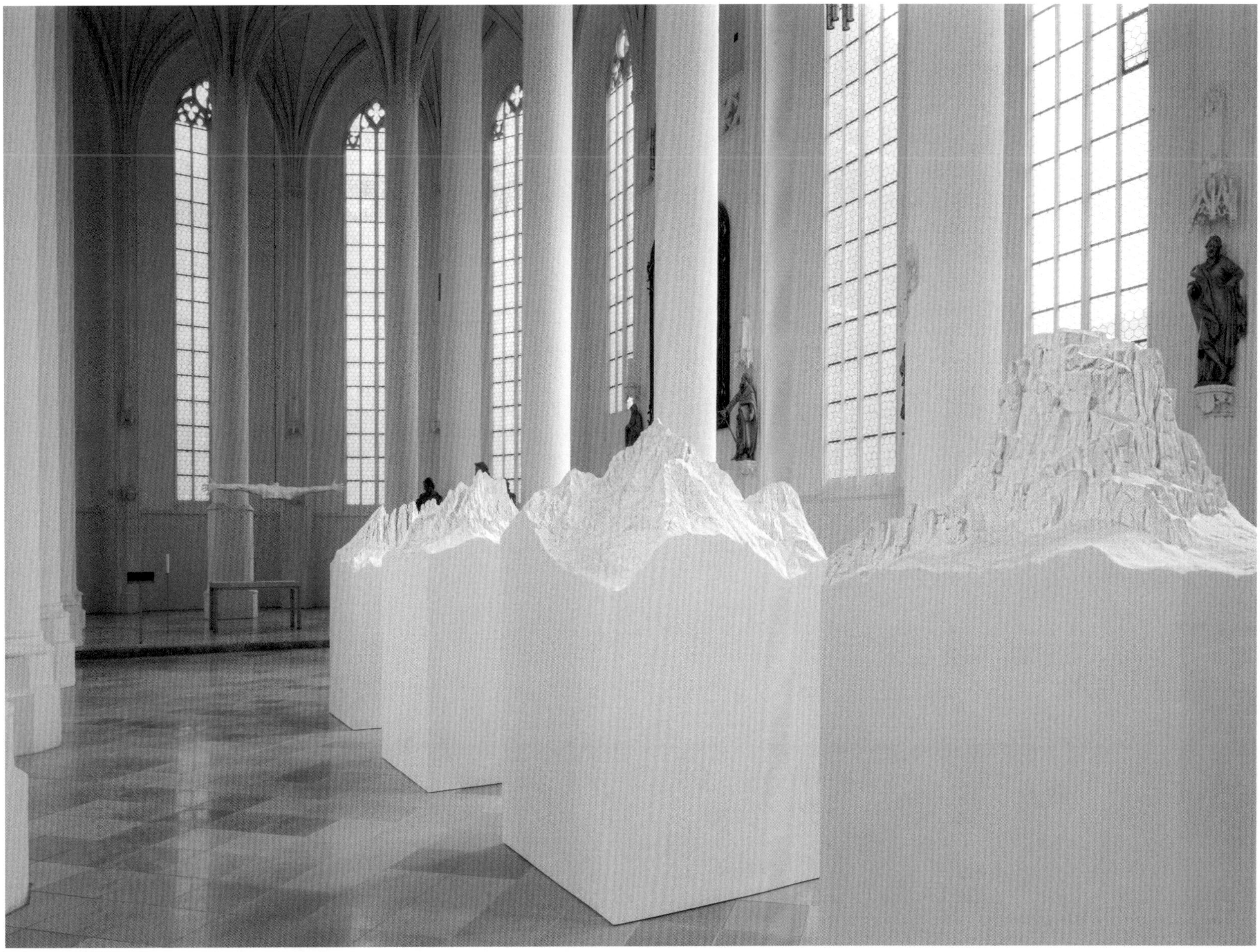

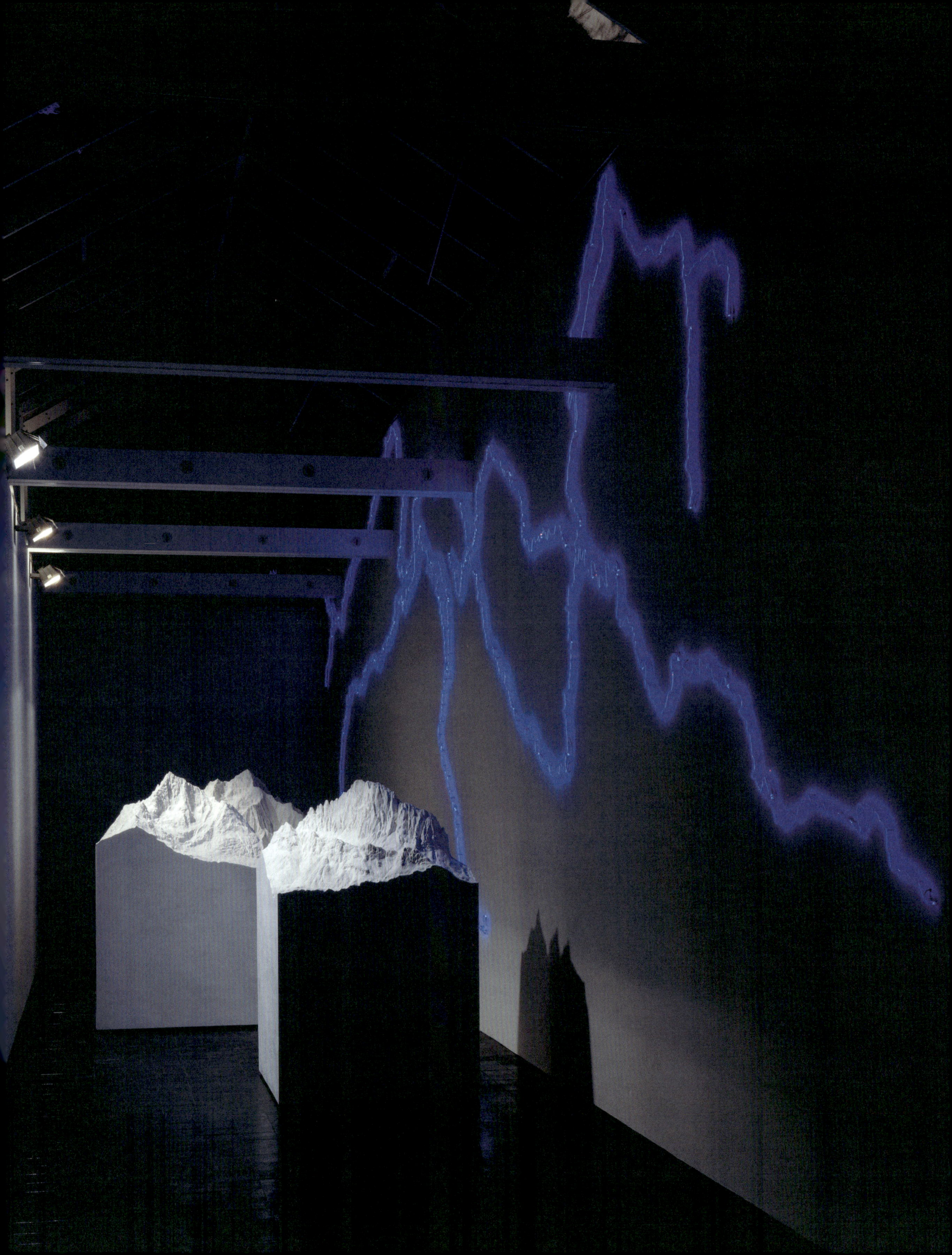

Gran Paradiso II
1998
Montblanc Kulturstiftung, Hamburg

Gran Paradiso II
1999
Hamburger Kunsthalle

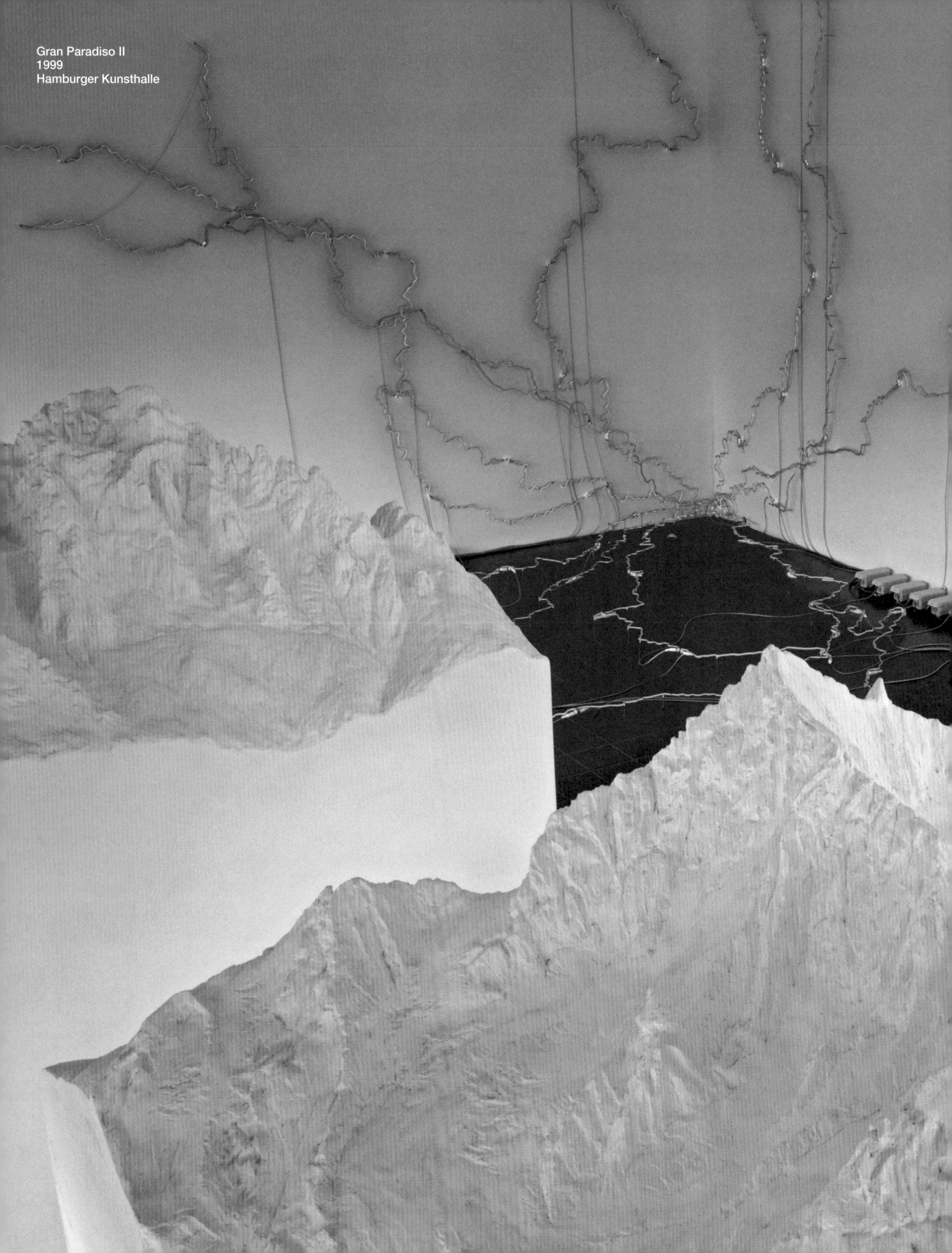

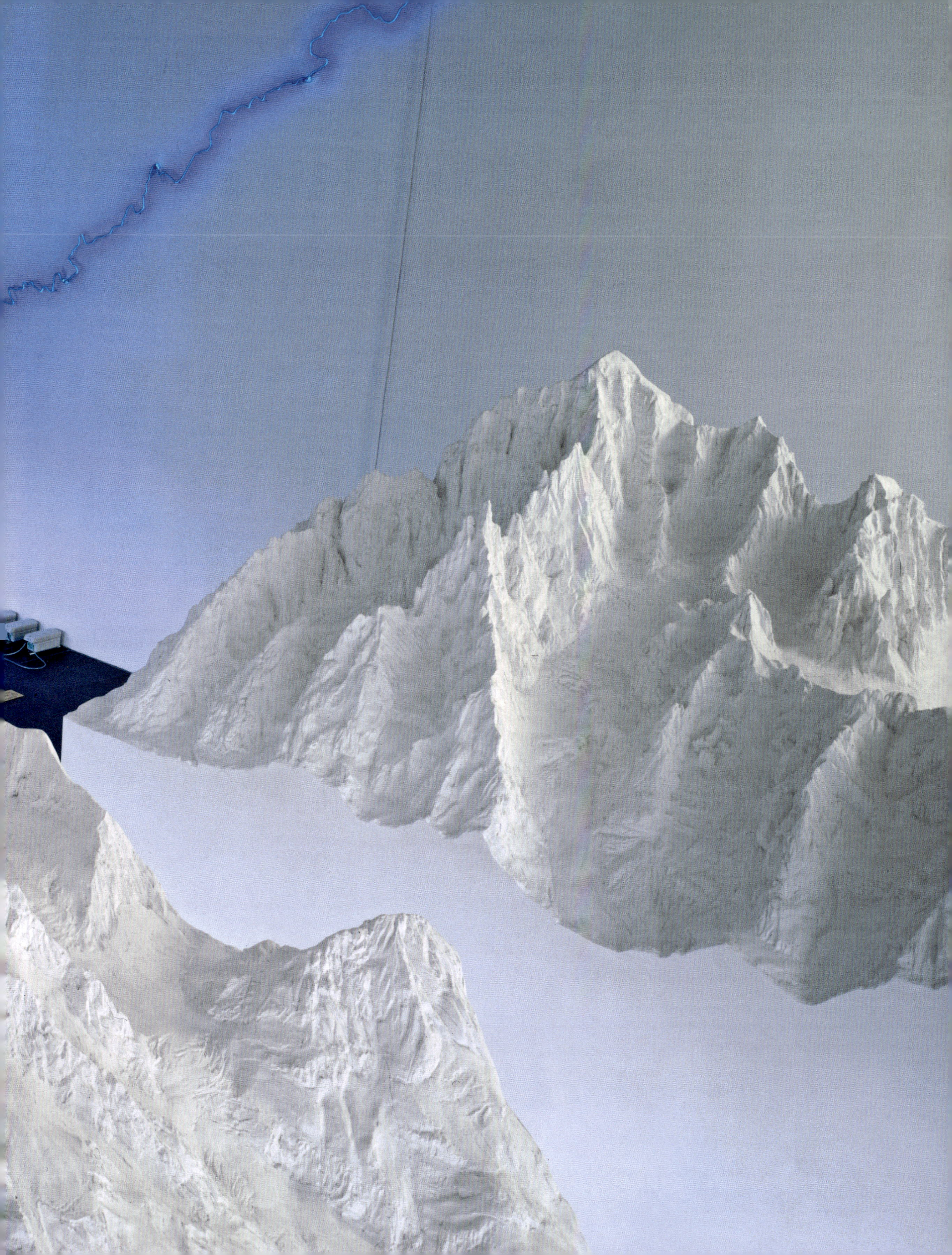

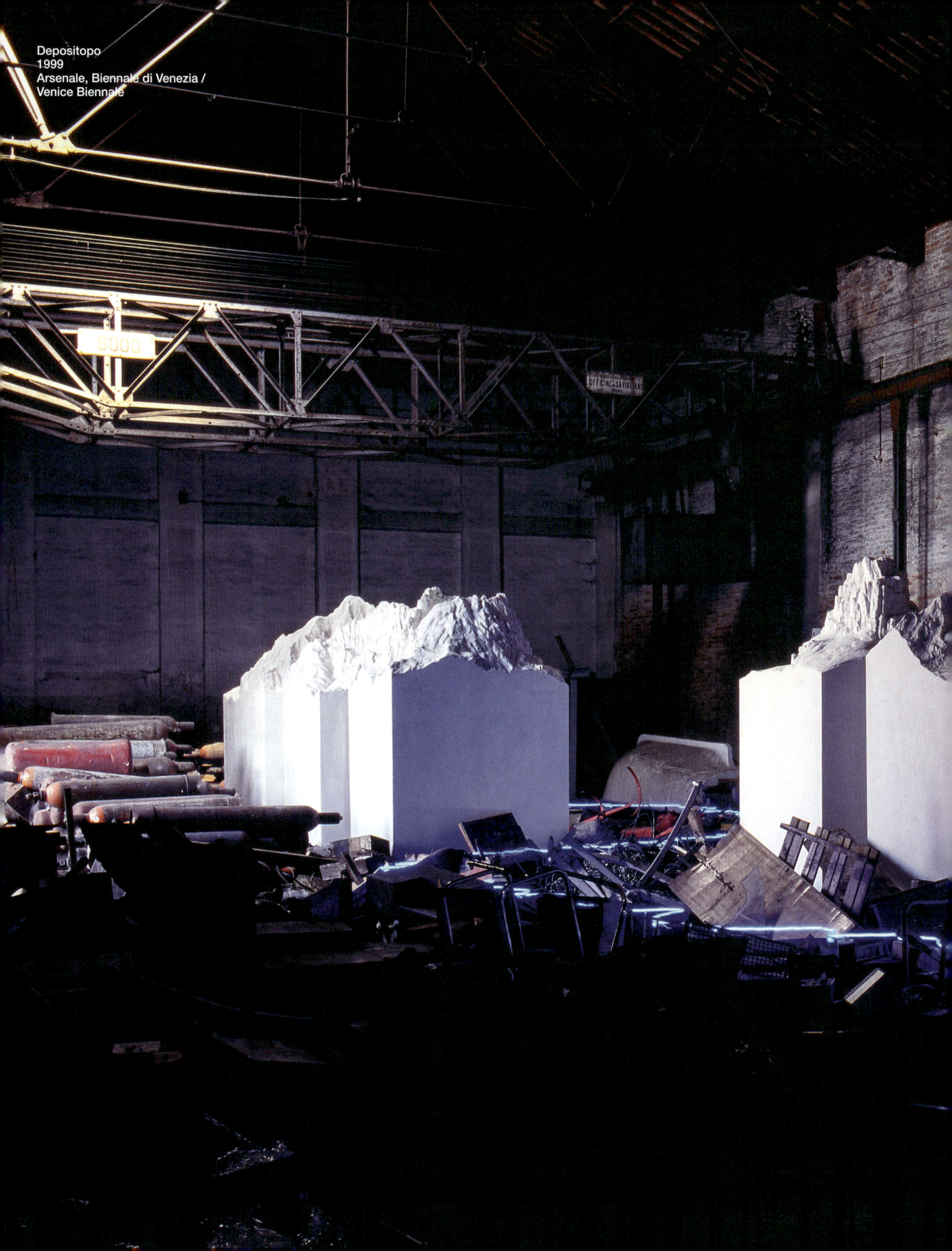

Depositopo
1999
Arsenale, Biennale di Venezia /
Venice Biennale

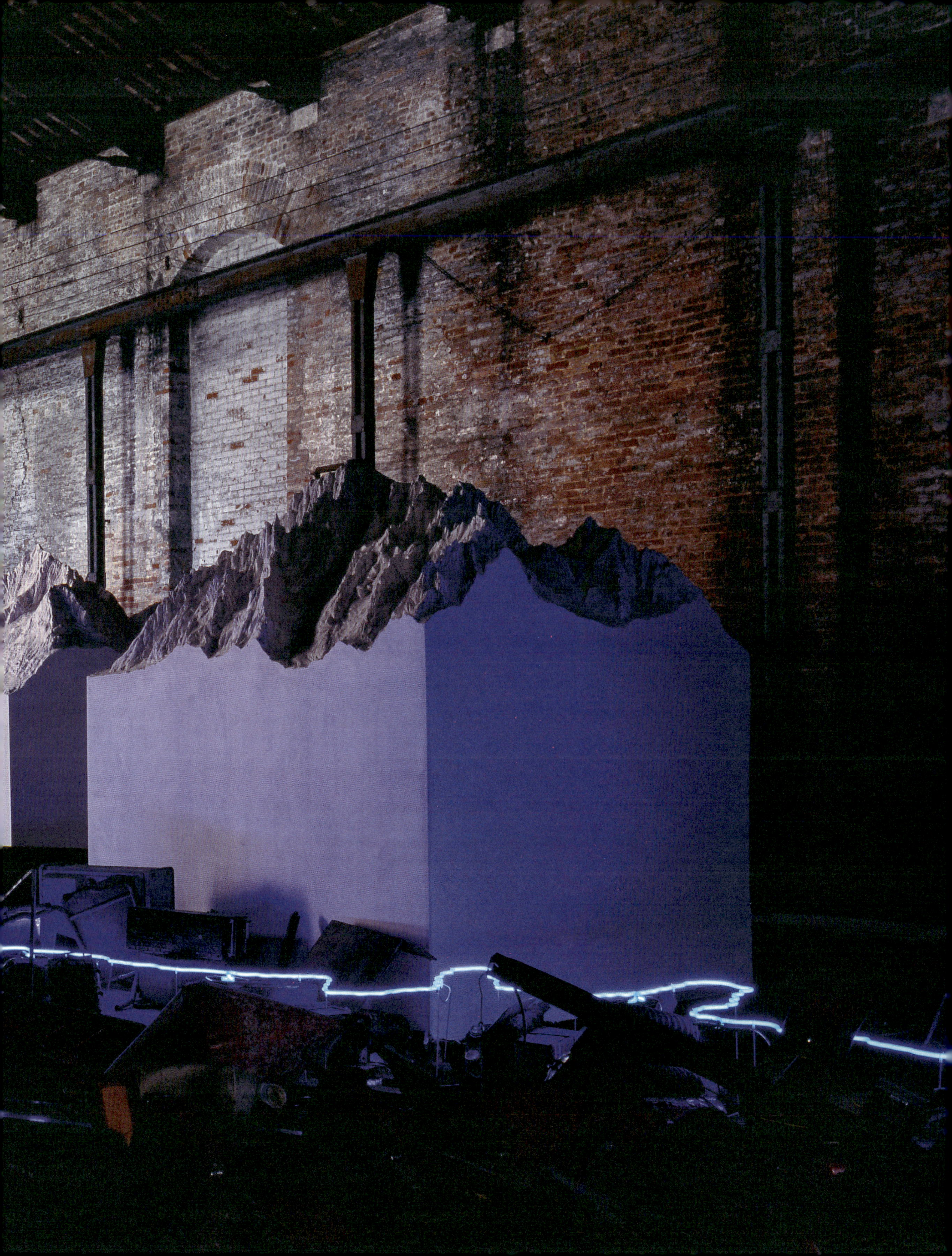

Depositopo
1999
Arsenale, Biennale di Venezia /
Venice Biennale

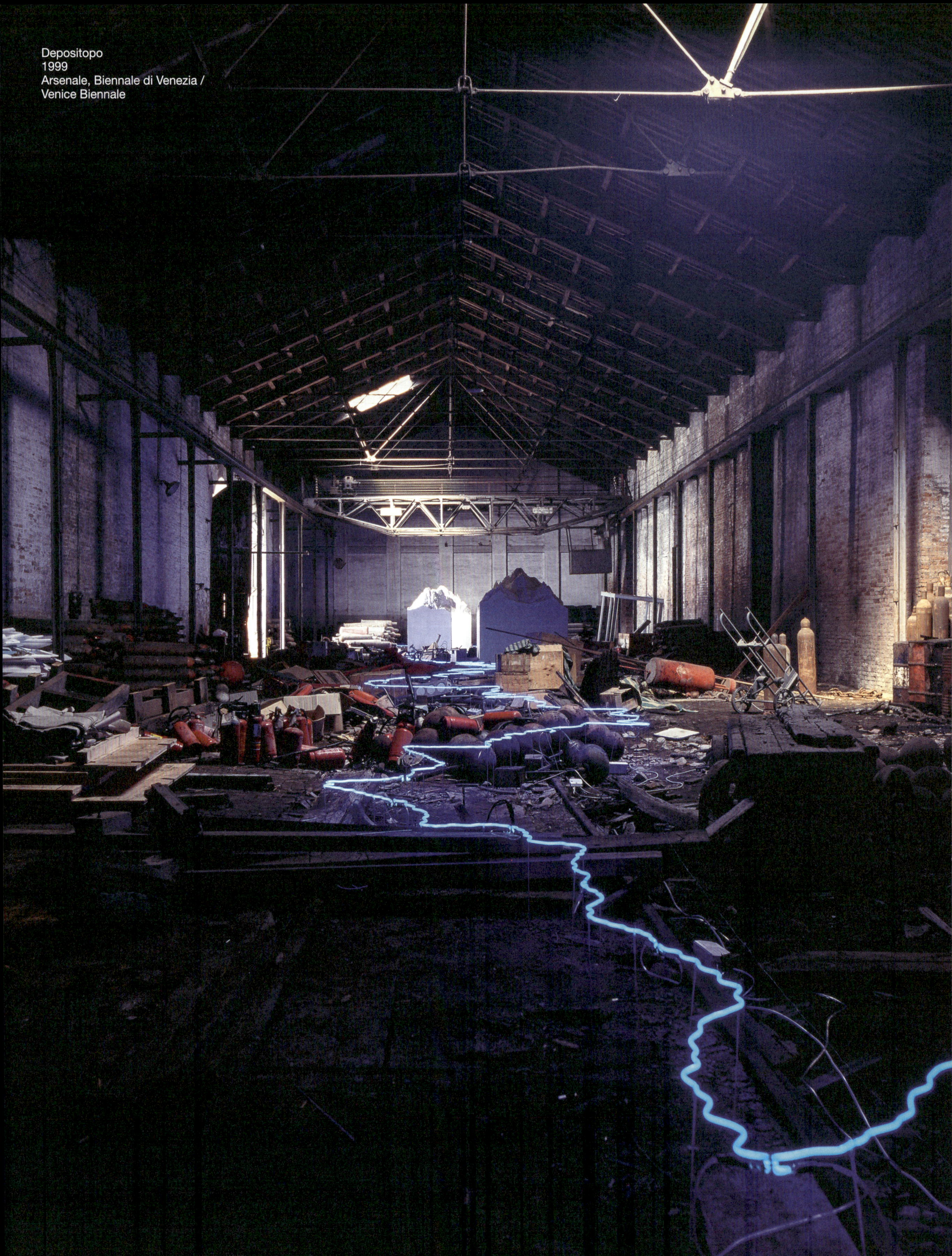

Großes Panorama
2006

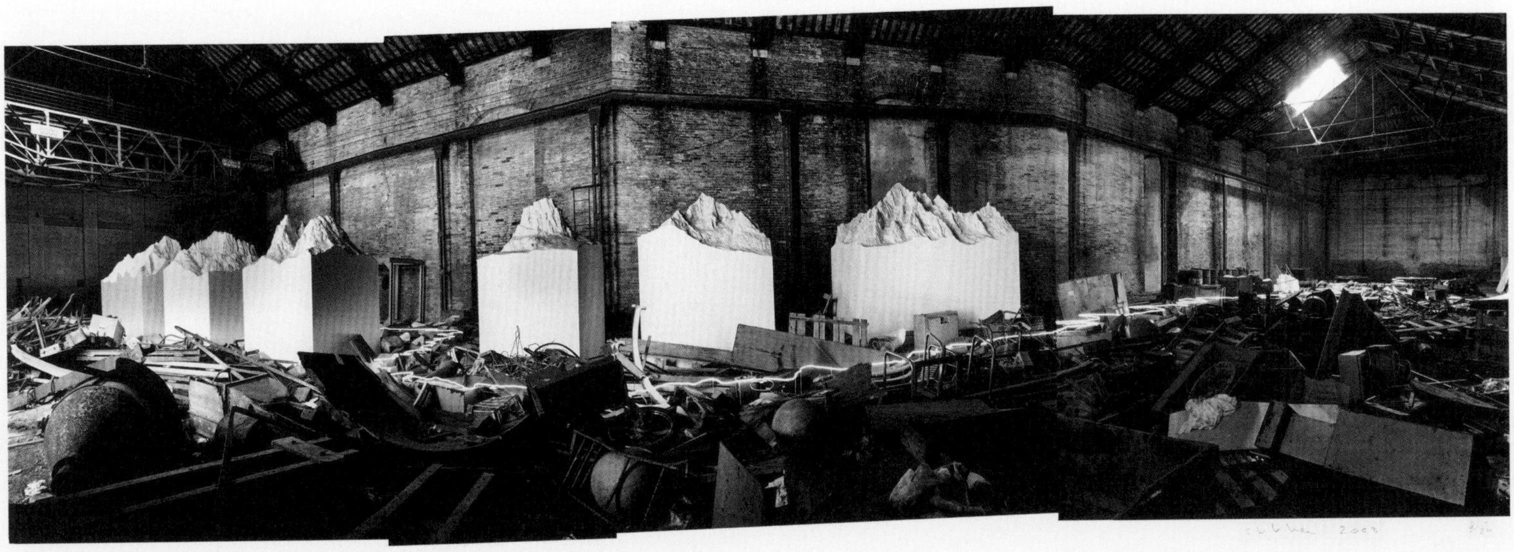

For Louis
2000

Krone
2000

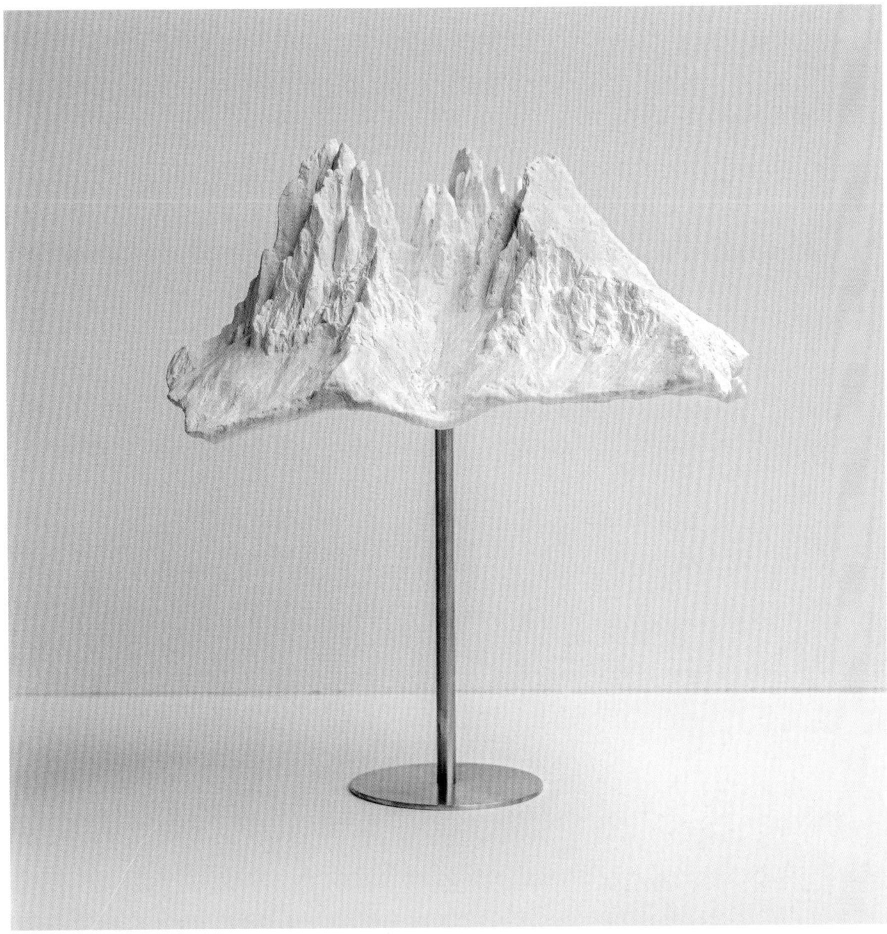

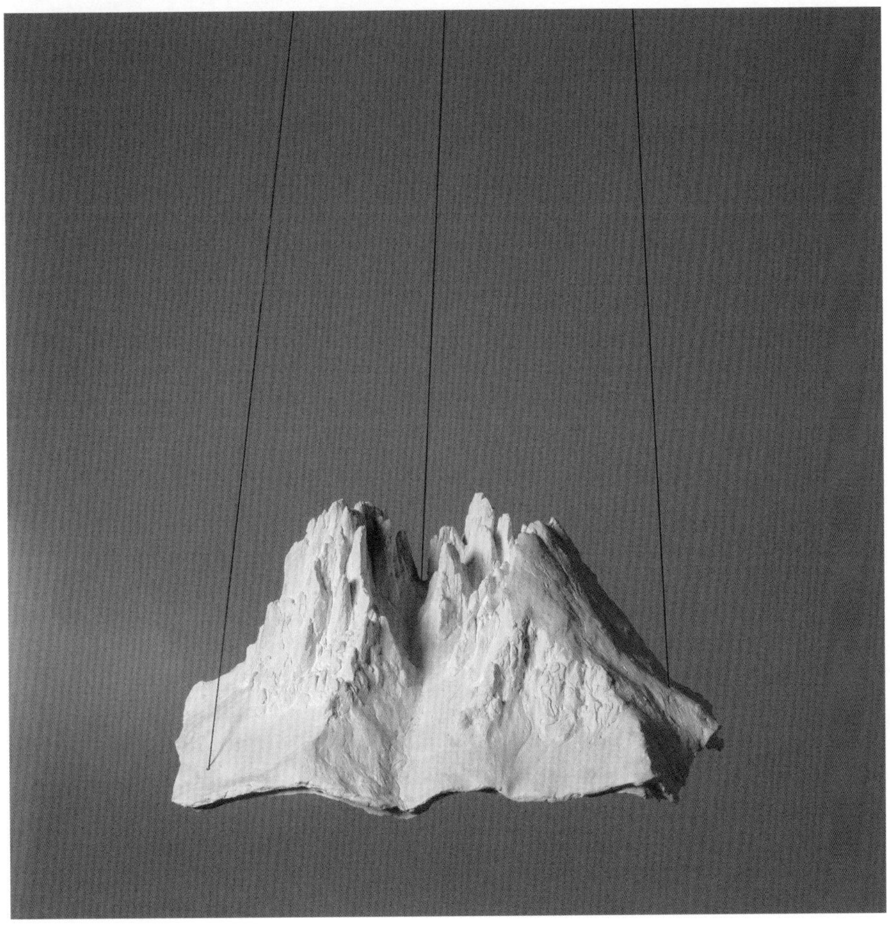

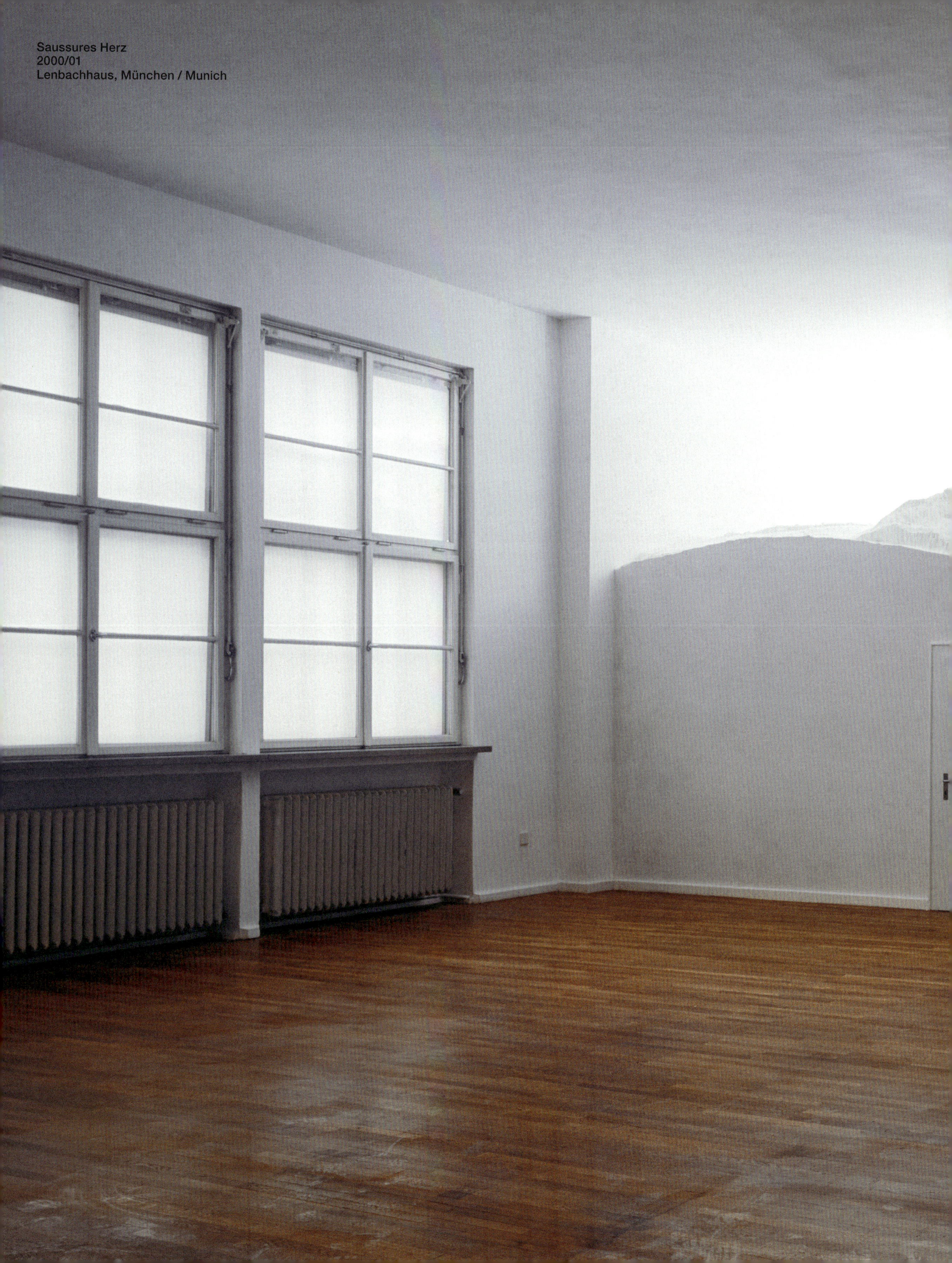

Saussures Herz
2000/01
Lenbachhaus, München / Munich

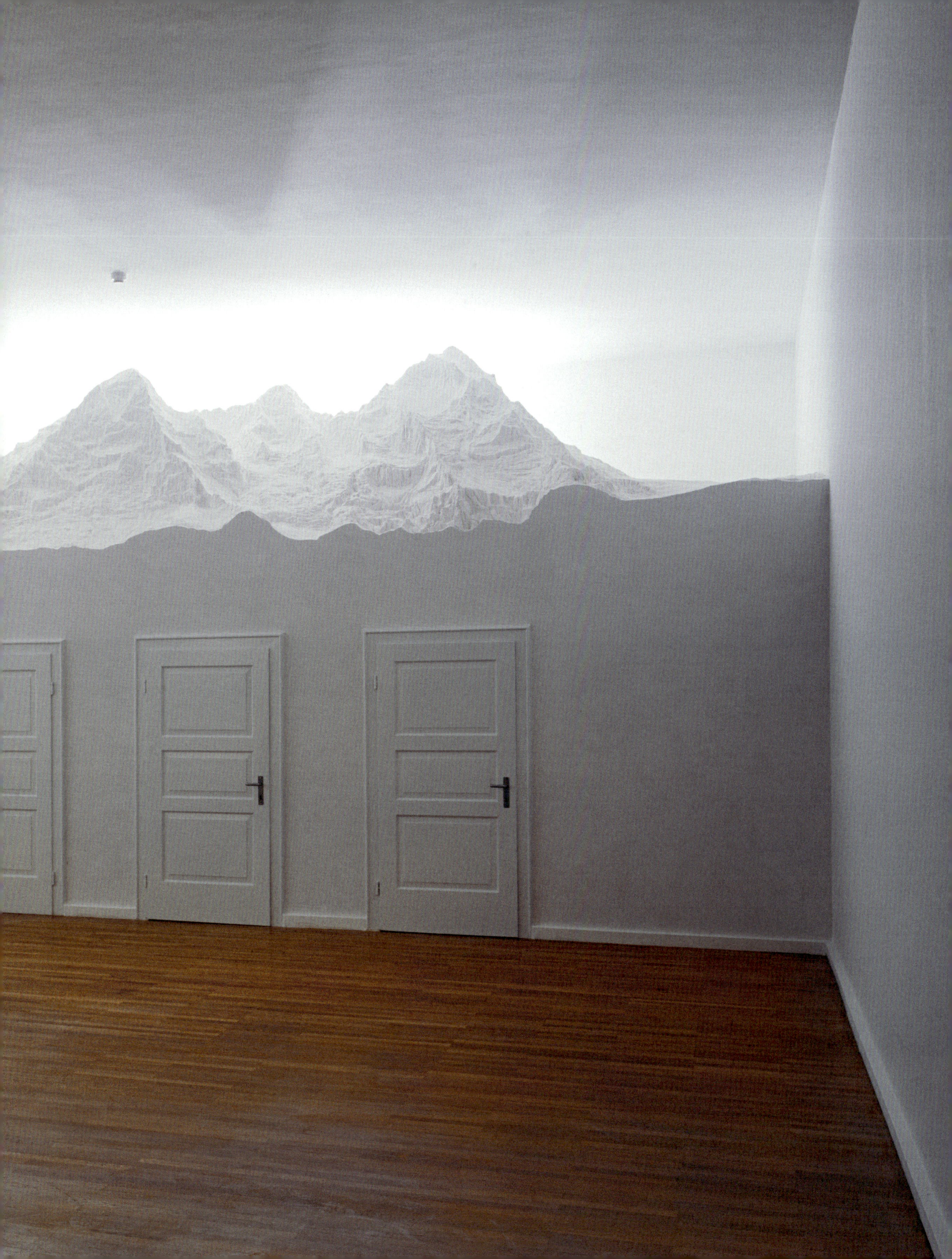

Saussures Herz
2000/01
Lenbachhaus, München / Munich

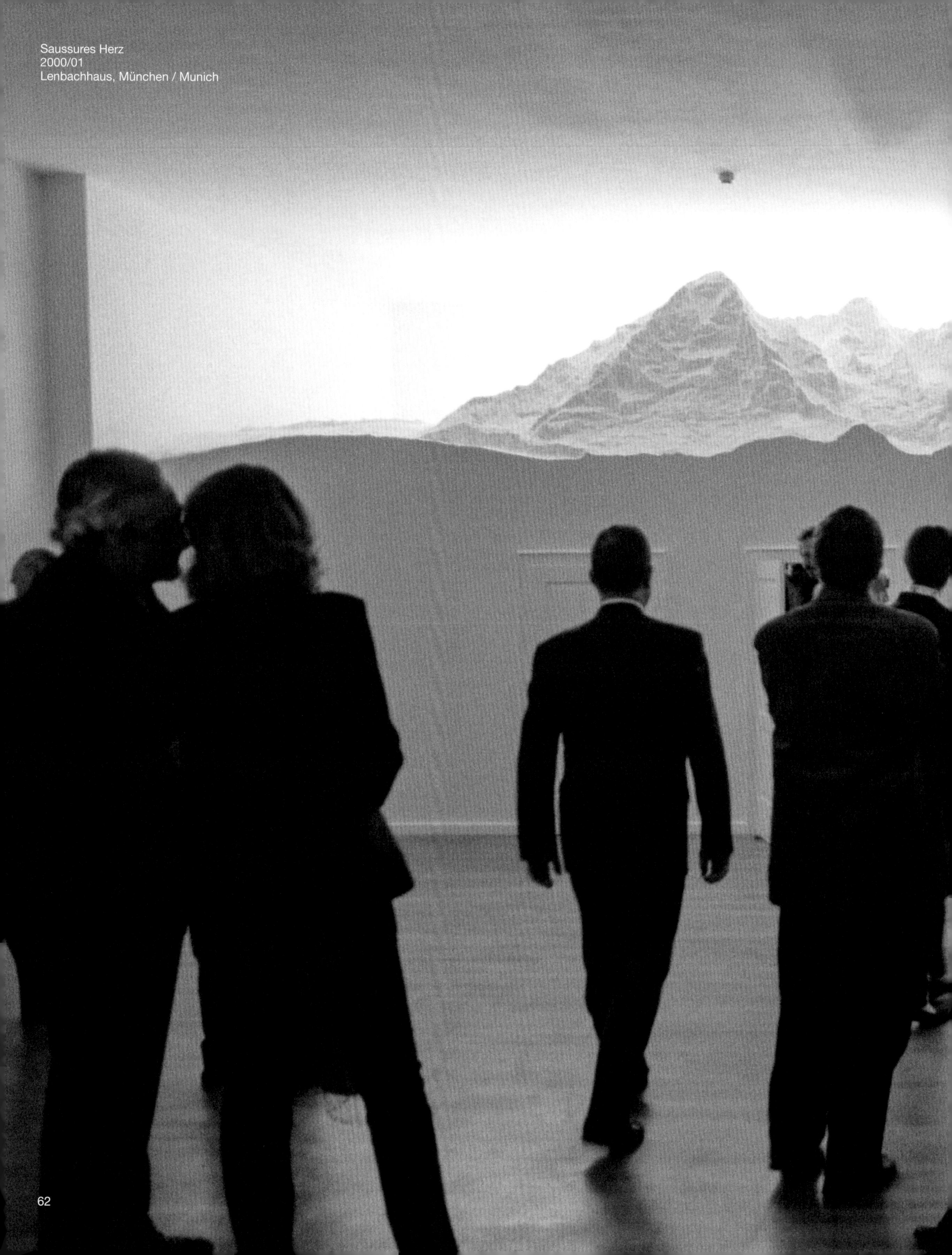

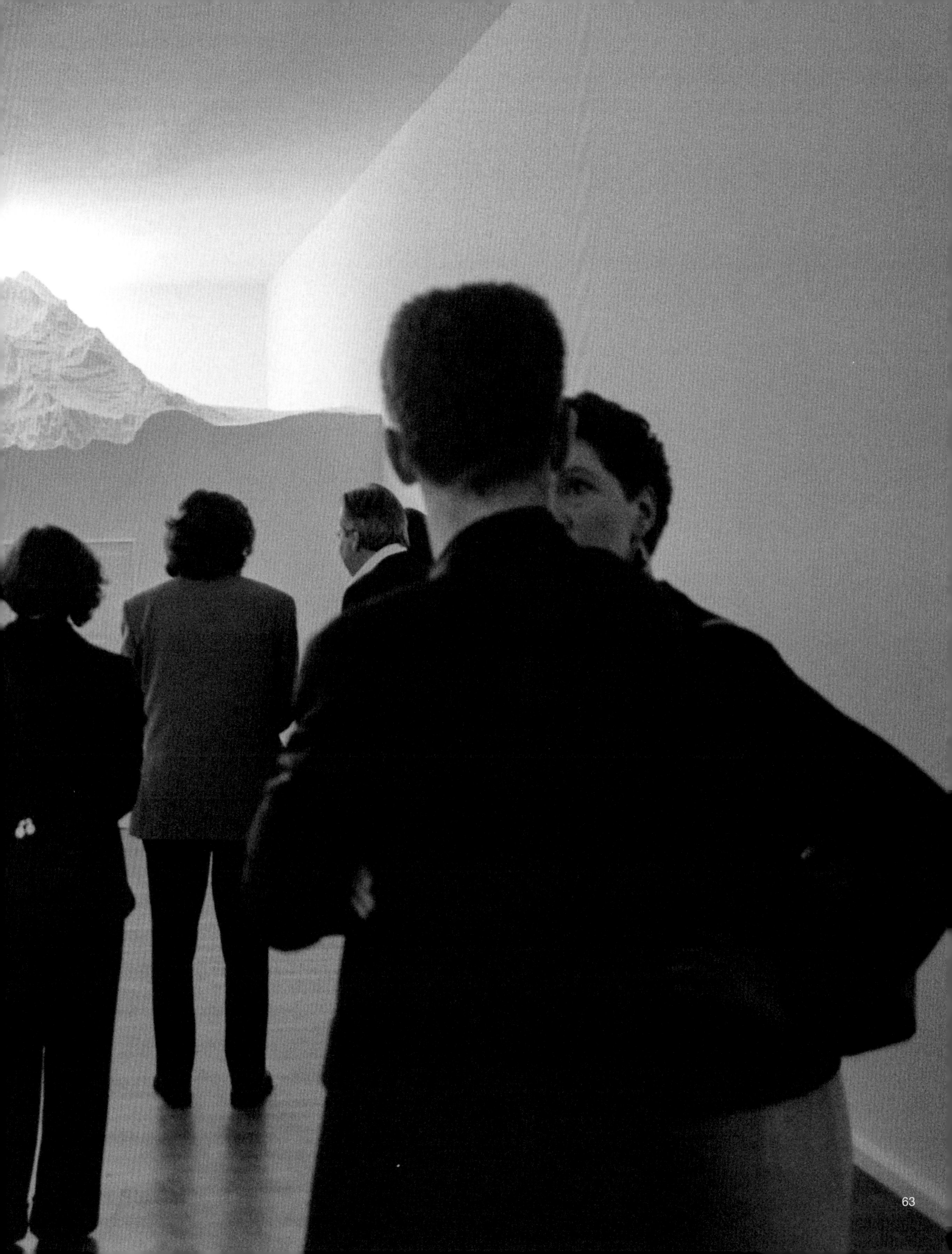

Saussures Herz
2000/01
Museum der bildenden Künste, Leipzig

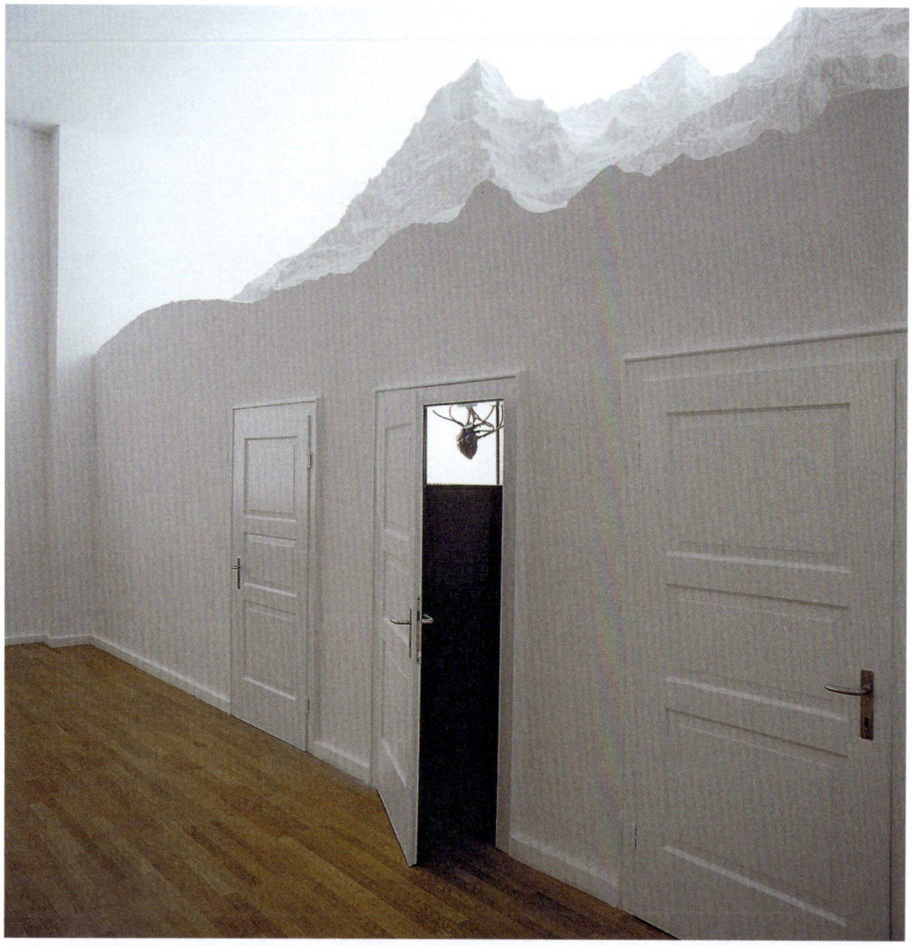

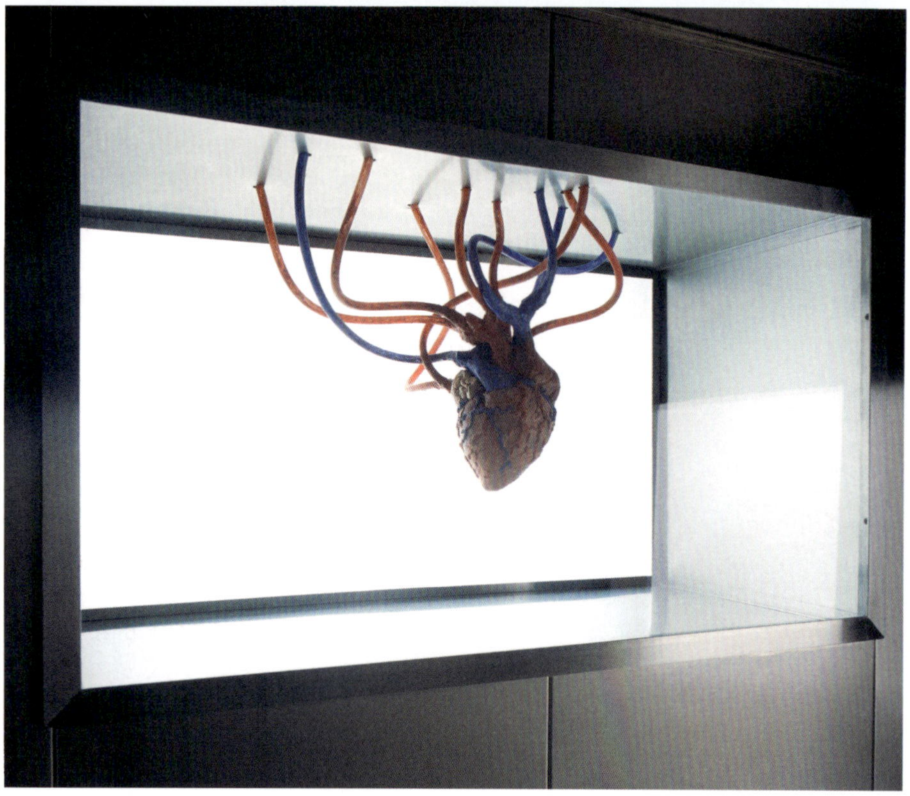

Ernstes Spiel
2006

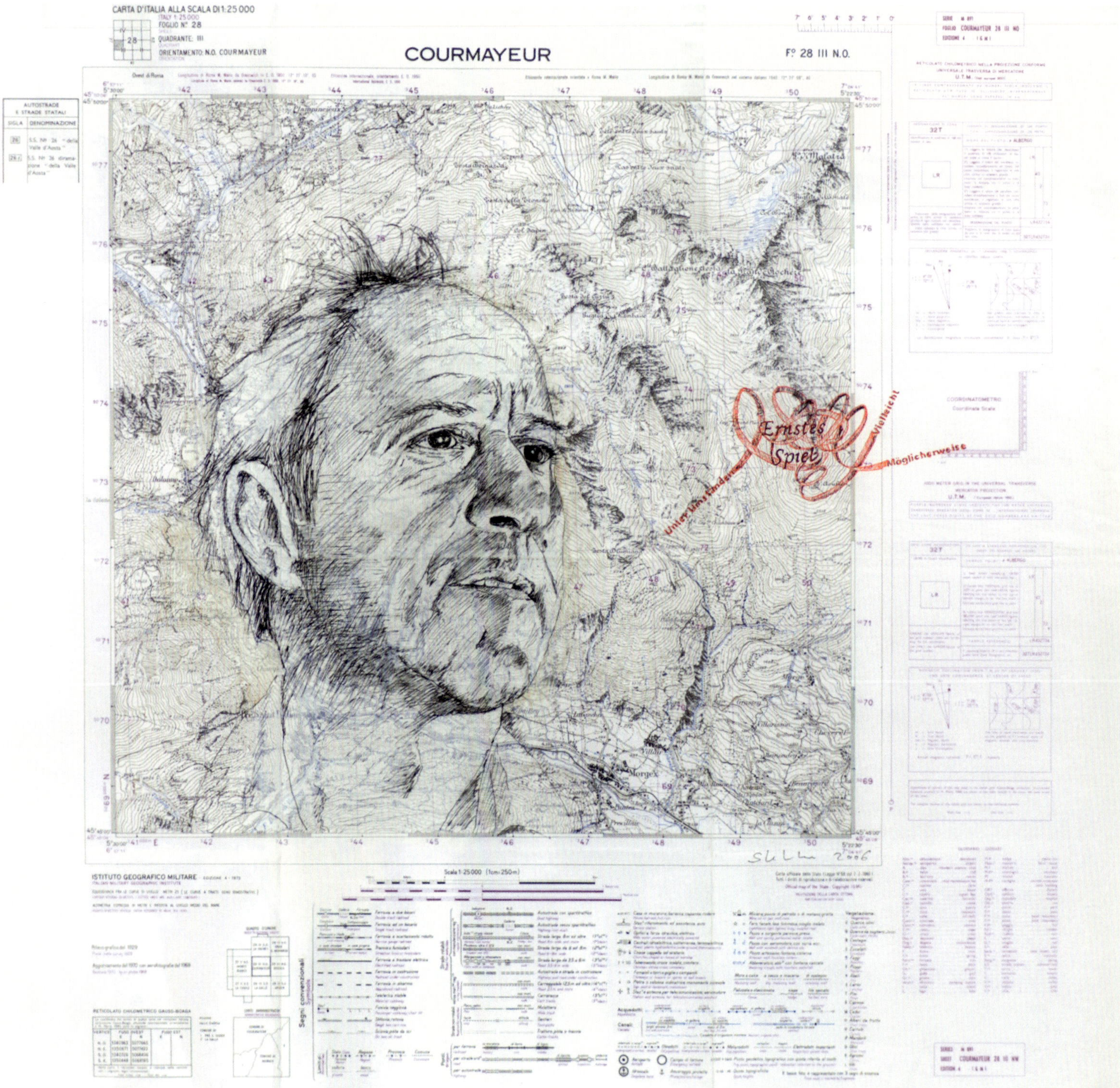

Hier und jetzt
2006

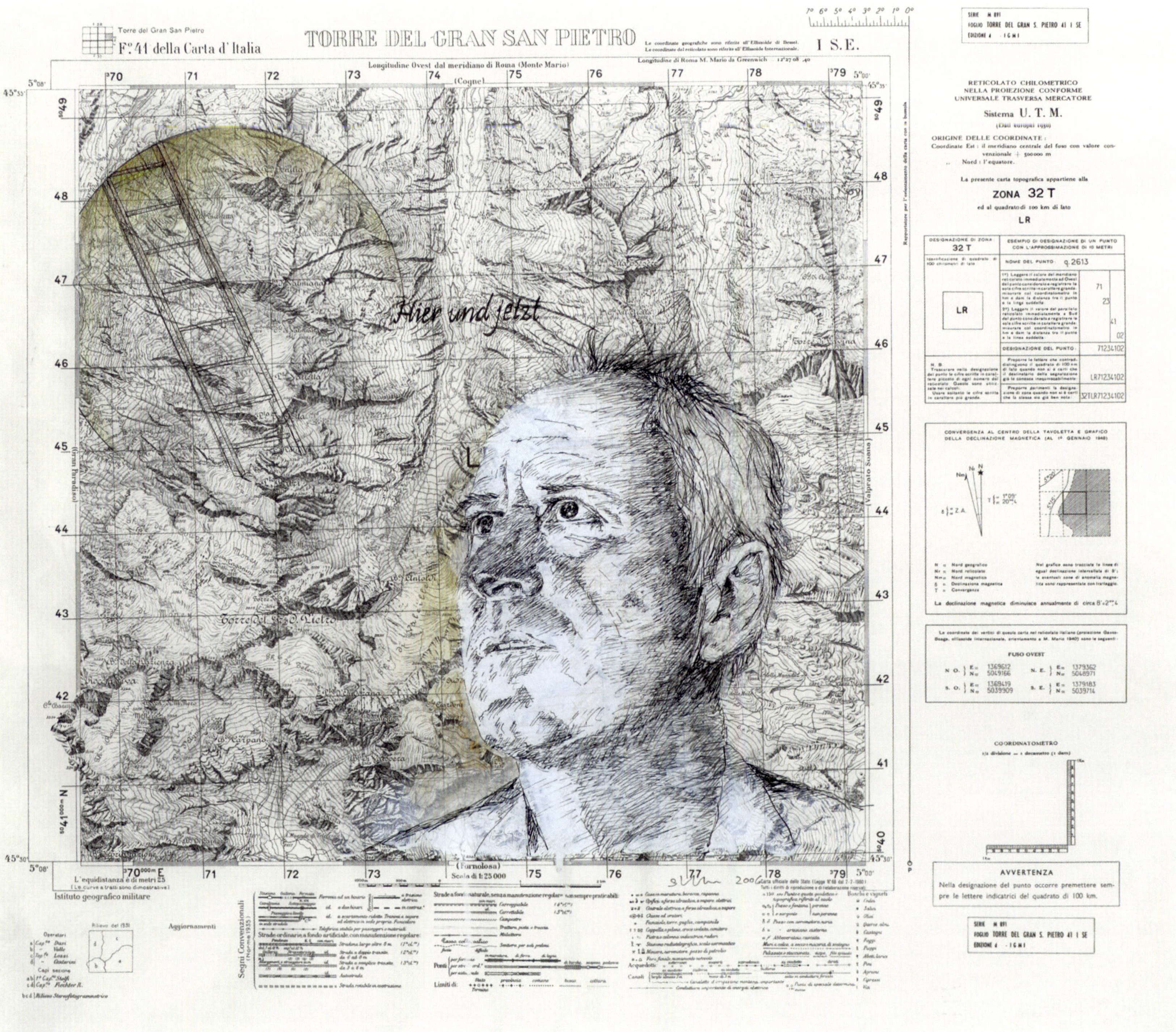

Mein Ausflug zum
Spiral Jetty im Jahr 1957
2003

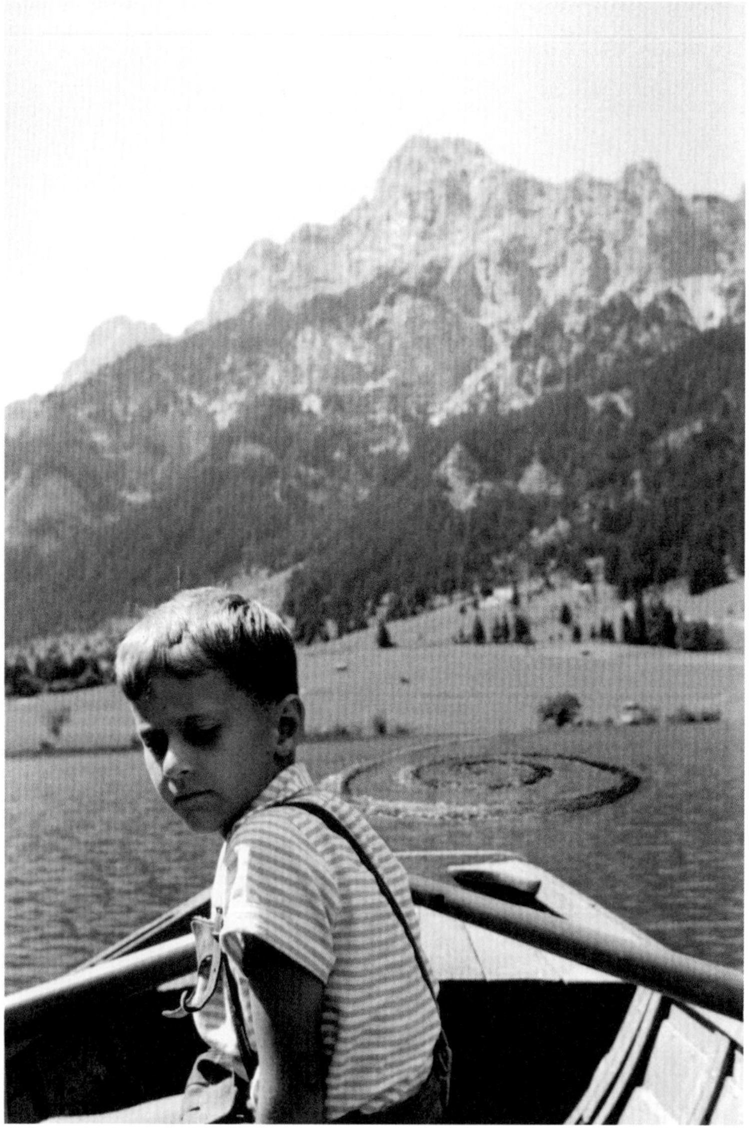

Mein zufälliges dabei sein
bei Asphalt Rundown im Jahr 1958
2003

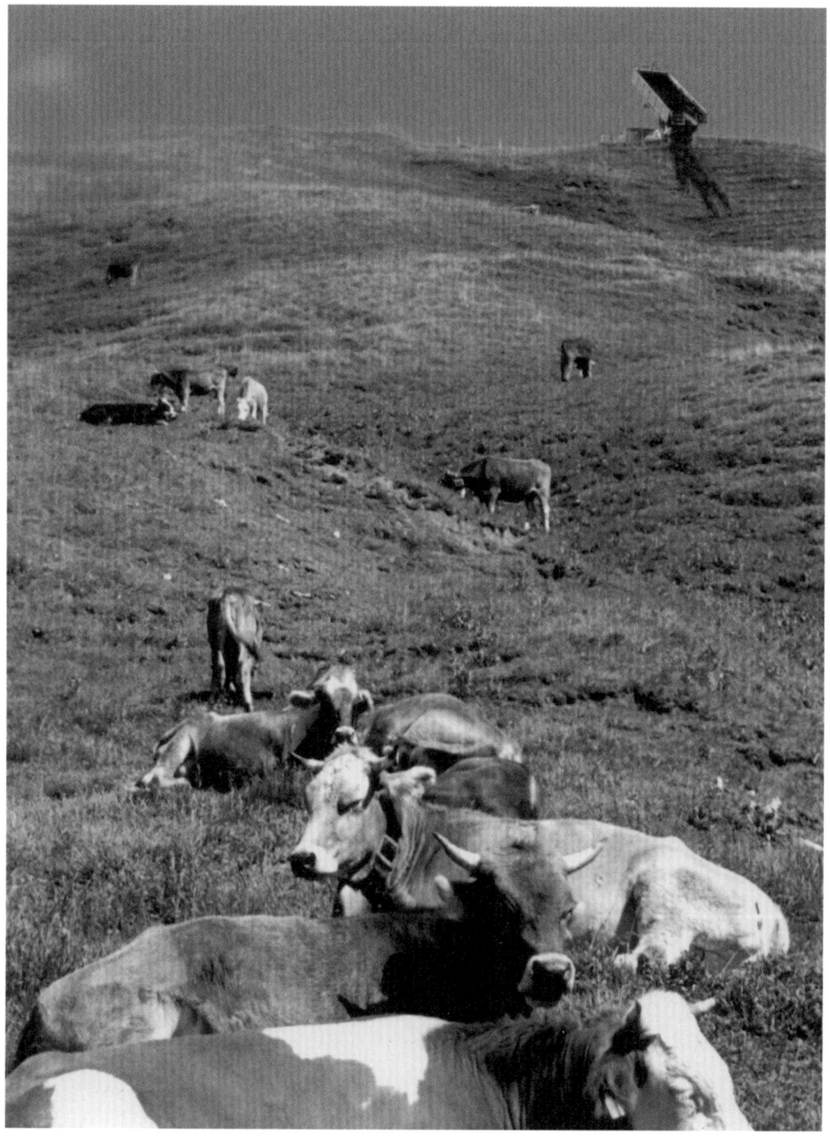

Shit Happens
2001

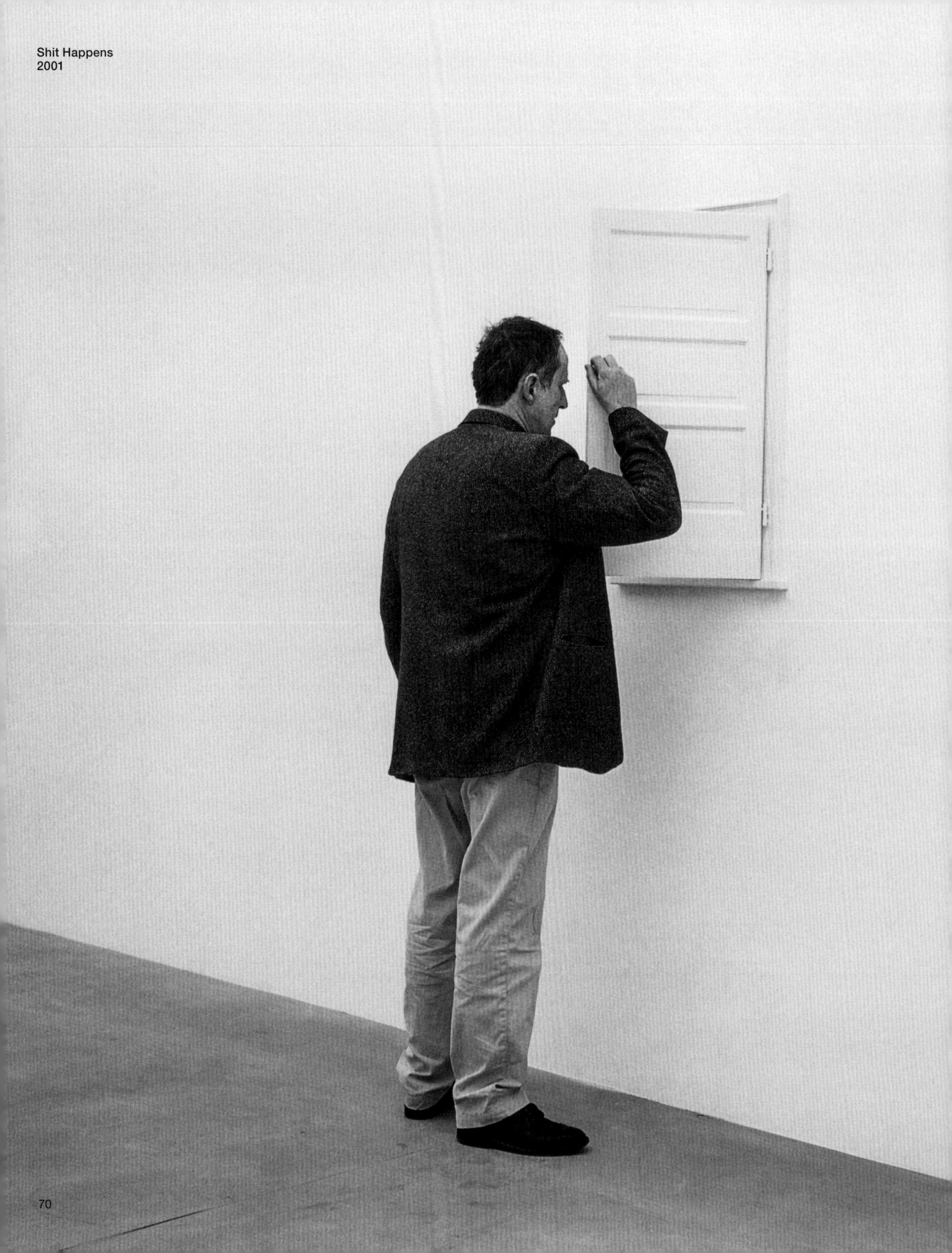

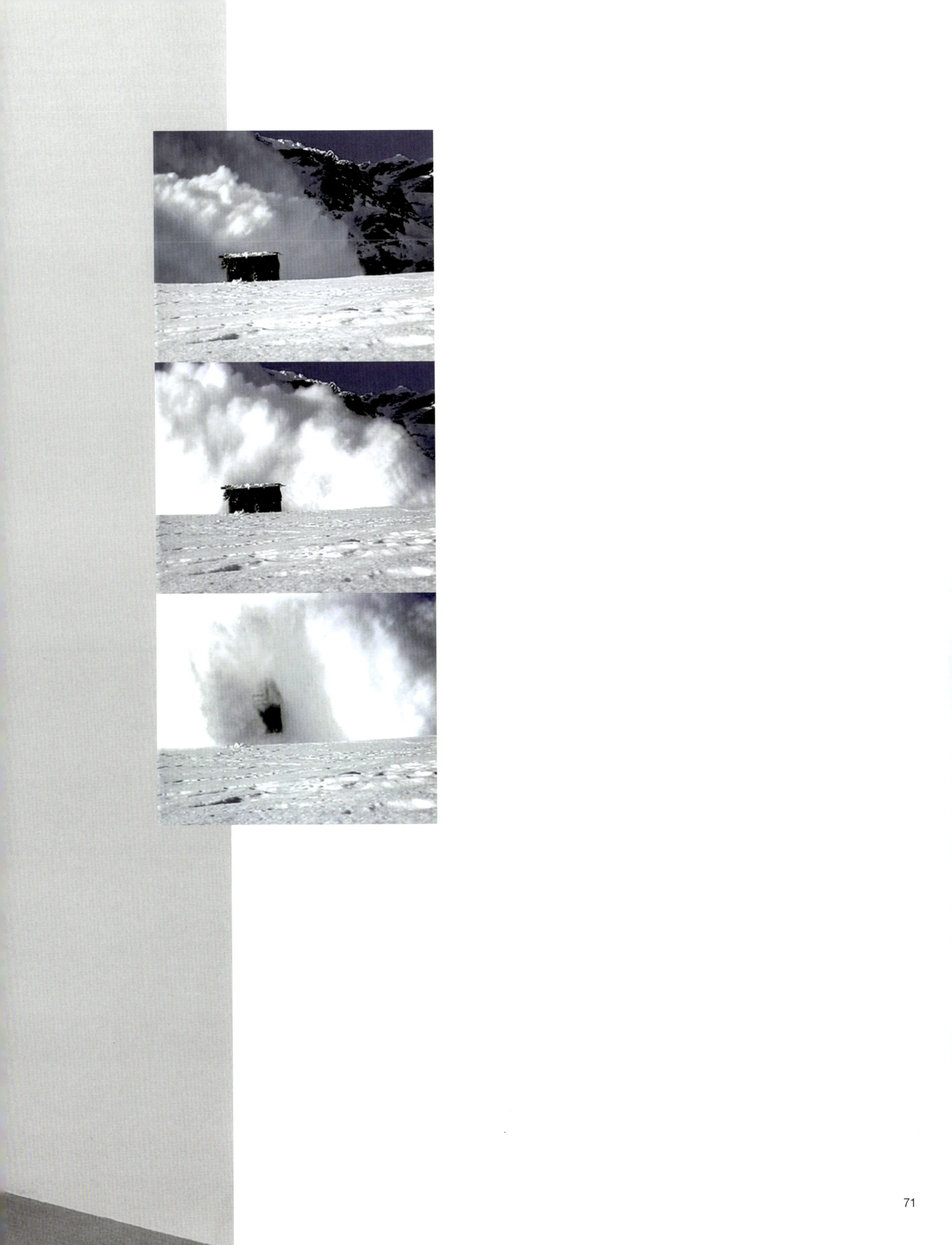

Shining
2004

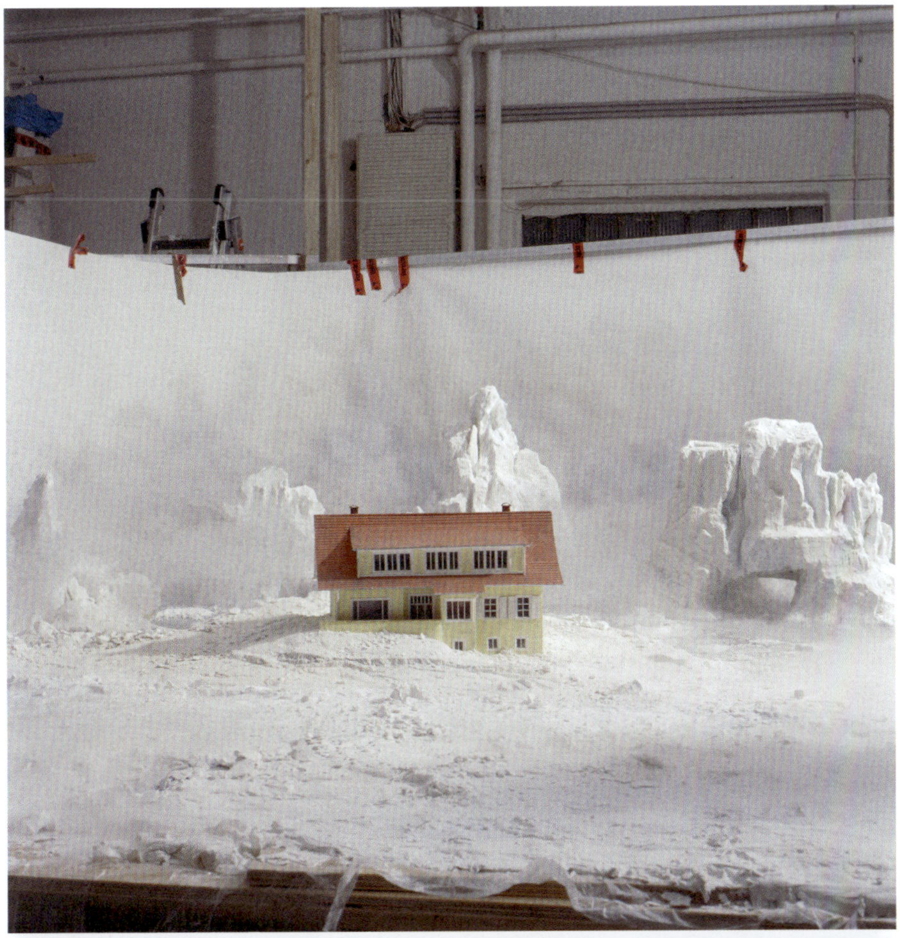

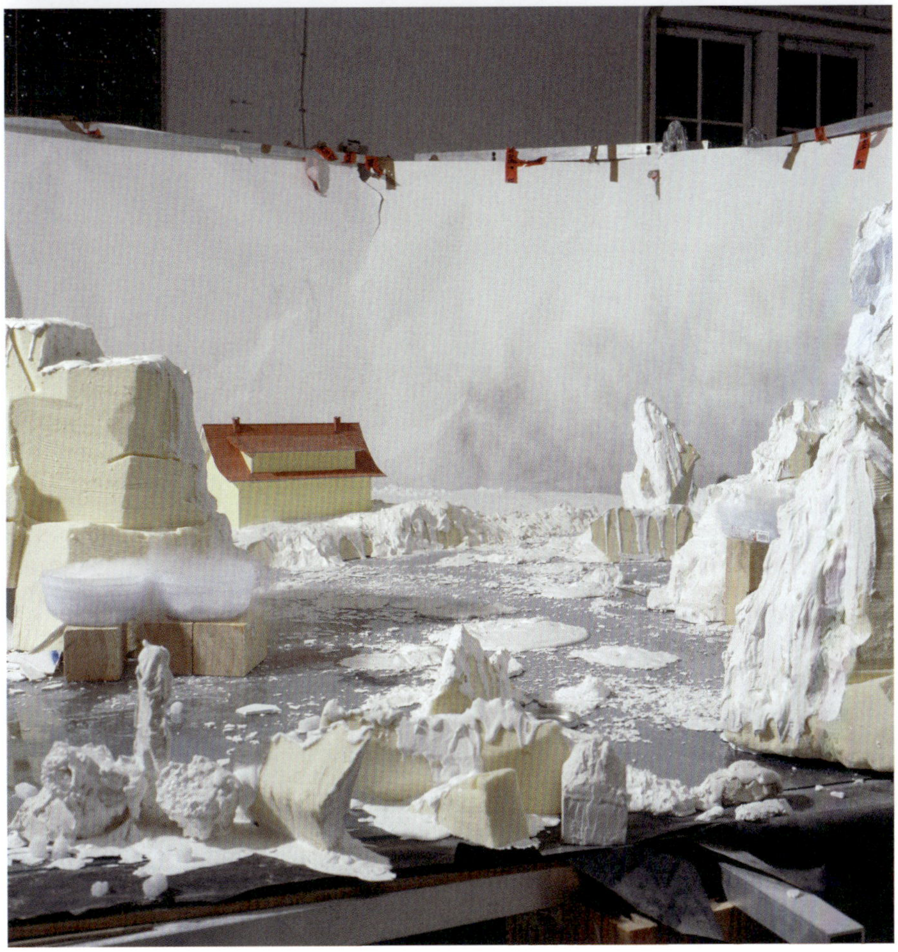

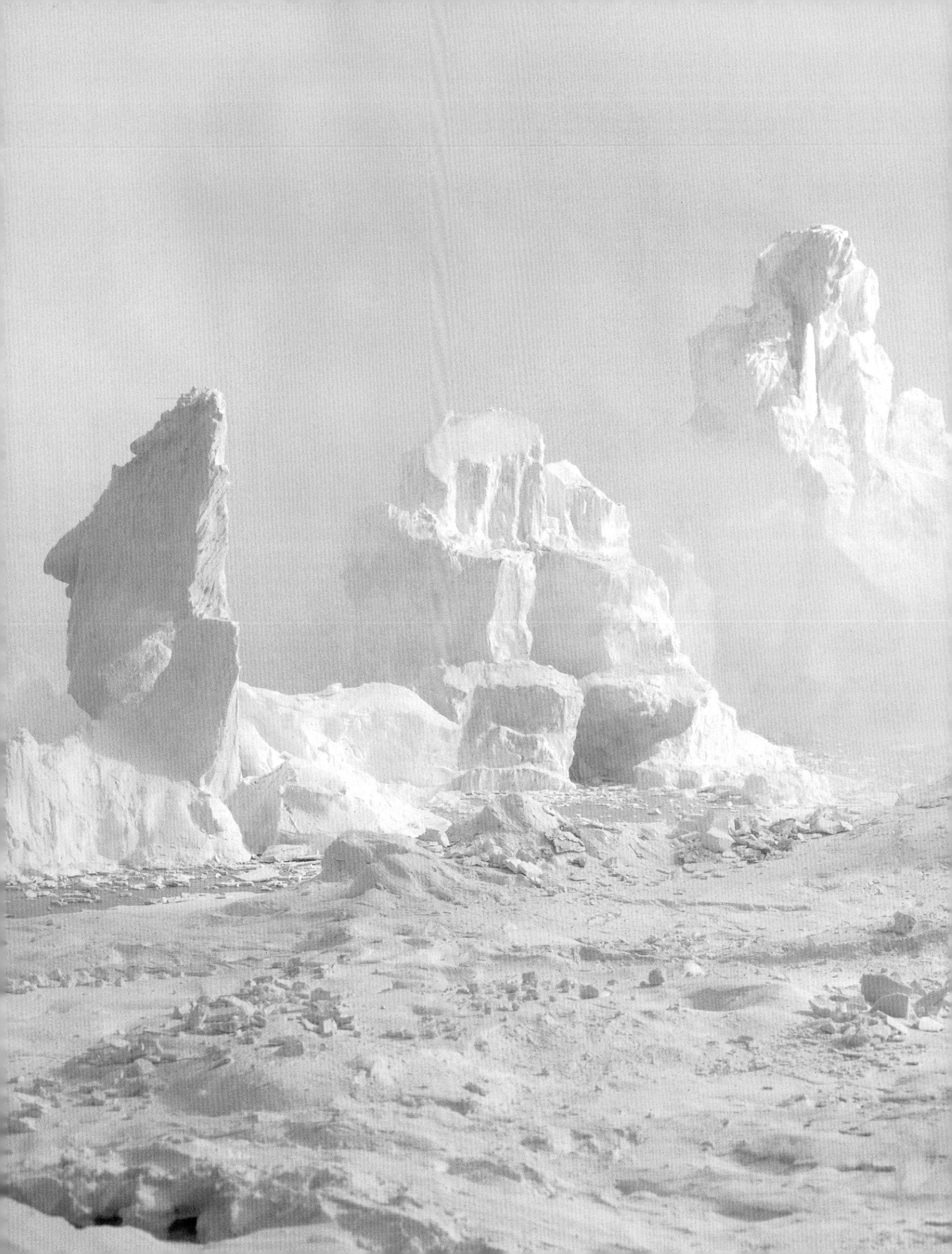

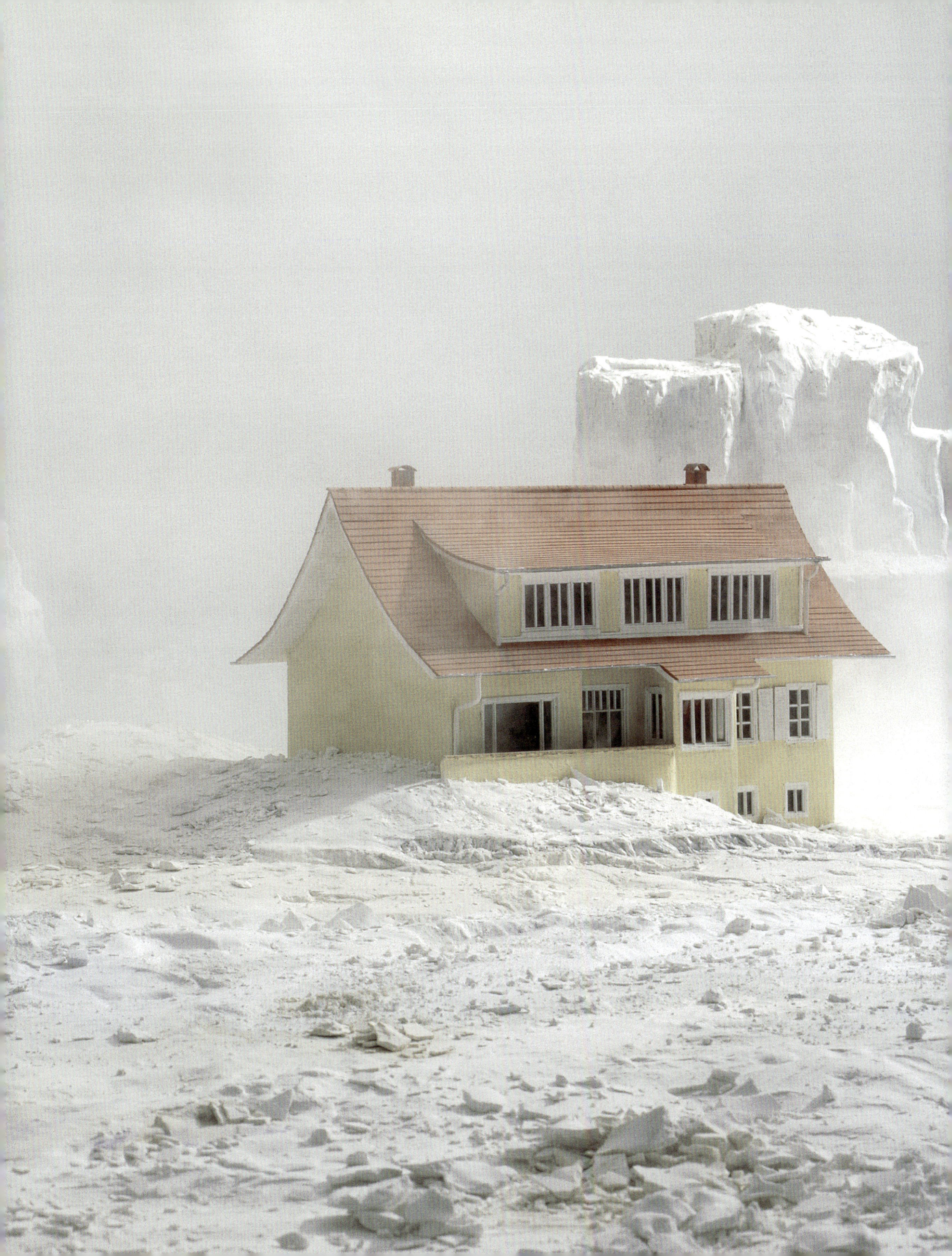

Shining
2001

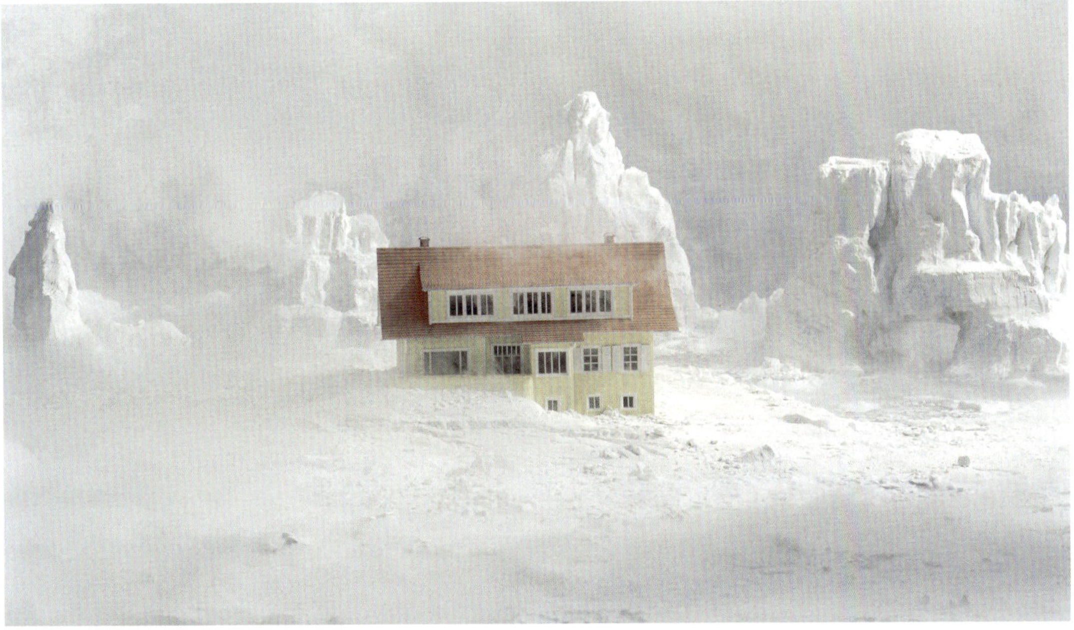

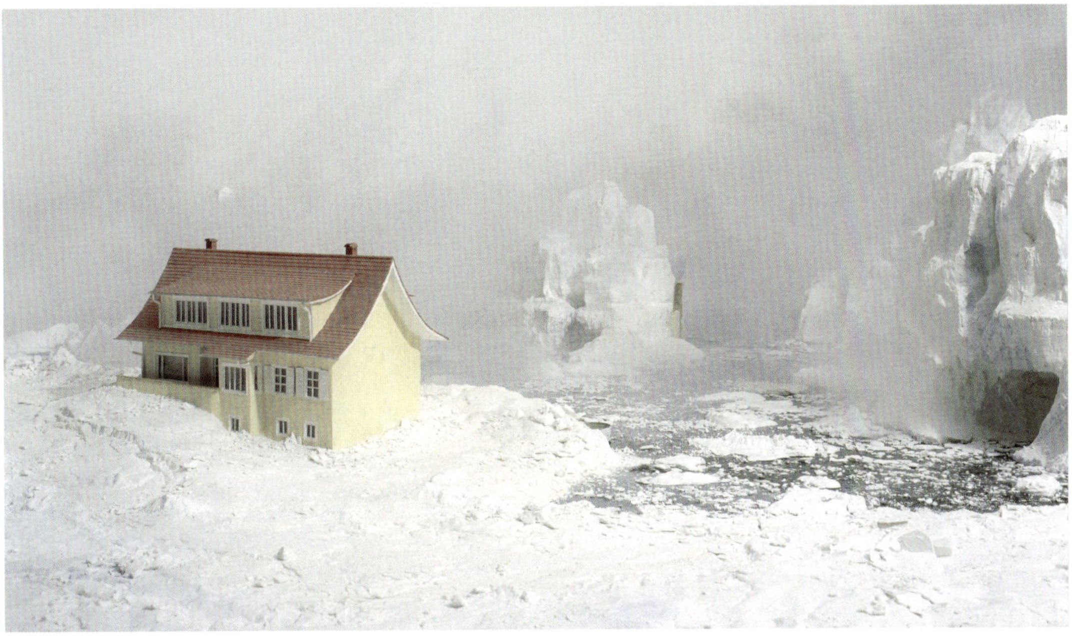

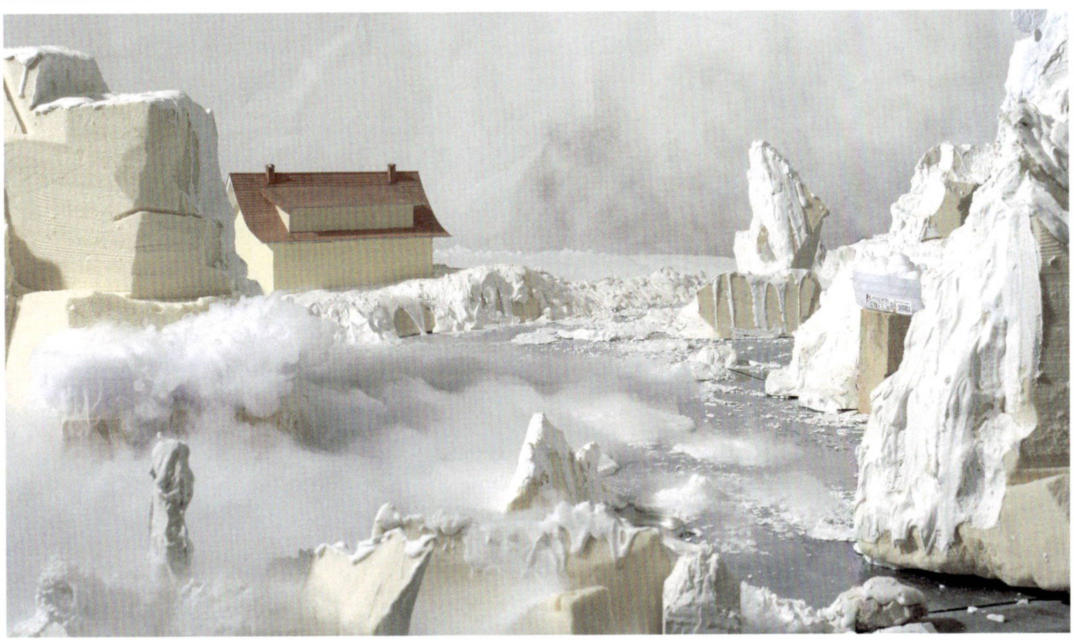

Ohne Titel
1998

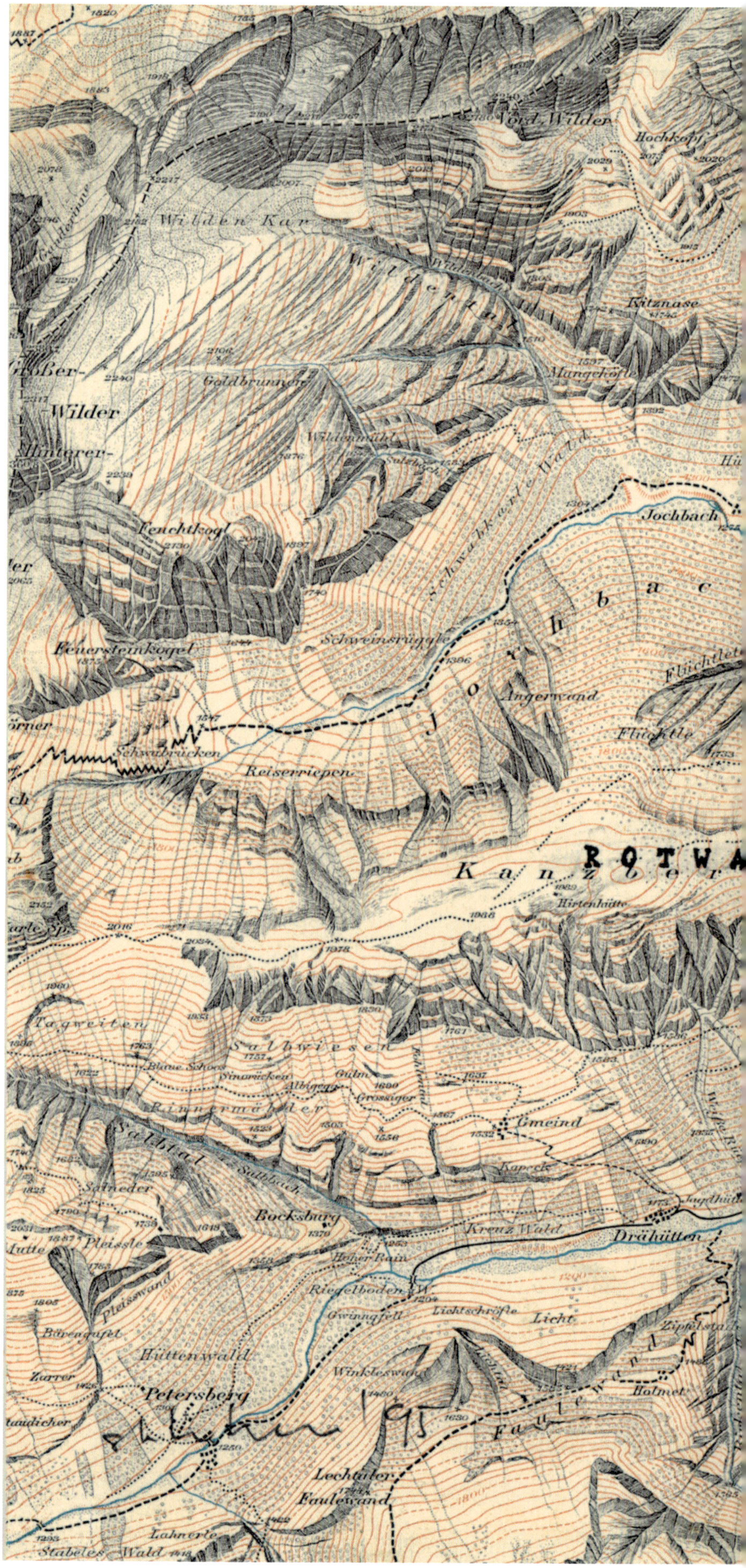

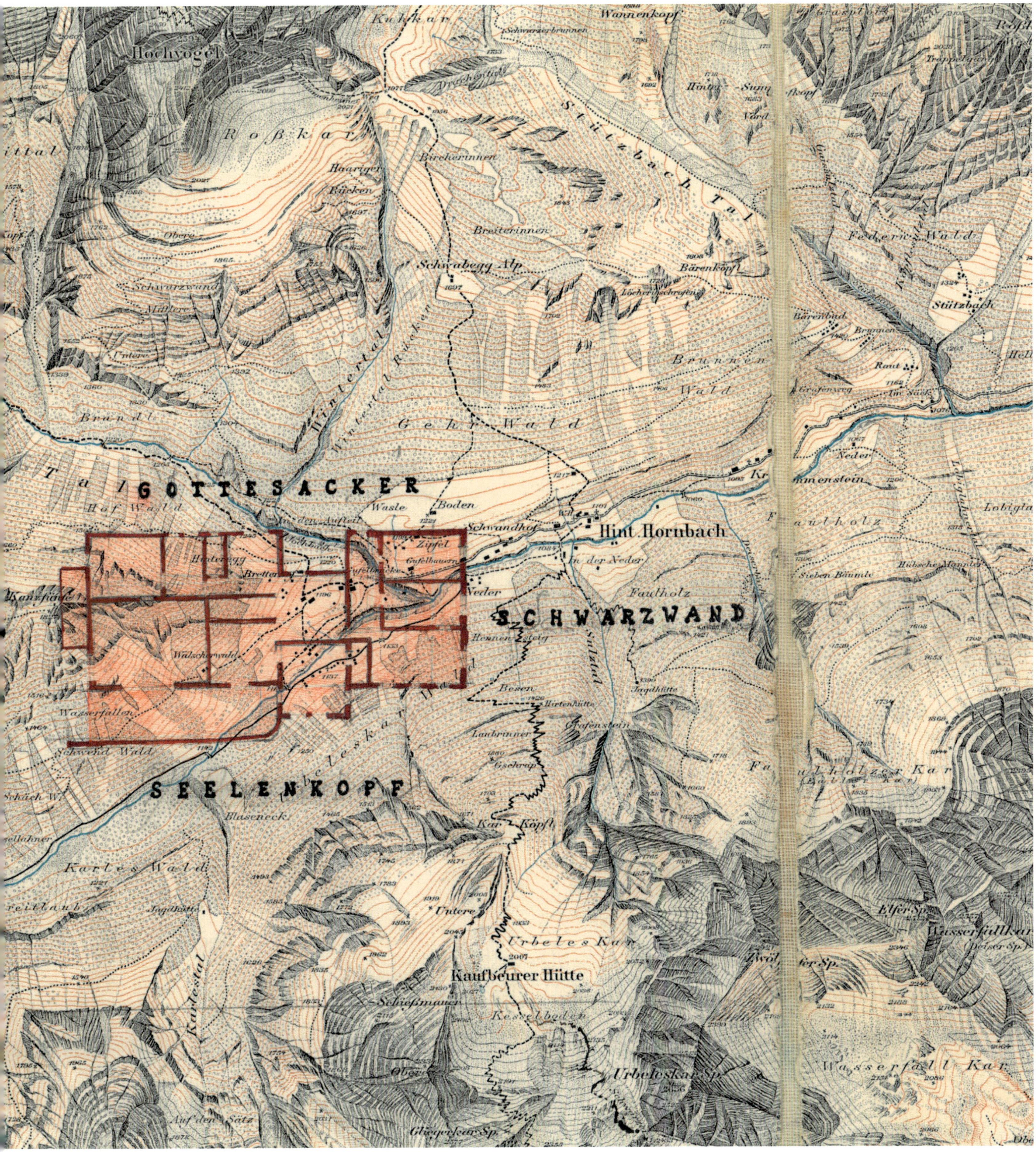
GOTTESACKER
SCHWARZWAND
SEELENKOPF
Hochvogel
Wannenkopf
Schwabegg Alp
Hint. Hornbach
Kaufbeurer Hütte
Stützbach

Lager A–E
2003/2019
Privatsammlung München /
Private collection, Munich

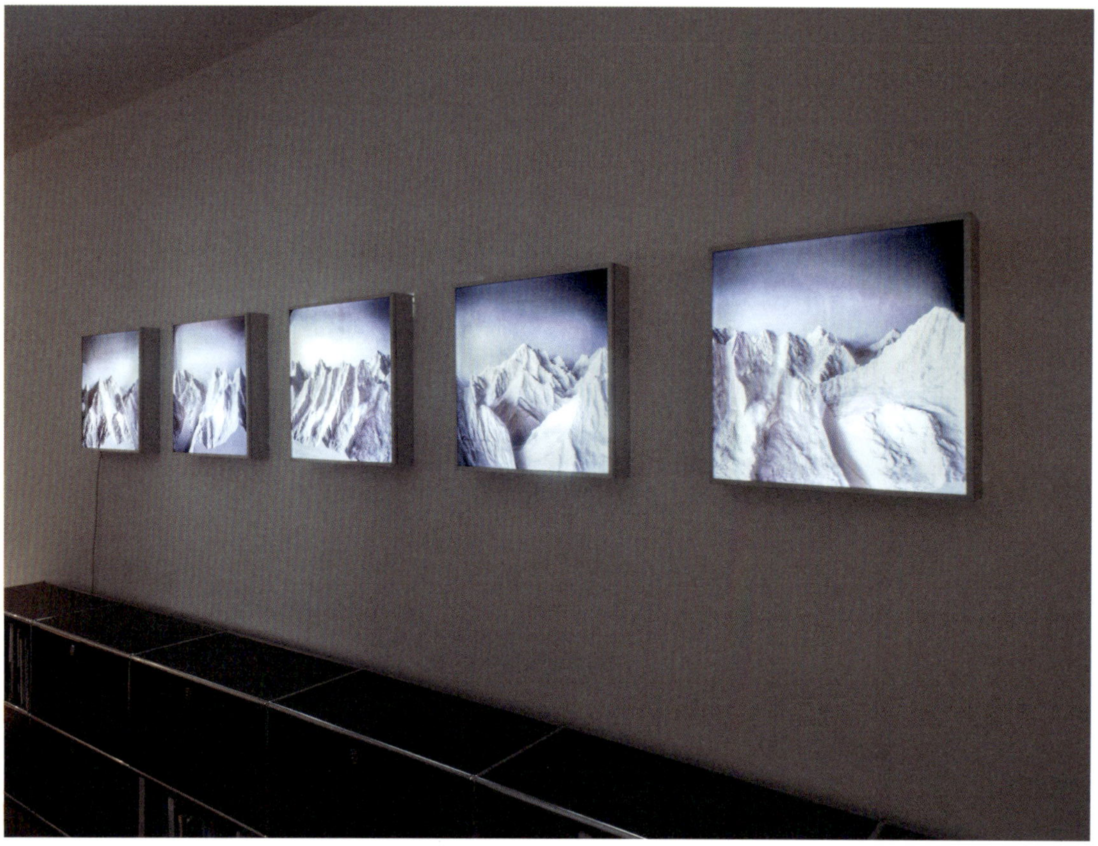

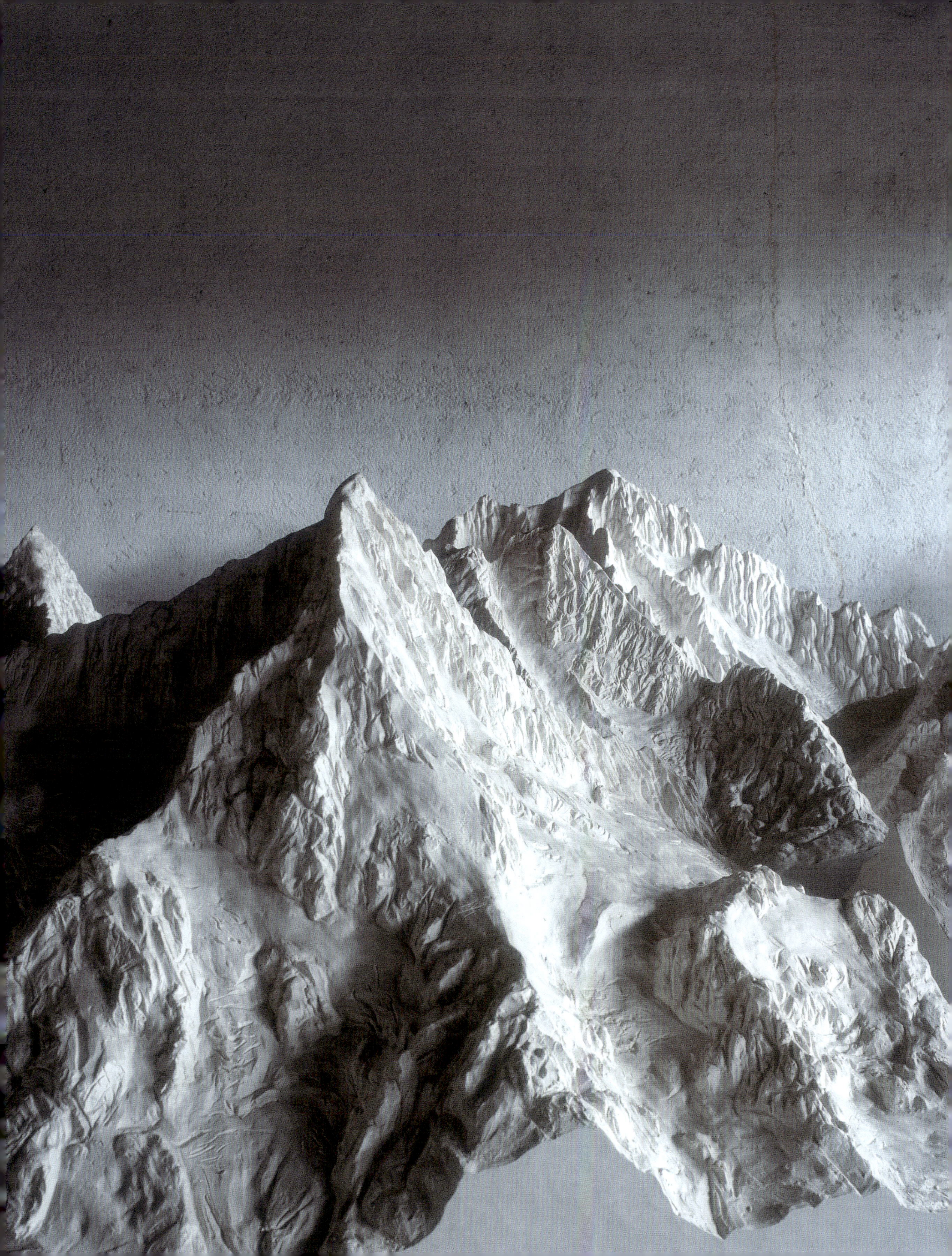

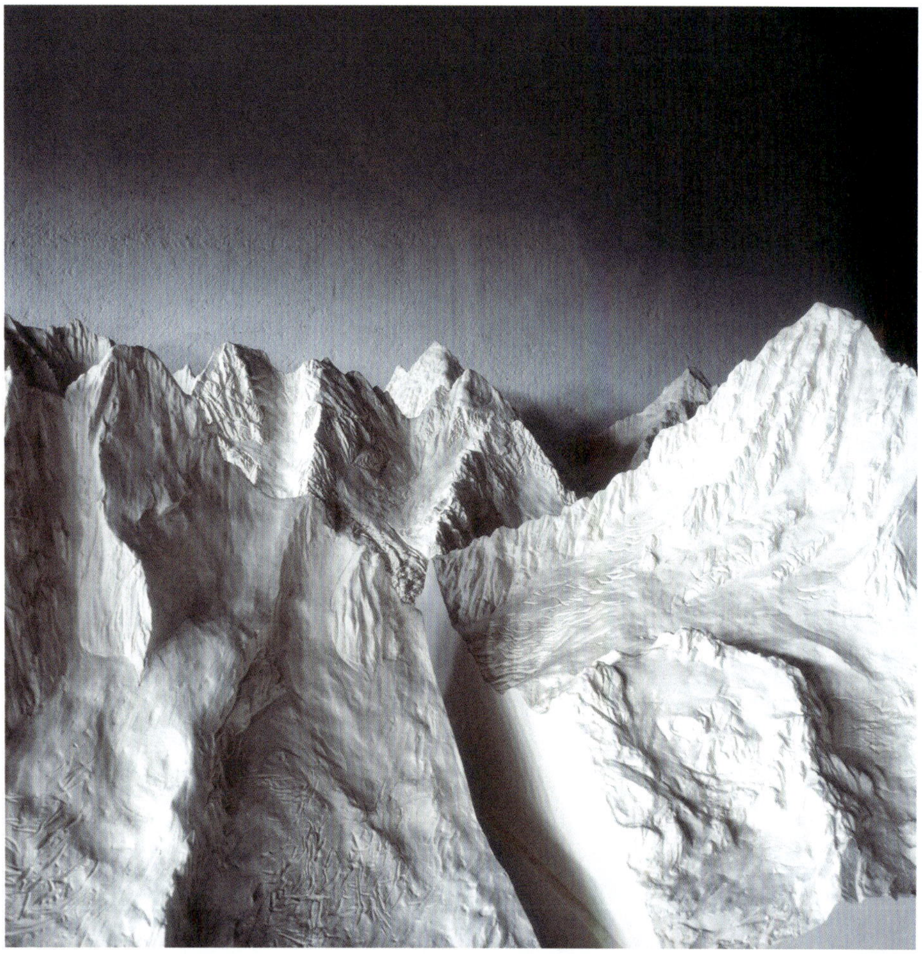

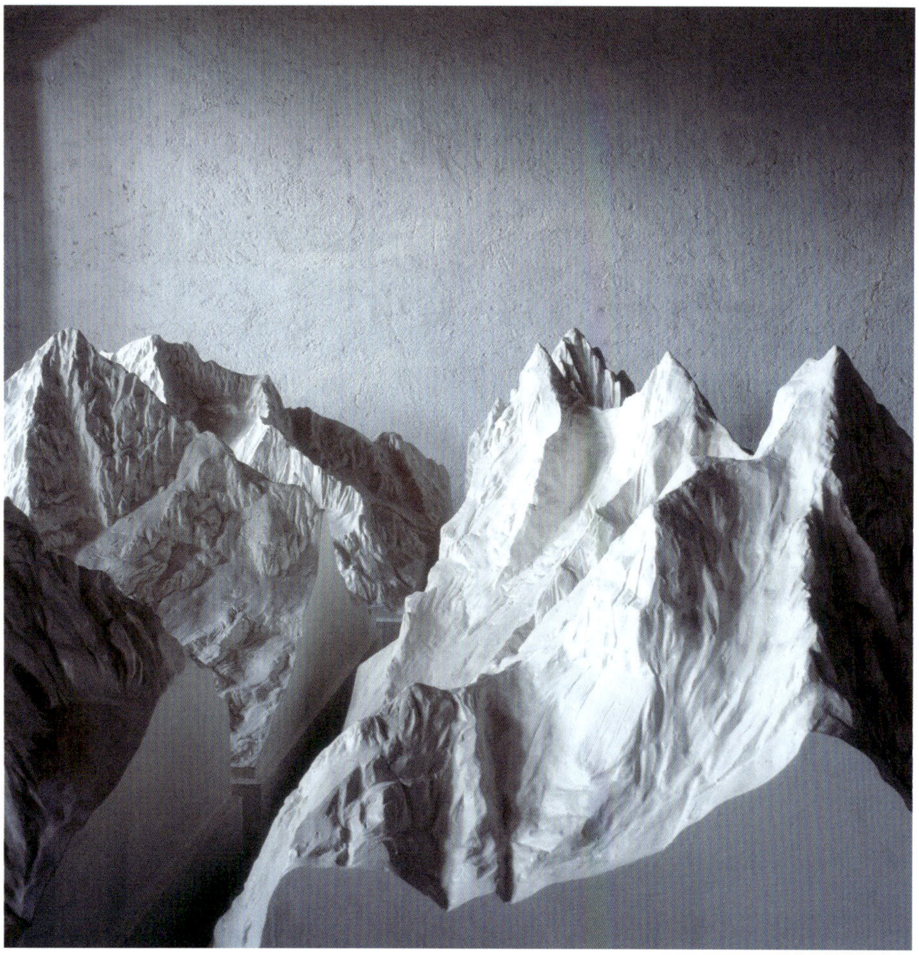

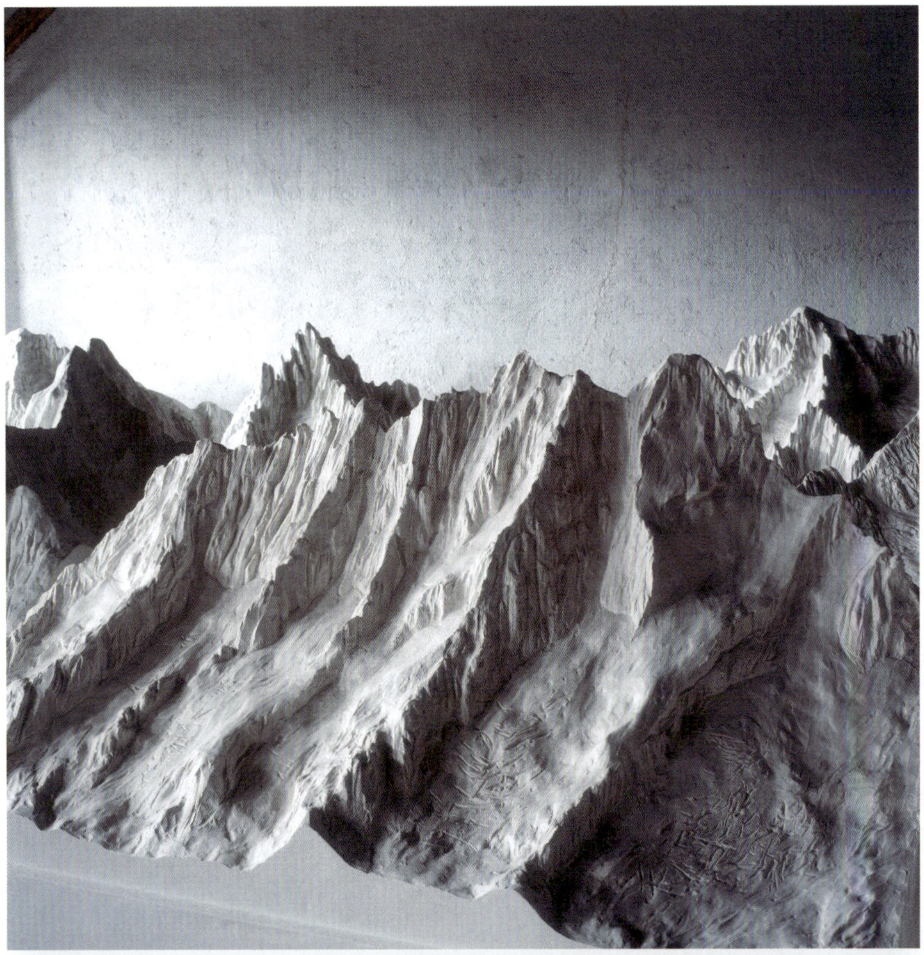

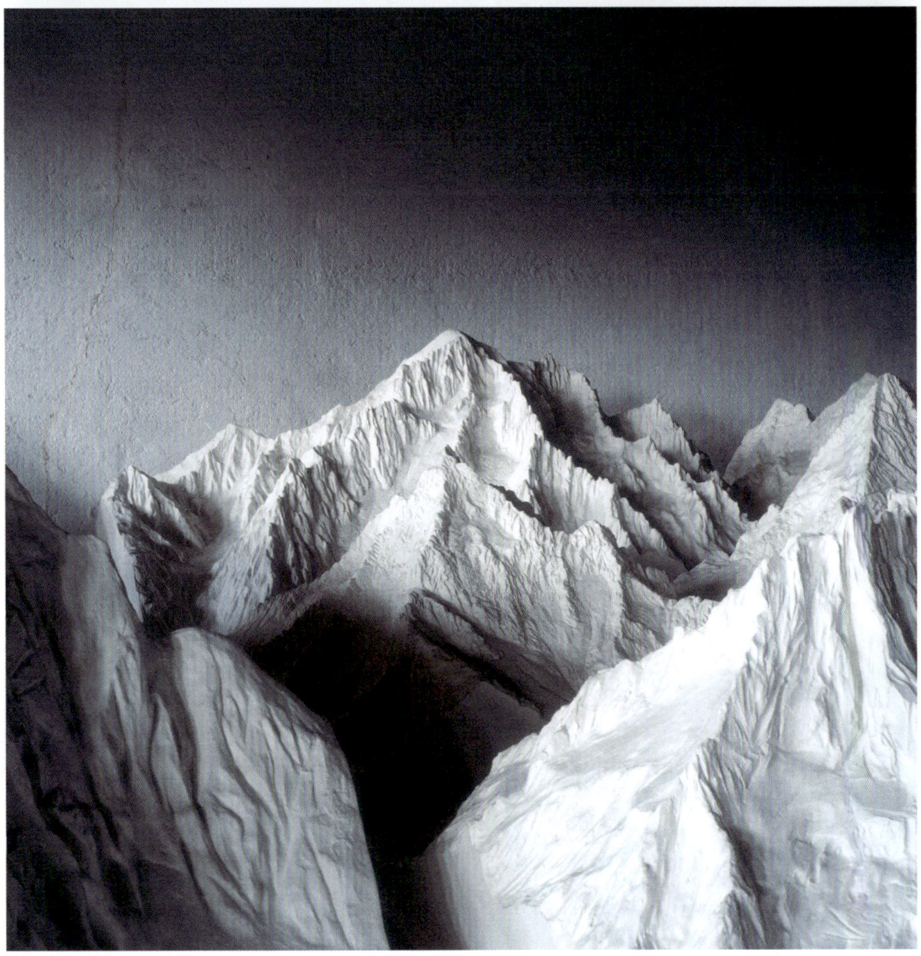

Die perfekte Linie
The Perfect Line

Ein Gespräch zwischen
Stephan Huber
und Reinhold Messner
A conversation between
Stephan Huber
and Reinhold Messner

Stephan Huber

In der Kunsthalle Kiel im Jahr 2000 bist du das erste Mal auf eine meiner Arbeiten gestoßen. Dort stand meine Skulptur des Langkofel.

Reinhold Messner

Ich erinnere die Umstände nicht mehr genau, sehe aber deinen Langkofel genau vor mir.

SH Zwei Jahre später hast du dein erstes Museum auf dem Monte Rite eröffnet und dafür Arbeiten von mir erworben. Ich fand es damals aufregend, dass du Berge wie die Civetta oder die Tre Cime, die Drei Zinnen, gewählt hast. Also Berge, an denen du selbst die schwierigsten Routen geklettert bist. Für mich war es wie eine doppelte, eine bergsteigerische und eine künstlerische Aneignung. Danach fing ich an, mich mehr mit dir zu beschäftigen, und habe gemerkt, dass es zwischen uns Ähnlichkeiten gibt.

RM Ja, ich kam profaner zu dir und deiner Kunst, ich habe damals angefangen, meine Museumsidee zu entwickeln. Der Hintergrund dazu: Das traditionelle Bergsteigen, das traditionelle Abenteuer Berg ist ja mehr eine rein sportliche als eine kulturelle Erscheinung. Ein Berg lebt für mich nicht nur von seiner Form, seiner Erhabenheit, sondern auch von seiner Geschichte, die dahintersteht. Wenn ich einen Berg anschaue, wie den Cerro Torre in Patagonien, lese ich aus seinen Rissen, Leisten und Wänden, was darauf passiert ist. Er erzählt mir die ganze Geschichte. Und ich wollte mit meinem Museum nichts anderes, als die Berge als Ganzes zu fassen. Ich habe meine Erzählform gewählt, in erster Linie erzähle ich mithilfe von Bildender Kunst, Reliquien – also Überbleibseln von berühmten Bergsteigern, aber nichts Knöchernem – und Gerätschaften sowie kurzen Texten. Mein Bergmuseum auf Schloss Sigmundskron, wo du ja mitgearbeitet hast, ist das Zentrum dieser Erzählung: Was passiert zwischen Mensch und Natur? Die Antwort gebe ich in erster Linie mithilfe von Kunst. Deswegen brauchte ich deine Arbeiten, die inzwischen in allen

Stephan Huber

You first encountered a work of mine in the Kunsthalle Kiel in 2000. My sculpture *Sassolungo* was shown there.

Reinhold Messner

I no longer remember the circumstances exactly, but I can see your *Sassolungo* right in front of me.

SH **Two years later you opened your first museum on Monte Rite and acquired works for it from me. I found it exciting that you chose mountains such as Civetta and the Tre Cime, the Three Pinnacles. That is, mountains you had climbed yourself up the most difficult routes. For me, this was like a double appropriation, a mountaineering one and an artistic one. That is when I began to find out more about you and noticed that there were similarities between us.**

RM **Yes, I discovered you and your art in a simpler manner. It was when I began to develop my idea for a museum. Of course the background was that traditional mountain climbing, the traditional adventure of the mountain, looks more like pure sport rather than culture. For me, a mountain not only expresses its form, its sublimity, but also the history behind it. When I look at a mountain, such as the Cerro Torre in Patagonia, I can read what has happened on it from its cracks, crests and walls. It tells me the whole story. With my museum I wanted nothing less than to understand mountains in their entirety. I chose my narrative form, above all I tell my story with visual art, with relics, that is, vestiges from famous mountain climbers – but no bones – and tools, as well as brief texts. My mountain museum in Sigmundskron Castle, in which you also participated, is the centre of this story: what takes place between man and nature? I provide an answer with the help of art. For this reason I need your works, which today are present in all the museums. The large sculptures *Civetta*, *Monte Pelmo* and *Sassolungo* have their home in the building by Zaha Hadid at the Kronplatz, and the *Antelao* is currently still in the middle of the space at Monte Rite. I am planning a new museum on the**

Museen präsent sind. Die großen Skulpturen *Civetta, Monte Pelmo* und *Langkofel* haben ihren Platz im Zaha-Hadid-Bau am Kronplatz, der *Antelao* steht momentan noch mitten im Raum im Museum am Monte Rite. Ich plane ein neues Museum zum Thema Fels, dort soll er endgültig seinen Platz finden. Aber kommen wir doch nun zu uns.

SH Ich selbst erklettere meine Berge nur im nassen Modellierton im Atelier. Zwar auch mit den Händen, aber anders als du. Es ist körperlich ungefährlicher. Ich finde, dich unterscheidet fundamental von den meisten Bergsteigern, dass du das Bergsteigen von diesen Kameradschaftsgeschichten, vom Pathetischen und von nationalen Attitüden gelöst hast. Du hast das Bergsteigen individualisiert.

RM Richtig.

SH In dieser Individualisierung liegt für mich eine Modernisierung des ganzen alpinen Milieus. Heute muss das Individuum hochgehalten werden gegen stets nivellierende Kollektive. Für mich gab es zwischen uns Übereinstimmungen, wie zum Beispiel: einsame Entscheidungen treffen, nur für sich selbst verantwortlich sein oder, wie auf dem Caspar-David-Friedrich-Bild *Der Wanderer über dem Nebelmeer*, die Niederungen verlassen, oben auf dem Berg stehen und sich von der Welt abheben. Eine wunderbare Erhabenheit.

RM Auch ich arbeite an diesen Ideen, aktuell mit dem neuen Museum am Helm in Sexten. Ich versuche, Bilder zu finden, Kunstwerke, die starke Geschichten erzählen. Zum Beispiel, „vereint am Seil auf Leben und Tod", ein alter Spruch, eine Botschaft. Wir Kletterer sind durch das Seil verbunden, auf Leben und Tod.

Kürzlich habe ich eine Geschichte recherchiert, eine Tragödie. Ich kannte die Bergsteiger – drei der besten Bergsteiger der Welt – der jungen Generation. Sie waren in Kanada am Howse Peak in den Rockies schon 400 Meter vom Gipfel abgestiegen, eine sehr kühne Route durch eine

subject of the cliff, and that is where it will ultimately be housed. But let's talk about us.

SH **I myself only climb my mountains in wet modelling clay in the studio. With my hands, too, but differently than you. It is physically less dangerous. I think you are fundamentally different from most mountaineers in that you have detached mountaineering from these stories of comradeship, from pathos and nationalistic attitudes. You have individualised mountaineering.**

RM **That's right.**

SH **For me, this individualisation is a modernisation of the whole alpine scene. Today, the individual must be defended against the collective that is continuously levelling it down. For me, there were similarities between us, such as making lonely decisions, being responsible only for oneself or, as in Caspar David Friedrich's painting *The Wanderer above the Sea of Fog*, leaving the lowlands, standing on top of the mountain and standing out from the world. A wonderful sublimity.**

RM **I am also working on such ideas, currently with the new Museum am Helm in Sexten. I try to find images, works of art that tell vibrant stories. For example, 'bound by the rope, for life and death', an old saying, a message. We climbers are united by the rope, for life and death.**

Recently I was researching a story, a tragedy. I knew the climbers, three of the best climbers in the world from the younger generation. They were in Canada, on Howse Peak in the Rockies, and had already descended 400 metres from the summit, a very bold route through a gully that was sunlit in the morning. At the bottom of this gully they either tied themselves back together with ropes or were in the process of doing so. They probably had a couple of pitons with them for abseiling, which they used to secure themselves. But then a wet snow avalanche came down through the gully and fell upon the three climbers. The pitons were torn out and they were whirled 500 metres through the air. The three of them were found days later, all dead of

Rinne, die am Vormittag von der Sonne beschienen war. Am unteren Ende dieser Rinne haben sie sich entweder wieder zusammengebunden oder waren gerade dabei, dies zu tun. Sie hatten wohl ein paar Haken zum Abseilen dabei, an denen sie sich auch sicherten. Und dann kam der Schnee als Nassschneelawine die ganze Rinne herunter und hat die drei Bergsteiger erfasst. Die Haken wurden herausgerissen, und sie sind 500 Meter durch die Luft gewirbelt worden. Tage später hat man die drei gefunden, alle tot natürlich. Die Seile hatten sich durch den Wind und den Fall so um die drei herumgeschlungen, dass sie zuletzt ein einziges Knäuel bildeten.

SH Schrecklich, ein totes Menschenknäuel.

RM Verbunden durch das Seil, auf Leben und Tod. Die andere Seite von Kameradschaft: Du hältst deinen Kameraden am Seil auf Leben und Tod. Die Natur ist so mächtig, so ungemein vielfältig, so kreativ, dass wir dazu keine klare Aussage machen können. Jede Aussage bekommt in diesem Zusammenhang eine fürchterlich tragische Bedeutung.

SH Ein trauriges, aber überwältigendes Bild.

RM Zu diesem Bild mache ich ein Kunstwerk, um es emotional zu unterfüttern.

SH Das realisierst du selbst?

RM Ja, aber nicht handwerklich, sondern als Vorstellung, als Ideengeber. Ich bin kein Künstler, ich bleibe Erzähler, rege Künstler aber häufig an, Ausdrücke für Ideen zu finden.

SH Bleiben wir beim Handwerklichen. In der Kunst ist Handwerk in Ordnung, aber hierfür ist es nur eine Voraussetzung von vielen. Ist es in deinem Metier genauso? Ich mag diese ganzen El-Capitan-Kletterer, die kalifornischen Hippies. Eine verwegene, kreative Truppe, die sich an der Wand immer wieder versuchte und sie auf neuen Routen bezwang. Lynn Hill, die du – glaube ich – sehr schätzt, hat das später auch geschafft, aber war sie denn mehr als eine sensationelle Handwerkerin?

course. The ropes had twisted around the trio, due to the wind and the fall, so that they finally formed a single knot.

SH **Terrible, a dead tangle of people.**

RM **Bound by the rope, for life and death. The other side of comradeship: You hold your mate on the rope for life and death. Nature is so powerful, so immensely diverse, so creative, that we cannot make a clear statement about it. Every statement takes on a terribly tragic meaning in this context.**

SH **A sad, but overwhelming image.**

RM **I'm making a work of art to go with this image, to give it an emotional underpinning.**

SH **You're realising that yourself?**

RM **Yes, but not as a craft, as a concept, as a generator of ideas. I am not an artist, I remain a storyteller, but I often encourage artists to find expressions for ideas.**

SH **Let's talk about craft. In art, craft is fine, but it is only one prerequisite among many. Is it the same in your profession? I like all these El Capitan climbers, the California hippies. A daring, creative bunch that kept trying to climb the wall and discovered new routes up it. Lynn Hill, whom I think you hold in high esteem, later did it, but was she more than a sensational craftswoman?**

RM **Yes, she was more a dancer than a craftswoman. Lynn Hill was the best competitive climber, became a great mountain climber, and moved in her elegance – as a girl, small, light, dancing. Her climbing was more art form than sport. The moment she was at the top, her art seemed to be over.**

SH **Yes, but one of my heroes, Royal Robbins, didn't only climb perfect routes in the rock, he also wrote many wonderful sentences that still survive today.**

RM **Yes, Royal Robbins is a special figure, he's right up my street.**

SH **He was extraordinary. The clarity and the intellectual aspect are important, especially after climbing the mountain or finishing the exhibition in**

RM Ja, sie war eher eine Tänzerin als eine Handwerkerin. Lynn Hill war die beste Wettkletterin, wurde eine großartige Bergkletterin und war in ihrer Eleganz – als Mädchen, klein, leicht, tänzerisch – unterwegs. Ihr Klettern war mehr Kunstform als Sport. In dem Moment, als sie oben war, schien ihre Kunst vorbei zu sein.

SH Ja, aber einer meiner Heroen, Royal Robbins, hat eben nicht nur perfekte Routen in den Fels geklettert, er schrieb auch viele wunderbare Sätze, die heute noch Bestand haben.

RM Ja, Royal Robbins ist eine besondere Erscheinung, er liegt auf meiner Linie.

SH Er war außergewöhnlich. Die Klarheit und damit auch das Intellektuelle sind wichtig, vor allem nach der Besteigung des Berges oder der Fertigstellung der Ausstellung im Atelier. Deine Bücher und deine Vorträge unterscheiden dich stark von denen anderer Bergsteiger.

RM Na, es gab schon einige, die vor mir gut geschrieben haben. Paul Preuß, Lionel Terray, ein Walter Bonatti ...

SH Auch Ausnahmeerscheinungen.

RM Ja, richtig. Aber es gab nicht viele, die sich, wie ich, selbstkritisch mit dem Bergsteigen beschäftigt haben. Die allermeisten widmen sich der Route, die sie klettern wollen: Erstbegehung, Winterbesteigung, Erstbesteigung, was auch immer. Du hast in der Vorbereitung zum Gespräch den Satz geschrieben, dass die Engländer einen ganz anderen Zugang zu den Bergen hatten.

SH Um auf die Engländer zu sprechen zu kommen, muss ich ausholen. Ich komme aus dem Westallgäu, und vor mir lag die Nagelfluhkette als dioramenartige Sperre, als Grenze zum Süden.

RM Ja, als Widerstand.

SH Bei dir war es das von den Bergen eingeschlossene Villnößtal. Wir haben uns beide immer die Frage gestellt: Was ist dahinter? Du hast die Überwindung dieser Sperre oft als Entree für deine Vorträge genommen, als deine Initiation für den ersten Schritt in die Welt. Also ist unsere

the studio. Your books and your lectures are very different from those of other climbers.

RM **Well, there have been some who have written well before me. Paul Preuß, Lionel Terray, a certain Walter Bonatti...**

SH **Exceptional ones, too.**

RM **Yes, that's right. But there weren't many who, like me, dealt with mountaineering in a self-critical way. Most of them dedicated themselves to the route they wanted to climb: first cliff ascent, winter ascent, first ascent, whatever. You wrote a sentence in preparation for the interview that the English had a very different approach to the mountains.**

SH **To talk about the English, I have to backtrack. I come from the western Allgäu region, where I had the Nagelfluhkette range before me, a diorama-like barrier, as a border to the south.**

RM **Yes, as opposition.**

SH **For you it was the Villnößtal valley, enclosed by the mountains. We both always asked ourselves the question: What is behind them? You often use the overcoming of this barrier as an introduction to your lectures, as your initiation for the first step into the world. So our mountain obsession is also shaped by our biography. How did all the English climbers from London, from a big city that was already vibrant, stinking, and noisy at the time, suddenly begin to think alpine, to move alpine, and to also make daring first ascents?**

RM **You've already explained it. Because they had to endure the consequences of their times. Alpinism began with the Enlightenment, which first took hold in England, and with industrialisation. Industrialisation brought with it the consequences of living in these cities, in the smoke, in the dirt – the clean mountains were a counter-world, a playground. The English were the first to develop mountaineering out of their social situation. They were the colonial masters of the world and they also colonised the mountains. And they immediately started to reflect on what they were doing. The first mountain**

Bergobsession auch durch die Biografie geprägt. Wie kommen jetzt die ganzen englischen Kletterer aus London überhaupt dazu, aus einer damals schon vibrierenden Großstadt, die stank und laut war, plötzlich alpin zu denken, sich alpin zu bewegen und auch waghalsige Erstbesteigungen zu unternehmen?

RM Du hast es schon erklärt. Weil sie die Folgen ihrer Zeit zu ertragen hatten. Der Alpinismus beginnt mit der Aufklärung, die in England zuerst griff, und mit der Industrialisierung. Die Industrialisierung zog Folgen nach sich, wie man in diesen Städten lebte, im Rauch, im Dreck – und da waren die sauberen Berge als Playground eine Gegenwelt. Die Engländer waren die Ersten, die das Bergsteigen von ihrer sozialen Situation aus entwickelt haben. Sie waren die Kolonialherren, weltweit, und haben auch die Berge kolonialisiert. Und sie haben gleich angefangen, über ihr Tun nachzudenken. Erste Bergbücher erschienen. Die ersten großen Bergbesteigungen und Bergbilder sind von Engländern. Die Engländer haben anfangs nicht fotografiert, sondern gezeichnet und gemalt. Einer von ihnen war Albert Mummery. Es waren aber nicht nur Engländer, auch die deutschen Brüder Hermann, Adolf und Robert Schlagintweit haben großartige Kunst von ihren Expeditionen hinterlassen.

SH Die waren auch von Johann Georg Dillis ausgebildet.

RM Ich habe leider noch keines ihrer Kunstwerke für meine Museen bekommen können. Die Anfänge dieser alpinistischen Welt haben wir Mitteleuropäer gar nicht wahrgenommen. In dieser ersten Zeit, in den ersten Jahren, waren nur arbeitende Alpler mit den Engländern unterwegs. Da waren die Bergführer, die Träger, die Wegzeiger aus den Alpen. Aber die eigentliche Auseinandersetzung mit dem Berg haben die Engländer gesucht, sie haben dafür Hilfen gebraucht, es dabei so gemacht wie in den Kolonien. Sie haben sich die Burschen von den Almen geholt, die ihre Rucksäcke trugen, ihnen Feuer machten und ihr Zelt aufstellten. Und diese ersten

books were published. The first big mountain climbs and mountain pictures were made by the English. In the beginning, the English did not take photographs; they drew and painted. One of them was Albert Mummery. But it wasn't only Englishmen, the German brothers Hermann, Adolf, and Robert Schlagintweit also left great art from their expeditions.

SH **They were also trained by Johann Georg Dillis.**

RM **Unfortunately, I have not yet been able to get any of their art for my museums. We Central Europeans didn't even notice the beginnings of this Alpine world. In those early days, in the first years, only those who worked on the alps [mountain pastures] climbed with the English. The mountain guides, the porters, the trailblazers all came from the alps. But the English sought the actual encounter with the mountain, they needed help for that, they did it like in the colonies. They got the boys from the alps to carry their rucksacks, build them fires, and pitch their tents. And these first mountaineers, the traditional mountaineers, from Edward Whymper to Mummery – Whymper was a fantastic artist – made the first ascent of the Matterhorn in 1865. It was only because Whymper was an artist and also a good mountaineer that he became so successful: because he wrote books, all well written and accompanied by his engravings. He was able to make a good living from it, unlike most professional mountaineers today. Whymper was sent to the Alps as an artist and only then became infatuated with the mountains. He left a lasting legacy.**

SH **He also saw it intellectually, didn't he?**

RM **Right.**

SH **In a much larger context, so to speak, passionately, thoughtfully. You said just now that the Schlagintweit brothers left great art, and you would like to have a work by them. If I could choose an Alpine painting, I would always choose one by Giovanni Segantini. The precision, the clarity, the Cinemascope-like quality, and at the same time the deeply existential, should appeal to you.**

Bergsteiger, die traditionellen Bergsteiger, von Edward Whymper bis Mummery, Whymper ein fantastischer Künstler – Erstbesteigung des Matterhorns im Jahr 1865. Und nur weil Whymper Künstler und dazu ein guter Bergsteiger war, ist er so erfolgreich geworden. Weil er Bücher gemacht hat – allesamt gut geschrieben und mit seinen Stichen ergänzt. Davon konnte er gut leben, im Gegensatz zu den meisten Profibergsteigern heute. Whymper wurde als Künstler in die Alpen geschickt und hat sich dann erst in die Berge vernarrt. Er hat Bleibendes hinterlassen.

SH Der hat das auch intellektuell gesehen, oder?

RM Richtig.

SH Sozusagen im viel größeren Zusammenhang, leidenschaftlich, denkerisch. Du hast gerade eben gesagt, die Brüder Schlagintweit hätten großartige Kunst hinterlassen, du hättest gerne eine Arbeit von ihnen. Wenn ich ein alpines Bild wählen könnte, würde ich immer eines von Giovanni Segantini nehmen. Diese Präzision, diese Klarheit, das Cinemascope-Artige und gleichzeitig das tief Existenzielle müsste dir doch auch gefallen.

RM Gefallen ist nicht mein Kriterium. Ich möchte, dass die Bilder oder Skulpturen Geschichten erzählen – mehrschichtig und unverwechselbar.

SH Nochmals zum Komplexen: Das Gegenteil davon war für mich immer Hillarys Antwort auf die Frage, warum er auf den Mount Everest klettern wollte. Er sagte: „Weil er da ist." Das ist flapsig schön, aber auch sehr wenig.

RM Das war nicht Hillary, das ist ganz wichtig, sondern George Mallory. Mallory, der 1921 den ersten Versuch am Everest unternommen hat. Der kam nicht hoch. 1922 hat er dann ein zweites Mal versucht, am Everest den Gipfel zu erreichen. Beim dritten Versuch ist er umgekommen. Er war vorher in Amerika auf Vortragsreise, und dort hat ihn ein Journalist gefragt, warum er immer wieder zum Mount Everest müsse. Er hatte es schon zweimal gewagt und

RM **Pleasing is not my criterion. I want the pictures or sculptures to tell stories – multi-layered and unmistakable.**

SH **Let me return to the complex: The opposite of that for me was always Hillary's answer to the question why he wanted to climb Mount Everest. He said, 'Because it's there.' That's flippantly beautiful, but it's also not much of a reply.**

RM **It wasn't Hillary, that's very important: it was George Mallory. Mallory, who made the first attempt on Everest in 1921. He didn't make it to the top. Then in 1922 he tried a second time to reach the summit of Everest. He died on the third attempt. Before that, he was on a lecture tour in America and a journalist asked him why he always had to climb Mount Everest. He had already dared to do it twice and had just announced that he was going for the third time. That's when he said, 'Because it's there.' It was the only right answer at the time. But today that answer no longer satisfies.**

SH **It wouldn't satisfy anyone today?**

RM **In the meantime, everything has been climbed. That answer was only good because the mountain had not yet been climbed. Because attempts had been made. The journalist insinuates that you won't manage it the third time either. But he also says that as long as the mountain is there and unclimbed, pioneers will try – or else an alpinist will dare to climb it.**

SH **It's a fixation, an obsession, a compulsion.**

RM **Not a compulsion, but a challenge. Once it has taken hold – it takes place in the mind, not outside at first – it wants to be dared.**

SH **Obsessions are goal-promoting, but they can also make you blind. You quickly get to the tragic, and tragic fates have always interested me, also in mountaineers like Matthias Zurbriggen. I've read a lot about him.**

RM **Yes, he is an interesting and tragic figure.**

SH **He hanged himself in Geneva. He had completed many great tours before he died.**

gerade angekündigt, er gehe zum dritten Mal. Und da hat er gesagt: „Weil er da ist." Es war damals die einzig richtige Antwort. Aber heute trägt diese Antwort nicht mehr.

SH Sie würde heute nicht tragen?

RM Inzwischen ist alles bestiegen. Diese Antwort ist nur gut, weil der Berg noch nicht bestiegen war. Weil Versuche gemacht worden sind. Der Journalist unterstellt dir, du kommst das dritte Mal auch nicht hinauf. Aber er sagt auch, solange der Berg da ist und unbestiegen ist, werden Pioniere es versuchen – oder aber wird ein Alpinist den Aufstieg wagen.

SH Es ist ein sich Verbeißen, eine Obsession, ein Zwang.

RM Kein Zwang, eine Herausforderung. Wenn sich diese einmal festgesetzt hat – sie findet ja im Kopf statt, anfangs nicht draußen – will sie gewagt werden.

SH Obsessionen sind zielfördernd, können aber auch blind machen. Schnell ist man beim Tragischen, und die tragischen Schicksale haben mich immer interessiert, auch bei Bergsteigern wie Matthias Zurbriggen, von dem ich viel gelesen habe.

RM Ja, der ist eine interessante und tragische Figur.

SH Er hat sich in Genf erhängt. Er hatte zuvor viele großartige Touren gemacht.

RM Er hat in Neuseeland und Südamerika große Touren unternommen, als Erster hat er den Aconcagua bestiegen und war im Himalaya. Sein Problem war, dass er gescheit war, gebildet. Du musst dir klarmachen, dass diese Bergführer damals davon gelebt haben, daheim haben sie in Bauerndörfern, Berghöfen ein einfaches Leben geführt, sie hatten wenig Ahnung von Natur und Wissenschaft, von Kunst und Hintergründen. Zurbriggen war anders, er ist zum Beispiel bei einer Himalaya-Expedition vor Ort geblieben, um die lokale Sprache zu lernen. Bei der nächsten Expedition hat er seinen reichen Klienten, einen Engländer, geführt, der ihn mitgenommen hat, alles noch mit dem Schiff. Dieser ist dann draufgekommen, dass Zurbriggen den Herrn Baron an

RM He did great tours in New Zealand and South America; he was the first to climb Aconcagua, and he was in the Himalayas. His problem was that he was clever, educated. You have to realise that in those days these mountain guides made a living from it; at home they led a simple life in farming villages, on mountain farms; they had little idea of nature and science, of art and knowledge. Zurbriggen was different; for example, he stayed on after a Himalayan expedition to learn the local language. On the next expedition he guided his rich client, an Englishman, who took him along, at that time still by boat. The baron then realised that Zurbriggen had left him standing in terms of background knowledge. So he didn't take Zurbriggen with him any more from then onwards. He probably couldn't bear to be shamed by a simple mountain guide. That has also been my experience: clients want to be guided by you on the mountain, but not in the palace; that's what my friend Hans-Peter Eisendle told me. When the clients notice that you outdo them with regard to intellectual ability and knowledge, to their ability to grasp things, they no longer take you as their guide. They want to feel at least intellectually superior to the great mountaineer who has them on the rope.

SH Well, otherwise it would be totally depressing for them.

RM That's exactly how it is. That's why Zurbriggen broke in the end. Yes, he broke down from wanting more as a mountain guide than to lead the rope. No one took him on any more.

SH Sad.

RM Yes, sad. He withdrew and killed himself.

SH Let's move from the sad to the positive. When I model mountains, I usually choose them according to aesthetic sensations. Only sometimes do I choose a mountain with historical significance. For example, the pinnacles with holes made by the military. But actually, I'm always guided by the form, the pyramidal, the walls, the solitary. How did you choose your mountains in the past, according to the difficulty of the routes?

Hintergrundwissen überflügelt hat. Also hat er Zurbriggen künftig nicht mehr mitgenommen. Er hat es wohl nicht ertragen, vom einfachen Bergler beschämt zu werden. Das ist auch meine Erfahrung: Die Gäste wollen von dir als Bergführer am Fels geführt werden, nicht im Palast, so hat es mir auch mein Freund Hans-Peter Eisendle erzählt. Wenn die Gäste merken, dass du sie in ihrem geistigen Können und Wissen, in ihrem Erfassthaben überflügelst, nehmen sie dich nicht mehr als Führer. Sie wollen sich dem großartigen Bergsteiger, der sie am Seil hat, zumindest intellektuell überlegen fühlen.

SH Naja, sonst wäre es für sie total deprimierend.

RM Genauso ist es. Deswegen ist Zurbriggen zuletzt zerbrochen. Ja, er ist daran zerbrochen, als Bergführer mehr zu wollen, als das Seil zu führen. Niemand hat ihn mehr mitgenommen.

SH Traurig.

RM Ja, traurig. Er hat sich zurückgezogen, hat sich umgebracht.

SH Gehen wir vom Traurigen zum Positiven. Wenn ich Berge modelliere, suche ich sie meistens nach ästhetischen Empfindungen aus. Nur manchmal entscheide ich mich für einen Berg, der historisch besetzt ist. Zum Beispiel die militärisch durchlöcherten Zinnen. Aber eigentlich leitet mich immer die Form, das Pyramidale, die Wände, das Solitäre. Wie hast du früher deine Berge ausgesucht, nach Schwierigkeiten der Routen?

RM Angefangen habe ich natürlich an den paar Bergen, die über dem Dorf aufragten, logischerweise zuerst mit den Eltern, weil ich nicht allein hingefunden hätte. Schon sehr früh war ich mit meinen Brüdern unterwegs, hauptsächlich mit meinem jüngeren Bruder Günther, wir haben uns dann zunehmend schwierigere Routen gesucht. Wir wussten, dass da vor uns schon andere geklettert sind, aber uns ging es nicht mehr um die leichtesten Wege, sondern um die Schwierigkeit. Wir haben uns psychisch gesehen so stark gemacht, durch das Finden immer schwierigerer

RM I started, of course, on the few mountains that towered above the village, logically with my parents at first, because I wouldn't have found my way there alone. Very early on, I went climbing with my brothers, mainly with my younger brother Günther, and then we looked for increasingly difficult routes. We knew that others had climbed there before us; we were no longer interested in the easiest routes, but in the difficulty. We made ourselves strong psychologically; we grew by finding increasingly difficult routes. And then came the next step, which was only a small one for us, because we didn't have any tools in the wider sense to tempt us to climb the mountains. Renunciation became our motto. My alpinism was therefore pure 'renunciation alpinism' from the start. So I transferred my experience to the entire Alps: as few pitons as possible, no bolts, later no oxygen tanks. I later transferred this style to the eight-thousanders. When I started climbing eight-thousanders, the procedure involved a huge amount of effort. We had nine tonnes of equipment with us on Nanga Parbat in 1970. Imagine how expensive it was to bring all that to the foot of the mountain. Eight years later I climbed the mountain alone, with a total of 60 kilograms. And only then did it become clear that I had found a completely new approach to the mountain.

SH But now a very provocative question: Do you have to climb Nanga Parbat?

RM No, you don't have to.

SH Then why have so many climbers put so much effort into doing so? Because Hermann Buhl was there, because it is the German mountain of fate? But that wouldn't concern you at all; you're from South Tyrol.

RM No, not me. But the story of Nanga Parbat basically tells the whole story of alpinism. One of the great Englishmen, in this case Albert Mummery, tried to climb Nanga Parbat in 1895 with two comrades from England and a few locals. They failed. In the end, Mummery disappeared. The German writer Walter Schmidkunz has worked on this.

Routen sind wir gewachsen. Und dann kam der nächste Schritt, der für uns nur ein kleiner war, weil wir ja kein Instrumentarium im breiten Sinne zur Verfügung hatten, um auf die Berge zu steigen. Der Verzicht wurde unser Motto. Mein Alpinismus war demnach von Anfang an reiner Verzichtsalpinismus. So habe ich meine Erfahrung auf die ganzen Alpen übertragen: möglichst wenige Haken, keine Bohrhaken, später keine Sauerstoffflaschen. Ich habe später diesen Stil auf die Achttausender übertragen. Als ich anfing, Achttausender zu besteigen, war das Vorgehen mit riesigem Aufwand verbunden. Am Nanga Parbat hatten wir 1970 neun Tonnen Ausrüstung dabei. Das muss man sich vorstellen: wie teuer es war, das alles an den Fuß des Berges zu bringen. Acht Jahre später habe ich den Berg allein bestiegen, mit insgesamt 60 Kilogramm. Und da wird erst klar, dass ich einen ganz neuen Zugang zum Berg gefunden habe.

SH Aber jetzt einmal eine ganz provokative Frage: Muss man den Nanga Parbat besteigen?

RM Nein, muss man nicht.

SH Warum haben sich dann so viele Bergsteiger daran abgearbeitet? Weil Hermann Buhl da war, weil er der deutsche Schicksalsberg ist? Aber das würde dich gar nicht betreffen, du bist ja ein Südtiroler.

RM Nein, mich nicht. Aber die Geschichte vom Nanga Parbat erzählt im Grunde den ganzen Alpinismus. Einer der großen Engländer, in diesem Fall Albert Mummery, versucht 1895 den Nanga Parbat mit zwei Kameraden aus England und ein paar Einheimischen zu besteigen. Sie scheitern. Am Ende verschwindet Mummery. Das greift der deutsche Schriftsteller Walter Schmidkunz auf.

SH Damals?

RM Nein, 20 Jahre später. Weil er die Briefe von Mummery, die in England erschienen waren, ins Deutsche übersetzte. Diese Briefe liest Willo Welzenbach.

SH **At that time?**

RM **No, twenty years later. Because he translated Mummery's letters, which had been published in England, into German. Willo Welzenbach read these letters.**

SH **He was the municipal architect in Munich, a great mountaineer.**

RM **Willo Welzenbach was the best mountaineer of his time. He planned an expedition to Nanga Parbat from the Diamir side in 1932. However, he did not make it for several reasons. Firstly, because Paul Bauer, who had great influence in the expedition business at the time, thwarted it behind the scenes. How he thwarted it makes appalling reading – I wrote a book about it, *The Ice Pope: The Welzenbach File*, as Welzenbach was called at the time. But in 1932, when the expedition was finally supposed to take place, Welzenbach couldn't take part because the Great Depression would not let him out of his job. He handed over the expedition leadership to his friend Willy Merkl. He tackled the mountain in the spirit of the 1930s. But they only got as far as 7,000 metres. Two years later, more or less the same people returned, making a great effort. The most extensive, biggest expedition to date – Welzenbach was with them this time. A total of ten people died on this expedition, four sahibs and six sherpas, the biggest disaster up to then in the Himalayas. And in the wake of this catastrophe, Paul Bauer took over the leadership of German mountaineering. Supported by the National Socialists, he climbed up to 'avenge' the deaths on Nanga Parbat from 1934 to 1937: sixteen dead. An avalanche surprised them in the camp. The German people followed this heroism. But you can't avenge the dead: a mountain is unintentional.**

SH **That should be clear to everyone.**

RM **Thus this story became politically charged. Nanga Parbat is also exciting in that these entanglements become clear.**

SH **Before, I talked about the individual and the group. If you stay with Nanga Parbat now, you see these national groups struggling up. For me, the**

SH Er war Stadtbaurat in München, ein großer Bergsteiger.

RM Willo Welzenbach war der beste Bergsteiger seiner Zeit. Er plante 1932 eine Expedition zum Nanga Parbat zur Diamirseite. Er kommt aber aus mehreren Gründen nicht zum Zug. Einmal, weil Paul Bauer, der damals großen Einfluss im Expeditionswesen hatte, es im Hintergrund vereitelte. Wie er es vereitelt hat – ich habe ein Buch dazu geschrieben, *Der Eispapst: Die Akte Welzenbach*, so wurde Welzenbach damals genannt – ist ungut. Aber 1932, als die Expedition endlich stattfinden soll, kann er nicht teilnehmen, weil die Weltwirtschaftskrise ihn aus seiner beruflichen Position nicht frei lässt. Er übergibt das Leadership an seinen Freund Willy Merkl. Der geht, im Geist der 30er-Jahre, diesen Berg an. Sie kommen aber nur bis 7000 Meter hinauf. Zwei Jahre später kehren mehr oder weniger die gleichen Leute mit großem Aufwand zurück. Die umfangreichste, stärkste Expedition, die es bis dahin gab – Welzenbach ist diesmal dabei. Insgesamt zehn Menschen sterben bei dieser Expedition, vier Sahibs und sechs Sherpas, die größte Katastrophe bis dahin im Himalaya. Und auf diese Katastrophe hin übernimmt Paul Bauer das Leadership im deutschen Bergsteigen. Unterstützt von den Nationalsozialisten geht er hin, um die Toten vom Nanga Parbat 1934 bis 1937 zu „rächen": 16 Tote. Eine Lawine hatte sie im Lager überrascht. Das deutsche Volk folgt diesem Heldentum. Man kann die Toten aber nicht rächen, der Berg ist absichtslos.

SH Das sollte allen Menschen klar sein.

RM Und damit wird diese Geschichte politisch besetzt. Der Nanga Parbat ist auch insofern spannend, als diese Verstrickungen klar werden.

SH Vorher habe ich schon mal von Individuum und Kollektiv gesprochen. Wenn man jetzt beim Nanga Parbat bleibt, sieht man diese nationalen Kollektive, die sich hochquälen. Für mich ist das absolute Gegenteil das Bild des ausgemergelten Hermann Buhl, der völlig allein vom Nanga Parbat herunterkommt. Das ist so ein modernes Foto, weil es die Individualität hochhält.

absolute opposite is the image of the gaunt Hermann Buhl coming down from Nanga Parbat completely alone. That's such a modern photo, because it upholds individuality.

RM **Or the other way round, because that was when it was all seen otherwise. The expedition leader Karl Maria Herrligkoffer denied Buhl his individual achievement and said it was a team achievement. Although he had set out alone, against the will of the expedition leader – who had forbidden the ascent at that moment. However, it was not Buhl who had decided, but the older Hans Ertl. He said by radio: 'We'll go up there and you can talk all you want at base camp, but forget your ban.'**

SH **A very important decision towards individualism.**

RM **Right. The 1934 expedition was a team effort. It was already the time of the 'Third Reich', the pooling of forces, fascism.**

SH **Let's get back to the mountains: My two favourite mountains are Tre Cime and Ayers Rock. I have often modelled Tre Cime. The three blocks next to each other seem designed by an artist, nothing seems random; they have a perfectly harmonious form-mass relationship. Nature spoils us here with a perfect sculpture. Natural form and art form coincide. Ayers Rock is the opposite of Tre Cime, an alien in a flat desert like a huge red cowpat. Great, but in fact unmodifiable. An iron floor sculpture would work.**

RM **But it has a very interesting history.**

SH **Yes, Uluru, as it is called by the Aboriginal people, is a sacred mountain and may not be climbed today. Is there a mountain for you that is entirely complete, aesthetically and historically?**

RM **Yes. For me there is no doubt: it is the Machapuchare.**

SH **Really? I modelled it.**

RM **You modelled it?**

SH **Yes, of course, a fascinating structure.**

RM **It has the boldest form, an individual form. No other mountain is**

RM Oder umgekehrt, denn damals wurde das Ganze gedreht. Der Expeditionsleiter Karl Maria Herrligkoffer hat Buhl seine individuelle Leistung abgesprochen und gesagt, es sei eine kollektive Leistung gewesen. Obwohl er gegen den Willen des Expeditionsleiters – der hatte den Aufstieg in diesem Moment verboten – allein aufgebrochen war. Allerdings hatte nicht Buhl entschieden, sondern der ältere Hans Ertl. Der hatte per Funkgerät gesagt: „Wir gehen da hinauf und du kannst im Basislager gescheit reden, aber vergiss dein Verbot."

SH Eine ganz wichtige Entscheidung zum Individualismus hin.

RM Richtig. Die Expedition 1934 war Gemeinschaftsleistung. Es war schon die Zeit des „Dritten Reichs", Bündelung der Kräfte, Faschismus.

SH Lass uns wieder zu den Bergen kommen: Meine zwei Lieblingsberge sind Tre Cime und Ayers Rock. Tre Cime habe ich oft modelliert. Die drei Blöcke nebeneinander sind wie vom Künstler gestaltet, nichts erscheint zufällig, sie haben eine vollkommen harmonische Form-Masse-Beziehung. Die Natur verwöhnt uns hier mit einer perfekten Skulptur. Naturform und Kunstform decken sich. Ayers Rock ist das Gegenteil von Tre Cime, ein Alien in einer ebenen Wüste wie ein riesiger roter Kuhfladen. Toll, aber eigentlich unmodellierbar. Eine Bodenskulptur aus Eisen ginge.

RM Aber er hat eine sehr interessante Geschichte.

SH Ja, der Uluru, so heißt er bei den Aboriginal People, ist ein heiliger Berg und darf heute auch nicht mehr betreten werden. Gibt es für dich einen Berg, der völlig komplett ist, ästhetisch, geschichtlich?

RM Ja. Für mich gibt es keinen Zweifel: Es ist der Machapuchare.

SH Ehrlich? Den habe ich modelliert.

RM Den hast du modelliert?

SH Ja klar, ein faszinierendes Gebilde.

like it. The Matterhorn, they say, also has a unique shape, but the Machapuchare is more individual.

SH **Yes, the twisted thing at the top, as if El Greco had designed it.**

RM **But there are several mountains in the world that look similar. Mount Assiniboine, they say, is the Matterhorn in the Rockies.**

SH **I like it: I modelled it too. Even more imposing than in nature. I made it even more pyramidal. There's something godlike about simply reshaping nature.**

RM **But Machapuchare really is radically different. And the most important thing: it is unclimbed. For 30 years I begged all the way to the king in Nepal to get permission to try. I didn't get it. It is considered sacred. But how it became holy is interesting. In 1956, Colonel James Roberts got a permit to climb the mountain. They tried, but didn't get to the top. And then Roberts went to the king and asked that the mountain be closed forever. Just so that no one else could get up there either. That's how it became sacred. So it's profanely sacred.**

SH **I found it difficult to model, because it has huge sloping surfaces in parts, especially on the fishtail side, without the usual structuring. The extreme wall height is quite difficult to realise.**

RM **As you said, it is so twisted at the top.**

SH **That's what makes it so difficult to model. What does Machapuchare actually mean?**

RM **It translates as 'Fish Tail'. I have an artwork of it from Nepal, a large bronze, weighing 300 kilograms. The locals say it is a goddess who jumped into the sea, like a whale, and at the back the fin remained alive. The goddess disappeared into the water.**

SH **So this is one of the very few mountains that has never been climbed. As regards the Kailash, I don't believe no one has ever been up there. I just don't believe that.**

RM Er hat die kühnste Form, eine individuelle Form. So ist kein anderer Berg. Das Matterhorn, sagt man, hat auch eine einmalige Form, aber der Machapuchare ist eigenwilliger.

SH Ja, oben, das Gedrehte, als hätte ihn El Greco entworfen.

RM Es gibt aber mehrere Berge auf der Welt, die ähnlich ausschauen. Mount Assiniboine, heißt es, sei das Matterhorn in den Rockies.

SH Den mag ich gerne, den habe ich auch modelliert. Sogar imposanter als in der Natur. Ich habe ihn noch pyramidaler gemacht. Es hat etwas Gottgleiches, die Natur einfach umzuformen.

RM Aber wirklich radikal anders ist der Machapuchare. Und das Wichtigste: Er ist unbestiegen. 30 Jahre lang habe ich in Nepal bis zum König gebettelt, dass ich eine Genehmigung für einen Versuch bekomme. Ich habe sie nicht gekriegt. Er gilt als heilig. Aber wie er heilig geworden ist, ist interessant. 1956 hat Colonel James Roberts eine Genehmigung erhalten, den Berg zu besteigen. Sie haben es versucht, sind aber nicht zum Gipfel gekommen. Und dann ging Roberts zum König und hat gebeten, dass man den Berg für immer sperrt. Nur damit auch kein anderer hochkommt. So ist er heilig geworden. Also, profan heilig geworden.

SH Ich fand ihn schwierig zu modellieren, weil er zum Teil riesig abfallende Flächen hat, gerade an der Fischschwanz-Seite ohne die üblichen Strukturierungen. Die extreme Wandhöhe ist ganz schwer umzusetzen.

RM Wie du gesagt hast, er ist oben so gedreht.

SH Das macht es ja so schwierig, ihn zu modellieren. Was heißt Machapuchare eigentlich?

RM Übersetzt heißt es Fischschwanz. Ich habe ein Kunstwerk dazu aus Nepal, eine große Bronze, 300 Kilogramm schwer. Die Einheimischen sagen, er ist eine Göttin, die ins Meer gesprungen ist, wie ein Wal, und hinten ist die Flosse lebendig geblieben. Die Göttin ist im Wasser verschwunden.

RM The Kailash has been climbed, of course, by Milarepa, who rode on the rays of the sun and thus climbed the peak 3,000 years ago. Mythology says that the Kailash will be climbed again, but without disturbing the mountain, without raping the mountain.

SH That's a beautiful image. What does it mean now?

RM Yes, that is a very beautiful image. You must only touch the mountain, not conquer it, only do it like Milarepa. He flew up riding on sunbeams, at the speed of light. It was a competition. And his opponent didn't get to the top. But nowhere is it written that the Kailash cannot be climbed. It just can't be climbed by bad means, says the Tibetan-Nepali narrative.

SH If you were younger now, would you be tempted to secretly climb the Kailash today?

RM The Kailash is not a particularly difficult mountain.

SH No, not because of the difficulty. But because of crossing the boundary.

RM No. I would be much happier if I had been allowed to climb Machapuchare.

SH Where do you see the similarity between artists and mountaineers?

RM In the self-injury and the potential self-destruction. Well, with us alpinists, it is more radical. We waste all our energy, our strength, our imagination to reach, or envisage, some useless goal. We are prepared to pursue it to the point of self-destruction. Artists do the same when they disappear completely into their art and become absorbed. Most of them end up broke and hang themselves.

SH That's a very drastic way of putting it. Many artists live on the verge of poverty until they die of natural causes. The problem also exists with mountaineers who don't have a great career. When they are physically no longer capable of great tours and are also unable to write books or give lectures, they fall out of their profession and wake up in a world of poverty.

SH Das ist also einer der ganz wenigen Berge, der nie bestiegen wurde. Beim Kailash glaube ich nicht, dass da nie jemand oben war. Das glaube ich einfach nicht.

RM Der Kailash ist natürlich bestiegen, und zwar von Milarepa, der auf den Sonnenstrahlen ritt und so vor 3000 Jahren den Gipfel erklommen hat. Die Mythologie sagt, dass der Kailash wieder bestiegen wird, aber ohne den Berg zu stören, ohne den Berg zu vergewaltigen.

SH Das ist ein schönes Bild. Was heißt das nun?

RM Ja, das ist ein sehr schönes Bild. Man darf den Berg nur berühren, nicht bezwingen, nur so wie Milarepa. Er ist auf Sonnenstrahlen reitend raufgeflogen, rauf in Lichtgeschwindigkeit. War ein Wettkampf. Und sein Gegner ist nicht hinaufgekommen. Aber es steht nirgends, dass der Kailash nicht bestiegen werden darf. Er darf nur nicht mit unguten Mitteln bestiegen werden, sagt das tibetisch-nepalesische Narrativ.

SH Und angenommen du wärst jetzt jünger, würde es dich reizen, heute heimlich auf den Kailash zu steigen?

RM Der Kailash ist kein besonders schwieriger Berg.

SH Nein, nicht wegen der Schwierigkeit. Sondern wegen der Grenzüberschreitung.

RM Nein. Ich würde mich viel mehr freuen, wenn ich den Machapuchare hätte besteigen dürfen.

SH Wo siehst du die Ähnlichkeit zwischen Künstlern und Bergsteigern?

RM In der Selbstverschwendung und der möglichen Selbstzerstörung. Also, bei uns Alpinisten ist das Tun radikaler. Wir verschwenden alle unsere Energie, unsere Kraft, unsere Fantasie, um irgendein unnützes Ziel zu erreichen oder ins Auge zu fassen. Und sind bereit, es bis zur Selbstzerstörung zu verfolgen. Der Künstler tut es auch, wenn er völlig in seiner Sache verschwindet und aufgeht. Die meisten sind dann am Ende pleite und hängen sich auf.

RM **A similar situation, that is, self-injury and self-destruction – economically speaking – could have hit me with the Sigmundskron museum project. Because I put everything I had into it in terms of means, ideas, and strength.**

SH **But you always put everything you have into whichever project you're currently working on.**

RM **Yes, after the eight-thousander I had funds left over at the end, otherwise I wouldn't have been able to build the museums. But in the beginning it was really about economic survival. You know, I begged three museum directors to tell me whether the museum project made sense or not. All three said, 'no chance'. Today we have been open for almost twenty years. We got through the Corona crisis, and without subsidies. Many other museums needed financial support. I had signed a contract that we would have to do without state funding. We survived. I had given my daughter Magdalena, who is now the chief coordinator, the responsibility, even helped out, but she managed it. The first key factor was to put the museums where they carry the world outside – landscape, nature, and light. So Monte Rite stands grandly with the theme of rocks in the middle of the Dolomites.**

SH **In terms of location, it's my favourite museum.**

RM **The place is great. And the fact that we are using a former wartime fortress to explain the tension between man and mountain is a stroke of luck. A peaceful exhibition in former trenches. That this fortress is also in the right place and is basically good architecture, with this long corridor, is wonderful. It also works. But it's the weakest museum we have.**

SH **You mean in terms of what's inside, right?**

RM **No, no, no. The weakest in terms of entrance fees coming in.**

SH **Yes, people have to walk up. Actually, it's a wonderful idea that I have to work for art, or even culture, through a two-hour climb, that not everything is always available without any effort.**

SH Das ist jetzt sehr drastisch ausgedrückt. Viele Künstler leben am Rande der Armut oft bis zum natürlichen Tod. Das Problem gibt es auch bei Bergsteigern, die keine große Karriere machen. Wenn sie körperlich nicht mehr zu großen Touren fähig sind und auch nicht in der Lage sind, Bücher zu schreiben oder Vorträge zu halten, fallen sie aus ihrem Metier und wachen in einem Milieu der Armut auf.

RM Eine ähnliche Situation – auch Selbstverschwendung, Selbstzerstörung, wirtschaftlich gesehen – hätte mich beim Museumsprojekt Sigmundskron treffen können. Weil ich alles, was ich an Mitteln, Ideen und Kraft hatte, hineingesteckt habe.

SH Aber du hast doch immer alles, was du hattest, in dein jeweiliges Projekt gesteckt.

RM Ja, bei dem Achttausender hatte ich am Ende Mittel übrig, sonst hätte ich die Museen nicht aufbauen können. Doch am Anfang ging es wirklich um das wirtschaftliche Überleben. Du weißt, dass ich bei drei Museumsdirektoren gebettelt habe, mir zu sagen, ob das Museumsprojekt Sinn macht oder nicht. Alle drei haben gesagt: „No Chance." Heute sind wir bald 20 Jahre offen. Wir sind über die Coronakrise gekommen, und zwar ohne Subventionen. Viele andere Museen wurden subventioniert. Ich hatte einen Vertrag unterschrieben, dass wir ohne Zuschüsse auskommen müssen. Wir überleben es. Ich hatte meiner Tochter Magdalena, der heutigen Chefkoordinatorin, die Verantwortung übertragen, auch noch geholfen, aber sie hat das gestemmt. Der erste Schlüssel war, die Museen dorthin zu stellen, wo sie die Welt draußen – Landschaft, Natur und Licht – tragen. Also der Monte Rite steht grandios mit dem Thema Fels mitten in den Dolomiten.

SH Vom Ort her ist es mein Lieblingsmuseum.

RM Der Platz ist großartig. Und dass wir eine ehemalige Kriegsfestung nutzen, um die Spannung zwischen Mensch und Berg zu erklären, ist ein Glücksfall. Eine friedliche Ausstellung

Talking about ascents: How important is Pervitin [a German methamphetamine brand] in the history of alpinism? Many artists are accused of taking drugs, as are many alpinists. Do you think that plays a decisive role?

RM Yes, the issue exists with mountaineers. Especially with the English and Americans in the 70s. And today with the young. It has remained fashionable.

SH I read about Jim Bridwell that he climbed around on El Capitan on LSD without a rope. I can't imagine that, because I took LSD a few times in the past. It seems impossible to me to climb in such a trance-like state.

RM Apparently, fears then disappear. I had an experience like that with Doug Scott. Unfortunately he is already dead. We were at Chamlang and made a first ascent; it was a seven-thousand-metre peak. In the evening we crawled into a crevice, into a crevice at the edge, to seek shelter. We had no tents with us – we had planned it so. It was cold, the wind blew all over my face. Doug lay there, completely apathetic, had taken something in the evening and then slept. Admittedly it was a great advantage for him; fears, doubts; and pain could be controlled that way. People tell me that all this comes naturally to the young, the 20 to 30-year-olds or Generation Z, as they are called today. But I can't confirm that, because I don't belong to that generation.

SH Hermann Buhl allegedly took Pervitin when he climbed Nanga Parbat. I always found the analogy with the Japanese kamikaze pilots exciting. A kamikaze pilot knows he is going to die. The extreme mountaineer at least has a better chance of surviving.

RM Buhl probably wouldn't have come down without the stuff.

SH Have you ever taken drugs?

RM No, I have never used drugs. I still get together with young climbers. And they tell me it's common nowadays.

SH Well, so did the El Capitan climbers, all my Yosemite favourites, and many others.

in früheren Schützengräben. Dass diese Festung auch noch an der richtigen Stelle liegt und im Grunde gute Architektur ist, mit diesem langen Gang, ist top. Funktioniert auch. Ist allerdings das schwächste Museum, das wir haben.

SH Du meinst gemessen an dem, was drin ist, oder?

RM Nein, nein, nein. Das Schwächste, was an Eintrittsgeldern hereinkommt.

SH Ja, die Leute müssen hochlaufen. Eigentlich ist es eine wunderbare Vorstellung, dass ich mir Kunst oder auch Kultur erarbeiten muss, durch einen zweistündigen Aufstieg, dass nicht immer alles ohne Anstrengung zur Verfügung steht.

Wenn wir schon über Aufstiege reden: Wie wichtig ist Pervitin in der Geschichte des Alpinismus? Vielen Künstlern wird ja unterstellt, Drogen zu nehmen, vielen Alpinisten ebenso. Glaubst du, das spielt eine entscheidende Rolle?

RM Ja, bei den Bergsteigern ist das Thema da. Vor allem bei den Engländern und Amerikanern in den 70er-Jahren. Und heute bei den Jungen. Es ist Mode geblieben.

SH Ich habe von Jim Bridwell gelesen, dass er mit LSD am El Capitan ohne Seil herumgeklettert ist. Ich kann mir das nicht vorstellen, da ich ganz früher auch ein paarmal LSD genommen habe. Es scheint mir unmöglich, in so einem tranceartigen Zustand zu klettern.

RM Scheinbar fallen dann Ängste ab. Mit Doug Scott habe ich auch so ein Erlebnis gehabt. Leider ist er schon tot. Wir waren am Chamlang und haben eine Erstbegehung gemacht, es war ein Siebentausender. Am Abend sind wir in eine Spalte hineingekrochen, in eine Randspalte, um Schutz zu suchen. Wir hatten keine Zelte dabei – geplant keine Zelte dabei. Und es war kalt, es hat mir das Gesicht vollgeweht. Doug lag da, völlig apathisch, hatte sich am Abend etwas reingesteckt und dann geschlafen. Zugegeben war es ein großer Vorteil für ihn, Ängste, Zweifel und Schmerz ließen sich so beherrschen. Man sagt mir, alles das sei für die Jungen, die 20- bis 30-Jährigen oder

RM **But it didn't start then. It started with the British in the 1960s and 70s, in the hippie era. First it was amphetamines; the French mountaineers Maurice Herzog and Louis Lachenal also took amphetamines when they climbed Annapurna in 1950. The result was that when they went back down they were completely insane, really insane. They left their gloves at the top.**

SH **Then you're surprised that nothing happens. But it does.**

RM **Yes, because there's also an advantage.**

SH **Because the fear is gone.**

RM **Fear costs a lot of energy.**

SH **Your dealing with fear, your solitariness, your collecting, your writing, the interest in the universal has everything to do with your mental abilities.**

RM **I worked my way into it differently from most other people. I started very early to describe my world of mountains.**

SH **Was there any moment that influenced you very strongly?**

RM **Yes, reading Paul Preuß, around the age of sixteen or seventeen. Preuß was not available in Germany; there was no book to read. But there was an Italian book on him. Preuß was a Jew and was erased from history at that time. I read it in Italian and soon found out why it was only available in Italian. The author was a romantic, a terrible romantic, who glorified everything about Preuß. And later, through the original documents, I found out who Preuß really was and is. I wrote a biography on Paul Preuß in 1986, which I would like to add to soon, because I have found new documents again.**

SH **And what happened there? You read Preuß and then?**

RM **Then the mountains became something else for me. Then they were no longer just these towers or these possibilities to climb up. They became something spiritual, or works of art in terms of form. I still say that a sculpture of Cerro Torre is and remains a sculpture. But the real Cerro Torre can't be represented in an image: you have to make something of your own for that. For me it works best with the help of language.**

die Generation Z, wie man sie heute nennt, selbstverständlich. Kann ich aber nicht bestätigen, weil ich ja nicht dazugehöre.

SH Hermann Buhl hat angeblich bei der Nanga-Parbat-Besteigung Pervitin genommen. Ich fand die Analogie mit den japanischen Kamikaze-Piloten immer spannend. Ein Kamikaze-Pilot weiß, dass er sterben wird. Der Extrembergsteiger hat immerhin eine größere Chance, zu überleben.

RM Buhl wäre wohl ohne das Zeug nicht mehr heruntergekommen.

SH Hast du je Drogen genommen?

RM Nein, ich habe nie Drogen konsumiert. Ich komme ja immer noch mit jungen Kletterern zusammen. Und die erzählen mir, es sei heute üblich.

SH Gut, das taten die El-Capitan-Kletterer auch, meine ganzen Yosemite-Favoriten und viele andere.

RM Damals hat das aber nicht angefangen. Begonnen hat das schon bei den Briten in den 1960er- und 70er-Jahren, also in der Hippiezeit, zuerst waren es die Amphetamine. Die Franzosen Maurice Herzog und Louis Lachenal hatten bei der Annapurna-Besteigung 1950 auch davon eingenommen. Die Folge war dann, dass sie beim Runtergehen völlig irre waren, wirklich irre. Haben ihre Handschuhe oben liegen gelassen.

SH Da wundert es einen dann, dass da nichts passiert. Aber es ist so.

RM Ja, weil es auch ein Vorteil ist.

SH Weil die Angst weg ist.

RM Die Angst kostet sehr viel Energie.

SH Dein Umgang mit der Angst, dein Einzelgängertum, dein Sammeln, dein Schreiben, das Interesse am Universellen hat doch alles mit deinen mentalen Fähigkeiten zu tun.

SH **I never imitated the mountains. I took the model and modelled it according to my ideas, greatly exaggerated and cast in perfect white. If I don't like a side, I model it more impressively. Usually one or two views stay very close to reality. These are then my recognition views. I am always looking for the ideal mountain, the ideal sculpture. Moreover, the shift of context from nature to space creates a strange, surreal exaggeration.**

RM **The routes we climb are like drawings. It's not just the line behind them, but also what you have experienced. There is no sport that has produced as much art, especially literature, as mountaineering has.**

SH **You once mentioned in a lecture – it was in the Lenbachhaus in Munich, at my big exhibition – about how a certain line is climbed into the rock, like a drawing on a piece of paper. Royal Robbins once put it in a similar way. I like that because it's so conceptual. So you think about your exact route as a concept beforehand ?**

RM **Yes, I have the line in my head.**

SH **And the deviation must not be too big. Because otherwise it might be too dangerous.**

RM **Yes.**

SH **When the idea then collapses. This is all an artistic problem, too, which I experience all the time in the studio.**

RM **Going to the mountain with an idea in my head, of the line, of the wall, of the difficulties, of the possible dangers, is an emotional approach. That is, I approach this mountain and not only know where the mountain is: I also know what it is like, at this point, at that point. And then comes the balancing of whether I have the prerequisites to tackle this mountain of mine along this line at all. Whether I finally reach the summit or not is completely secondary. It is the confrontation between what I can do, how I assess myself, and what I expect. Isn't that similar in art?**

RM Ich habe mich in das Ganze anders hineingearbeitet als die meisten anderen. Ich habe sehr früh angefangen, meine Welt der Berge zu beschreiben.

SH Gab es irgendeinen Moment, der dich ganz stark beeinflusst hat?

RM Ja, die Lektüre von Paul Preuß, so mit 16, 17 Jahren. Preuß war in Deutschland nicht zu haben, den gab es nicht zu lesen, es gab auch kein Buch. Es gab dazu aber ein italienisches Buch. Preuß war Jude und wurde damals aus der Geschichte gestrichen. Und ich habe ihn auf Italienisch gelesen. Bald bin ich draufgekommen, warum es ihn nur in italienischer Sprache gab. Der Autor allerdings war ein Romantiker, ein fürchterlicher Romantiker, der alles an Preuß verherrlicht hat. Und später habe ich dann durch die originalen Unterlagen herausgefunden, wer Preuß war und ist. Ich habe 1986 eine Biografie zu Paul Preuß geschrieben, die ich bald ergänzen möchte, weil ich wieder neue Unterlagen fand.

SH Und was ist da passiert? Du hast den Preuß gelesen und dann?

RM Dann wurden die Berge für mich etwas anderes. Dann waren sie nicht mehr nur diese Türme oder diese Möglichkeiten, da hinaufzuklettern. Sie wurden etwas Spirituelles oder von der Form her Kunstwerke. Ich sage nach wie vor, eine Plastik vom Cerro Torre ist und bleibt eine Plastik. Aber der wahre Cerro Torre ist nicht in einem Bild darstellbar, du musst mir dazu etwas Eigenständiges machen, für mich geht es am besten mithilfe von Sprache.

SH Ich habe die Berge nie nachgemacht. Ich habe das Vorbild genommen und nach meinen Vorstellungen modelliert, stark überhöht und in perfektem Weiß gegossen. Wenn mir irgendeine Seite nicht gefällt, modelliere ich sie eindrücklicher. Meistens bleiben eine oder zwei Ansichten stark an der Realität. Das sind dann meine Wiedererkennungsansichten. Ich bin immer auf der Suche nach dem idealen Berg, nach der idealen Skulptur. Außerdem entsteht durch die Kontextverschiebung aus der Natur in den Raum eine seltsame, surreale Überhöhung.

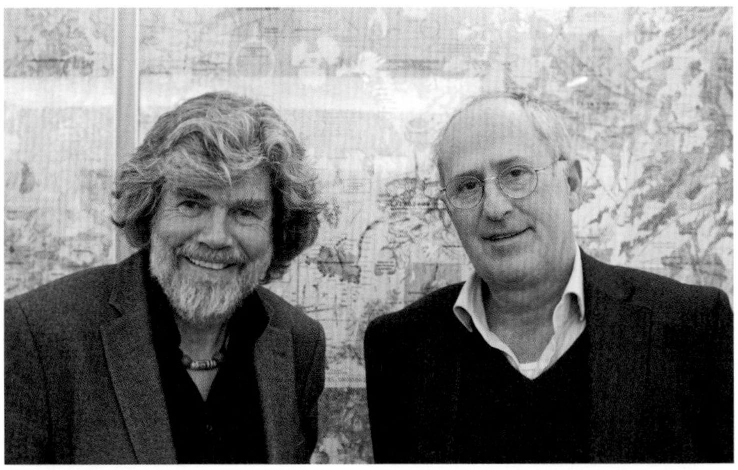

Reinhold Messner und Stephan Huber in der ERES Stiftung, München
Reinhold Messner and Stephan Huber in the Eres Foundation, Munich, Germany

SH **It is, but not as life-threatening. A difficult moment for artists is sometimes the exhaustion and emptiness after major exhibitions. A strange blues after reaching the goal. Actually, that's when the second part of my work starts, which is to deal with the work at the level of reception. I give interviews: I try to explain my ideas and starting points.**

RM **I don't think you should explain, but tell.**

SH **For me, explanation and narration blur, just as fiction and reality blur. That would be life-threatening for an alpinist.**

RM **The picture or the sculpture is always also a narrative. A narrative that tells how the summit was reached, or in your case, how the work of art came into being. That makes a whole. Since you hold it in such high regard, why don't you actually try to capture El Capitan and its route, the Salathé, on a canvas? A work of art of the path through the vertical.**

SH **Okay, I'll take the path through the vertical as a collaborative idea for once, but not on canvas: as a thin line of steel, floating slightly in front of the wall. That is more sculptural.**

RM Die Routen, die wir klettern, sind ja wie Zeichnungen. Da liegt eben nicht nur die Linie dahinter, sondern auch das, was du erlebt hast. Es gibt keine Sportart, die derart viel Kunst, vor allem Literatur, hervorgebracht hat wie die Bergsteigerei.

SH Du hast auch einmal im Vortrag darüber gesprochen – es war im Lenbachhaus, in meiner großen Ausstellung –, wie eine bestimmte Linie in den Fels geklettert wird, wie eine Zeichnung auf einem Blatt Papier. Ähnlich hat es Royal Robbins einmal formuliert. Ich mag das, weil es so konzeptuell ist. Du überlegst dir also deine genaue Route im Vorfeld also rein konzeptuell?

RM Ja, die Linie habe ich im Kopf.

SH Und die Abweichung darf nicht zu groß sein. Weil es sonst möglicherweise zu gefährlich wird.

RM Ja.

SH Wenn dann die Vorstellung zusammenbricht. Das ist alles auch eine künstlerische Problematik, die ich ständig im Atelier erlebe.

RM Das Hingehen zum Berg mit einer Vorstellung im Kopf, von der Linie, von der Wand, von den Schwierigkeiten, von den eventuellen Gefahren, ist eine emotionale Annäherung. Das heißt, ich nähere mich diesem Berg und weiß nicht nur, wo der Berg steht, ich weiß auch, wie er beschaffen ist, an dieser Stelle, an jener Stelle. Und dann kommt das Abgleichen, ob ich überhaupt die Voraussetzungen habe, um diesen meinen Berg auf dieser Linie anzugehen. Ob ich zuletzt den Gipfel erreiche oder nicht, ist völlig sekundär. Es ist die Auseinandersetzung zwischen dem, was ich kann, wie ich mich einschätze, und dem, was ich erwarte. Ist das nicht in der Kunst ähnlich?

SH Das ist so, jedoch nicht so lebensgefährlich. Ein schwieriges Moment für Künstler ist manchmal die Erschöpfung und die Leere nach großen Ausstellungen. Ein seltsamer Blues nach dem Erreichen des Ziels. Eigentlich fängt dann der zweite Teil meiner Arbeit an, nämlich die

Rezeptionsebene zu behandeln. Ich gebe Interviews, ich versuche, meine Ideen und Ausgangspunkte zu erklären.

RM Ich finde, du solltest nicht erklären, sondern erzählen.

SH Bei mir verschwimmen Erklärung und Erzählung, bei mir verschwimmen Fiktion und Realität. Das wäre für einen Alpinisten lebensgefährlich.

RM Das Bild oder die Plastik ist immer auch ein Narrativ. Ein Narrativ, das erzählt, wie der Gipfel erreicht wurde, oder bei dir, wie das Kunstwerk entstanden ist. Das ergibt ein Ganzes. Nachdem du Royal Robbins so schätzt, warum versuchst du dann eigentlich nicht, den El Capitan und seine Route, die Salathé, auf eine Leinwand zu bannen? Ein Kunstwerk vom Weg durch die Vertikale.

SH Okay, den Weg durch die Vertikale übernehme ich jetzt einmal als gemeinschaftliche Idee, aber nicht auf Leinwand, sondern als dünne Linie aus Stahl, leicht vor der Wand schwebend. Das ist skulpturaler.

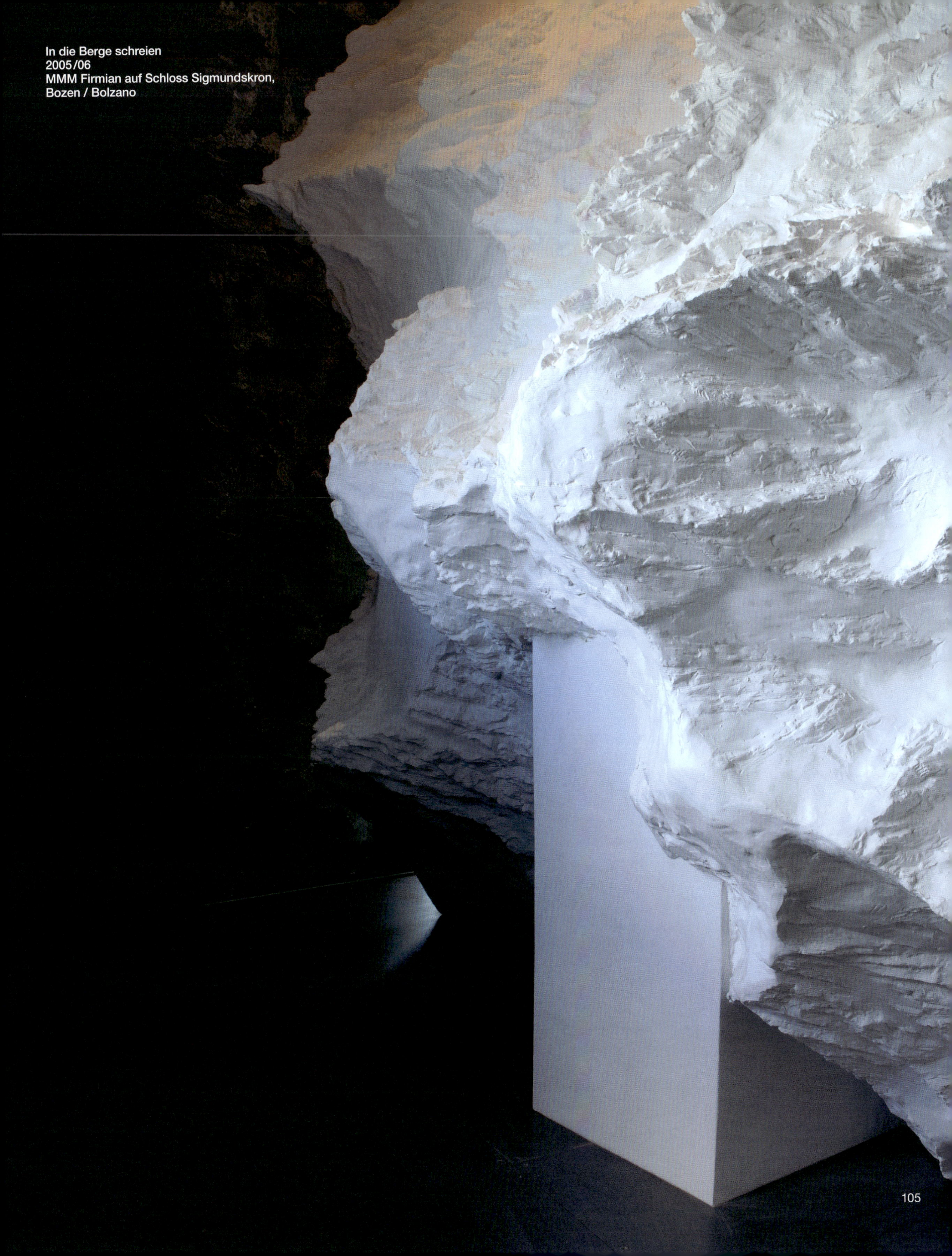

In die Berge schreien
2005/06
MMM Firmian auf Schloss Sigmundskron,
Bozen / Bolzano

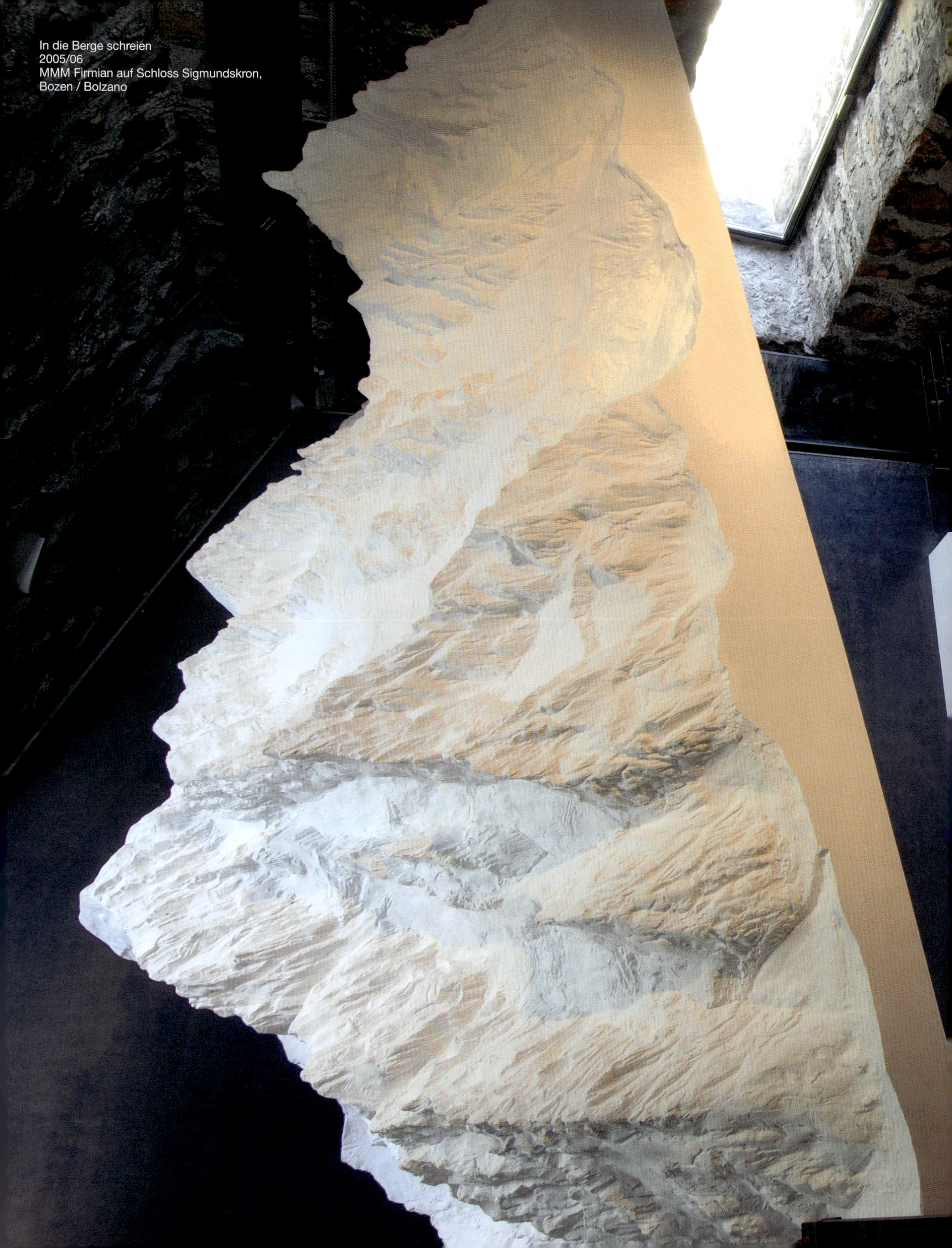

In die Berge schreien
2005/06
MMM Firmian auf Schloss Sigmundskron,
Bozen / Bolzano

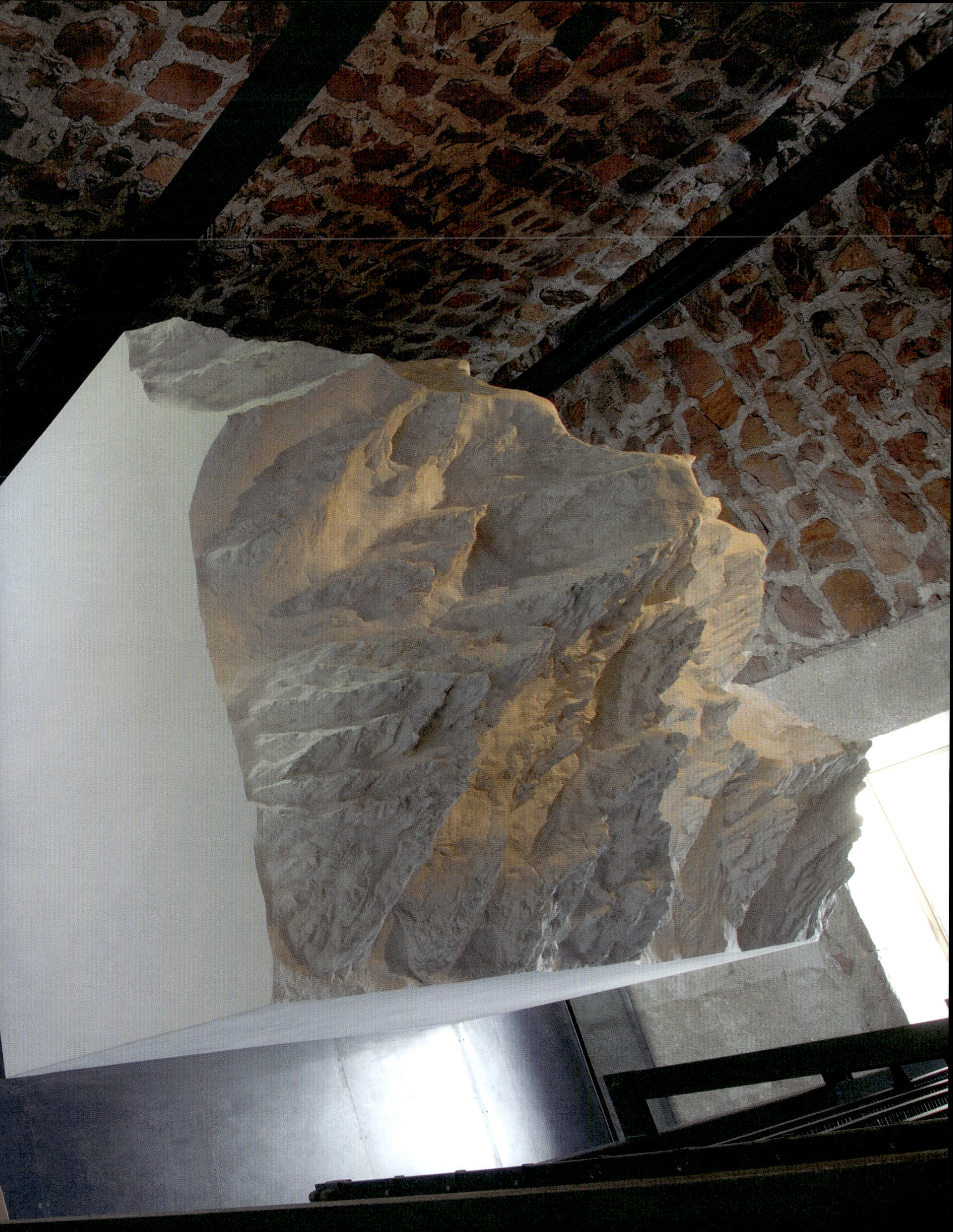

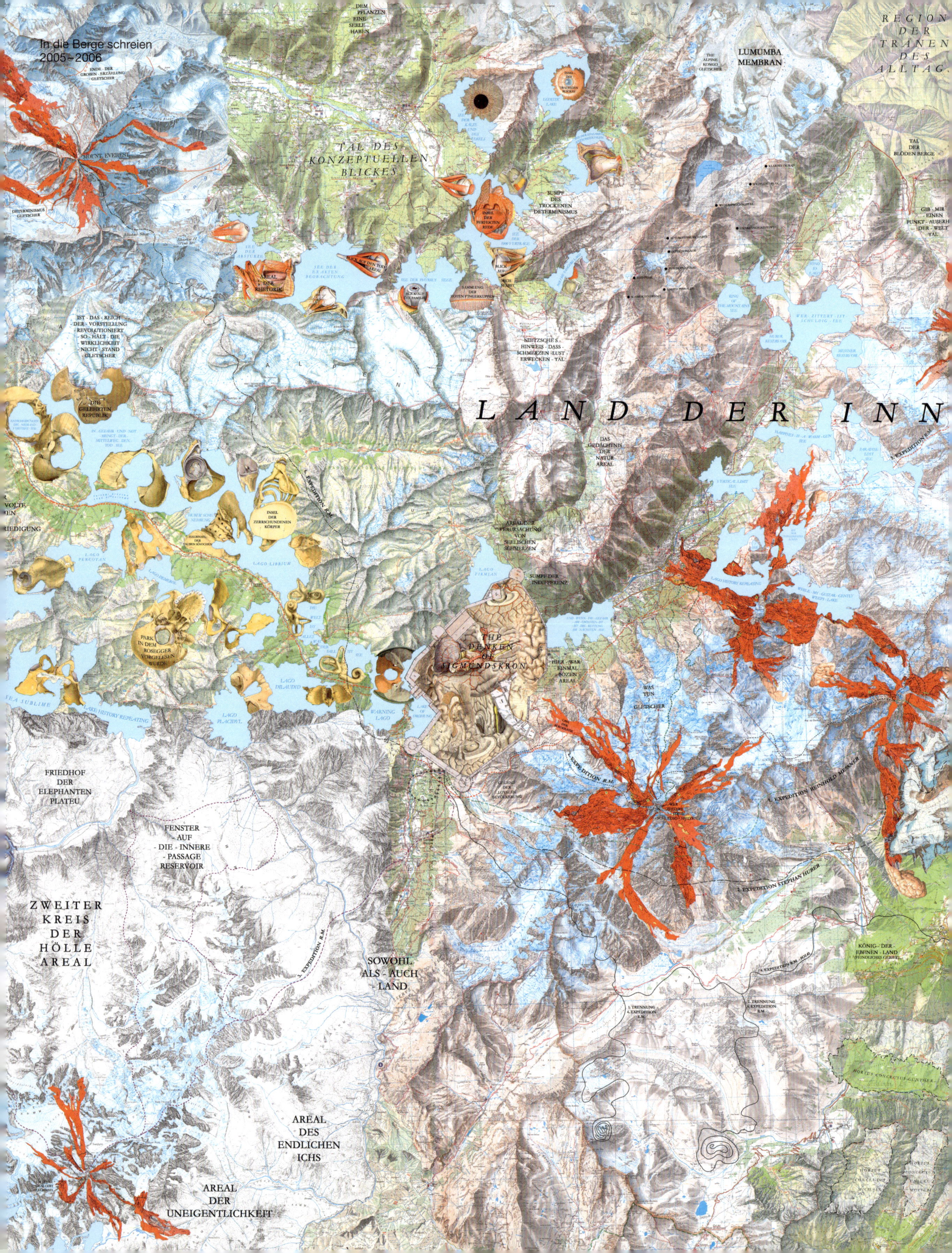
In die Berge schreien
2005–2006
REGION DER TRÄNEN DES ALLTAG
LUMUMBA MEMBRAN
TAL DES KONZEPTUELLEN BLICKES
SUMPF DES TROCKENEN DETERMINISMUS
TAL DER BLÖDEN BERGE
MOUNT EVEREST
IST · DAS · REICH · DER · VORSTELLUNG · REVOLUTIONIERT · SO · HÄLT · DIE · WIRKLICHKEIT · NICHT · STAND GLETSCHER
NIETZSCHE'S · HINWEIS · DASS · SCHMERZEN · LUST · ERWECKEN · TAL
L A N D D E R I N N
DAS GEDÄCHTNIS DER NATUR AREAL
SUMPF DER INDIFFERENZ
FRIEDHOF DER ELEPHANTEN PLATEAU
FENSTER · AUF · DIE · INNERE · PASSAGE RESERVOIR
ZWEITER KREIS DER HÖLLE AREAL
SOWOHL · ALS · AUCH · LAND
AREAL DES ENDLICHEN ICHS
AREAL DER UNEIGENTLICHKEIT

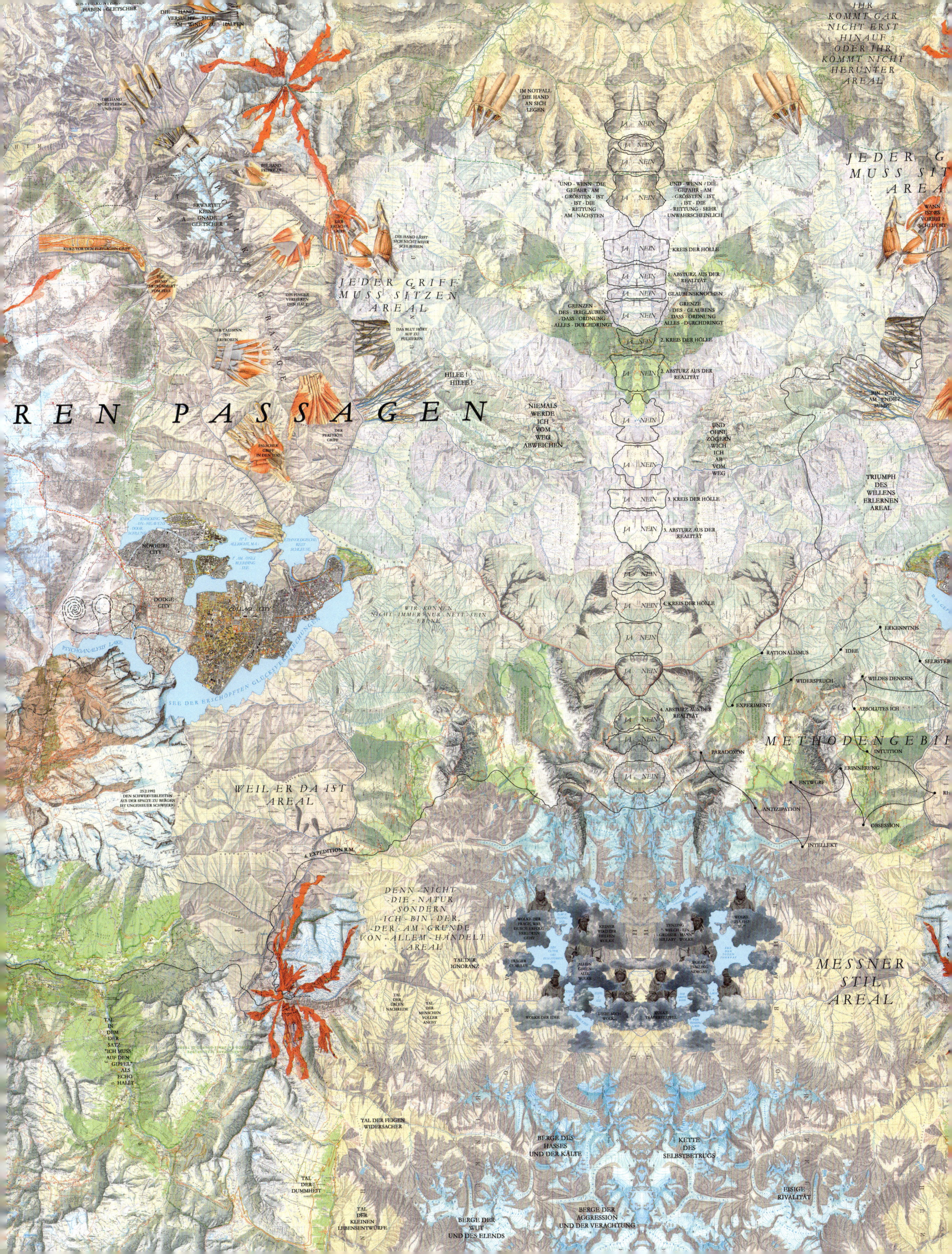

HABEN - GLETSCHER
DIE HAND VERSUCHT SICH AM WIND ZU HALTEN
DIE HAND SPÜRT FLEISCH UND FELS
DIE HAND FRIERT AB
ERWARTET KEINE GNADE GLETSCHER
KURZ VOR DEM PERFEKTEN GRIFF
DIE HAND "ZERTRÜMMERT" VOM FELS
DER FALSCHE GRIFF
DIE HAND LÄSST SICH NICHT MEHR SCHLIESSEN
DIE FINGER VERLIEREN DEN HALT
JEDER GRIFF MUSS SITZEN AREAL
DER TASTSINN IST ERFROREN
DAS BLUT HÖRT AUF ZU PULSIEREN
HILFE ! HILFE !
REN PASSAGEN
DER PERFEKTE GRIFF
FALSCHER GRIFF IN DEN TOD
KNOCKING - ON - HEAVENS - DOOR SCHLUND
NOWHERE CITY
IT'S - ALLRIGHT, MA -
ETHNOLOGISCHE REST - SCHLEUSE
I' AM - ONLY - BLEEDING - SEE
DODGE CITY
COLLAGE CITY
PSYCHOANALYSIS LAKE
SEE DER ERSCHÖPFTEN GLÜCKSVERSPRECHUNGEN
WIR - KÖNNEN NICHT - IMMER - NUR - NETT - SEIN EBENE
23.2.1992 DEN SCHWERVERLETZTEN AUS DER SPALTE ZU BERGEN IST UNGEHEUER SCHWIERIG
WEIL ER DA IST AREAL
4. EXPEDITION R.M.
DENN - NICHT - DIE - NATUR - SONDERN - ICH - BIN - DER, - DER - AM - GRUNDE - VON - ALLEM - HANDELT - AREAL
TAL DER IGNORANZ
TAL DER ÜBLEN NACHREDE
TAL DER MENSCHEN VOLLER ANGST
TAL IN DEM DER SATZ "ICH MUSS AUF DEN GIPFEL" ALS ECHO HALLT
TAL DER FEIGEN WIDERSACHER
TAL DER DUMMHEIT
TAL DER KLEINEN LEBENSENTWÜRFE
BERGE DER WUT UND DES ELENDS
IHR KOMMT GAR NICHT ERST HINAUF ODER IHR KOMMT NICHT HERUNTER AREAL
IM NOTFALL DIE HAND AN SICH LEGEN
JA NEIN
UND - WENN - DIE GEFAHR - AM - GRÖSSTEN - IST - IST - DIE - RETTUNG - AM - NÄCHSTEN
UND - WENN - DIE - GEFAHR - AM - GRÖSSTEN - IST - IST - DIE - RETTUNG - SEHR - UNWAHRSCHEINLICH
JEDER G MUSS SIT AREA
WANN IST ES VORBEI ? SCHLUCHT
KREIS DER HÖLLE
1. ABSTURZ AUS DER REALITÄT
GLAUBENSKNOCHEN
GRENZEN - DES - IRRGLAUBENS - DASS - ORDNUNG - ALLES - DURCHDRINGT
GRENZE - DES - GLAUBENS - DASS - ORDNUNG - ALLES - DURCHDRINGT
2. KREIS DER HÖLLE
2. ABSTURZ AUS DER REALITÄT
BIN ICH AM ENDE ? SUMPF
NIEMALS WERDE ICH VOM WEG ABWEICHEN
UND OHNE ZÖGERN WICH ICH AB VOM WEG
TRIUMPH DES WILLENS ERLERNEN AREAL
3. KREIS DER HÖLLE
3. ABSTURZ AUS DER REALITÄT
4. KREIS DER HÖLLE
4. ABSTURZ AUS DER REALITÄT
ERKENNTNIS
RATIONALISMUS
IDEE
WIDERSPRUCH
WILDES DENKEN
EXPERIMENT
ABSOLUTES ICH
METHODENGEBI
INTUITION
PARADOXON
ERINNERUNG
ENTWURF
ANTIZIPATION
OBSESSION
INTELLEKT
WOLKE DER FRAGE, WAS DURCH ERFOLG VERLOREN GEHT
KEINER WIRD DIR HELFEN WOLKE
TENZING - WELCH - EIN - GROSSER - MANN HILLARY - WOLKE
WOLKE 23.5.1953 11.°°
TRÄGER CUMULUS
ALLEIN GEGEN ALLE WOLKE
WOLKE TENZING NORGAY
WOLKE DER IDEE
LIEBE MICH WOLKE
WOLKE TRÄGERSTAFFEL
MESSNER STIL AREAL
BERGE DES HASSES UND DER KÄLTE
KETTE DES SELBSTBETRUGS
EISIGE RIVALITÄT
BERGE DER AGGRESSION UND DER VERACHTUNG

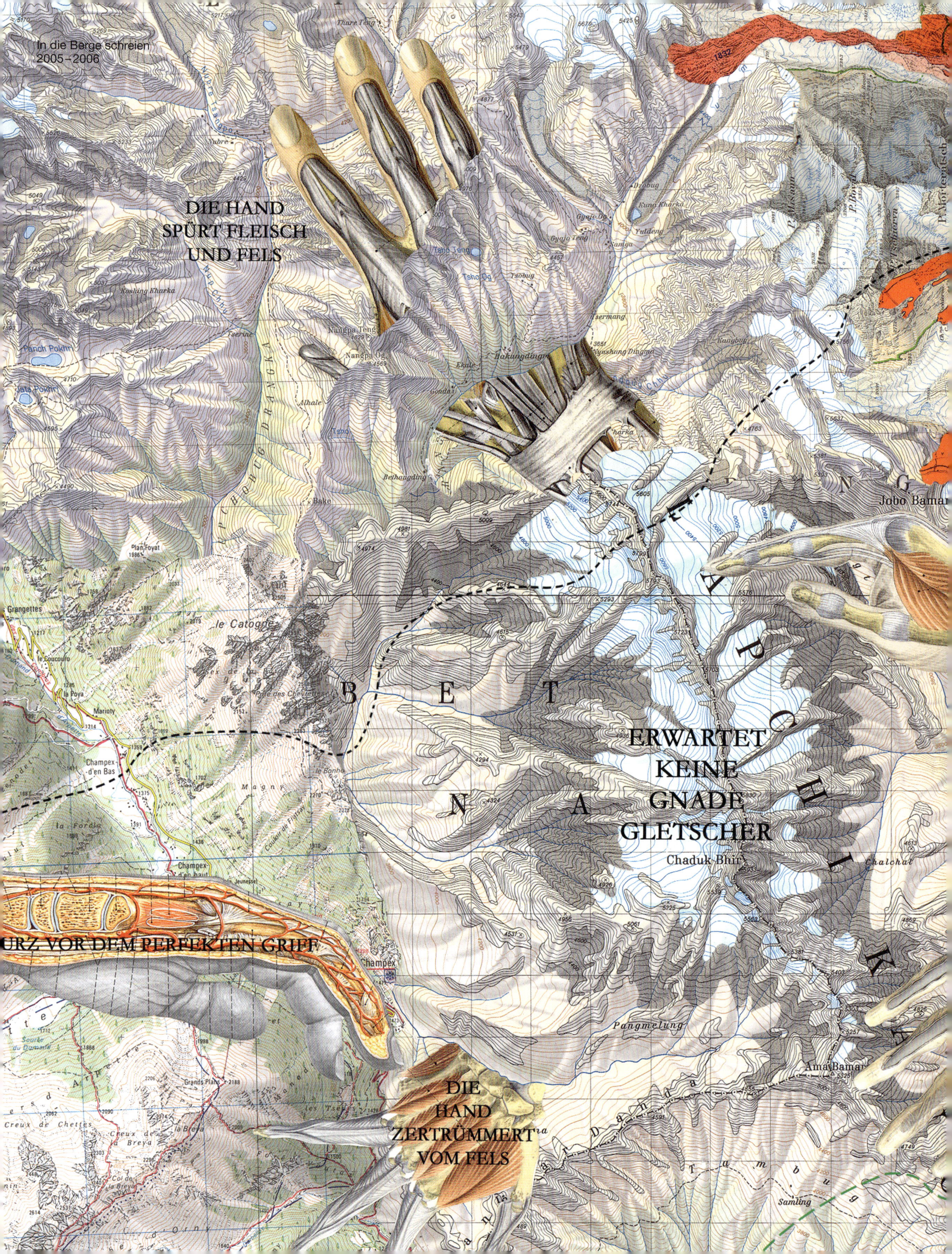

In die Berge schreien
2005 – 2006

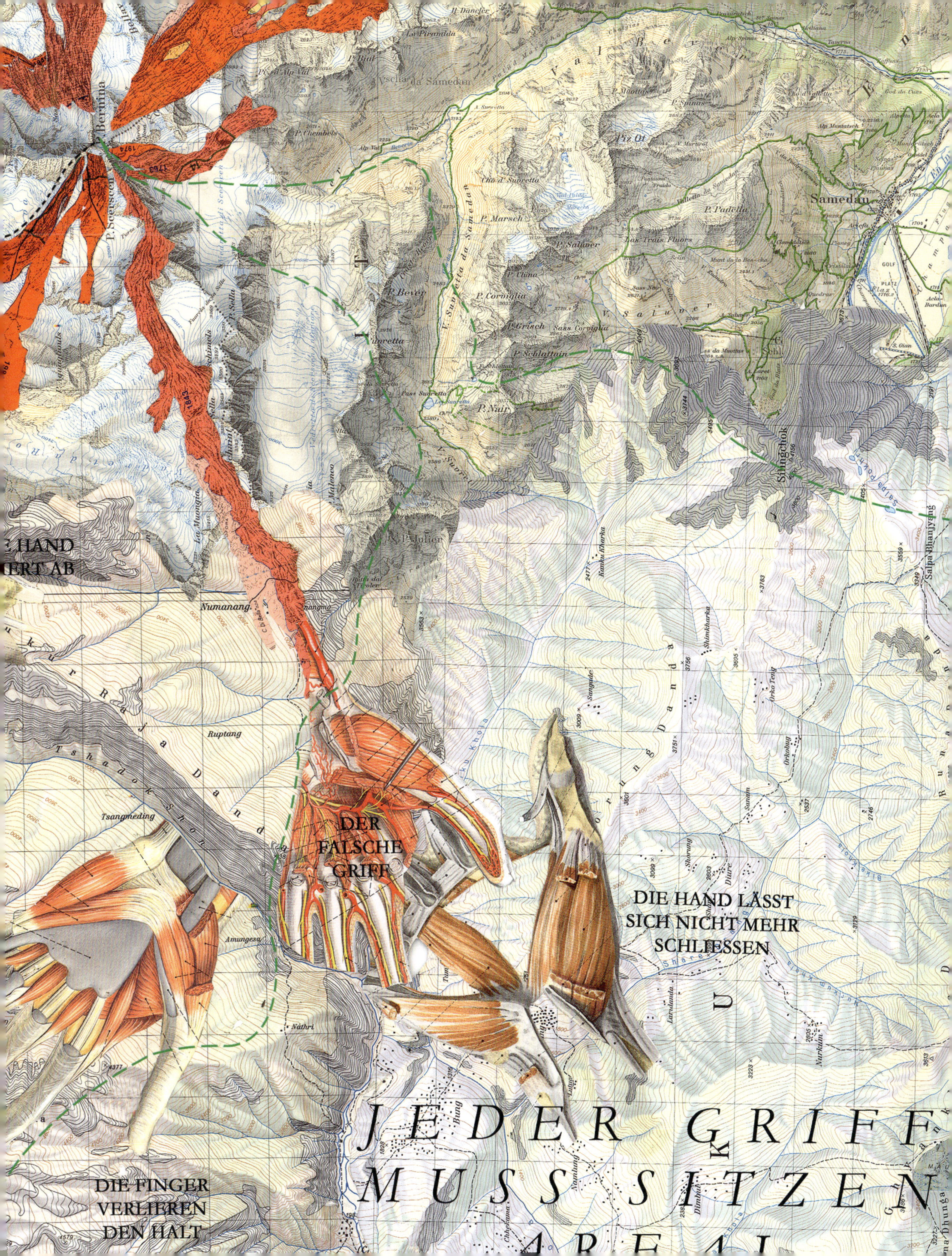

E HAND
IERT AB
DER
FALSCHE
GRIFF
DIE HAND LÄSST
SICH NICHT MEHR
SCHLIESSEN
JEDER GRIFF
MUSS SITZEN
DIE FINGER
VERLIEREN
DEN HALT

Perfect Sculpture, 6 (Tre Cime)
2016
MMM Corones, Kronplatz bei St. Vigil /
Kronplatz near St. Vigil

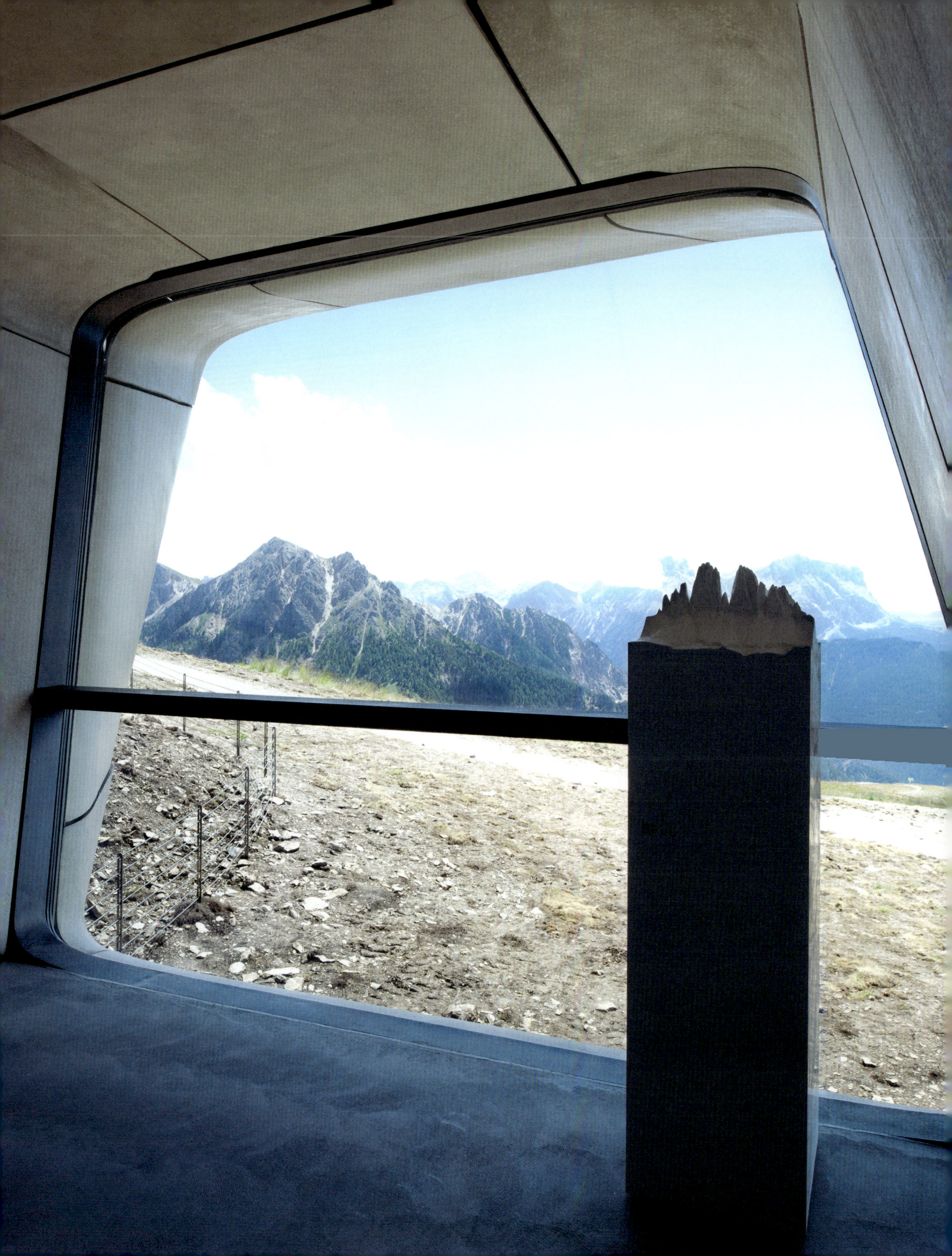

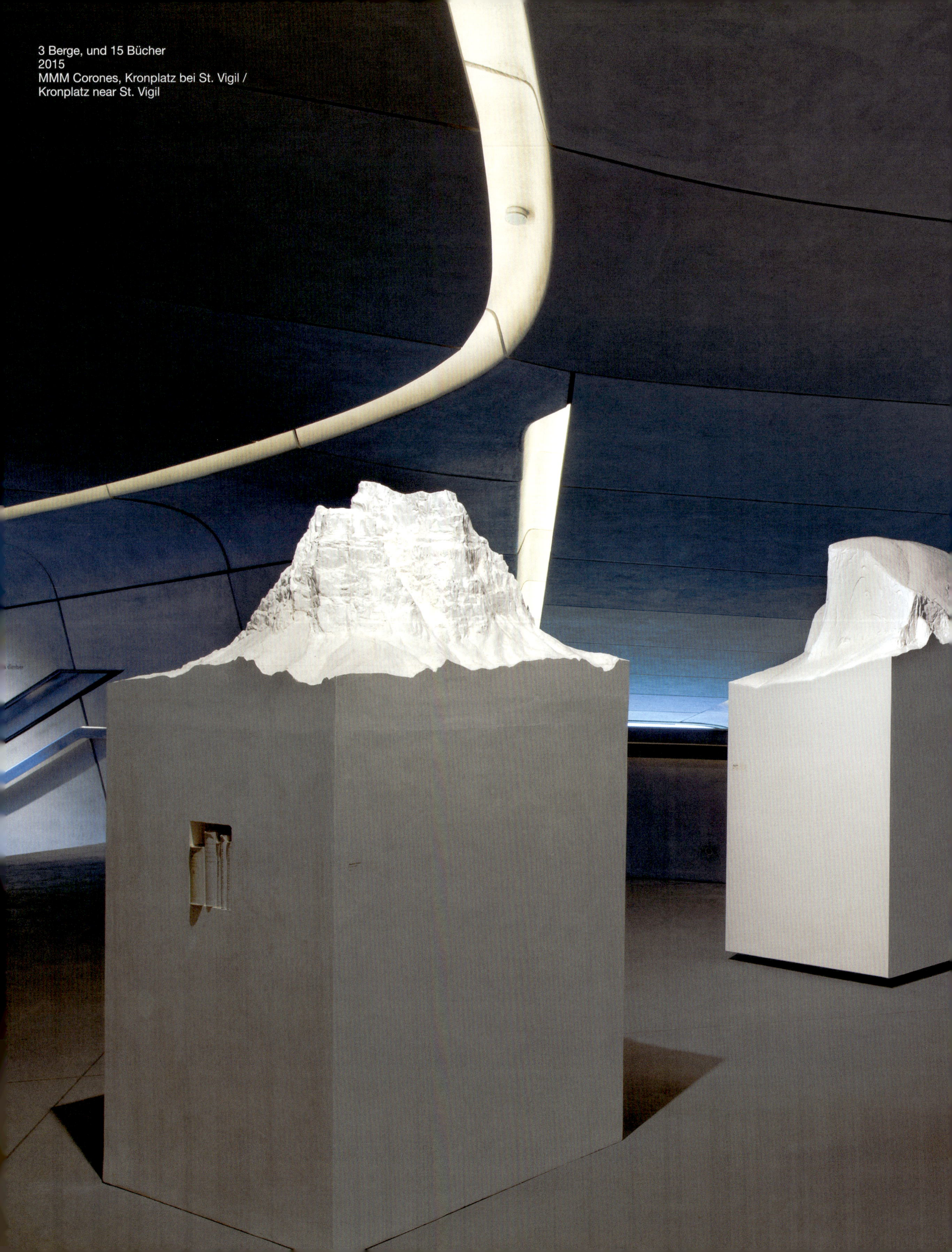

3 Berge, und 15 Bücher
2015
MMM Corones, Kronplatz bei St. Vigil /
Kronplatz near St. Vigil

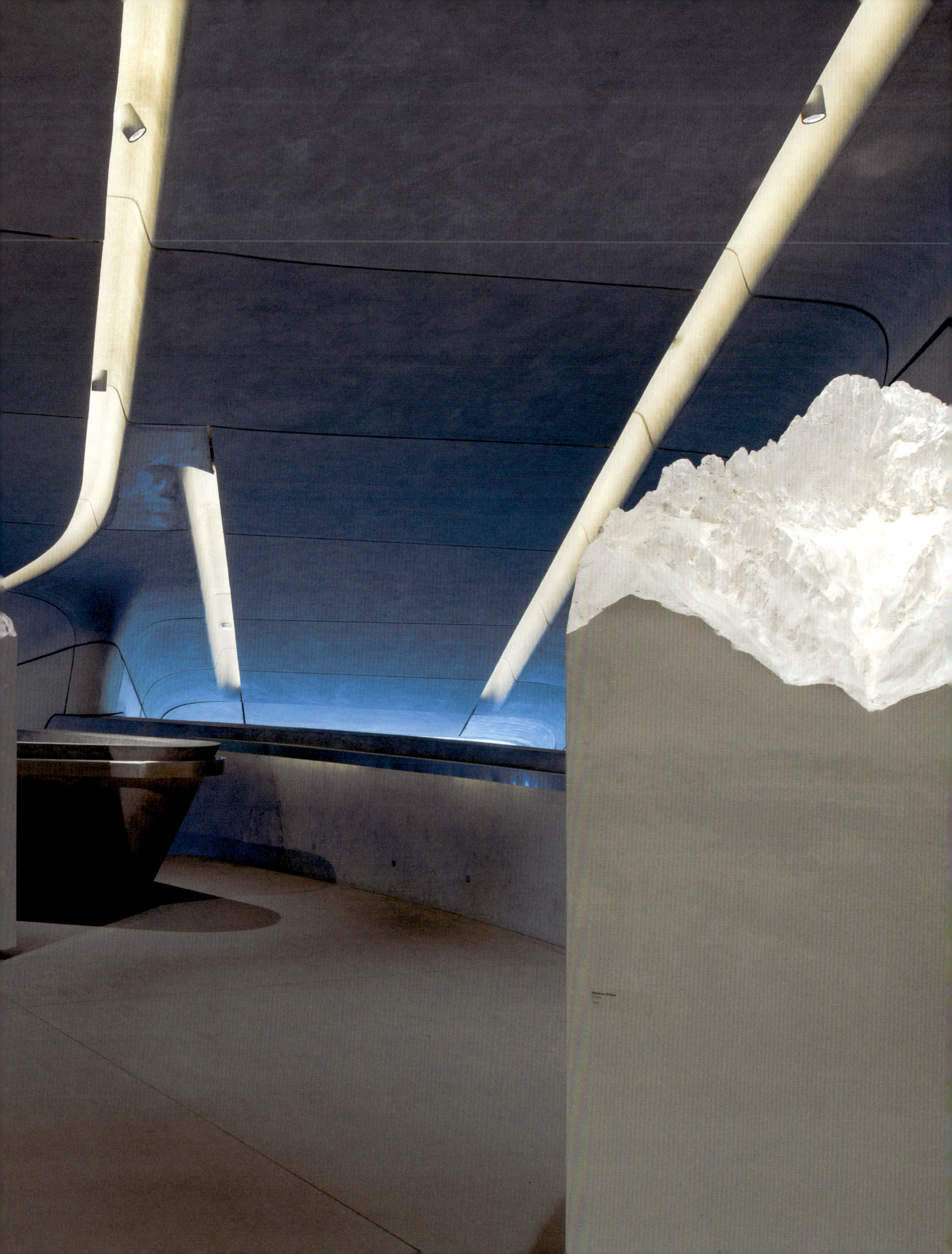

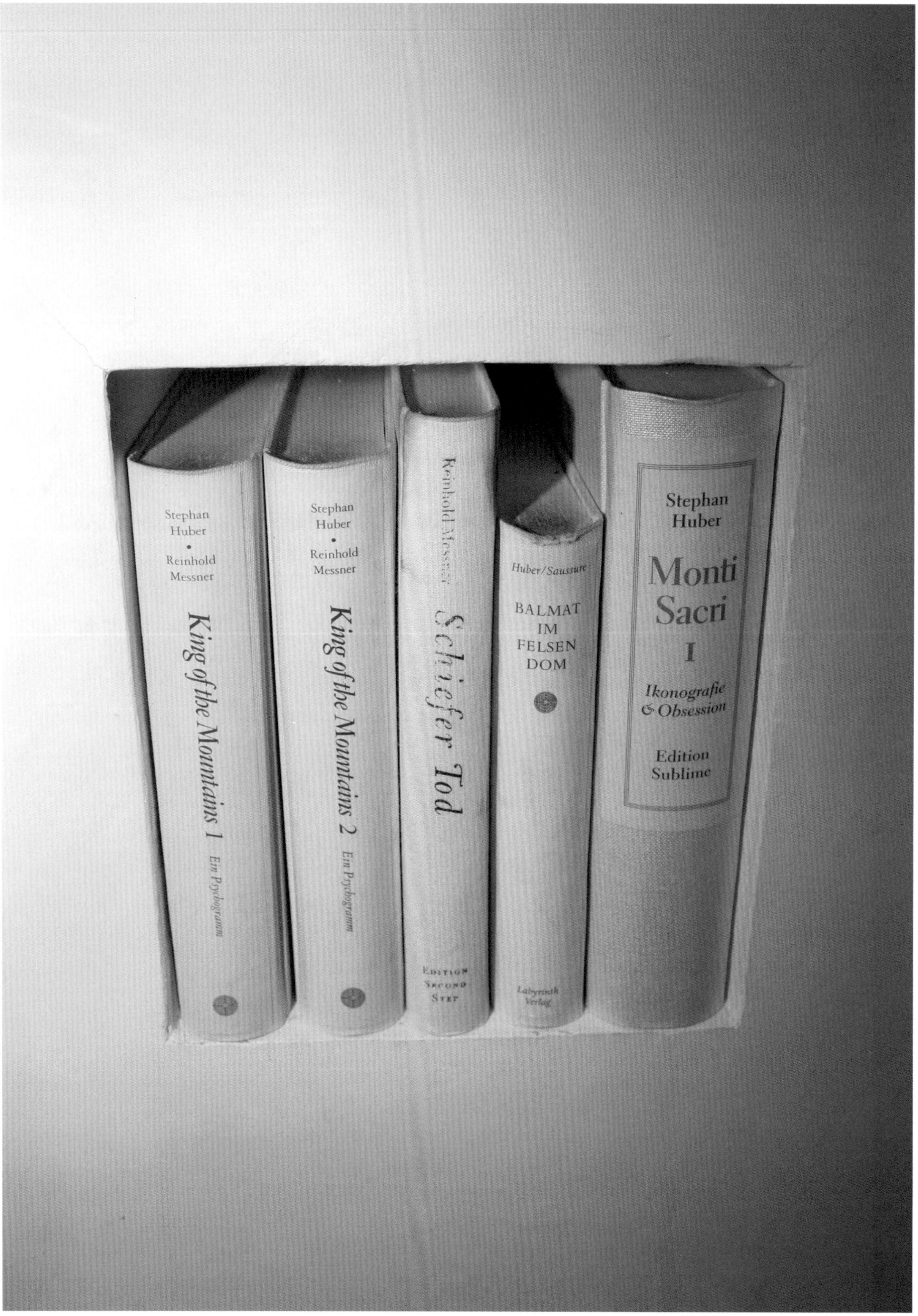
Stephan
Huber
•
Reinhold
Messner
King of the Mountains 1
Ein Psychogramm
Stephan
Huber
•
Reinhold
Messner
King of the Mountains 2
Ein Psychogramm
Reinhold Messner
Schiefer Tod
Edition
Second
Step
Huber/Saussure
BALMAT
IM
FELSEN
DOM
Labyrinth
Verlag
Stephan
Huber
Monti
Sacri
I
Ikonografie
& Obsession
Edition
Sublime

3 Berge und 15 Bücher
2015
MMM Corones, Kronplatz bei St. Vigil /
Kronplatz near St. Vigil

Bergederweltremix
2015
MMM Corones, Kronplatz bei St. Vigil /
Kronplatz near St. Vigil

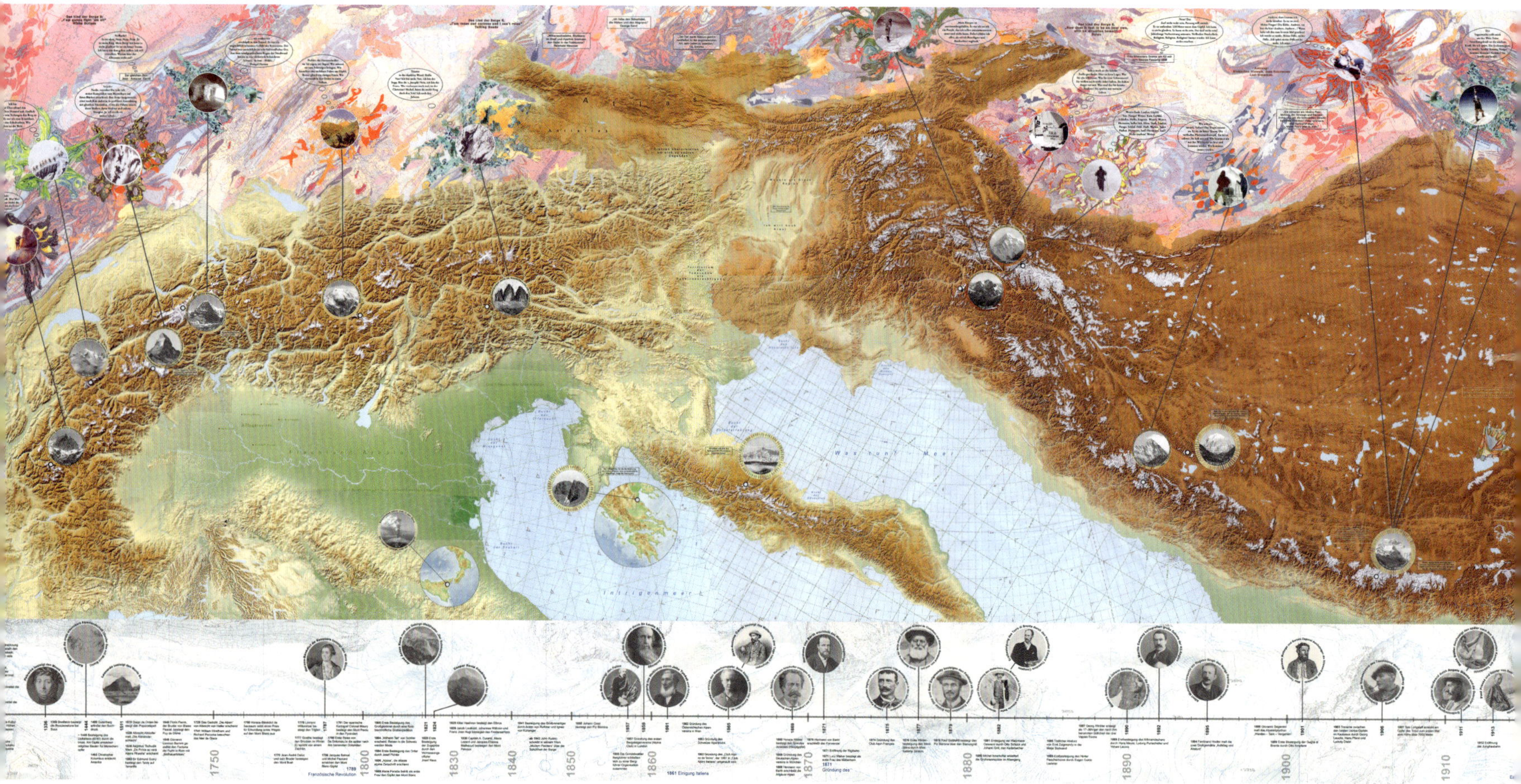

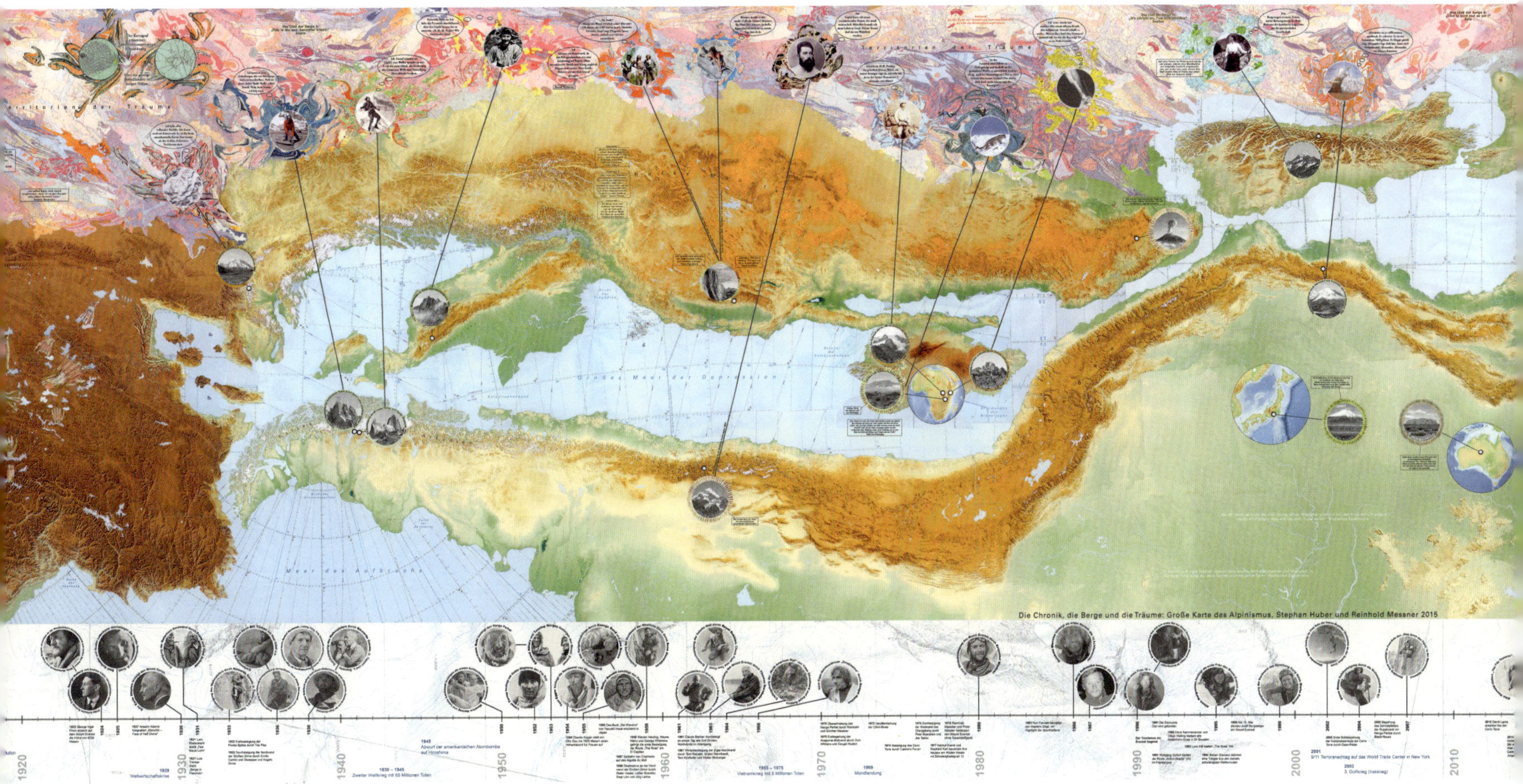

Die Chronik, die Berge und die Träume: Große Karte des Alpinismus, Stephan Huber und Reinhold Messner 2015

Bergederweltremix
2015
MMM Corones, Kronplatz bei St. Vigil /
Kronplatz near St. Vigil

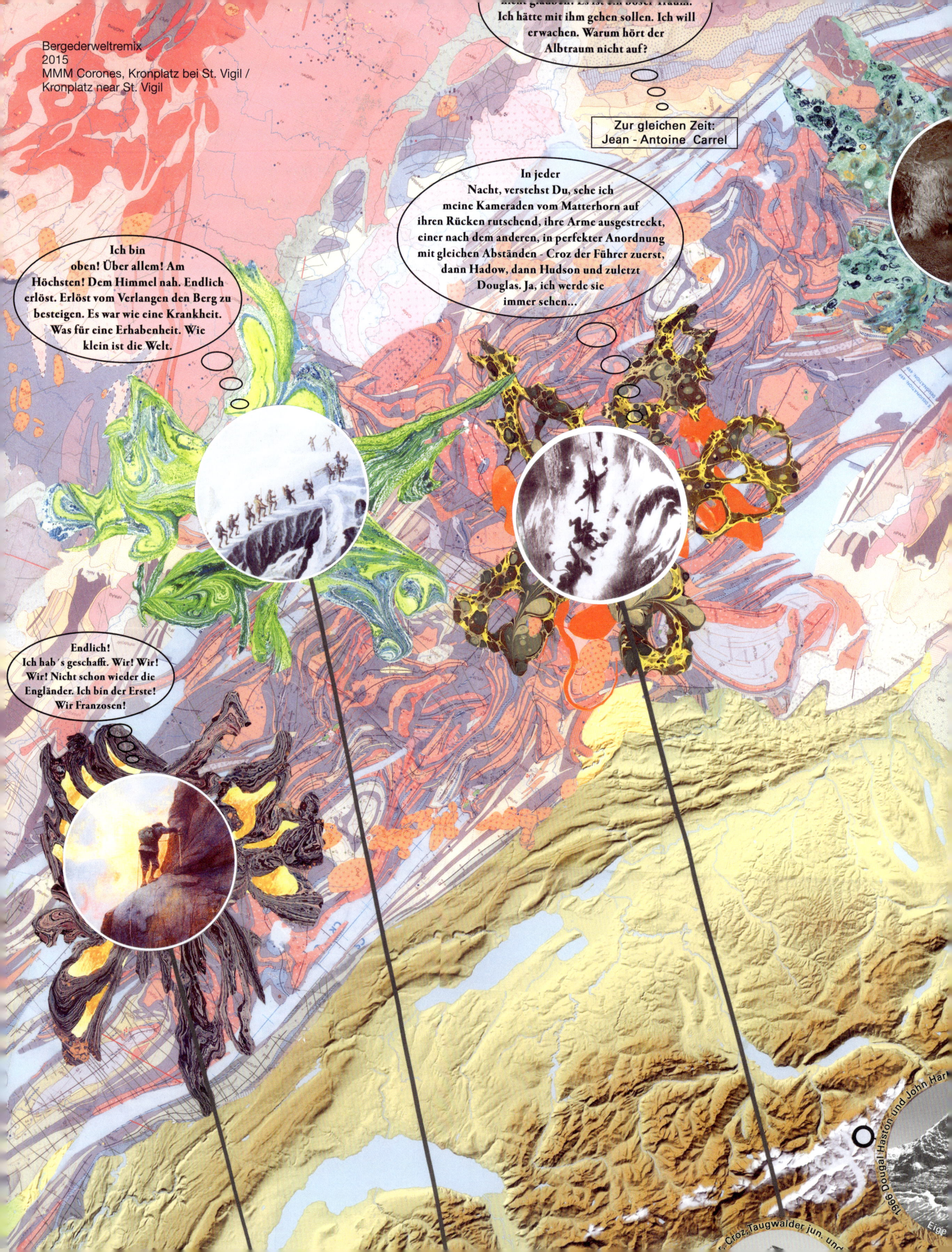

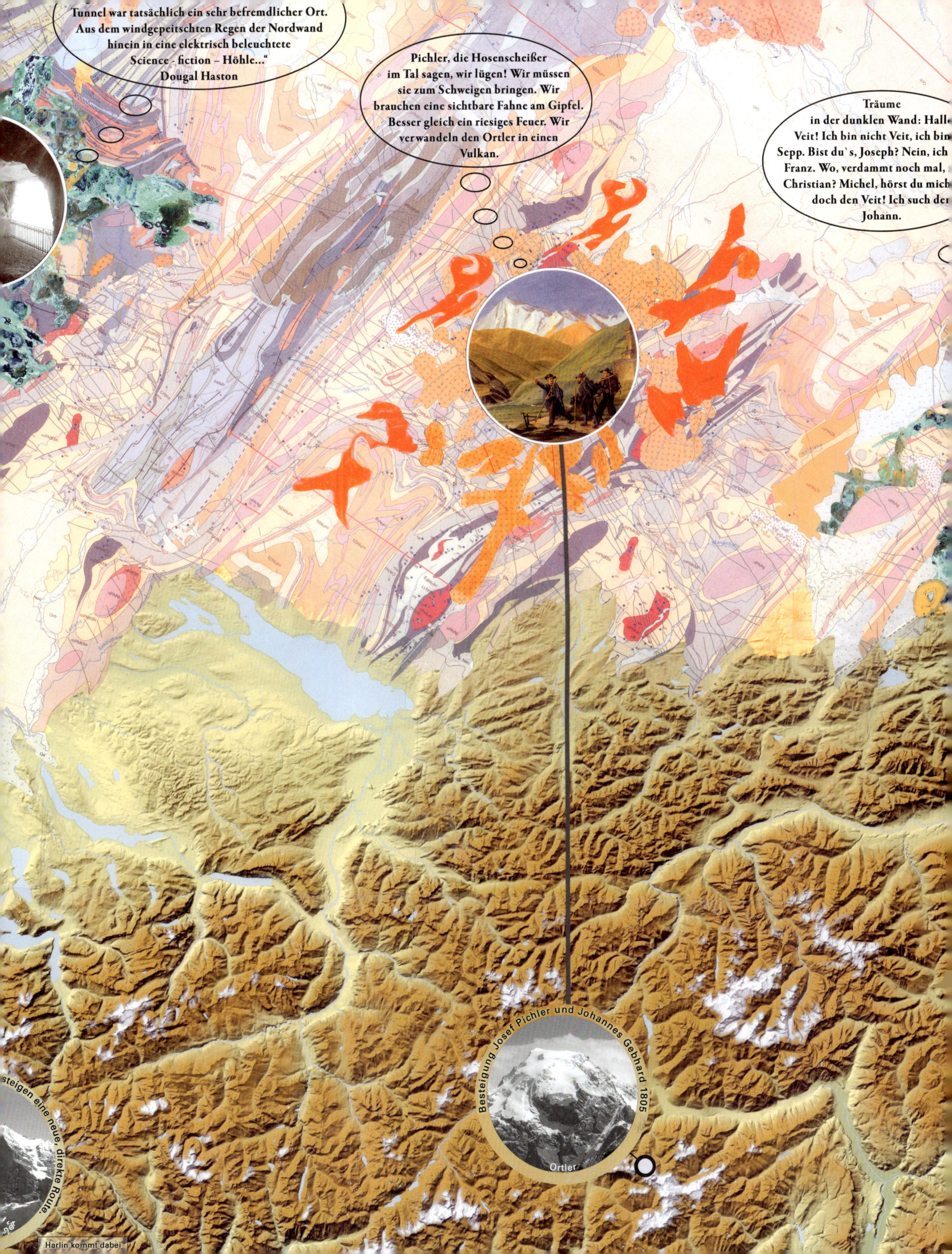
Tunnel war tatsächlich ein sehr befremdlicher Ort. Aus dem windgepeitschten Regen der Nordwand hinein in eine elektrisch beleuchtete Science - fiction – Höhle..." Dougal Haston
Pichler, die Hosenscheißer im Tal sagen, wir lügen! Wir müssen sie zum Schweigen bringen. Wir brauchen eine sichtbare Fahne am Gipfel. Besser gleich ein riesiges Feuer. Wir verwandeln den Ortler in einen Vulkan.
Träume in der dunklen Wand: Halle Veit! Ich bin nicht Veit, ich bin Sepp. Bist du`s, Joseph? Nein, ich Franz. Wo, verdammt noch mal, Christian? Michel, hörst du mich doch den Veit! Ich such der Johann.
Besteigung Josef Pichler und Johannes Gebhard 1805
Ortler
steigen eine neue, direkte Route.
Harlin kommt dabei

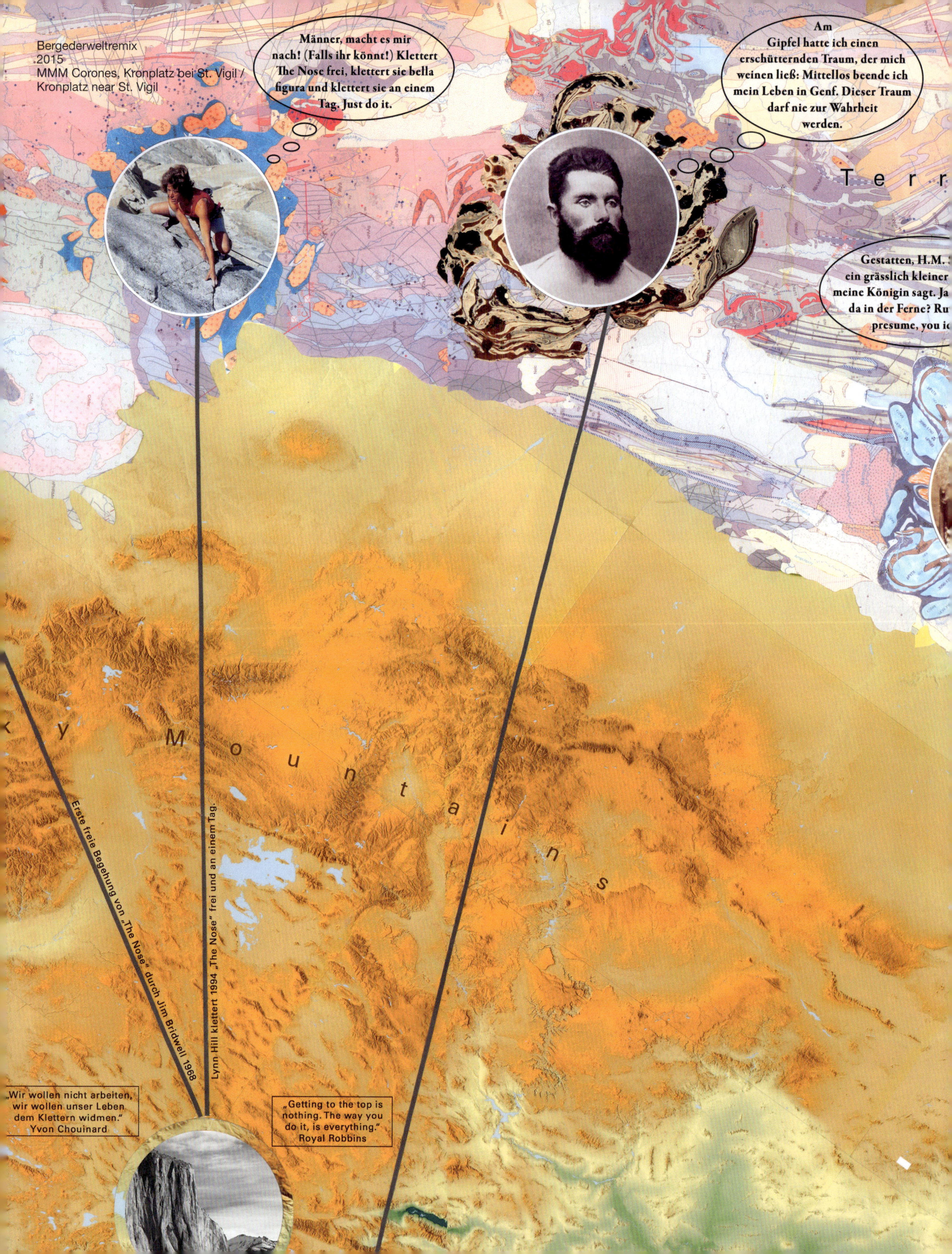

Bergederweltremix
2015
MMM Corones, Kronplatz bei St. Vigil / Kronplatz near St. Vigil

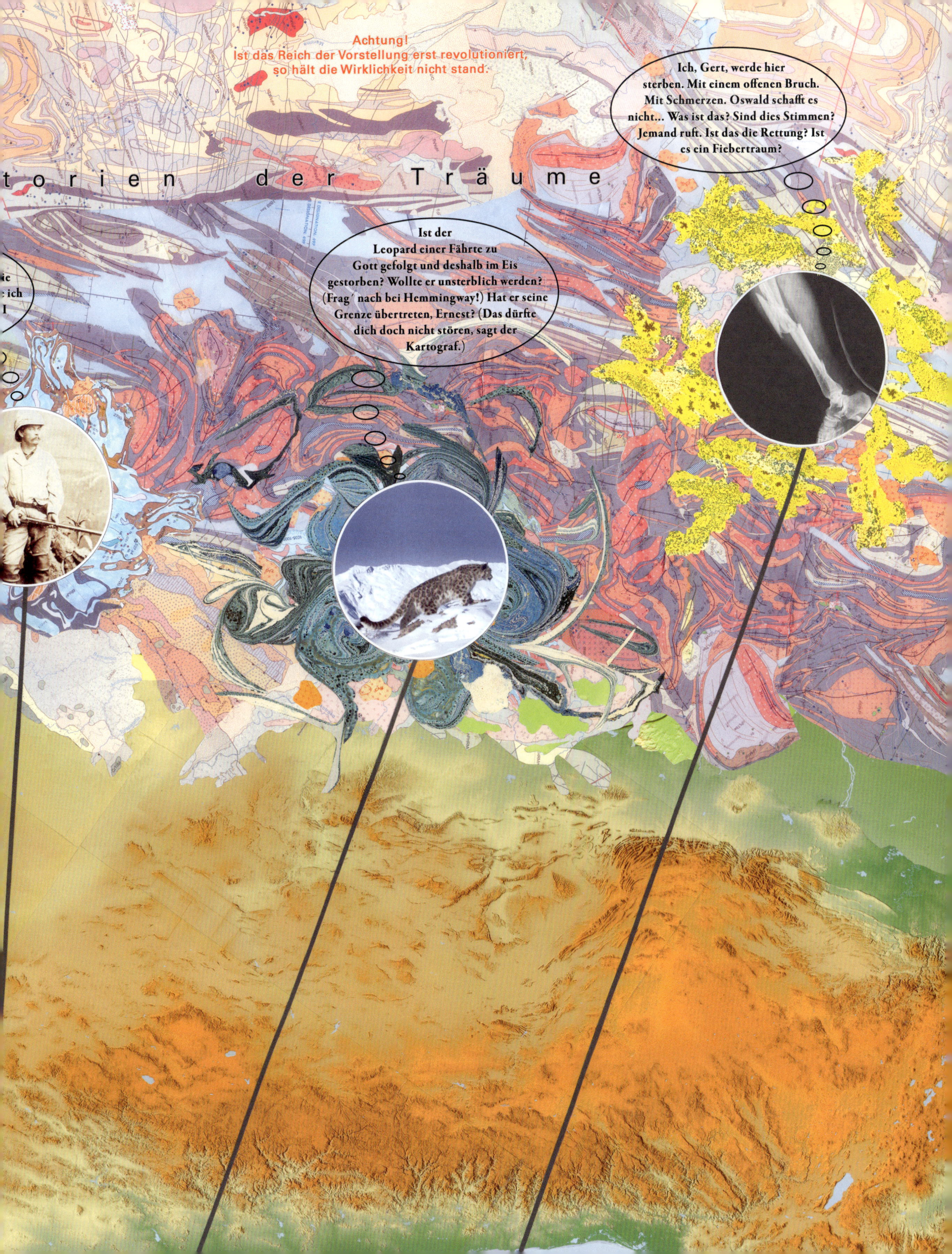
Achtung!
Ist das Reich der Vorstellung erst revolutioniert, so hält die Wirklichkeit nicht stand.
torien der Träume
Ich, Gert, werde hier sterben. Mit einem offenen Bruch. Mit Schmerzen. Oswald schafft es nicht... Was ist das? Sind dies Stimmen? Jemand ruft. Ist das die Rettung? Ist es ein Fiebertraum?
Ist der Leopard einer Fährte zu Gott gefolgt und deshalb im Eis gestorben? Wollte er unsterblich werden? (Frag´ nach bei Hemmingway!) Hat er seine Grenze übertreten, Ernest? (Das dürfte dich doch nicht stören, sagt der Kartograf.)

Auf dem Monte Rite
On Monte Rite

Uschi Demeter

Im Herzen der Dolomiten, zwischen Cortina und Belluno, steht ein Berg wie ein Podest, von dem die Panoramisten des 19. Jahrhunderts nur träumen konnten: der 2181 Meter hohe Monte Rite. Von seinem Gipfelplateau aus geht die Rundsicht in die idyllischen Täler des Cadore, auf das Grün verlassener Almen und – darüber – auf die spektakulärsten Dolomitengipfel: den Monte Agner, den Cimon della Pala, die Civetta, die Marmolata, den Monte Pelmo, den Monte Cristallo. Für Stephan Huber skulpturale Modelle, für Reinhold Messner die begehrenswertesten Kletterfelsen, und für Le Corbusier die schönsten Bauwerke der Welt. Wie die Zacken einer Krone umrunden sie den Monte Rite, und bei Nacht sieht man die Lichter in den Dörfern des Cadore, von Cortina, von Longarone, bei Vollmond zwischen zwei Felsnasen sogar die Lichter der Adriaküste von Istrien.

Für Botaniker ist der Monte Rite eine Oase, wo sie auf dem Sentiero Botanico die seltensten Alpenblumen finden, für Ästheten eine Insel für die aufregendsten Sonnenauf- und untergänge in geradezu existenzverwirrendem Rosa und Blau, vergleichbar mit den Eindrücken, derentwegen sich im 19. Jahrhundert Engländerinnen in Sänften auf die Rigi tragen ließen, um bei ihrem Anblick in Ohnmacht zu fallen.

Und genau hier, auf diesem paradiesischen Plateau, haben die Italiener 1914 ein Fort gebaut, mit dem sie die Soldaten des österreichischen Kaisers Franz Joseph in Schach halten wollten. 1917 besetzten die Österreicher den Monte Rite, 1918 mussten sie abziehen, nicht ohne vorher große Teile des Forts zu sprengen. Im Zweiten Weltkrieg hausten Partisanen in den Ruinen, und dann begann ein langer Dornröschenschlaf. Bis Reinhold Messner 1997 auf einer Tour durchs Cadore zufällig dieses Fort entdeckte. Langgestreckt wie ein Schiff, mit drei Gefechtsständen, die Fata Morgana eines Bergmuseums.

Cibiana ist ein kleines Dorf am Fuß des Monte Rite, die Einwohner eng zusammengeduckt in Häusern aus Stein, die mit ihren Blechdächern wie rostige Osternester in den Talfurchen der

In the heart of the Dolomites, between Cortina and Belluno, a mountain rises like a pedestal, one that nineteenth-century painters of panoramas could only dream of: Monte Rite, 2,181 metres high. From its summit plateau the panoramic view extends to the idyllic valleys of the Cadore, to the green of abandoned alpine pastures and – above them – to the most spectacular Dolomite peaks: Monte Agner, Cimon della Pala, Civetta, Marmolata, Monte Pelmo and Monte Cristallo. Sculptural models for Stephan Huber, the most desirable climbing cliffs for Reinhold Messner, and the most beautiful buildings in the world for Le Corbusier. They encircle Monte Rite like the points of a crown, and at night you can see the lights in the villages of Cadore, Cortina and Longarone – and with a full moon, between two rocky outcrops, even the lights of the Adriatic coast of Istria.

For botanists, Monte Rite is an oasis where they can find rare alpine flowers on the 'Sentiero Botanico' path. For aesthetes, it is a promontory for the most exciting sunrises and sunsets in almost existentially confusing pinks and blues, comparable to the impressions for which English ladies in the nineteenth century had themselves carried up the Rigi in sedan chairs, in order to swoon at the sight of them.

It was precisely here, on this paradisiacal plateau, that the Italians built a fort in 1914 to keep the soldiers of the Austrian Emperor Franz Joseph at bay. In 1917 the Austrians occupied Monte Rite, but in 1918 they had to withdraw, not without first blowing up large parts of the fort. During the Second World War, partisans housed in the ruins. Afterwards, a long slumber began, until Reinhold Messner, on a tour through Cadore, discovered this fort by accident in 1997. Stretched out like a ship, with three command posts, the mirage of a mountain museum.

Cibiana is a small village at the foot of Monte Rite, where the inhabitants huddle together in stone houses with tin roofs, like rusty Easter nests in the furrows of the mountain slopes along the old pass road. The village is in reality

Berghänge entlang der alten Passstraße liegen. Richtig bewohnt ist das Dorf eigentlich nur im Winter. Wenn die Familien der Eismacher in Deutschland ihre Läden den Teppichhändlern überlassen und in den Bars von Cibiana die *Bild*-Zeitung lesen. Als der italienische Staat begann, seine militärischen Anlagen zu verkaufen, hat Cibiana zugeschlagen. Irgendetwas ganz besonders Attraktives wollten sie da oben gestalten, vielleicht sogar ein Museum, noch keine Ahnung mit welchem Inhalt.

Als Messner ins Dorf kam, fragte man auch ihn um Rat. Den hatte er schon parat. Das war der Beginn des gemeinsamen Projekts „Museum in den Wolken" – das MMM Dolomites. Cibiana hatte damals einen genialen Bürgermeister, Guido de Zordo, im Hauptberuf Griechischlehrer am Humanistischen Gymnasium von San Vito di Cadore und politisch bestens vernetzt. So wurde mit EU-Zuschüssen, mithilfe der Repubblica Italiana, der Region Belluno und unter Aufsicht der Soprintendenza per i Beni Architettonici das Messner-Mountain-Museum-Dolomites-Projekt auf die Beine gestellt. Als Architekten wurden Enzo Siviero und Paolo Faccio aus Padua engagiert.

1999 entdeckte ich in Venedig auf der Harald-Szeemann-Biennale *dAPERTutto* in einer heruntergekommenen Lagerhalle voller Gerümpel die eindrucksvollste Landkarte Italiens, die ich je gesehen hatte: zwischen dem stumpfen Orangerot, das diesen Schrott mit Rost überzogen hatte wie Samt, schlängelte sich eine kobaltblaue Neonröhre, der Flusslauf des Po. Darin erhoben sich weiß und riesig Berge, von denen ich die meisten kannte – Dolomitengipfel. *Deposito Po!* Das ist meine erste Begegnung mit Stephan Huber gewesen. Ein Jahr später traf auch Reinhold Messner Stephan Huber. Auf einer Vortragsreise begegnete er der Skulptur des *Langkofel* in der Kunsthalle Kiel. Als ich 2001 die Projektleitung für die Einrichtung des Museums auf dem Monte Rite übernahm, besuchte ich Stephan in seinem Münchner Atelier am Harras und lud ihn zu einer Besichtigung des Monte Rite ein.

only inhabited in winter, when the families of the ice-cream makers in Germany leave their shops to the carpet dealers and read the popular *Bild* newspaper from their northern home in the bars of Cibiana. When the Italian state began to sell off its military installations, Cibiana snatched it up. They wanted to create something particularly attractive up there, maybe even a museum, with no idea of what to put in it.

When Messner came to the village, he was asked for advice. He already knew the answer. That was the beginning of the joint project 'Museum in the Clouds', the MMM Dolomites. At that time, Cibiana had an ingenious mayor, Guido de Zordo, whose primary profession was teaching Greek at the Humanistic High School in San Vito di Cadore, and who was politically well connected. Thus, the Messner Mountain Museum Dolomites project was set up with EU subsidies and support from the Repubblica Italiana and the Belluno region, under the supervision of the Soprintendenza per i Beni Architettonici. Enzo Siviero and Paolo Faccio from Padua were engaged as architects.

In 1999, at the Harald Szeemann Biennale in Venice, dAPERTutto, I discovered the most impressive map of Italy I had ever seen in a run-down warehouse full of junk: a cobalt-blue neon tube symbolising the course of the Po River as it wound its way between the dull orange-red that had covered this junk with rust like velvet. Huge white mountains rose alongside, most of which I knew – the Dolomite peaks. *Deposito Po!* That was my first encounter with Stephan Huber. A year later, Reinhold Messner met Stephan Huber too. He encountered the sculpture of the Sassolungo in the Kunsthalle Kiel while on a lecture tour. When I took over the project management for the installation of the museum on Monte Rite in 2001, I visited Stephan in his Munich studio on the square called Harras and invited him to visit Monte Rite.

In the meantime, the ruinous fort had changed enormously. On the roof, in place of the three command posts with their cannons, sculptures made of steel and glass, like crystals, shone from afar, providing daylight for the museum

Inzwischen hatte sich das ruinöse Fort gewaltig verändert. Auf dem Dach anstelle der drei Gefechtsstände mit ihren Kanonen leuchteten weithin Skulpturen aus Stahl und Glas, Kristallen gleich, Tageslichtspender für den darunterliegenden Museumsparcours. Innen gleicht die renovierte „Ex-Batteria" heute einem langen Kirchenschiff mit 20 Nischen für Seitenaltäre, Kabinetten, in denen einst wachhabende Soldaten schliefen und in denen Messner nun Phase für Phase die Erschließungsgeschichte der Dolomiten und ihrer Protagonisten erzählt.

Stephan kam mit seiner kleinen Tochter Philippa nach Brixen, wir frühstückten gemeinsam im Hotel Elephant, und dann fuhr uns Reinhold im Auto zum Monte Rite. Während der fast dreistündigen Fahrt durch die Dolomiten sprachen wir ständig – sehr zum Leidwesen von Stephans Tochter – über das Wunschbild und das Ideal eines Bergmuseums. Als wir ankamen, stiegen wir gemeinsam aufs Museumsdach und betranken uns an dem Wahnsinnsblick und waren plötzlich kleine Menschen in einem überwältigenden alpinen 360-Grad-Panorama. Die Dolomiten! Korallenriffe ohne Meer! Tizian, selbst im Cadore geboren, hat sie gemalt. Arthur Schnitzler hat sie in *Fräulein Else* (1924) als Metapher benutzt. Gustav Mahler hat dort das Lied von der Erde vertont, und Oskar Kokoschka hat Mahlers abenteuerlustige Frau unter ihren Wänden als *Windsbraut* (1913) gemalt. Gio Ponti schließlich wollte sie in den 1930er-Jahren durch ein gigantisches Hotel-und-Seilbahn-Netz zwischen Bozen, Gröden und Cortina zu einer Hochburg des Tourismus ausbauen. 340 Millionen Jahre sind diese Berge alt, älter als die ersten Menschen und Sehnsuchtsorte, deren Schönheit noch heute Schmerzen verursachen kann.

Stephan entschied sich, in den Hauptgang des Kirchenschiffs drei voluminöse Berge zu stellen, die erratischen Blöcken gleich den Weg versperren. Aber die Skulpturen des Antelao, des Monte Pelmo und der Civetta sind mehr: In ihre Sockel sind kleine Nischen geschnitten, Miniregale für Bücher mit der weltweiten Auflage von einem einzigen Exemplar, mit Titeln wie

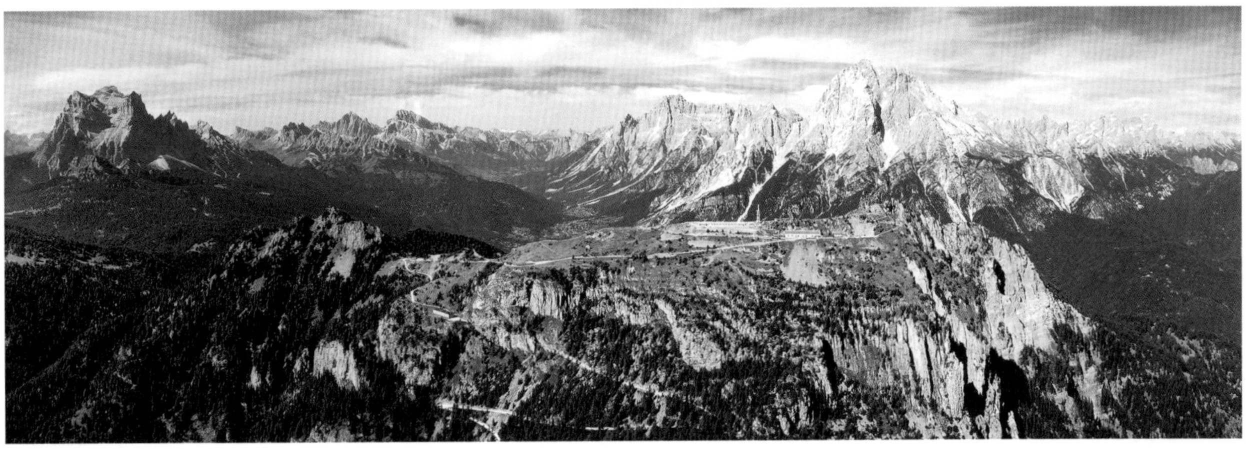

Monte Rite

below. Inside, the renovated "ex-batteria" now resembles a long nave with twenty niches for side altars, cabinets where soldiers on guard duty once slept and where Messner now tells the story, stage by stage, of the development of the Dolomites and their protagonists.

Huber came to Bressanone with his little daughter Philippa. We had breakfast together at the Hotel Elephant, and then Messner drove us to Monte Rite.

During the almost three-hour drive through the Dolomites, we talked constantly – much to Philippa's disappointment – about the essence and ideal of a mountain museum. When we arrived, we climbed up to the museum roof together and got drunk on the insane view; suddenly we were tiny persons in an overwhelming 360-degree alpine panorama. The Dolomites! Coral reefs without the sea! Titian himself, born in Cadore, had painted them. Arthur Schnitzler

Stephan Huber, Tod im Tiefland. Eine Studie über die Verdrängung, Labyrinth Verlag, oder *Stephan Huber, Soziales Milieu im Höllengebirge, Verlag Second Step*, wie meist bei seinen fiktiven Büchern haben diese Werke einen psychosozialen Bezug.

Hamish Fulton ist auf dem Sentiero Botanico rund um den Monte Rite gewandert und hat als Ergebnis im Lichtschacht der ersten Kristallkuppel die Arbeit *Mountain Skylines July* 2002 realisiert. Hubers damaliger Assistent David Regehr hat eine Gewitternacht auf dem Gipfel verbracht, die ihm spontan zu seiner Ätzarbeit auf Metall *Nachts im Norden* (2002) mit zuckenden Blitzen verhalf. Der Designer Peter Seipelt stattete die 20 Kabinette mit Vitrinen voller Bergsteiger-Devotionalien aus und war verantwortlich für die Hängung der Gemälde. Eines der Kabinette wurde zum Schluss ad hoc ausgestattet, als Stephan aus einem wilden Konglomerat von Seilen, Steinschlaghelmen und Felsbrocken die Arbeit *Bergsturz* (2002) schuf.

Grandios war der Blick im Museum am Abend. Wenn man durch die Fenster die „echten" Berggipfel sah, die der Sonnenuntergang rosa und blau und grünlich färbte, während sich gleichzeitig von innen in denselben Fenstern die weißen Huber-Gipfel spiegelten und das alles umgeben war von Gemälden von Thomas Ender, E. T. Compton und Christian Morgenstern. Das perfekte Dolomiten-Nirwana.

Wir wohnten auf dem Gipfelplateau im nebenan liegenden Rifugio, einer ehemaligen Mannschaftskaserne, oder in den warmen Nächten des Frühsommers von 2002 in Schlafsäcken auf dem Museumsdach, hauptsächlich aber unten in Cibiana im Albergo Remauro. Da gab es eine wunderbare Bar, mit einer üppigen Dekoration aus alten, rostigen Eisenschlüsseln, von den Vorfahren der Eismacher hergestellt. Hier erkundigten sich die Einheimischen bei uns nach dem Stand der Dinge auf dem Berg und bedankten sich mit einem Grappa. Der junge Chef des Albergo war ein exzellenter Koch, und seine Mama bemutterte auch uns. Mein Büro war unterm Dach,

had used them as a metaphor in *Fräulein Else* (Miss Else, 1924). Gustav Mahler had set the 'Song of the Earth' to music there, and Oskar Kokoschka had painted Mahler's adventurous wife under their walls as *Windsbraut* (Bride of the Winds, 1913). Finally, in the 1930s, Gio Ponti wanted to turn them into a tourist stronghold by building a gigantic hotel and cable car network between Bolzano, Val Gardena and Cortina. These mountains are 340 million years old, older than the first humans, and are places of longing whose beauty can still cause pain today.

Stephan Huber decided to place three voluminous mountains in the main aisle of the nave, blocking the way like erratic blocks. But the sculptures of the Antelao, Monte Pelmo and Civetta are more than that: small niches are cut into their bases, mini-racks for books with the worldwide edition of a single copy: titles like *Stephan Huber, Death in the Lowlands; A Study of Displacement, Labyrinth Verlag*, or *Stephan Huber, Social Milieu in the Mountains of Hell, Verlag Second Step*. As is usually the case with his fictional books, these works have psychosocial references.

Hamish Fulton hiked the Sentiero Botanico around Monte Rite and subsequently realised the work *Mountain Skylines July 2002* in the light well of the first crystal dome. Huber's assistant at the time, David Regehr, spent a stormy night on the summit, which spontaneously helped him to create his etching on metal, *Night in the North* (2002), with twitching lightning. Designer Peter Seipelt furnished the 20 cabinets with display cases full of mountaineering memorabilia and was responsible for hanging the paintings. One of the cabinets was furnished ad hoc at the end, when Huber created the work *Bergsturz* (2002) from a wild conglomeration of ropes, rockfall helmets and boulders.

The view from the museum in the evening was grandiose, when you saw the 'real' mountain peaks through the windows, coloured pink and blue and green by the sunset, while at the same time Huber's white peaks were

ein Doppelzimmer mit Kinderbett, in dem die Projektunterlagen ruhten. Zur Eröffnung am 30. Juni 2002 kam gefühlt das halbe Cadore, die Schickeria von Cortina, und viele Münchner herauf. Hamish fand, das reizvollste an einem richtigen Bergmuseum sei, dass der Aufstieg mühsam und anstrengend ist, aber zu seinem Leidwesen hatte die Gemeinde von Cibiana einen Jeep-Shuttle organisiert.

Ein paar hundert Meter unterhalb des Gipfels gibt es ein weiteres Kasernengebäude aus dem Ersten Weltkrieg, das leer stand. Bis der Professor Stephan Huber von der Akademie der Bildenden Künste in München auf die Idee kam, mit seiner Klasse im Sommer 2010 dort einzuziehen. Geplant war eine Ausstellung, die vor Ort erarbeitet und mit einfachsten Materialien und Mitteln hergestellt werden sollte. Es gab keinen Strom, kein Licht und keine Fensterscheiben. Die Ausstellung und der Aufenthalt wurden von der Gemeinde Cibiana und von Reinhold unterstützt. Untergebracht waren die Studenten und ihr Professor im Rifugio gleich neben dem Museum. Nachts saßen sie oft auf dem flachen Betondach des Forts inmitten des grandiosen Panoramas. Dann war die Natur stärker als die Kunst. Die Umgebung und das über den Berg verteilte architektonische Areal mit der Kaserne, dem Tunnel, dem Rifugio und dem Museum besaßen eine magische Faszination.

Die Ausstellung hieß *Ultima Vista* und thematisierte im weitesten Sinne Einsamkeit und Rückzug – das Menschenferne des Monte Rite, aber natürlich auch den militärischen Kontext. Es gab unter vielen anderen einen Raum mit Eisenbetten, auf denen jeweils eine mit einem Text bestickte Soldatendecke lag. Einen Raum mit bemalten Uniformen. Überdimensionierte Bienenwaben. Ein Plateau mit einer abstrakten Berglandschaft. Abends auch Performances am Feuer. Hoch oben in den Bergen arbeiteten die jungen Künstler intensiv, aber nicht militärisch kollektiv, sondern frei und unabhängig. Es war eine in sich geschlossene, gelungene Ausstellung. Sie war

reflected in the same windows from the inside, all this surrounded by paintings by Thomas Ender, E.T. Compton and Christian Morgenstern. The perfect Dolomite nirvana.

We stayed on the summit plateau in the adjacent 'Rifugio', a former military barracks, or in sleeping bags on the museum roof during the warm nights of the early summer of 2002, but mainly down in Cibiana in the Albergo Remauro. There was a wonderful bar there, with a lavish decoration of old, rusty iron keys, made by the ice cream makers' ancestors. The locals asked us about the state of affairs on the mountain and thanked us with a grappa. The young head of the Albergo was an excellent cook, and his *mamma* also mothered us. My office was under the roof, a double room with a cot, on which the project documents lay. For the opening on 30 June 2002, it felt as if half of Cadore, the chic set from Cortina, and many people from Munich came up. Hamish thought the most appealing thing about a real mountain museum was that the climb was tedious and exhausting, but to his chagrin the municipality of Cibiana had organised a jeep shuttle.

A few hundred metres below the summit, there is another barracks building from the First World War that had stood empty until Professor Stephan Huber from the Academy of Fine Arts in Munich came up with the idea of moving in there with his class in the summer of 2010. The plan was for an exhibition to be developed on-site and produced with the simplest materials and means. There was no electricity, no light and no window panes. The exhibition and the residency were supported by the municipality of Cibiana and by Messner. The students and their professor were accommodated in the Rifugio right next to the museum. At night, they often sat on the flat concrete roof of the fort amidst the grandiose panorama. Then nature was stronger than art. The surroundings and the architectural zone spread over the mountain, with the barracks, the tunnel, the Rifugio and the museum, radiating a magical fascination.

zwar öffentlich, hatte aber mehr mit Selbsterfahrung als mit Repräsentation zu tun, konnte einen Monat lang von den vorbeiziehenden Bergwanderern betrachtet werden. Zur Eröffnung kamen trotz der gefühlten Lage am Ende der Welt viele Protagonisten aus dem Kulturbereich Südtirols und Münchens, die alle vom Zauber des Monte Rite angesteckt wurden.

Seitdem sind etliche Jahre vergangen. Reinhold kann inzwischen sogar Berge versetzen. Zum Beispiel die von Stephan. So ist jetzt der *Antelao* vom Monte Rite hinunter ins Tal versetzt worden, in eine Art Basecamp, das er dort mit einem Großteil der Gemälde teilt. Man kriegt die Probleme mit der Feuchtigkeit oben im Fort nicht in den Griff. Die *Civetta* und der *Monte Pelmo* sind zurzeit im Zaha-Hadid-Bau auf dem Kronplatz gelandet. Wer weiß, wie lange, denn Reinhold plant ein weiteres Museum: das MMM Rocca in Sexten.

The exhibition was called *Ultima Vista* and addressed loneliness and withdrawal in the broadest sense – the remoteness of Monte Rite, but of course also the military context. Among much else, there was a room with iron beds, each with a soldier's blanket embroidered with a text. A room with painted uniforms. Oversized honeycombs. A plateau with an abstract mountain landscape. In the evenings, performances by the fire. High up in the mountains, the young artists worked intensively, not as a military group, but freely and independently. It was a self-contained, successful exhibition. Although it was open to the public, it had more to do with self-awareness than representation, and could be seen for a month by passing mountain hikers. Despite the location at what seemed like the end of the world, many protagonists from the cultural scene of South Tyrol and Munich came to the opening, all of whom were infected by the magic of Monte Rite.

Several years have passed since then. Messner can even move mountains in the meantime. Stephan's, for example. So now the Antelao has been moved from Monte Rite down into the valley, into a kind of base camp, which it shares there with most of the paintings. They can't get a grip on the problems with the humidity up at the fort. The Civetta and Monte Pelmo have currently ended up in the Zaha Hadid building on the Kronplatz. Who knows for how long, because Messner is planning another museum: the MMM Rocca in Sesto.

Rauminstallation
Room installation
2002
MMM Dolomites, Monte Rite, Cibiana di Cadore

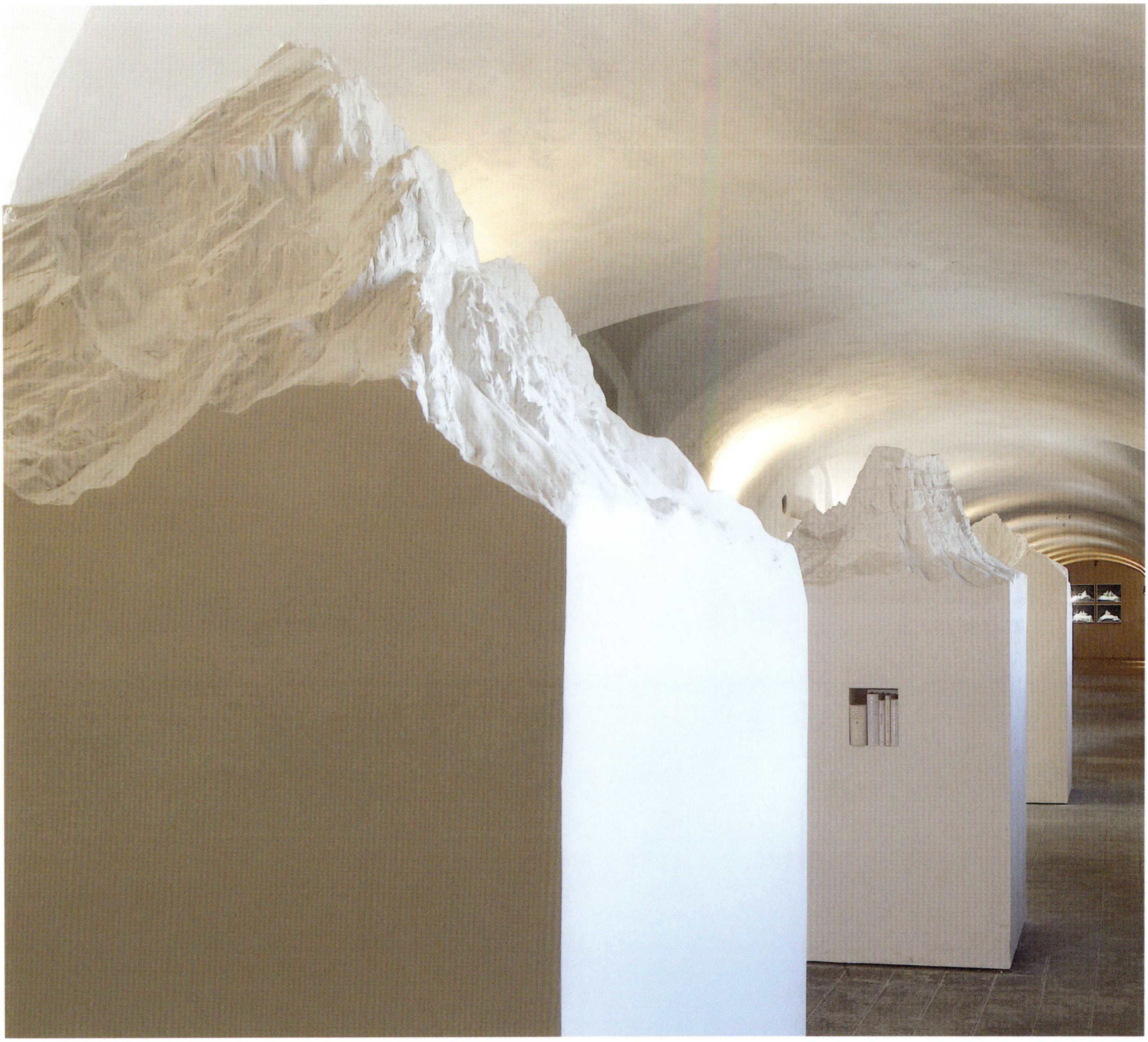

Panorama Nr. 2
1999

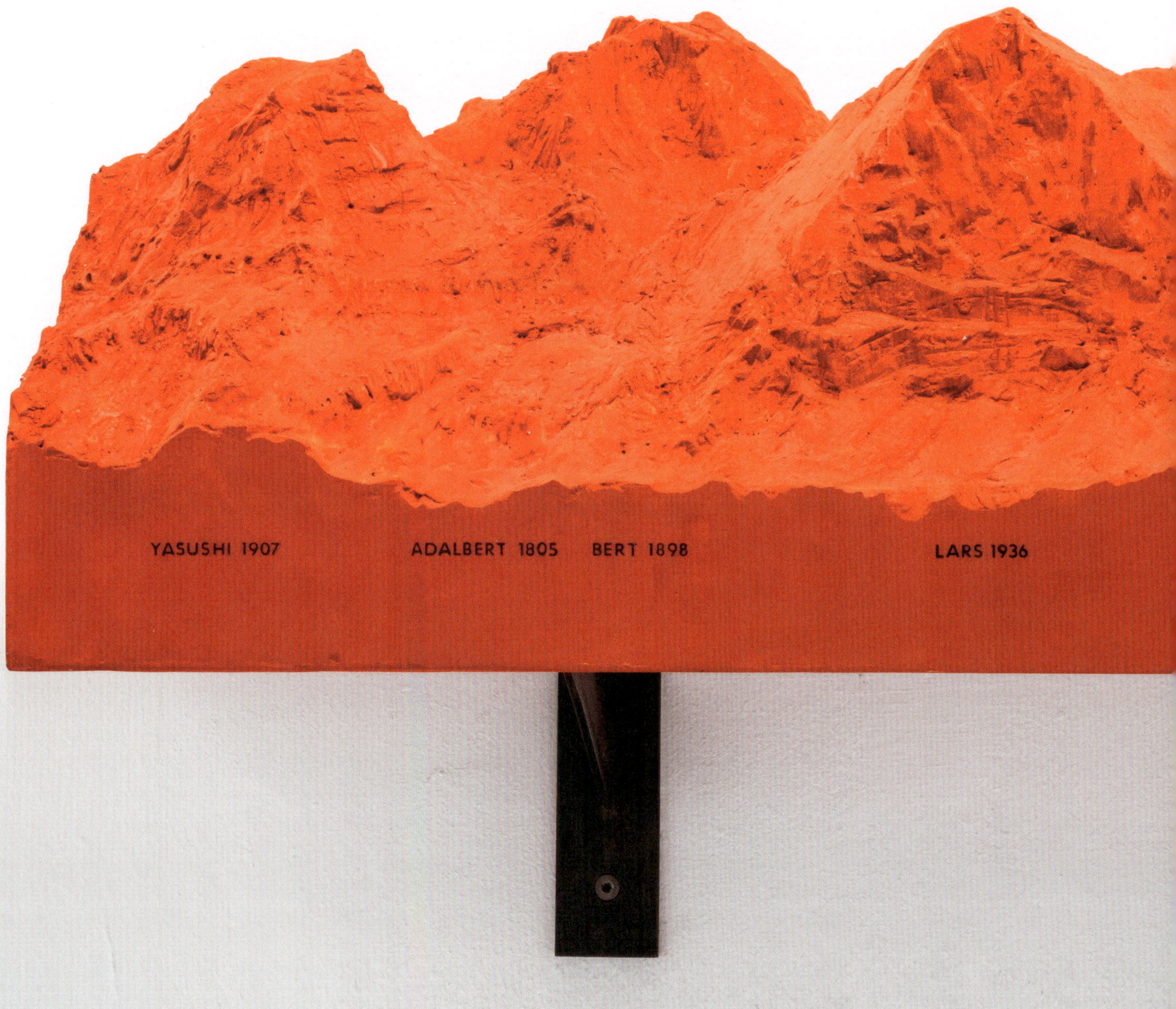

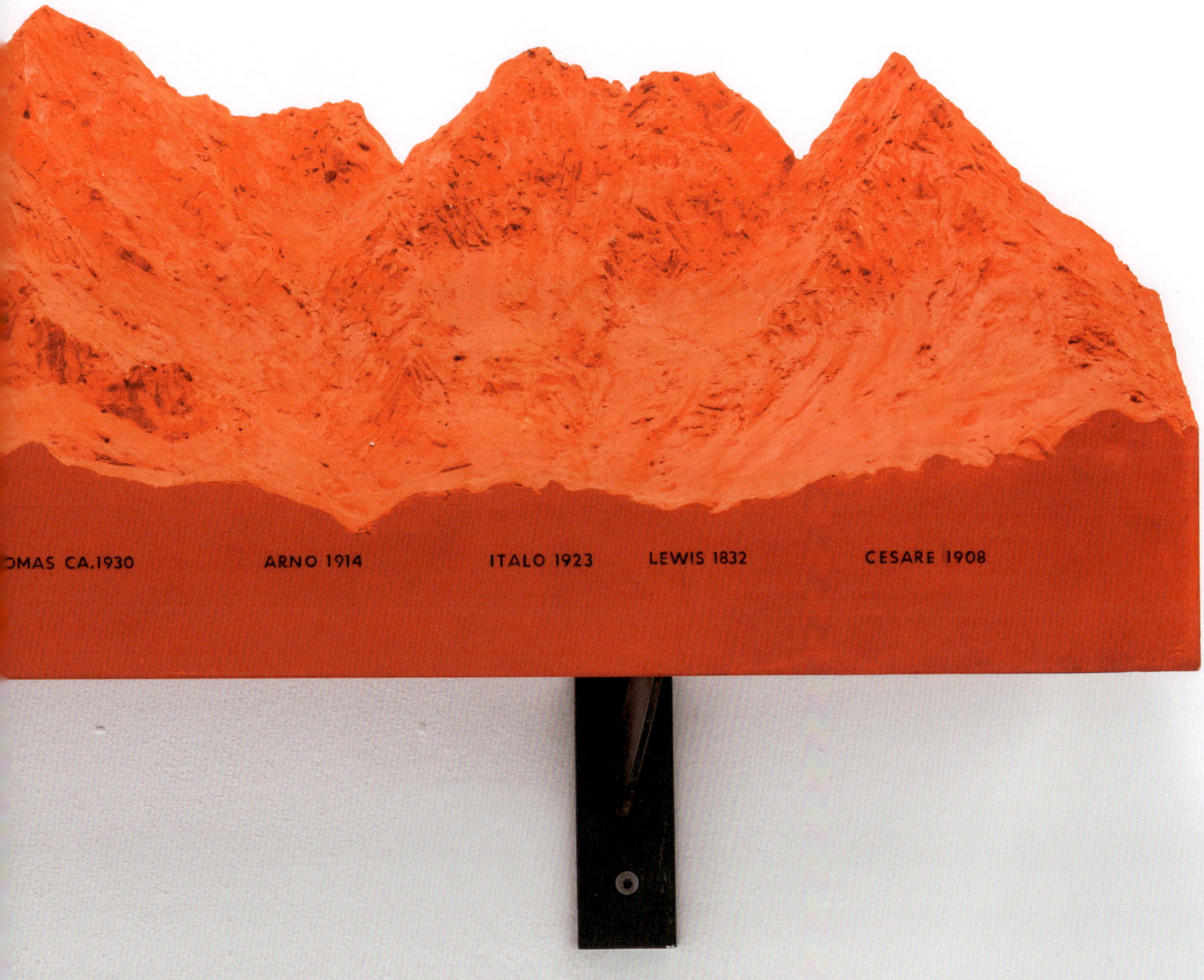
OMAS CA.1930
ARNO 1914
ITALO 1923
LEWIS 1832
CESARE 1908

Panorama Nr. 4
1999

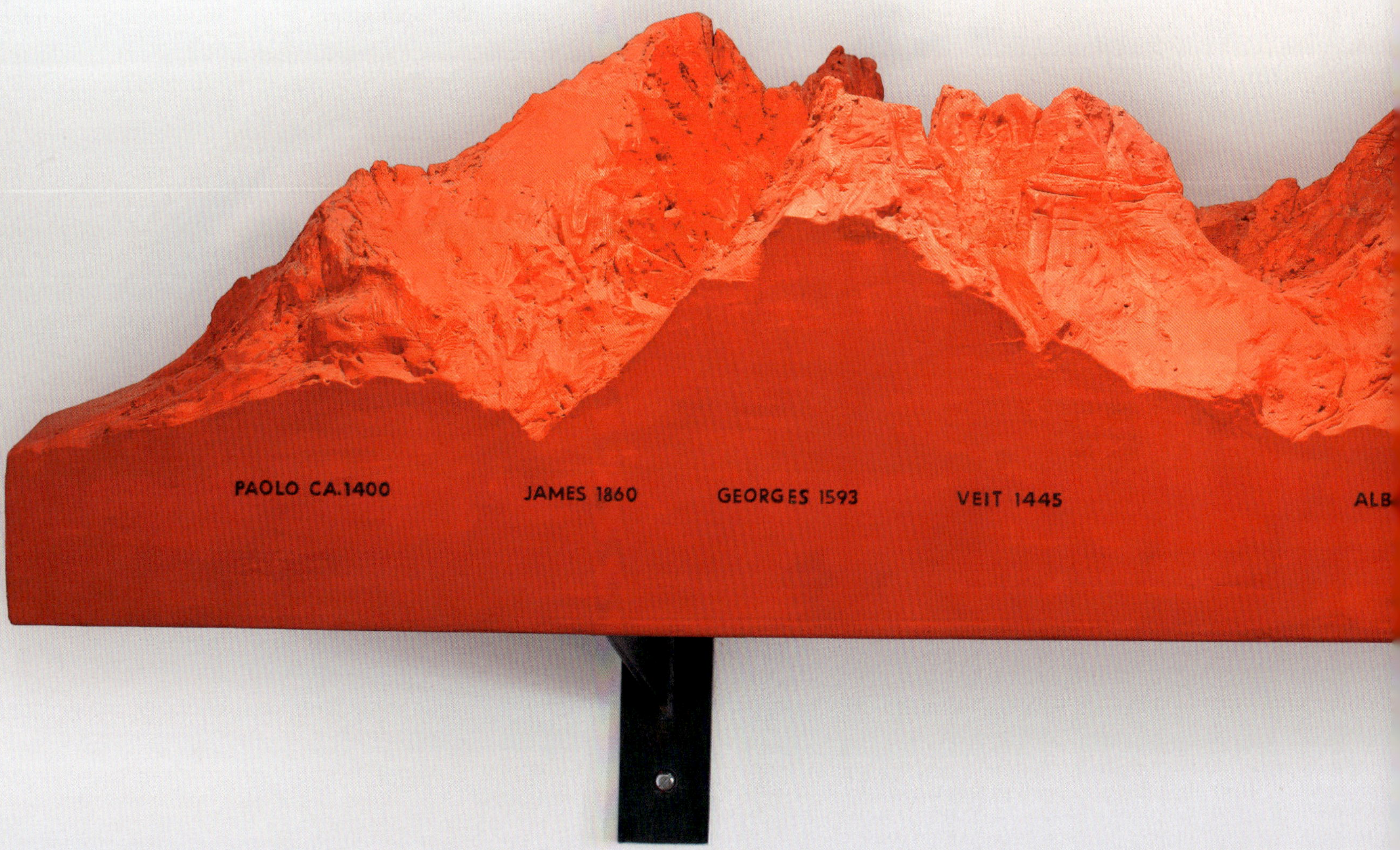

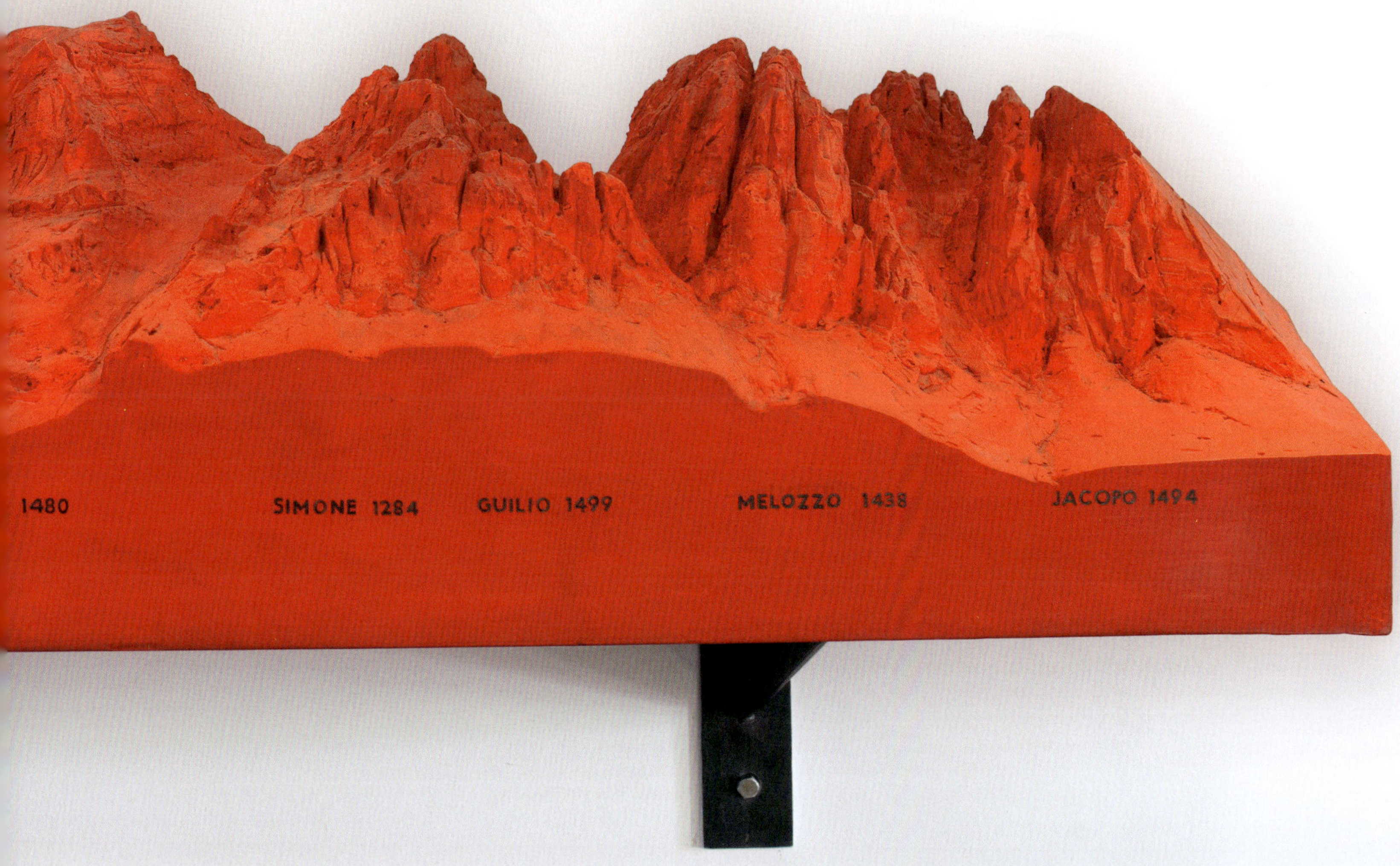
1480
SIMONE 1284
GUILIO 1499
MELOZZO 1438
JACOPO 1494

Expedition Nr. 3
2005
Privatsammlung München /
Private collection, Munich

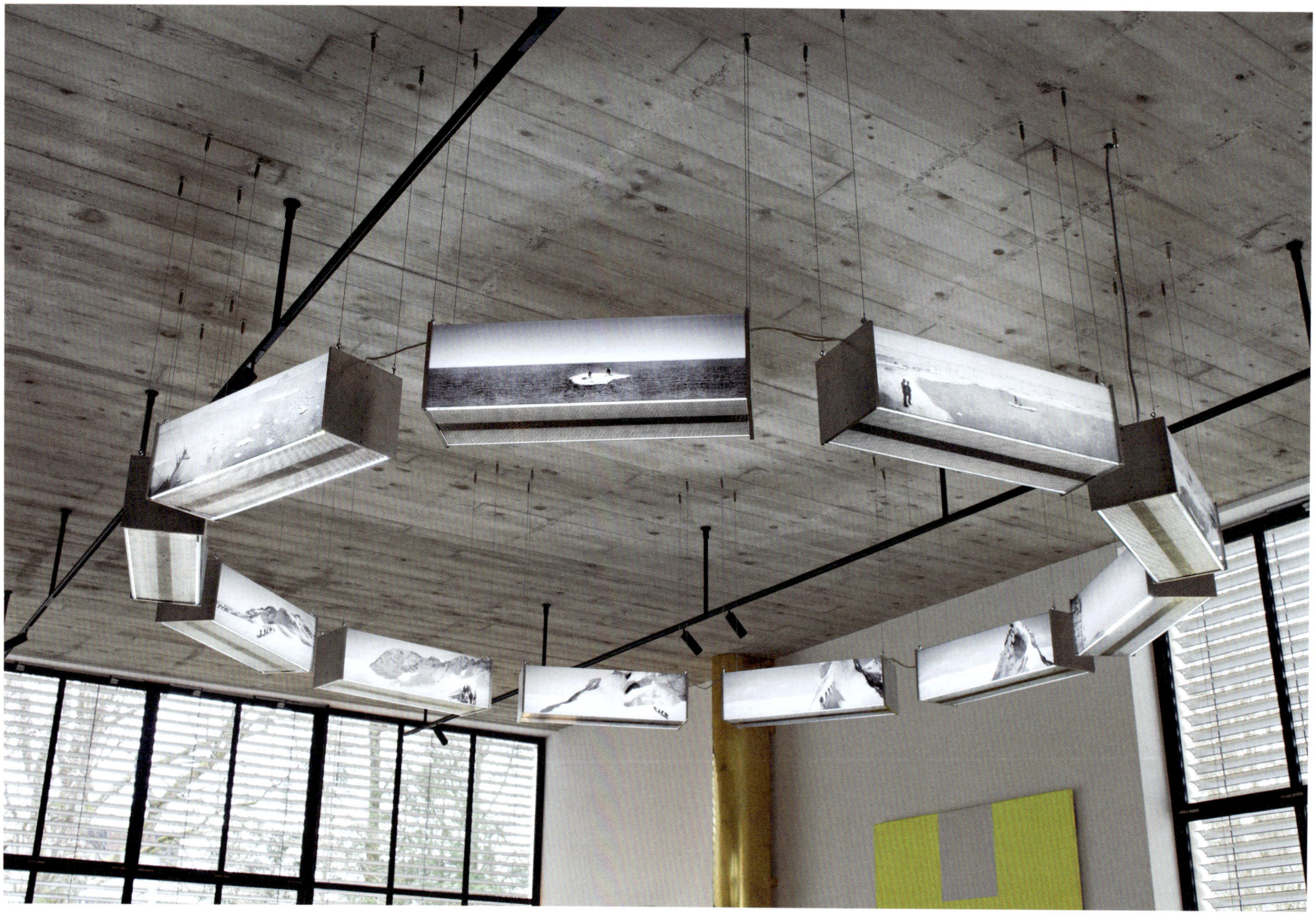

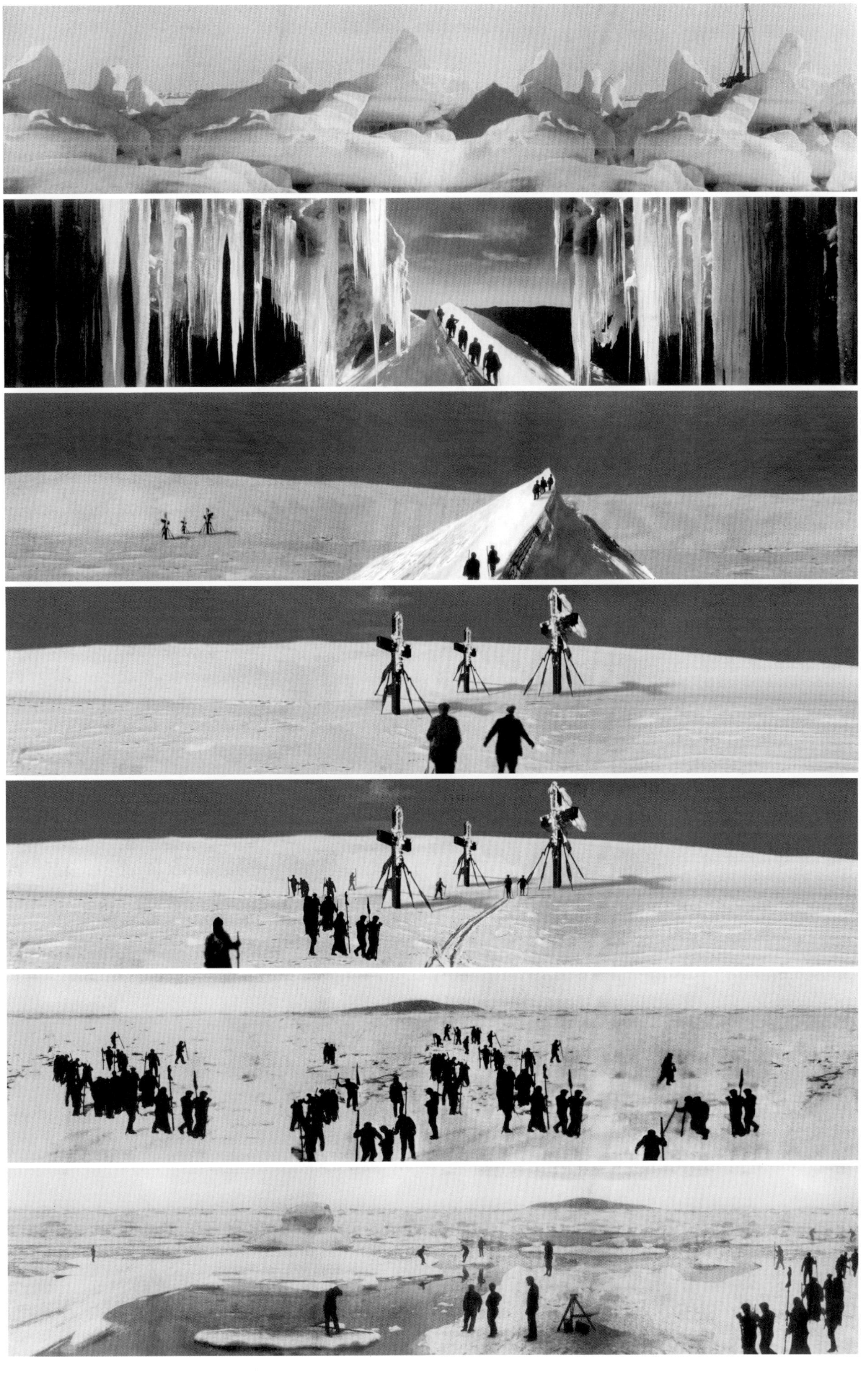

Expedition Nr. 3
2005

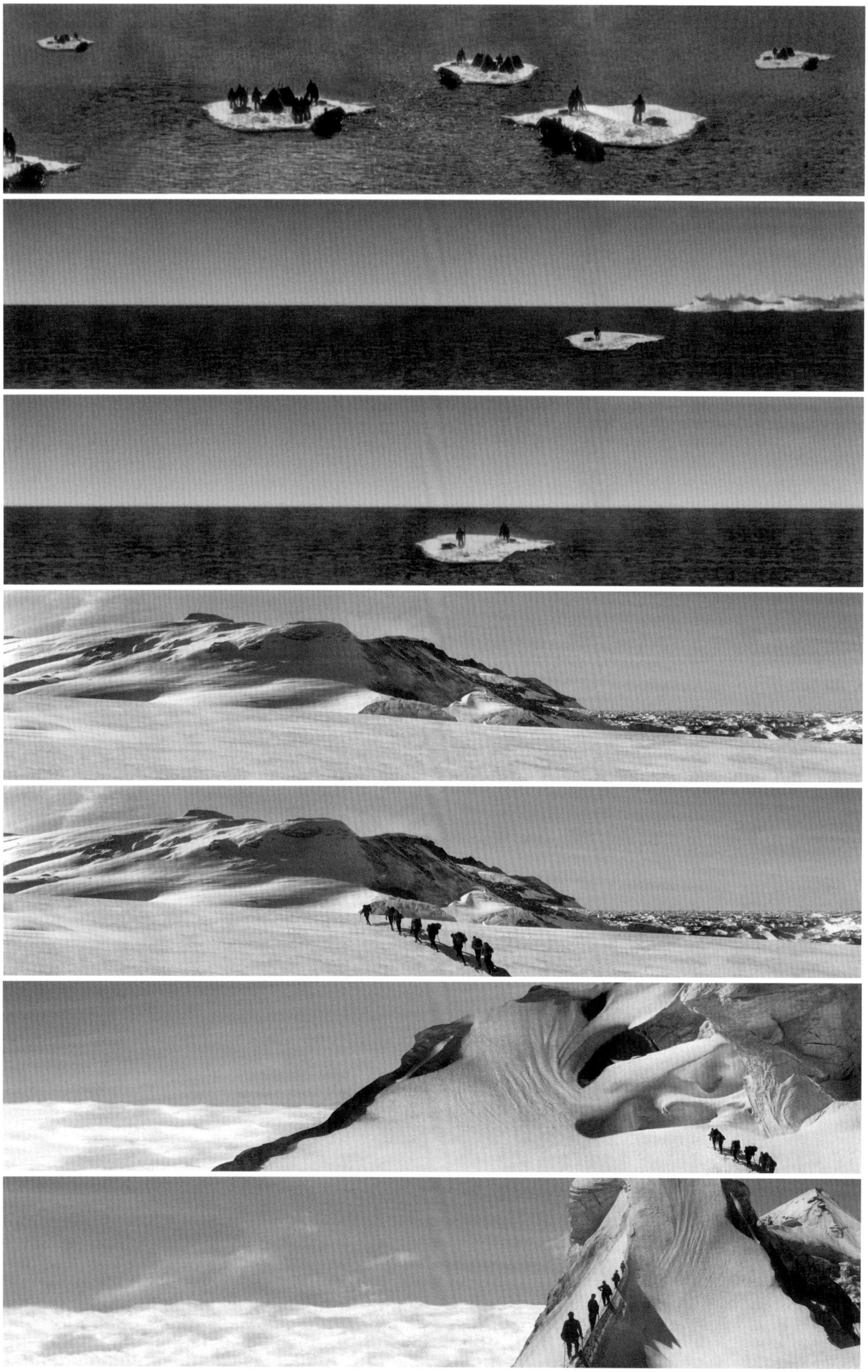

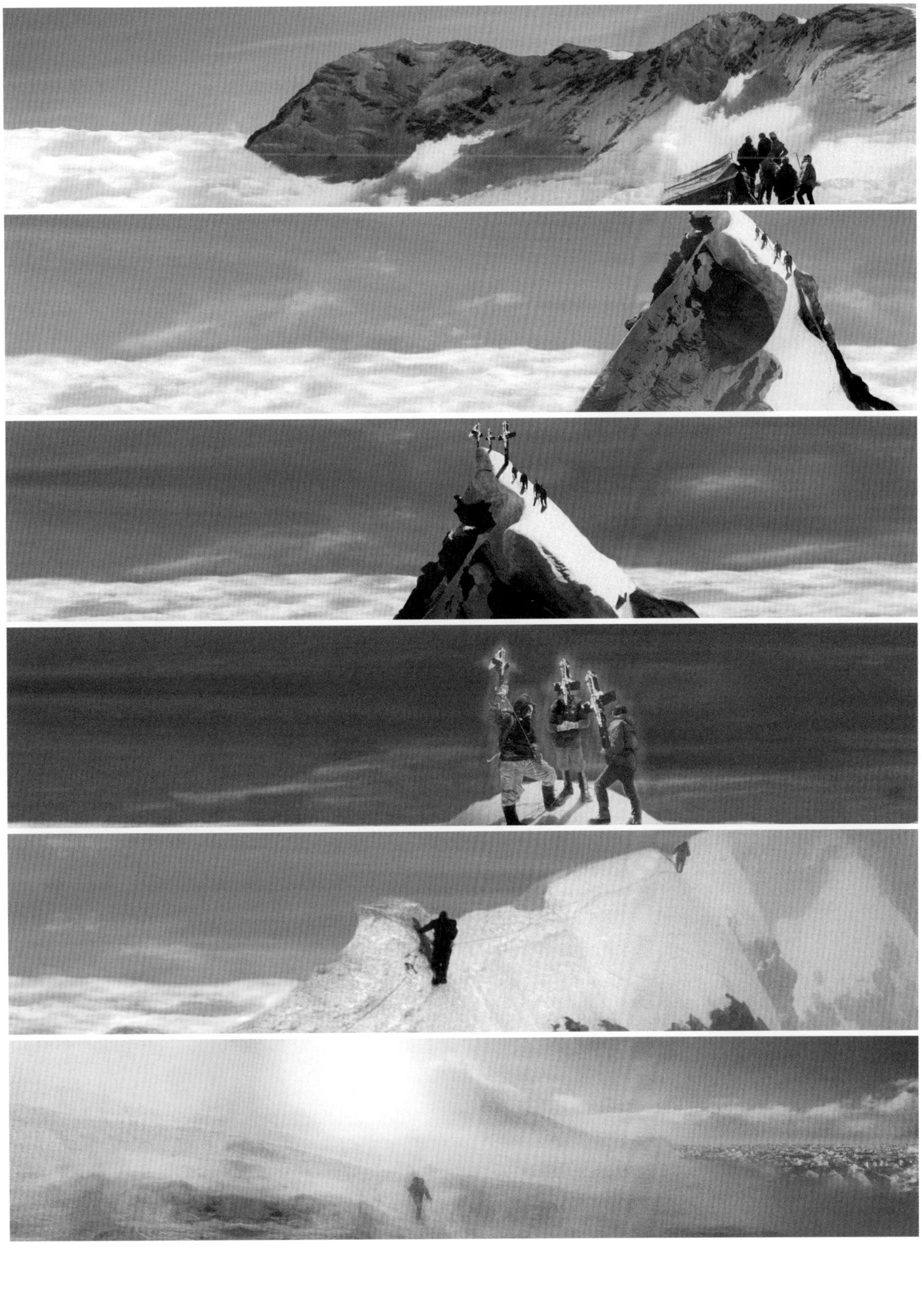

Expedition Nr. 3
2005

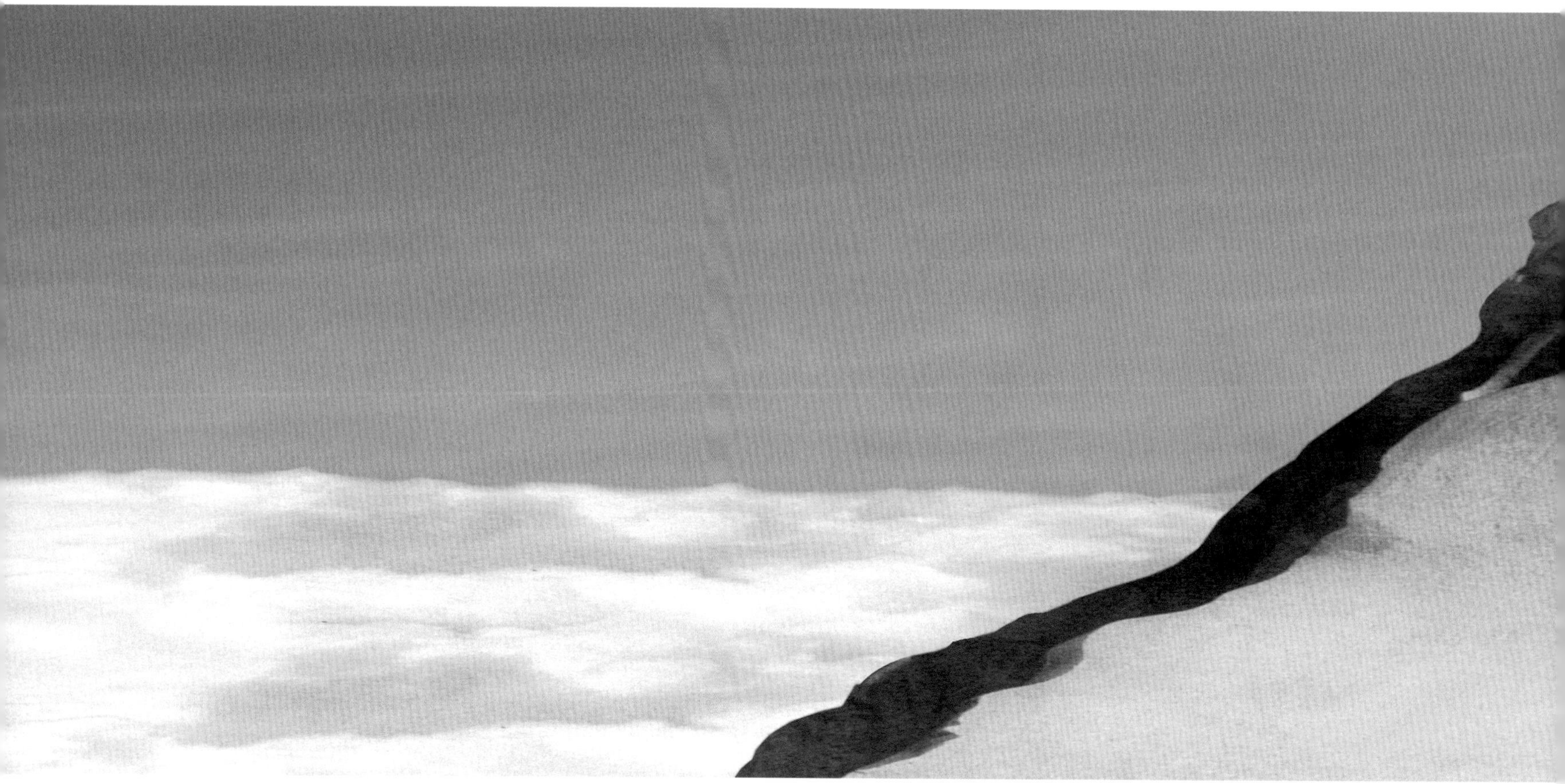

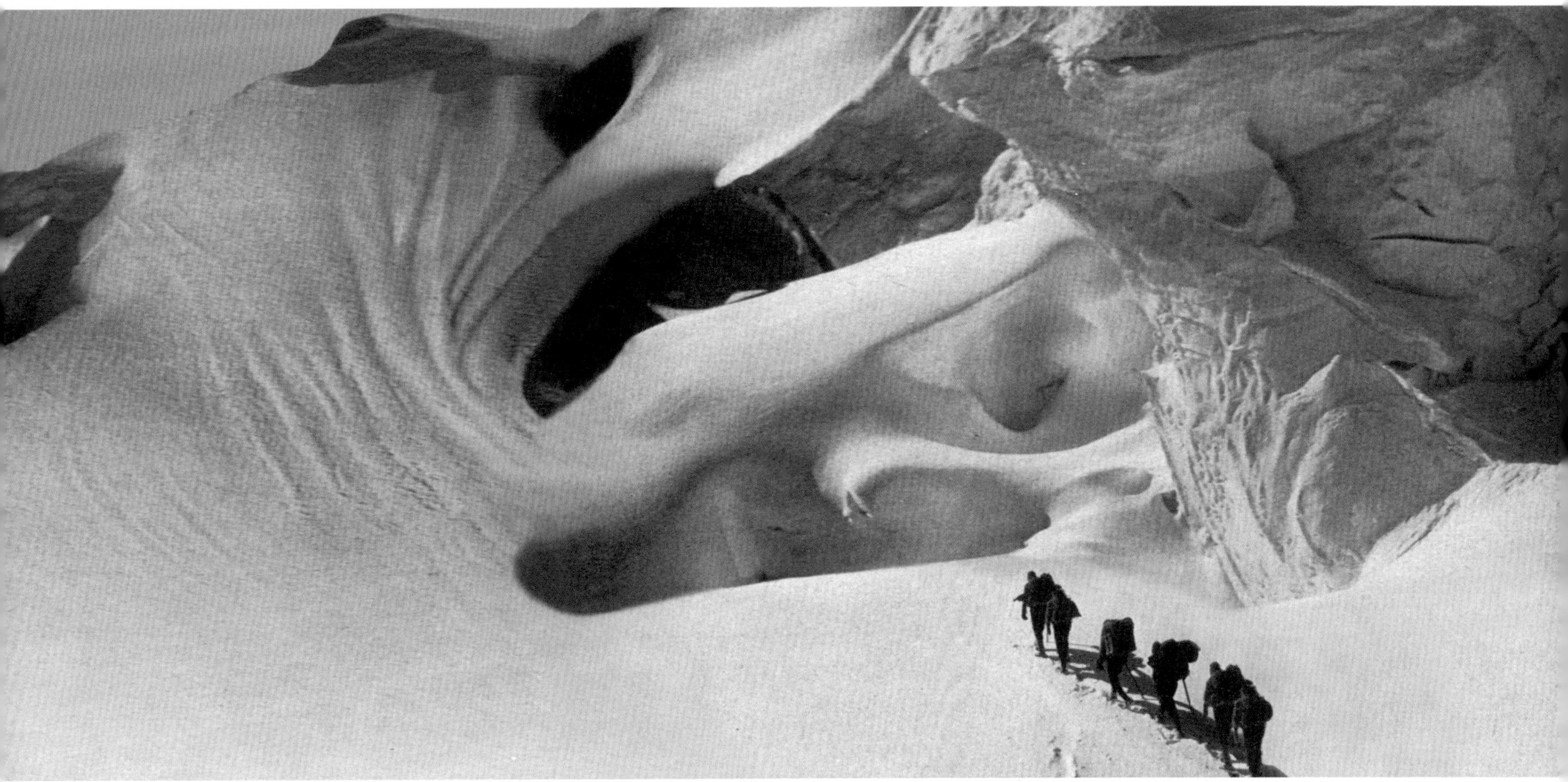

Rauminstallation
Room installation
2005
49 Nord 6 Est Frac Lorraine, Metz

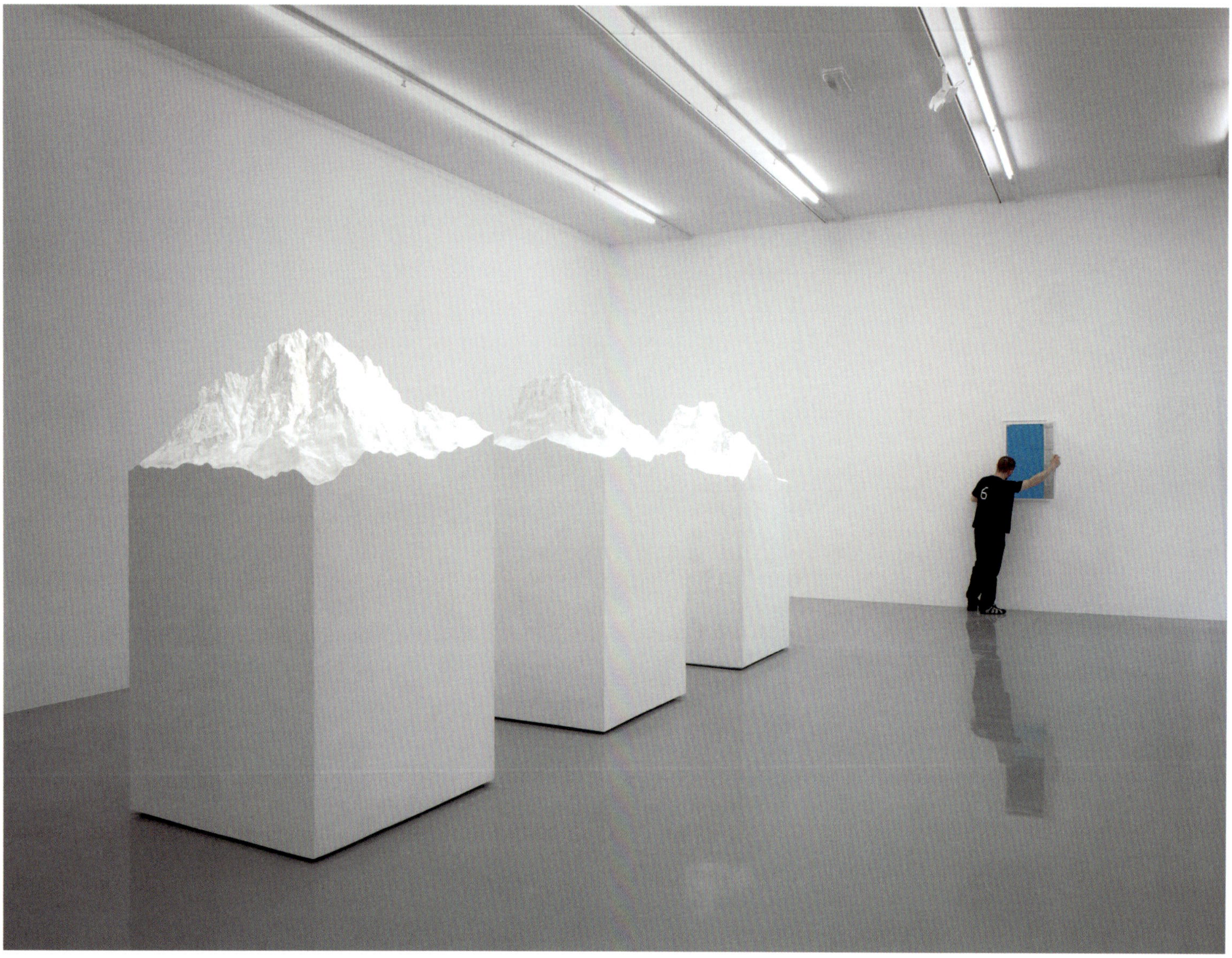

Doppelberg
2013

Antelao / Berlin
2011/2016

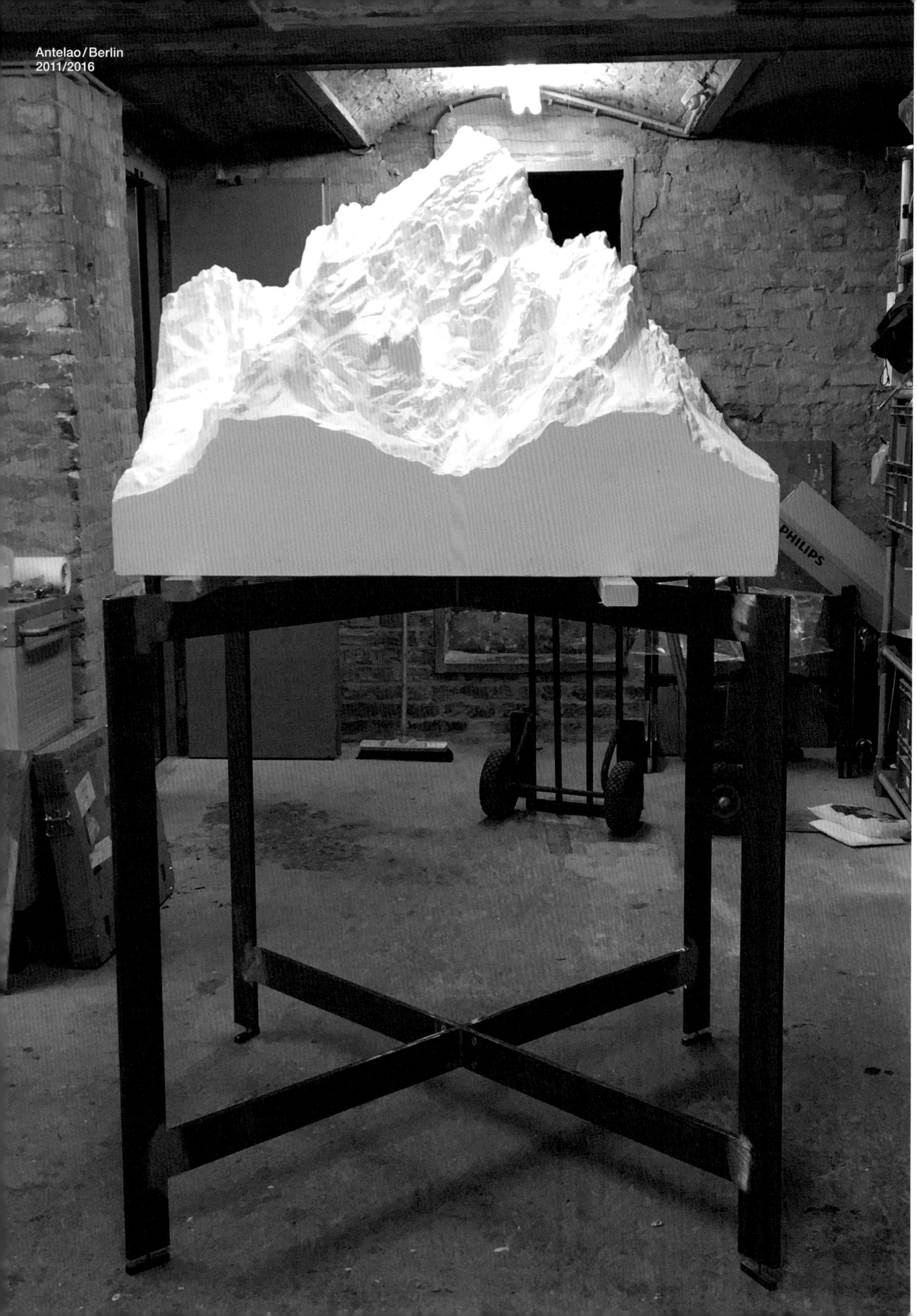

Watzmann
Detail
2013

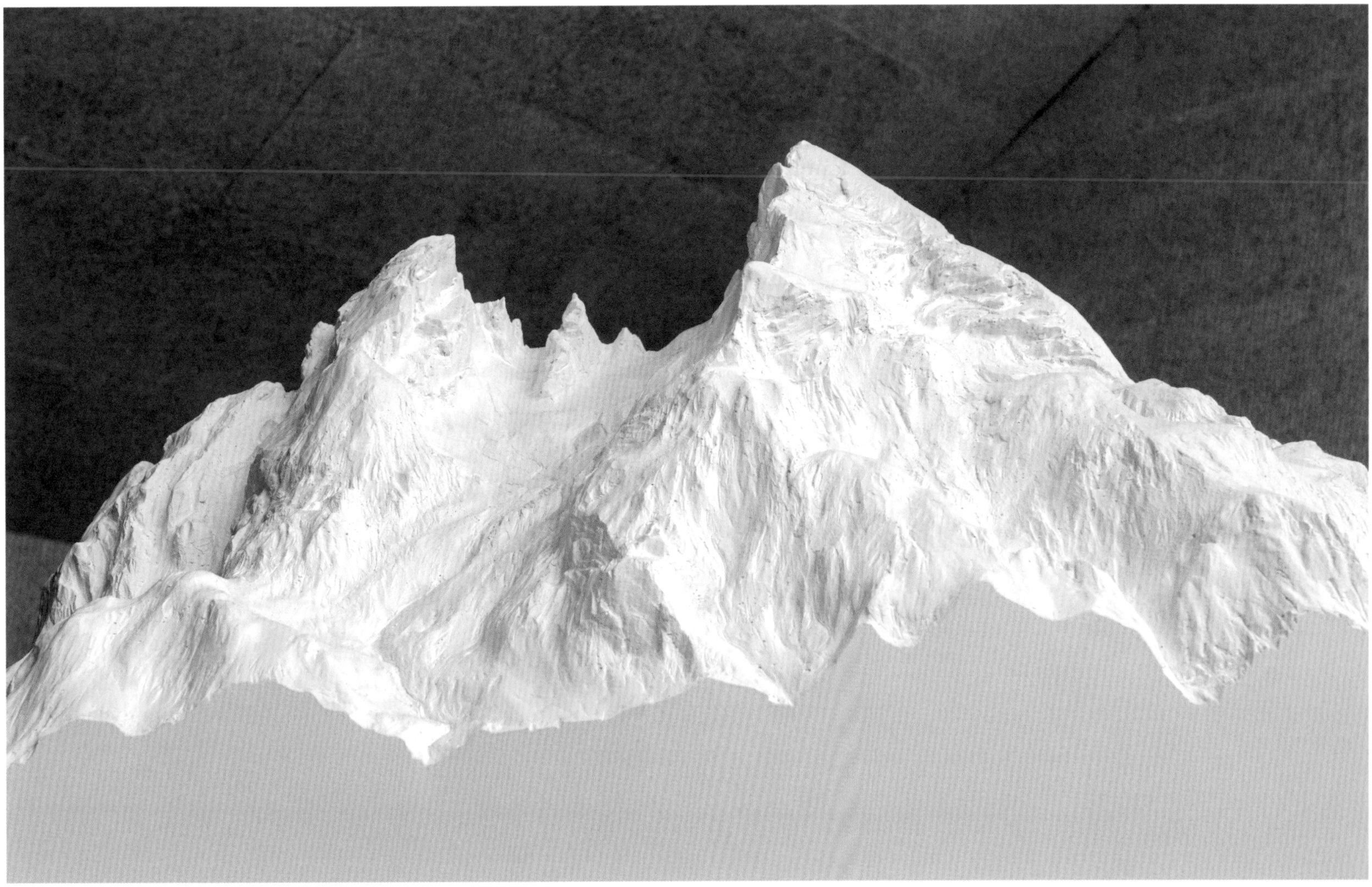

L'Allgäu probablement
Hochvogel
2012/13
Löwenbrauerei Meckatz, Heimenkirch

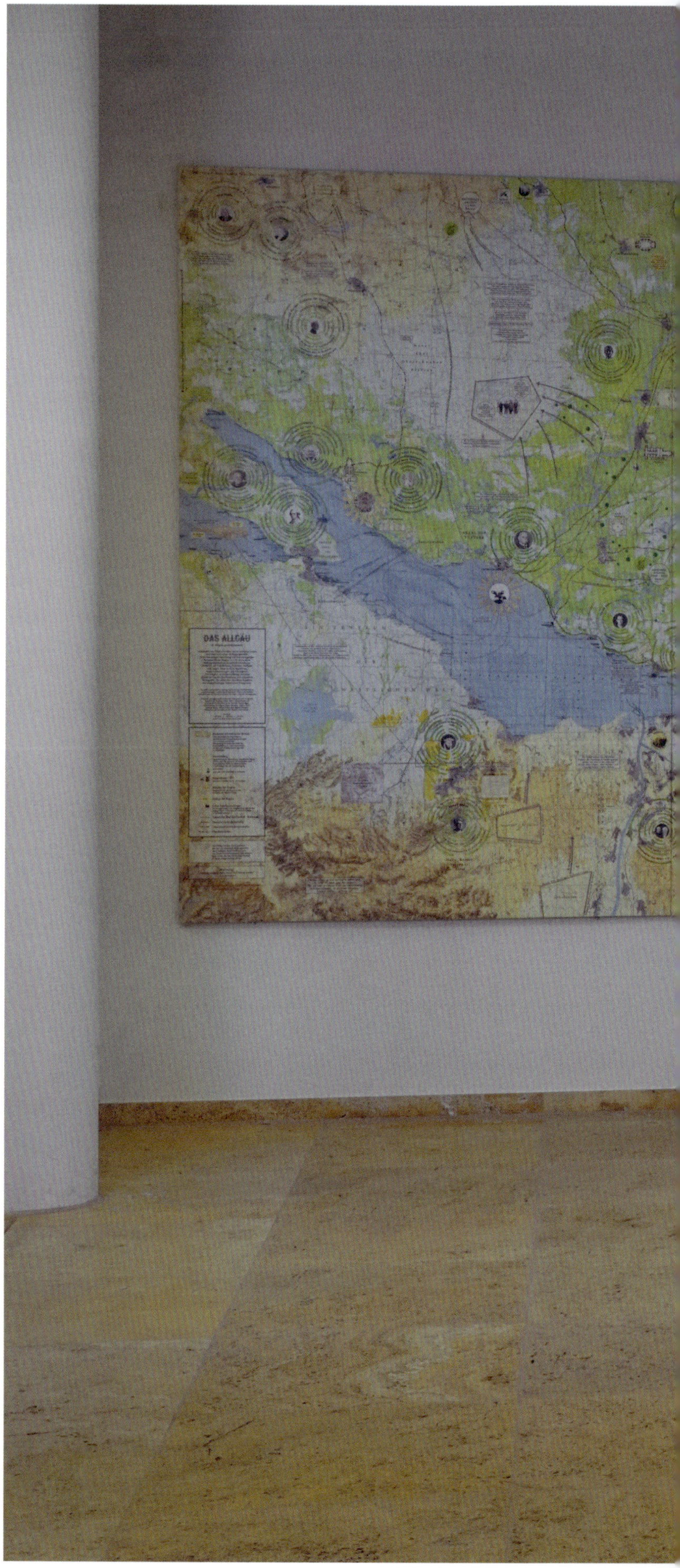

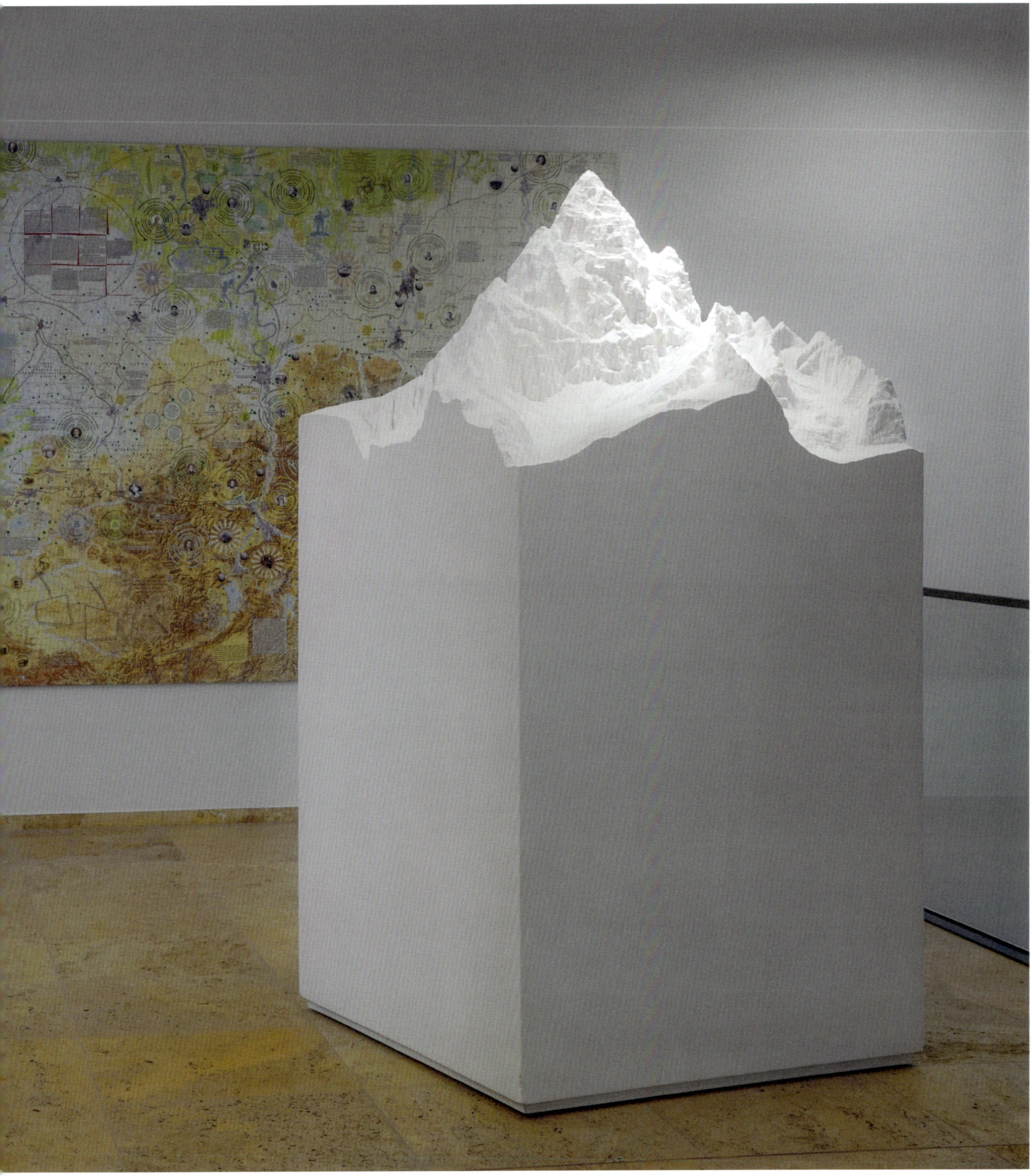

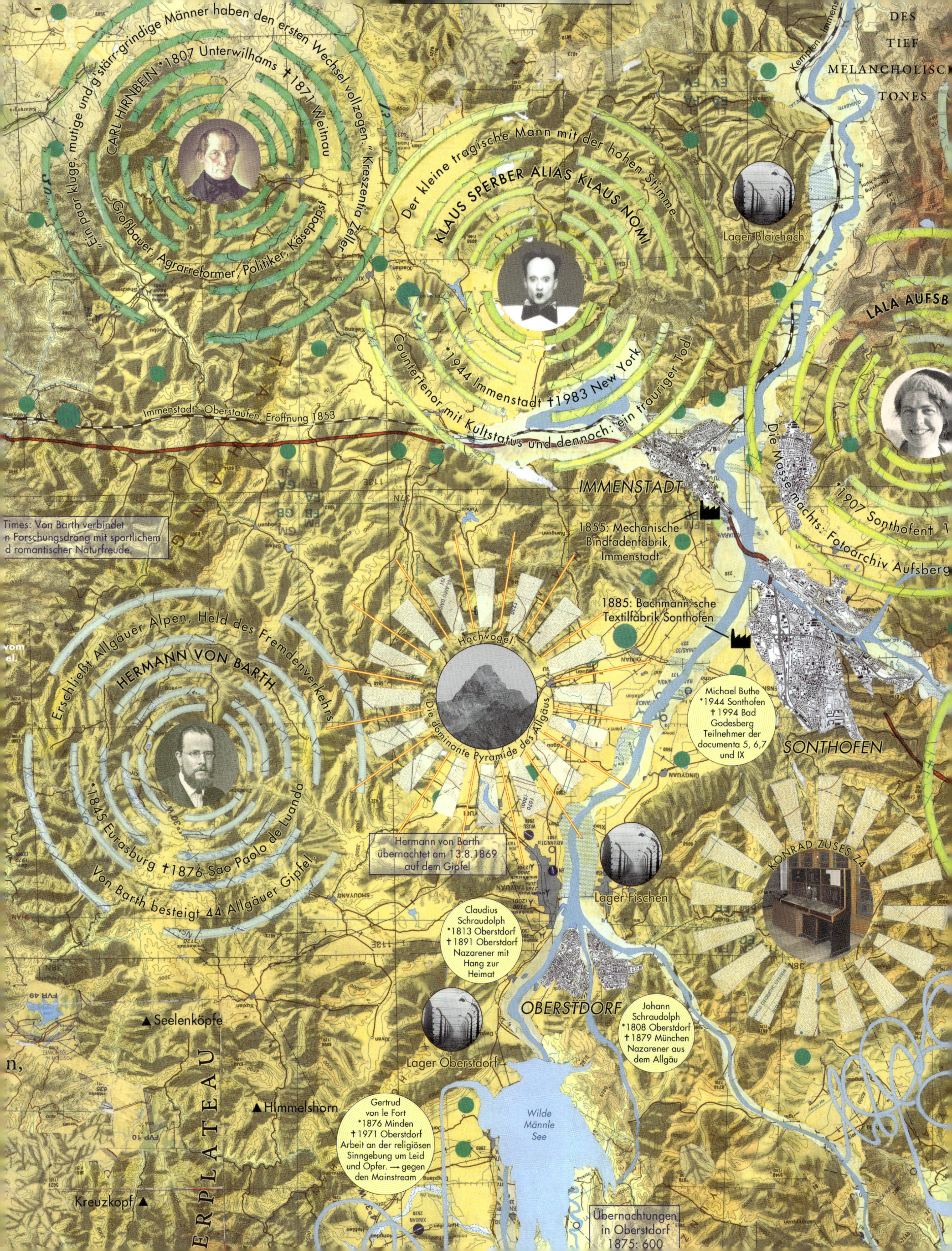

„Ein paar kluge, mutige und g'stärr-grindige Männer haben den ersten Wechsel vollzogen." Kreszentia Zeiler
CARL HIRNBEIN *1807 Unterwilhams †1871 Weitnau
Großbauer, Agrarreformer, Politiker, Käsepapst
Der kleine tragische Mann mit der hohen Stimme.
KLAUS SPERBER ALIAS KLAUS NOMI
*1944 Immenstadt †1983 New York
Countertenor mit Kultstatus und dennoch: ein trauriger Tod.
Lager Blaichach
DES
TIEF
MELANCHOLISC
TONES
LALA AUFSB
Die Masse machts: Fotoarchiv Aufsberg
Immenstadt - Oberstaufen, Eröffnung 1853
IMMENSTADT
1855: Mechanische Bindfadenfabrik, Immenstadt
1885: Bachmann'sche Textilfabrik Sonthofen
Erschließt Allgäuer Alpen, Held des Fremdenverkehrs
HERMANN VON BARTH
*1845 Eurasburg †1876 Sao Paolo de Luanda
Von Barth besteigt 44 Allgäuer Gipfel
Hochvogel
Die dominante Pyramide des Allgäus
Michael Buthe *1944 Sonthofen †1994 Bad Godesberg Teilnehmer der documenta 5, 6,7 und IX
SONTHOFEN
Hermann von Barth übernachtet am 13.8.1869 auf dem Gipfel
Lager Fischen
KONRAD ZUSES Z4
Claudius Schraudolph *1813 Oberstdorf †1891 Oberstdorf Nazarener mit Hang zur Heimat
OBERSTDORF
Johann Schraudolph *1808 Oberstdorf †1879 München Nazarener aus dem Allgäu
Lager Oberstdorf
Seelenköpfe
Himmelshorn
Kreuzkopf
ERPLATEAU
Gertrud von le Fort *1876 Minden †1971 Oberstdorf Arbeit an der religiösen Sinngebung um Leid und Opfer. → gegen den Mainstream
Wilde Männle See
Übernachtungen in Oberstdorf 1875: 600

L'Allgäu probablement
Hochvogel
2012/13
Löwenbrauerei Meckatz, Heimenkirch

Shiny Marmolada I & II
2015

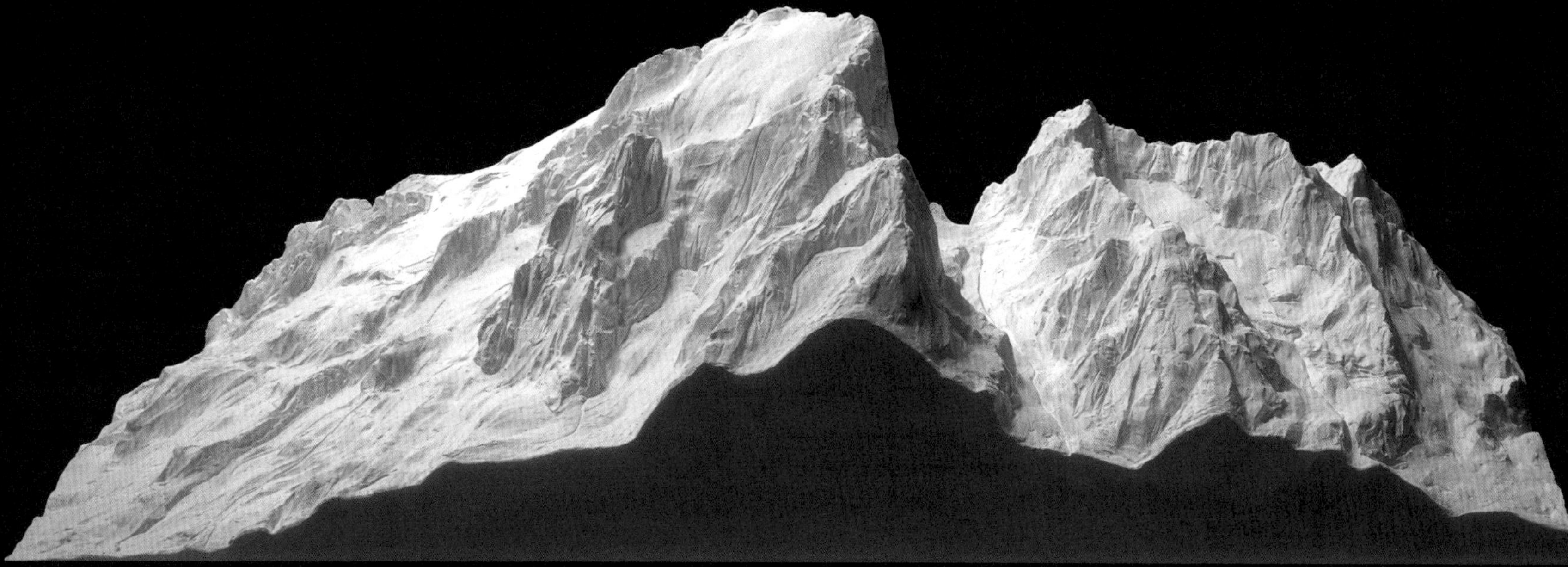

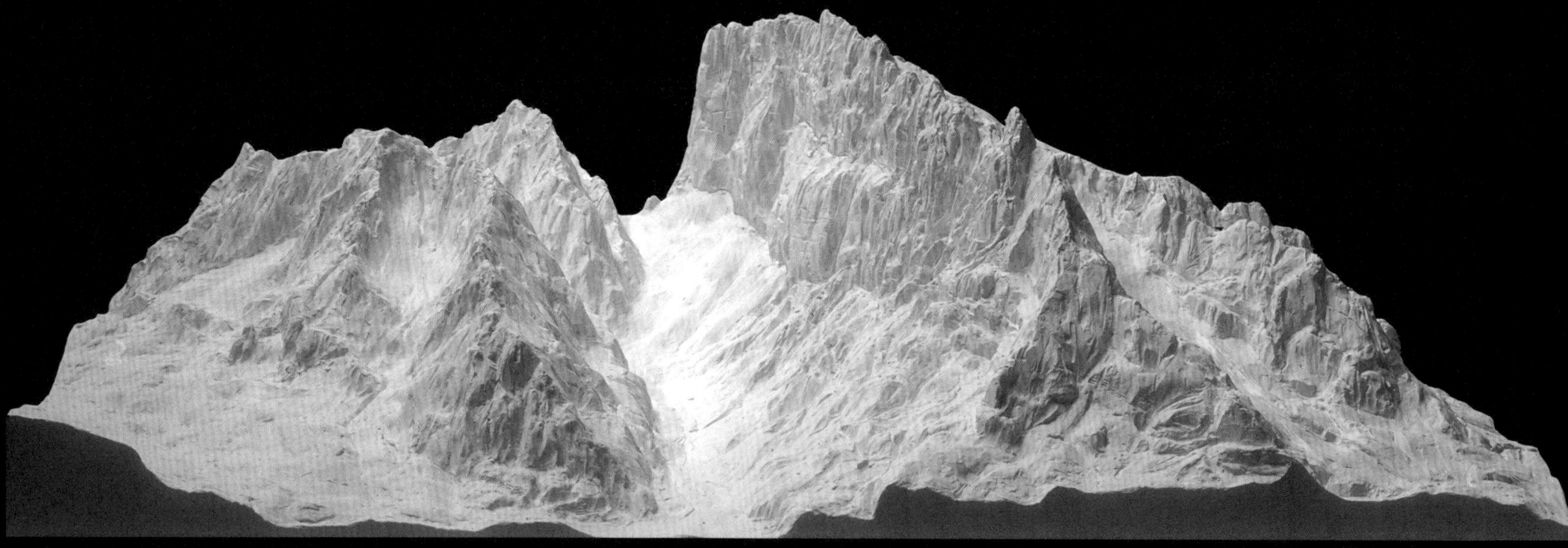

Expedition I & IV
2010

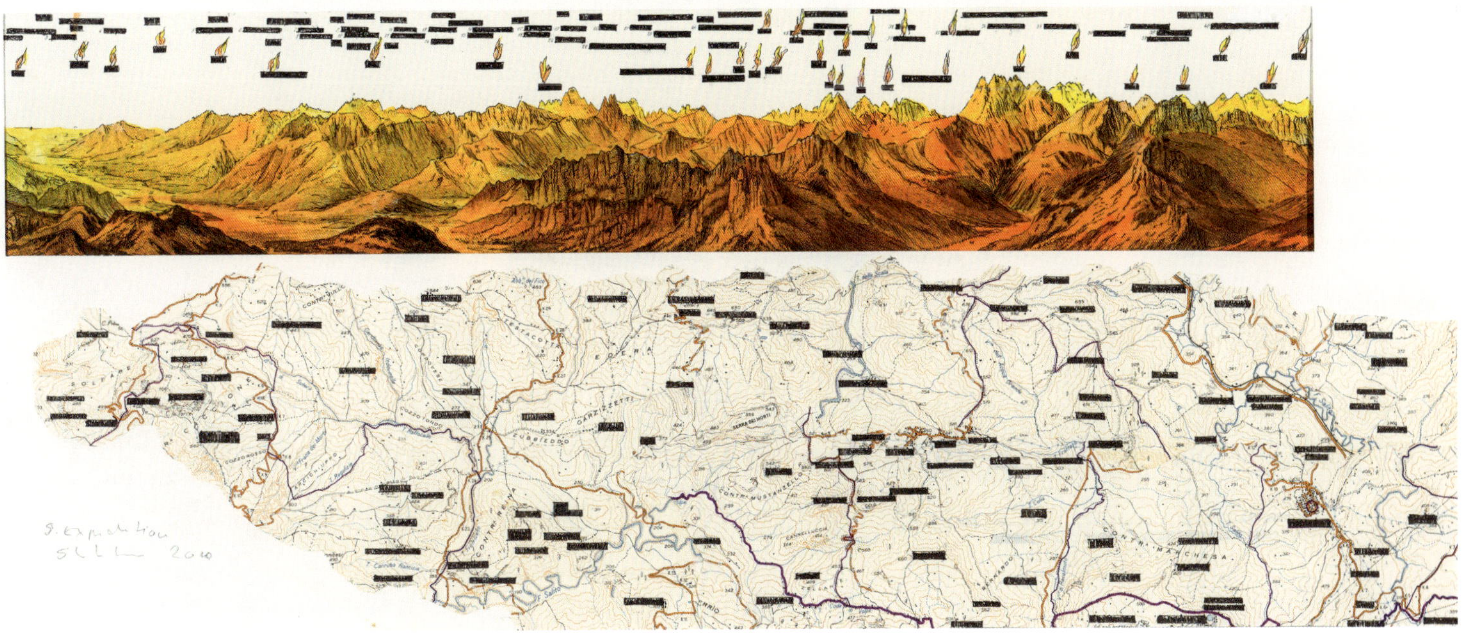

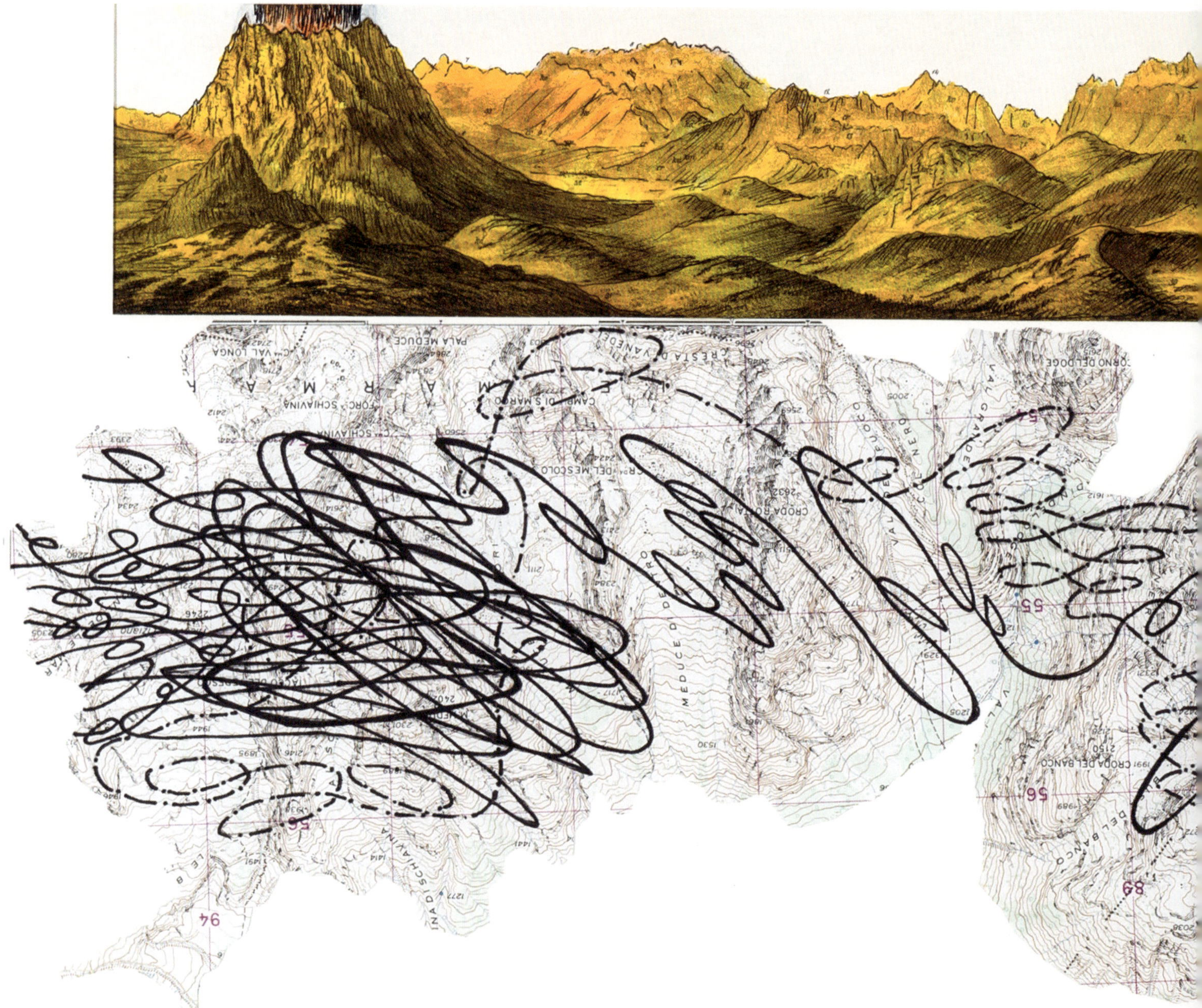

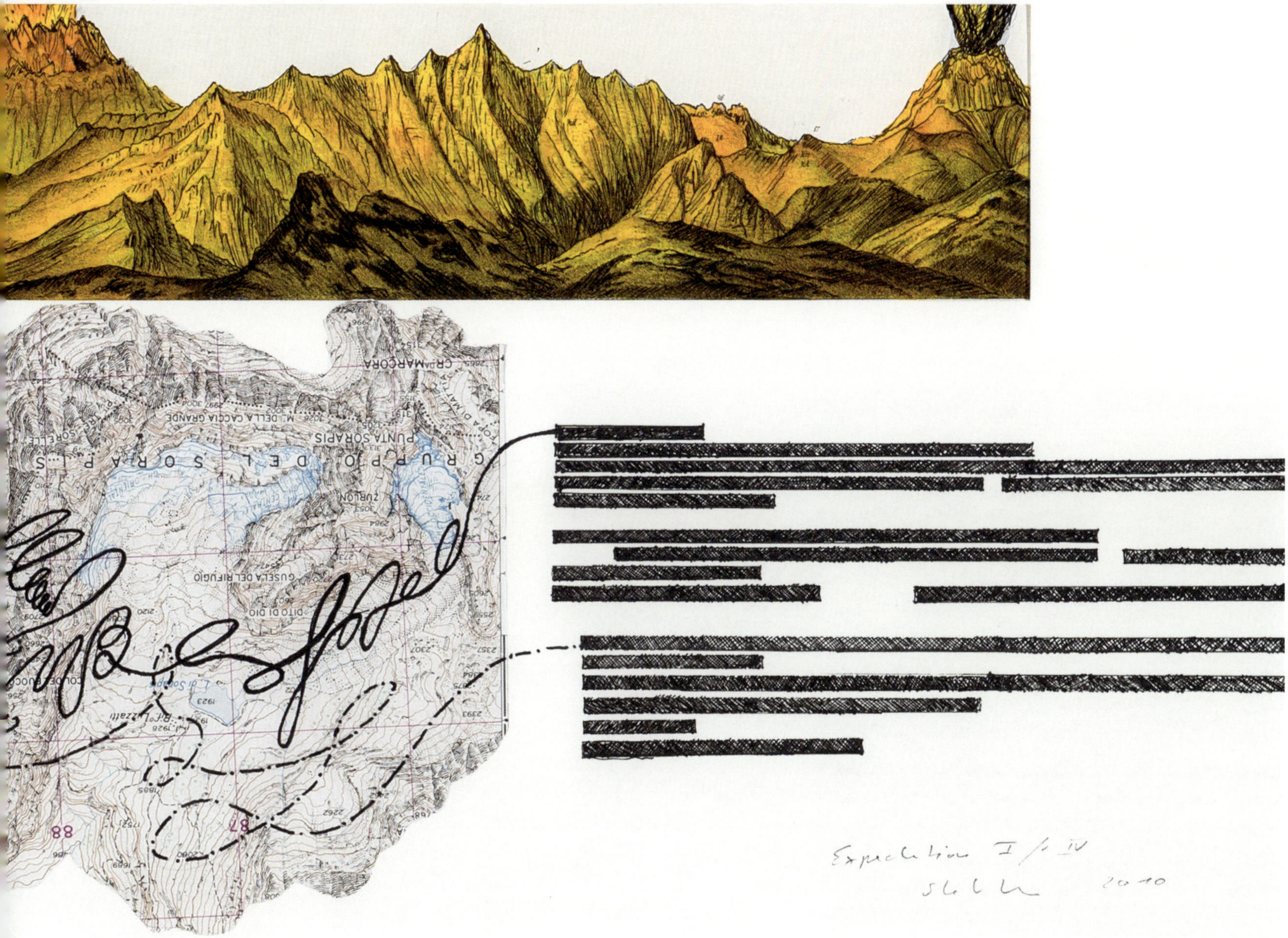

Tre Cime
2012

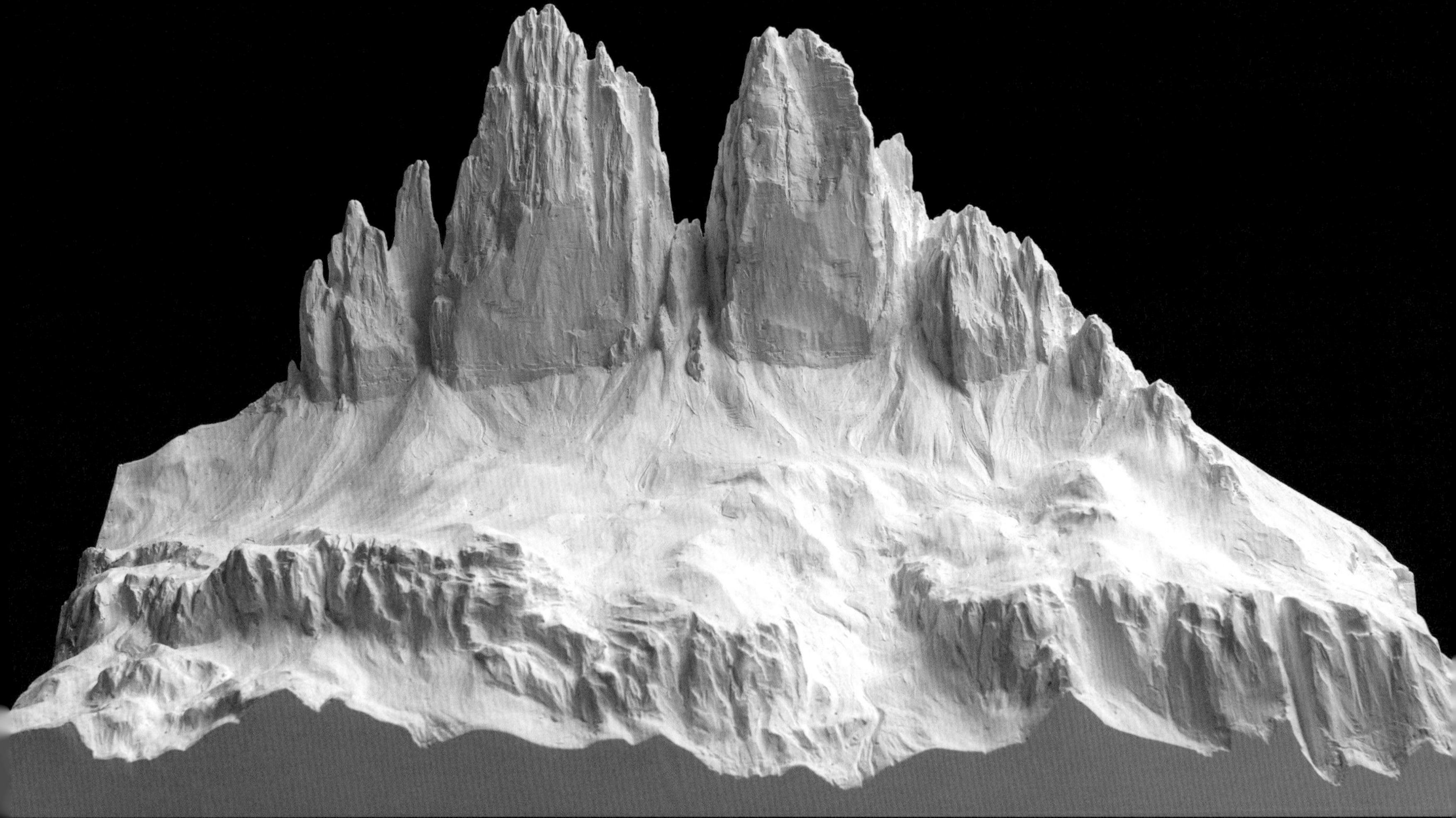

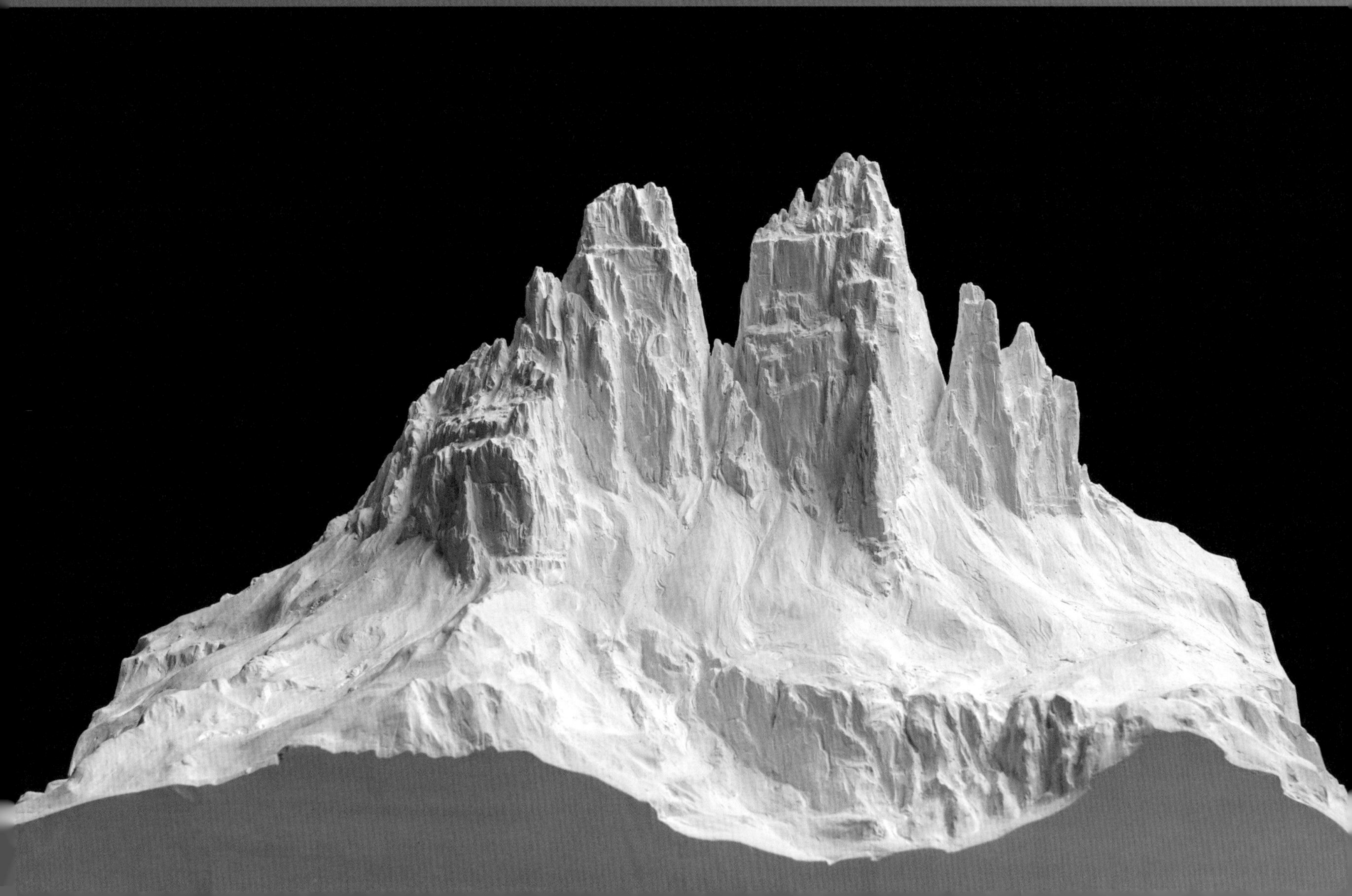

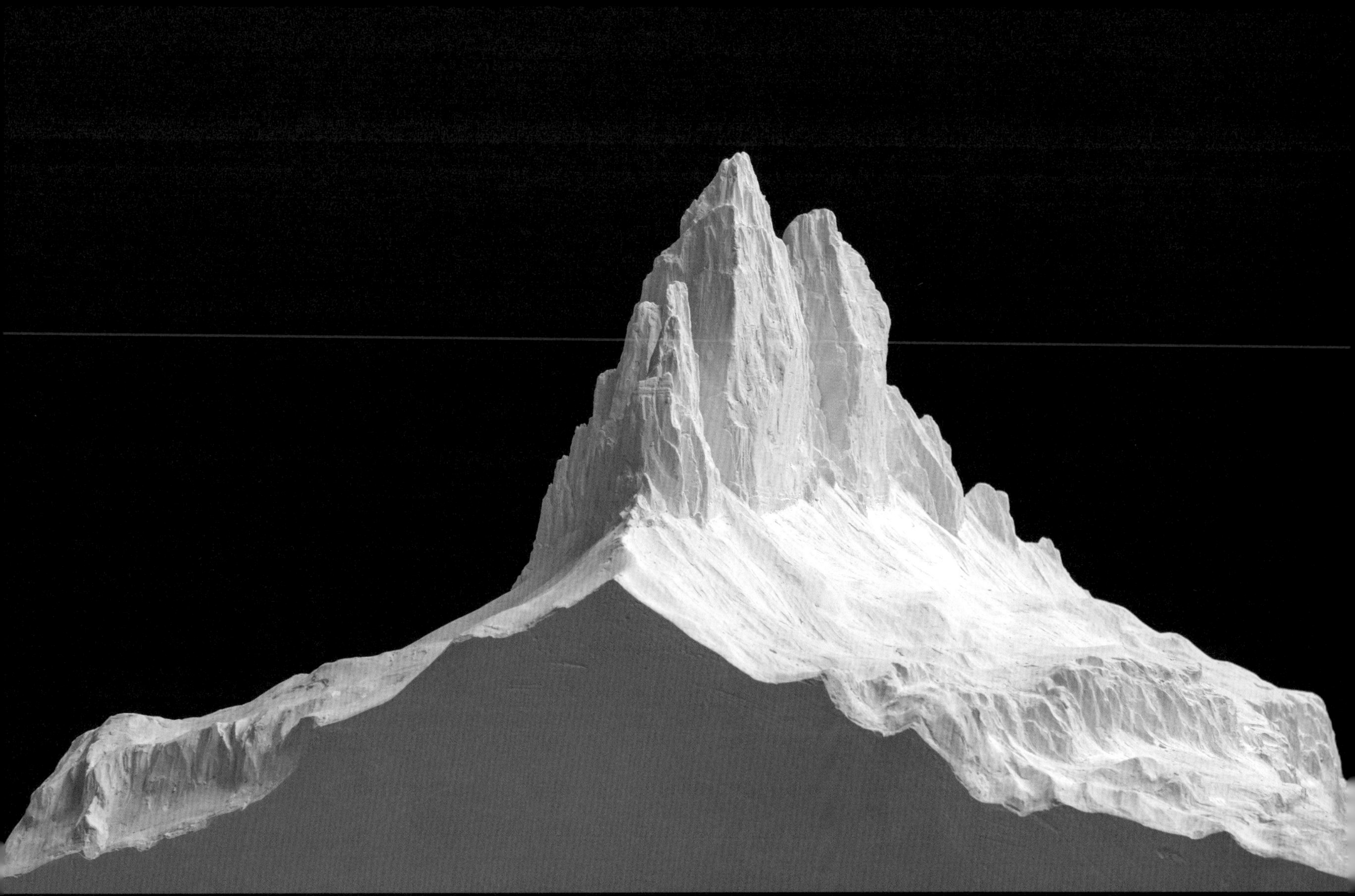

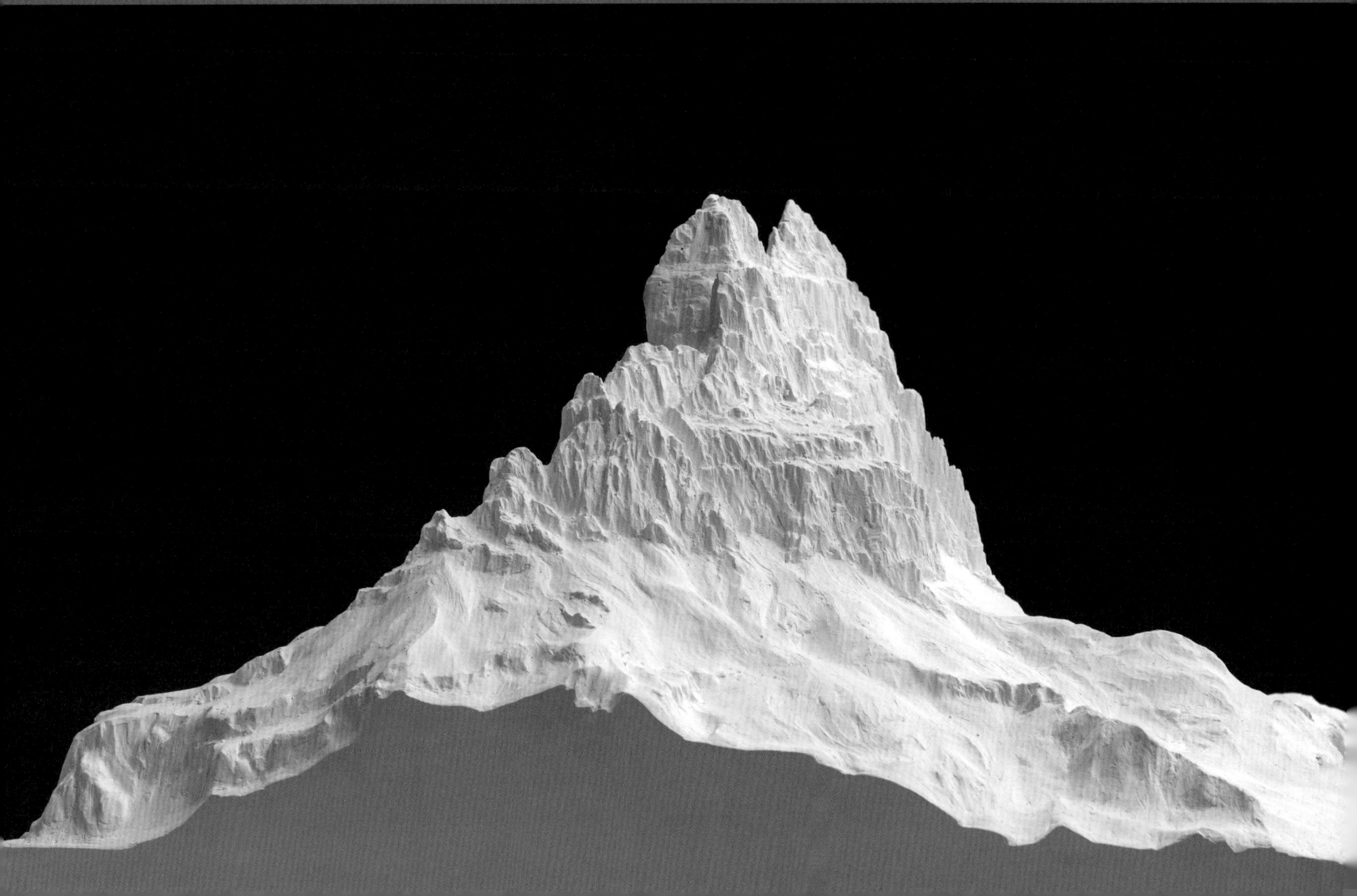

Großes Panorama II
2021

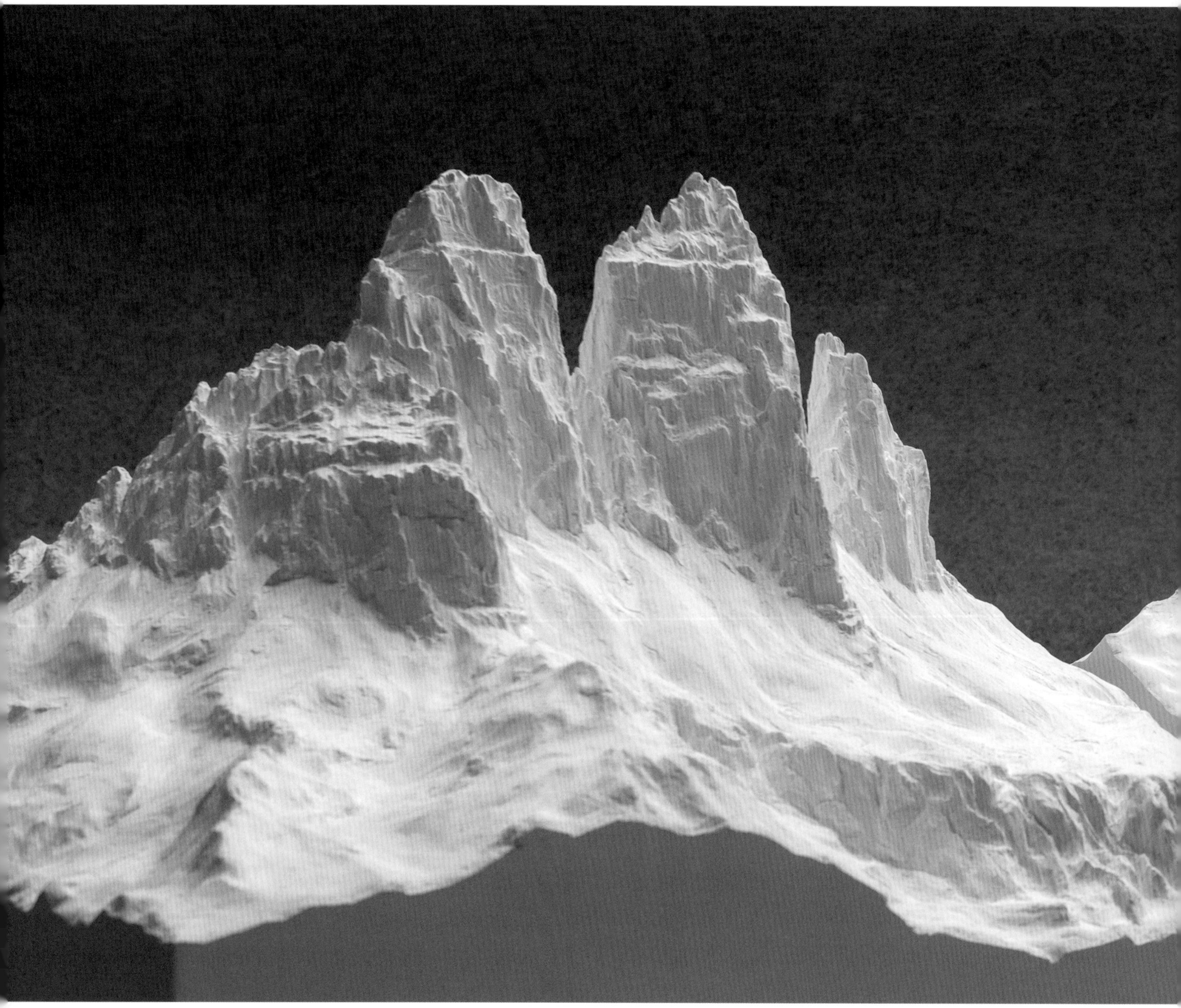

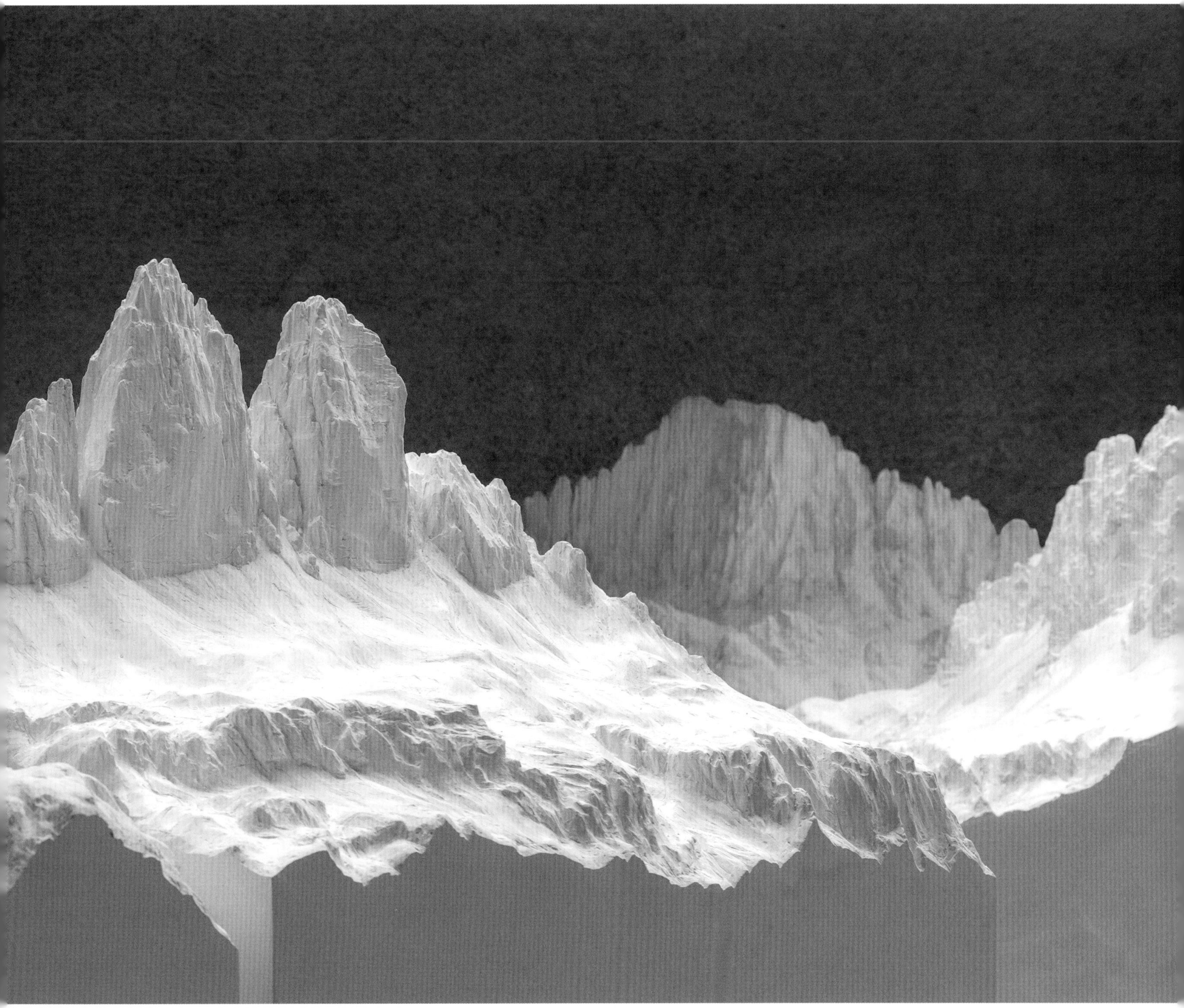

Pelmo
2006

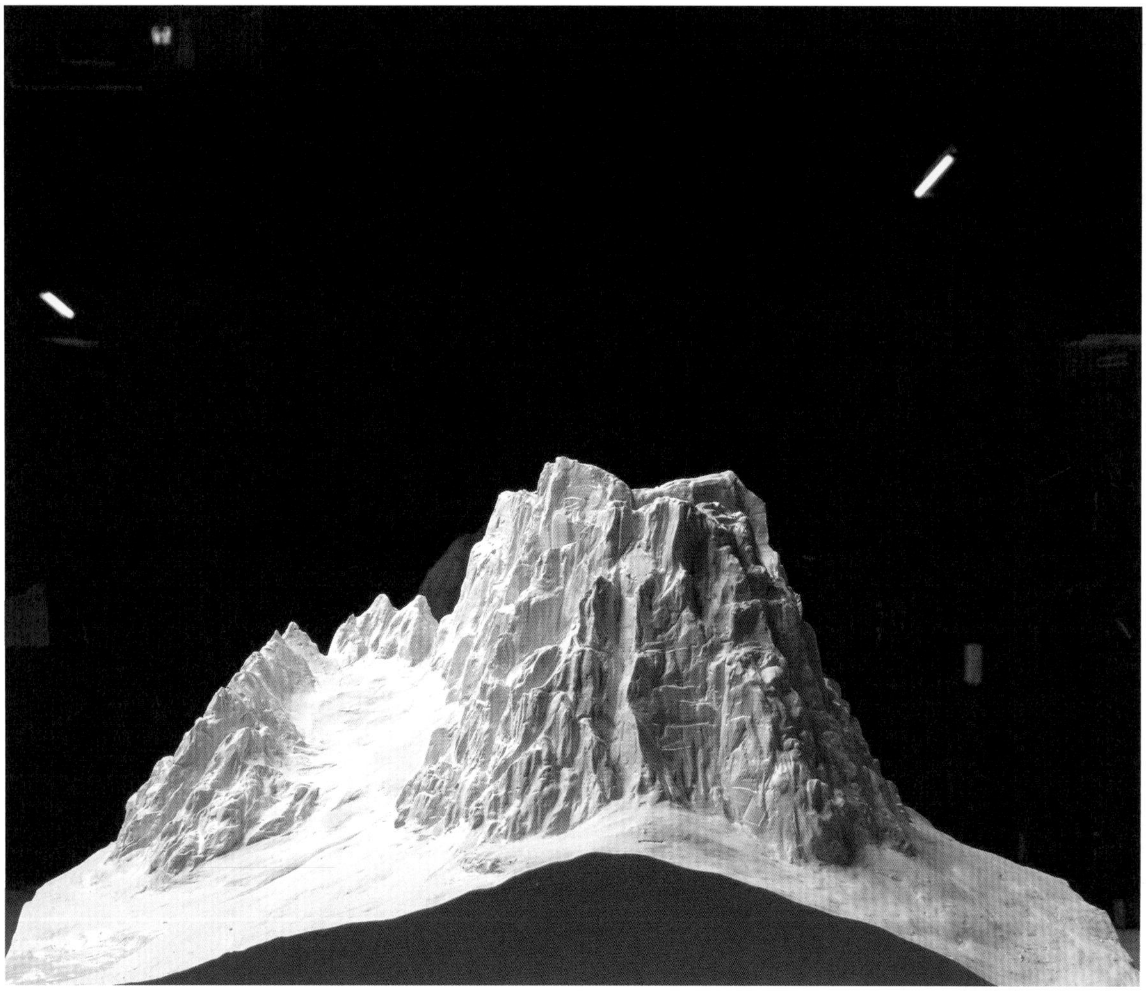

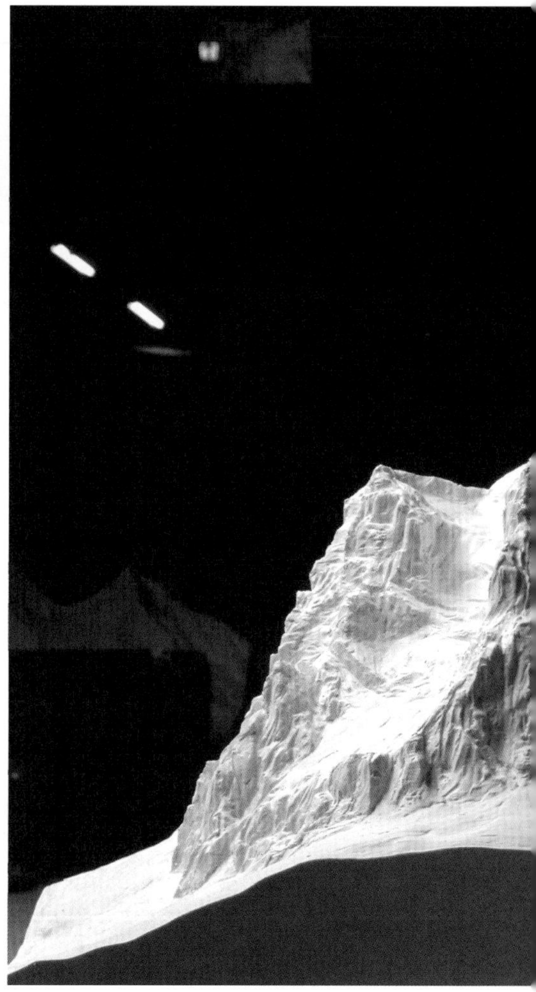

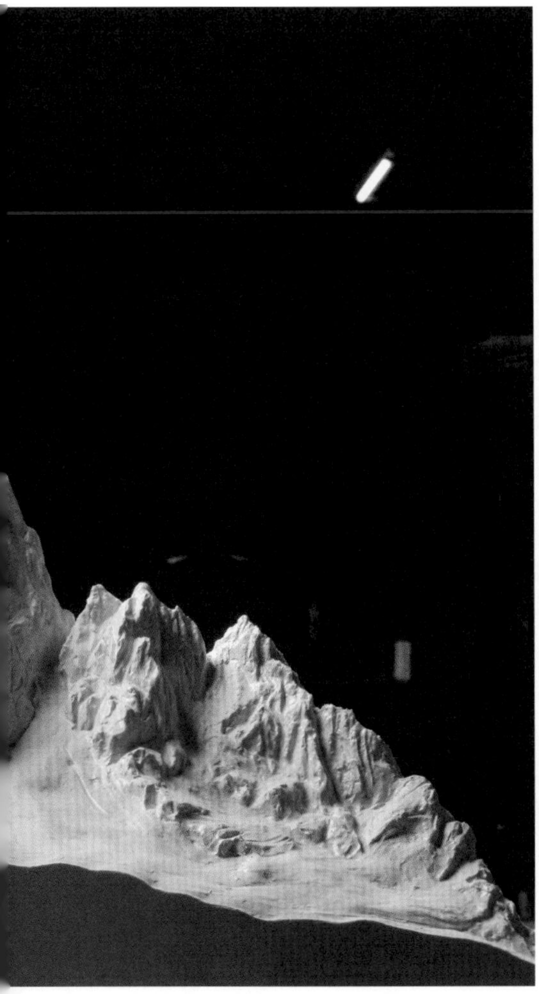
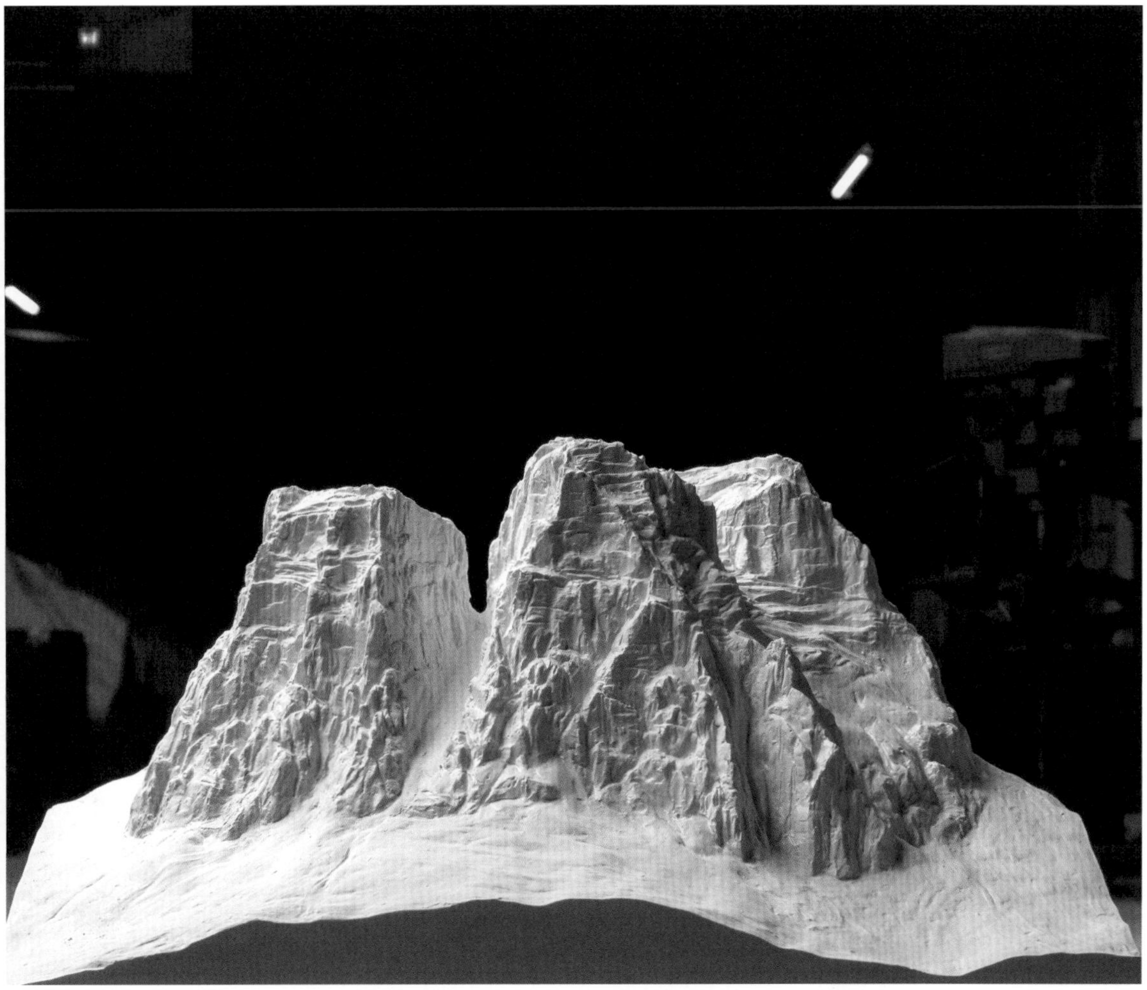

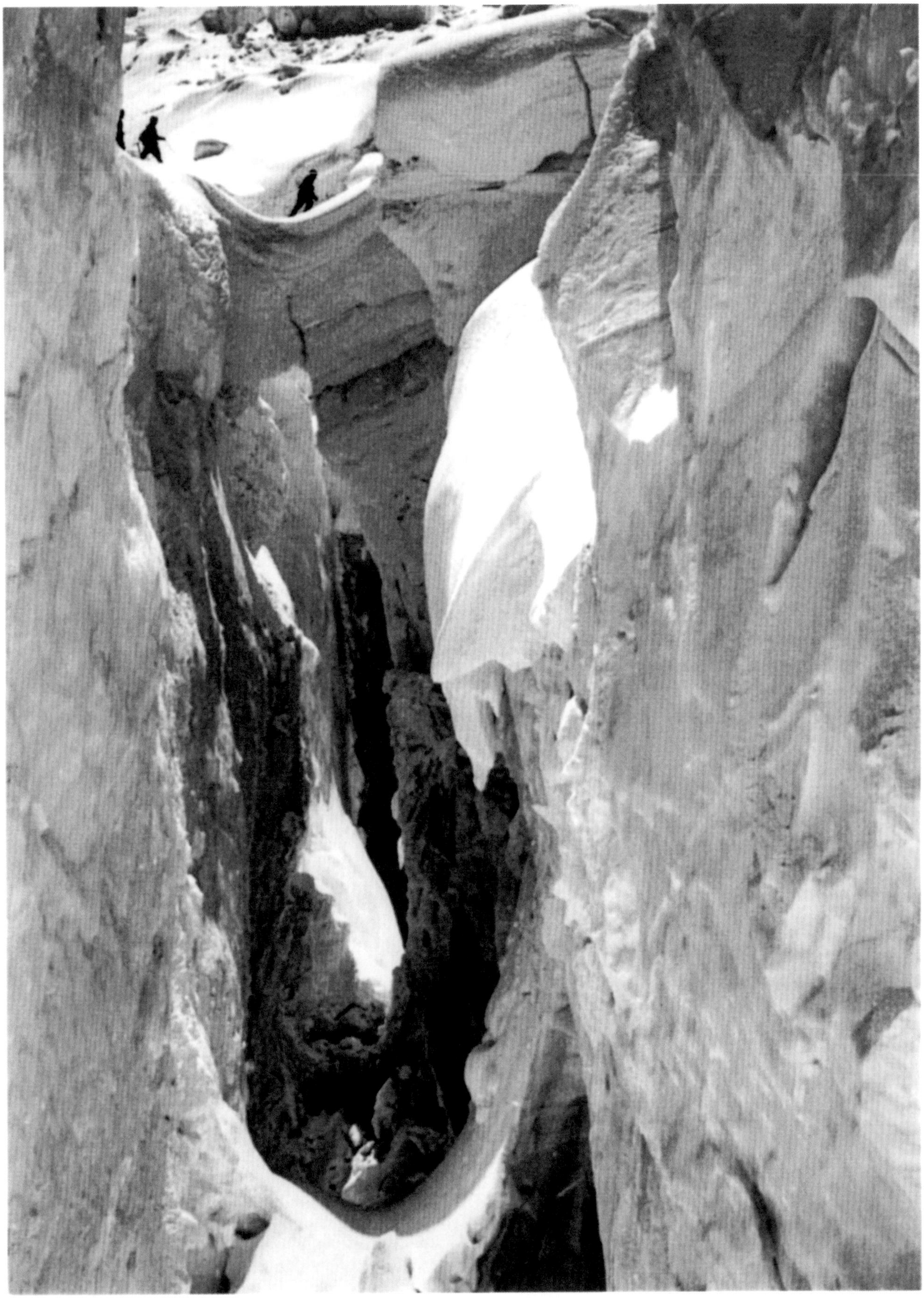

Expedition Nr.17
12.8.1931 – 27.8.1931: Erforschung des Borromäischen Knotens
(volkstümlich: Lumumbaspalte), östliche Wienerberge.
Teilnehmer: Sigmund Freud, Stephan Huber, Jacques Lacan
Abb.: Überquerung des Emotionsbruches,
Foto am 15.8. 1931. Ernste Auseinandersetzungen über die weitere Route.
Lacan erzwingt drei tägige Pause wg. psychischer Erschöpfung.
Expedition ausgestattet von Anton Meßmer und Georges Bataille

9/15
2008

Expedition Nr. 17
2008

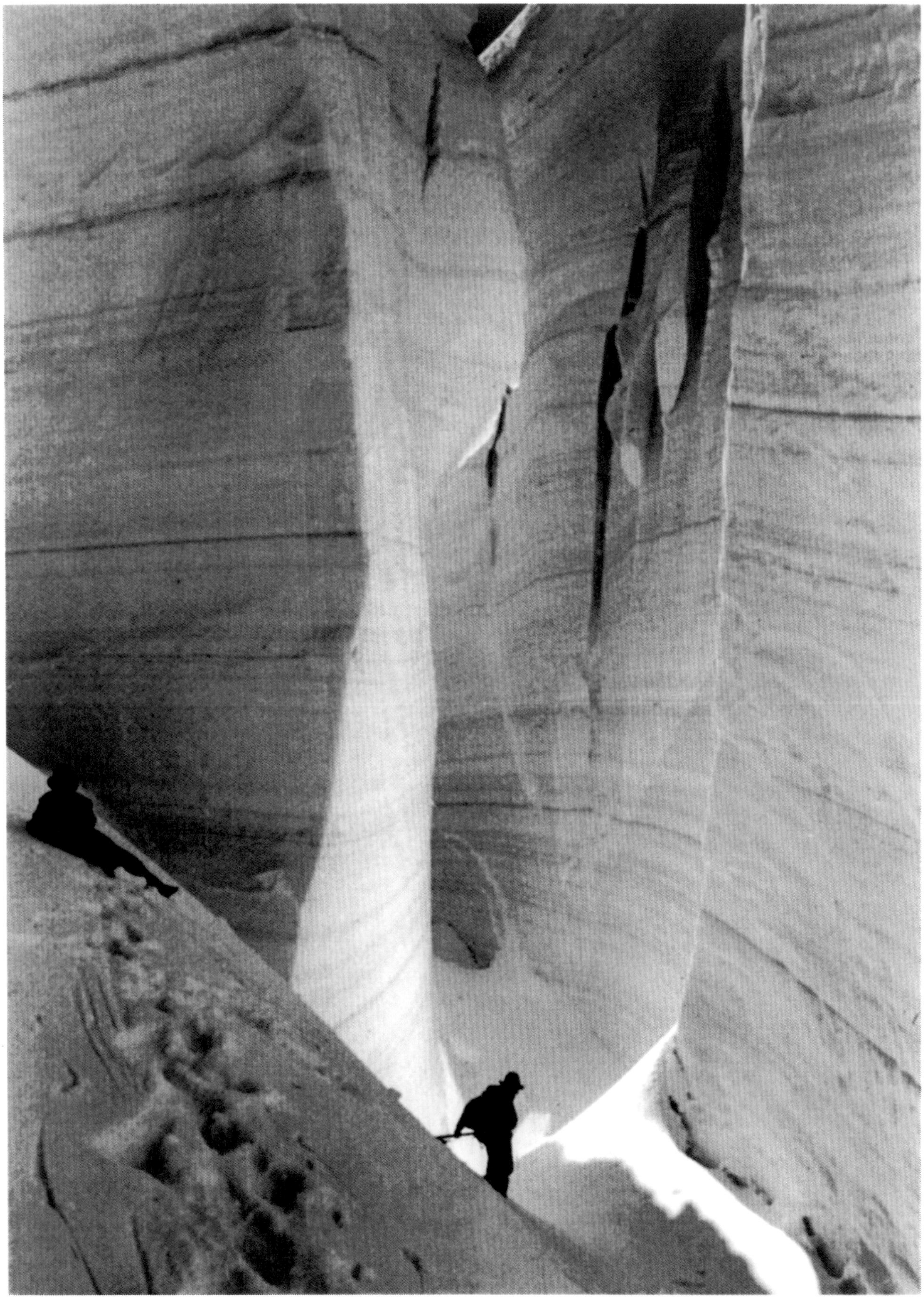

Expedition Nr.17
12.8.1931 – 27.8. 1931: Erforschung des Borromäischen Knotens
(volkstümlich: Lumumbaspalte), östliche Wienerberge.
Teilnehmer: Sigmund Freud, Stephan Huber, Jacques Lacan
Abb.: Durchquerung des Borromäischen Knotens, westlich Triglav,
Foto am 20.8.1931. Aufgabe Freuds am 18.8.1931 wegen starker Kehlkopschmerzen.
Abbruch der Expedition am 27.8.1931 aufgrund schwerer Differenzen zwischen S.H. und J.L.
Rückkehr von Lacan nach Paris. Rückzug von Huber in die Bourdieuhütte.
Expedition ausgestattet von Anton Meßmer und Georges Bataille.

9/15
2008

Expedition Nr. 16
2008

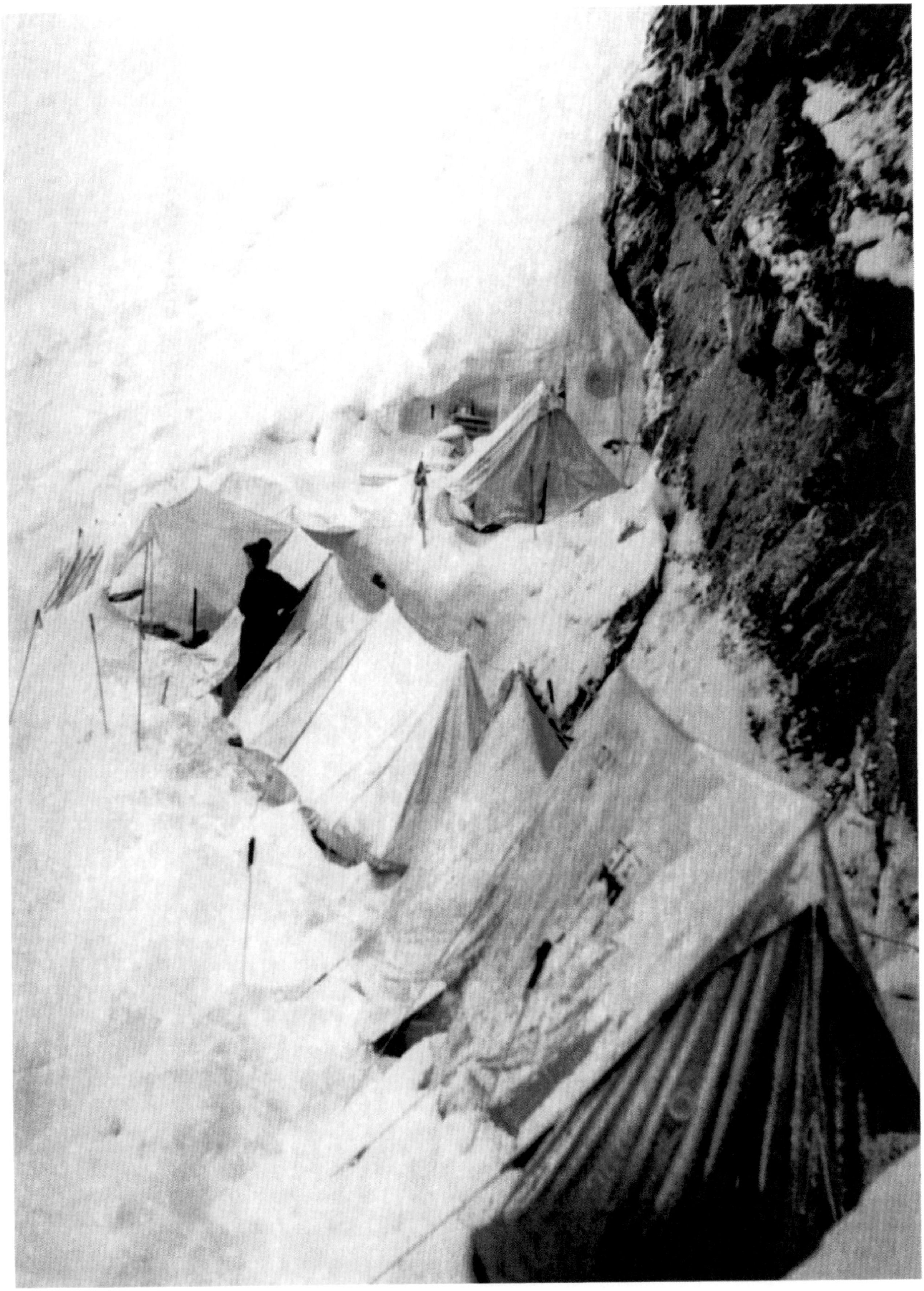

Expedition Nr.16
10.3.1623 – 5.4.1623: Auf der Suche nach Artemisia Gentileschi
Teilnehmer: Hélène Cixous, Stephan Huber, Luce Irigaray
Abb.: Refugio Gentileschi, Speculumwand (nördl. Abruzzen),
Person Mitte: A. Gentileschi, Foto: H. Cixous, am 17.3.1623.
Heftige Stürme während des Aufstieges (unerklärlicher roter Schnee),
S.H. verschollen seit 16.3.1623. Abbruch der Suche am 18.3.1623.
Expedition ausgestattet von Cosimo II, Florenz und Ecole Freudienne de Paris (EFP)

14/15

Expedition Nr. 16
2008

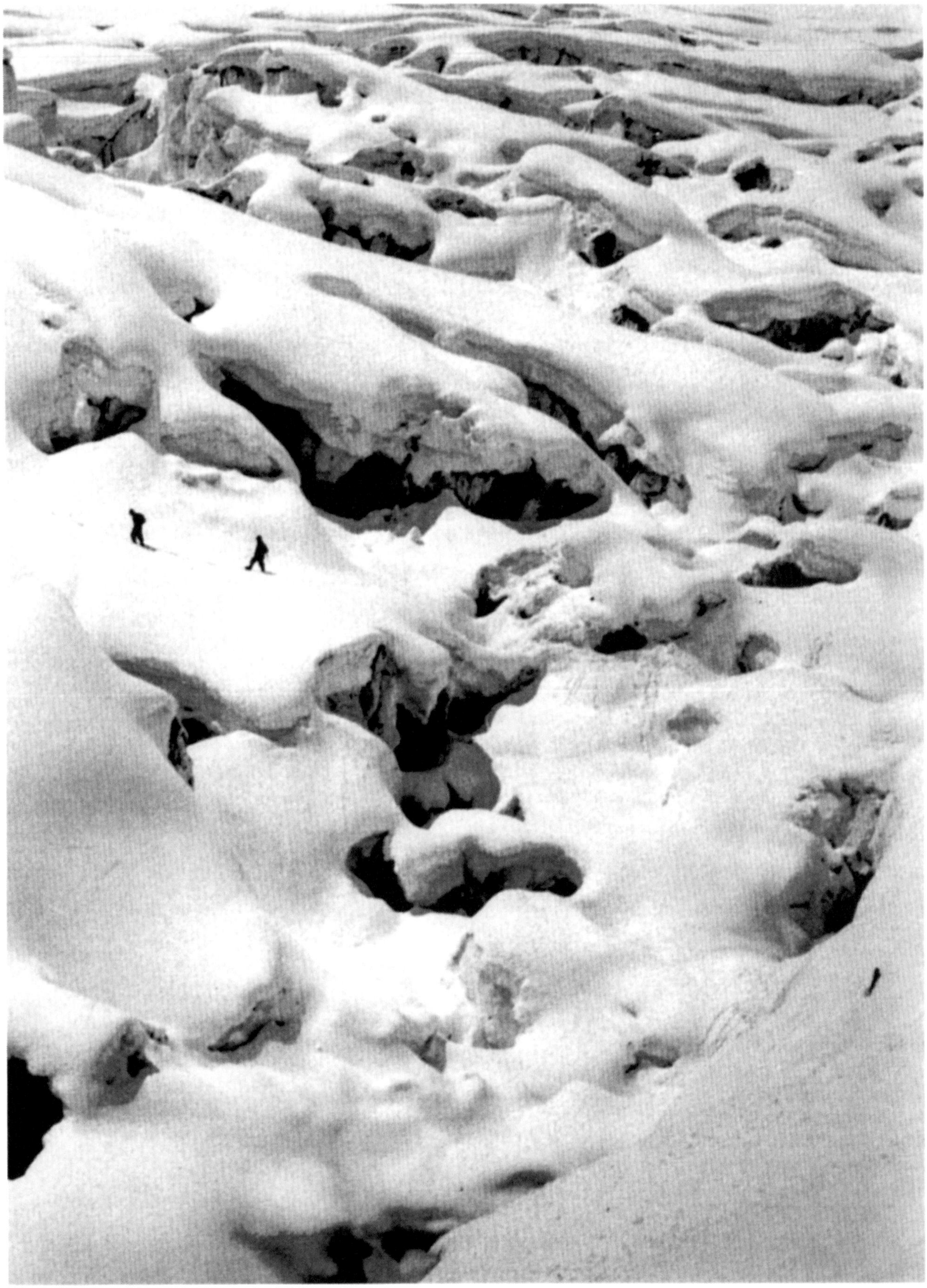

Expedition Nr. 16
10.3.1623 – 5.4.1623: Auf der Suche nach Artemisia Gentileschi
Teilnehmer: Hélène Cixous, Stephan Huber, Luce Irigaray
Abb.: Durchquerung des Holofernesgletscher (nördl. Abruzzen), Foto: H. Cixous, am 15.3.1623;
Halluzinationen von S.H. am Abend des 15.3.1623 (Erscheinung eines fliegenden Kopfes).
Expedition ausgestattet von Cosimo II, Florenz und Ecole Freudienne de Paris (EFP)

14/15
2008

Zugang Atelier Stephan Huber
2008

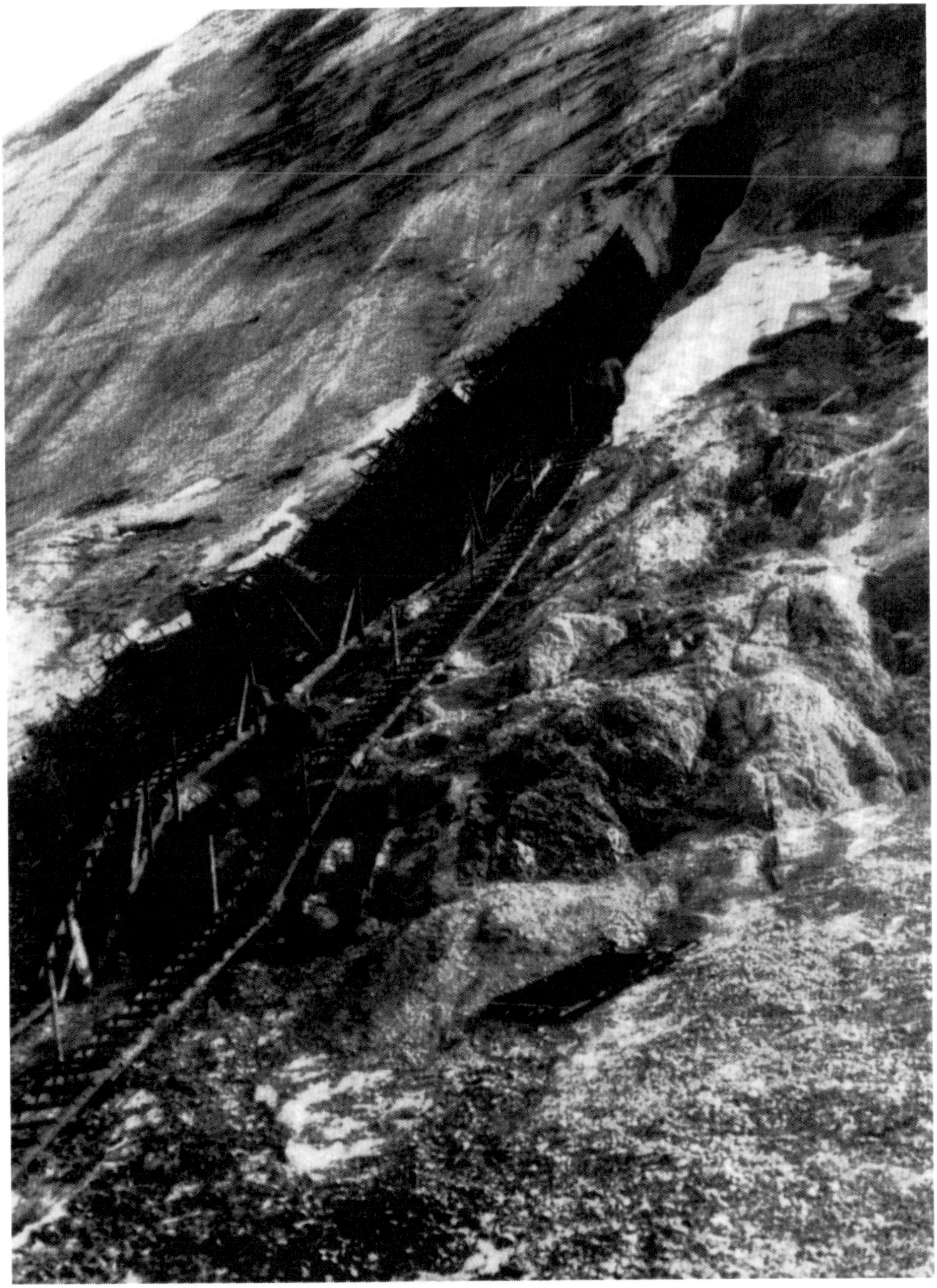

Zugang Atelier Stephan Huber
1998 – 2007
Oberhalb Morusgletscher, Bauphase.
Rechts: Zugang Links: Abgang
Mitarbeit: A. Meaulnes, H. Lee
Wegzeit von Talort Hinteröd bis Atelier SH 7 h.

Atelier Stephan Huber mit Wohnhütte
2008

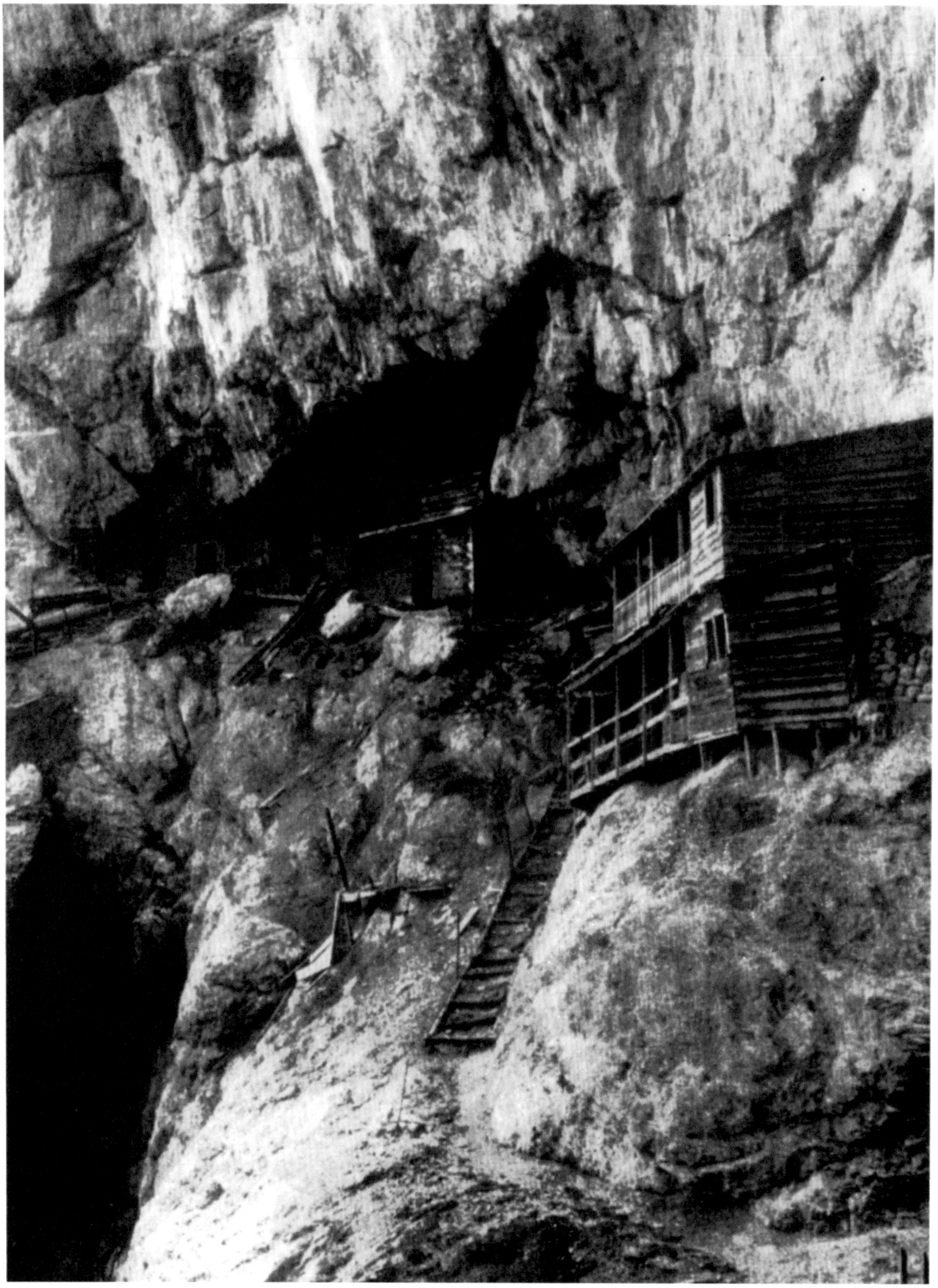

Atelier Stephan Huber mit Wohnhütte
1998 – 2007
Ostwand Seelenkopf (gesperrtes Gebiet)
Links: Schlafraum / Bibliothek Rechts: Atelier / Lager
entdeckt 7.5.2007, erfolglose Verteidigung, aufgegeben 8.5.2007
Flucht über Macondoplateau nach Sforzinda

Das skulpturale Gipfeltreffen
The Sculptural Summit

Stephan Berg

Mit den Bergen greift Stephan Huber ein Motiv auf, dem in der Bildenden Kunst und der Literatur im Grunde erst seit dem 18. Jahrhundert eine wichtige Bedeutung zukommt. Über viele Jahrhunderte wurden Berge dagegen nicht als ästhetische Erscheinungen wahrgenommen, sondern allein als menschenfeindlicher Gegensatz zur bewohnbaren, zivilisierten Welt. Aufgrund ihrer Unzugänglichkeit, ihrer zum Himmel strebenden Vertikalität galten sie seit der Antike als legitimer Sitz der Götter. Und die bis weit ins 16. Jahrhundert reichende Hemmung der Menschen, die Welt von oben zu betrachten, hatte genau darin ihren Ursprung: In einer göttlichen Sphäre hat der Mensch nichts zu suchen. Die Beschreibung von Hannibals Überquerung der Alpen in einem Schneesturm durch den römischen Geschichtsschreiber Titus Livius, die William Turner im 19. Jahrhundert zu einem eindrucksvollen Bild verdichtete, verfestigt über lange Zeit die Vorstellung des Gebirges, und insbesondere der Alpen, als *locus horribilis*. Eine entsprechend marginale Rolle spielen Berge lange Zeit in der Kunst. Wenn überhaupt, bilden sie, wie in der Sieneser Malerei des 13. Jahrhunderts, nicht lokalisierbare Hintergründe für Altarbilder.

Als ältestes Landschaftsbild, das einen präzise benennbaren Berg zeigt, darf der *Genfer Altar* von Konrad Witz aus dem Jahre 1444 gelten, der neben dem Genfer See im Hintergrund den Mont Blanc zeigt, gefolgt von Albrecht Dürers Alpenaquarellen (1494/95). Wichtige Impulse für eine künstlerische Auseinandersetzung mit dem Berg liefert auch Leonardo da Vincis *Traktat von der Malerei* (1517) mit seinen Gebirgsnotizen, welche die Gebirgsdarstellungen bis hin zur Romantik beeinflussten. Den Menschen des Mittelalters erschienen die Berge schon aufgrund der Tatsache, dass sie landwirtschaftlich nicht nutzbar waren, ausschließlich als Hindernis zwischen den Städten, die miteinander nur schlecht verbunden waren. Dem horizontalen Prinzip der Erschließung der Welt stellte ihre Vertikalität eine fundamentale Barriere entgegen, die zunächst mit Sinn gefüllt werden musste, bevor man die Berge als ein Ziel begreifen konnte. In seiner

Stephan Huber has taken up a motif – mountains – that has only acquired importance in the fine arts and in literature since the eighteenth century. For hundreds of years, mountains were not perceived as aesthetic phenomena, but only as an inhospitable counterpart to the habitable, civilised world. On account of their inaccessibility and the way their forms strove vertically heavenwards, they have been regarded since antiquity as the legitimate seat of the gods. The reluctance of humans to observe the world from above, which lasted well into the sixteenth century, was rooted in precisely this: the human has no business intruding into the divine sphere. Livy, the Roman historian Titus Livius, wrote an account of Hannibal crossing the Alps in a snowstorm which consolidated the idea of mountains – and the Alps in particular – as a *locus horribilis* across the centuries, inspiring William Turner to a striking painting in the nineteenth century. Consequently, mountains have long played only a marginal role in the arts. If they do appear, as in the Sienese paintings of the thirteenth century, than merely as the non-specific background for altar pictures.

The oldest landscape painting showing a precisely nameable mountain is the *Geneva Altarpiece* by Konrad Witz from 1444, which shows Mont Blanc in the background next to Lake Geneva. It was followed chronologically by Albrecht Dürer's *Alpine Watercolours* (1494/95). Leonardo da Vinci's *Treatise on Painting* (1517), with its notes on mountains, also supplied important impulses for an artistic examination of mountains, influencing their depiction right up to the Romantic period. If only because they could not be used for agriculture, mountains appeared to people of the Middle Ages exclusively as obstacles between cities that were poorly connected to each other. The horizontal principle of opening up the world was opposed by their verticality, a fundamental barrier that first had to be filled with meaning before mountains could be understood as a destination. In his *Divine Comedy* (1321), Dante describes ascending the Mount of Purgatory together with Virgil on three April days in the year 1300 as a process of progressive purification, thus laying the basis for the connection

Göttlichen Komödie (1321) beschreibt Dante den Aufstieg auf den Läuterungsberg zusammen mit Vergil an drei Apriltagen des Jahres 1300 als Prozess einer fortschreitenden Reinigung und legt damit die Basis für eine Verknüpfung zwischen der Bergbesteigung und einem Prozess der Transzendierung des Materiellen zum Geistigen. Antipodisch mit den Höllenkreisen verknüpft, wird der Läuterungsberg so zu einem Ort der Offenbarung transzendenter Wahrheiten.

Einen entscheidenden Bedeutungswandel erfährt der Berg in Francesco Petrarcas berühmter Beschreibung seiner Besteigung des Mont Ventoux am 26. April 1336. Sein Entschluss, diesen Gipfel „lediglich aus dem Verlangen, die namhafte Höhe des Ortes kennenzulernen", zu erklimmen, begründet ein neues Verhältnis zur (Berg)Natur, das seine Erfüllung allein in der ästhetischen Wahrnehmung findet. Der Berg ist hier kein Ort, an dem sich göttliche Wahrheiten offenbaren, sondern der von einem selbstbewussten Subjekt gewählte Gegenstand für einen ästhetischen Blick, mit dem sich die umgebende Natur in eine überschaubare, genießend betrachtbare Landschaft verwandeln lässt. Damit wird dieser Bericht auch zum Zeugnis für ein neues humanistisches Weltbild, das den Menschen mit seinen eigenen Fähigkeiten in den Mittelpunkt stellt und damit einen Vorschein auf den neuen Menschen der Renaissance liefert, der sich vom mittelalterlichen Ich zu einem die Welt formenden Subjekt emanzipiert. In der Folge rücken die zunächst vorwiegend als Hintergrundkulisse eingesetzten Berge vom Quattrocento bis ins 18. Jahrhundert immer mehr in den Vordergrund und beanspruchen dort ihren Ort als autonomes Thema.

In Edmund Burkes *Philosophischen Untersuchungen über den Ursprung unserer Ideen vom Erhabenen und Schönen* (1757) wird der Berg dann zum Kulminationspunkt eines Schönheitsbegriffs, der gerade auf dessen Menschenfeindlichkeit aufbaut. Die schneeig-weißen, unbetretbaren Gipfel strahlen eine eisige Schönheit aus, deren Kraft genau darin liegt, dass sie den Menschen nicht braucht, dass sie das völlig unabhängige Walten der von Gott geschaffenen Natur verdeut-

between climbing a mountain and a process of transcending the material to reach the spiritual. Antipodally linked to the circles of hell, the Mount of Purgatory thus becomes a place of revelation of transcendent truths.

The mountain underwent a decisive change of meaning in Francesco Petrarch's famous description of his ascent of Mont Ventoux on 26 April 1336. His decision to climb this peak, 'merely out of a desire to know the notable height of the place', establishes a new relationship to (alpine) nature that finds its fulfilment solely in aesthetic perception. Here, the mountain is not a place where divine truths are revealed, but the object chosen by a self-confident subject for an aesthetic gaze, via which the surrounding nature can be transformed into a manageable landscape that can be enjoyed. In this manner, Petrarch's description also testifies to a new humanistic world view that places human beings with their own abilities at the centre, thus providing a glimpse of the new human being of the Renaissance, who emancipates themself from the medieval ego to become a subject that shapes the world. From the Quattrocento to the eighteenth century, then, mountains – initially used mainly as background scenery – increasingly moved into the foreground and claimed their place there as an autonomous subject.

In Edmund Burke's (1729–1797) *Philosophical Enquiry into the Origin of Our Ideas of the Sublime and the Beautiful* (1757), the mountain embodies the culmination of a concept of beauty that rests on its hostility to man. The snowy-white, impassable peaks radiate an icy aesthetic whose power lies precisely in the fact that it has no need of man, that it illustrates the completely independent rule of nature created by God. Caspar Wolf's (1735–1783) mountain paintings such as *The Sustenstraße against the Pass Heights* (1777) are based on the close observation of nature, with their tiny figures set against the powerful landscapes. They are a striking example of the double strategy at work in depictions of mountains of this period, celebrating on the one hand a concept of nature whose sublimity lies in its independence from man and on

licht. Caspar Wolfs auf genauer Naturbeobachtung basierende Gebirgsbilder, etwa *Die Sustenstraße gegen die Passhöhe* (1777), mit ihren winzigen Figuren vor den gewaltigen Naturszenen sind ein bestechendes Beispiel für die Doppelstrategie, die in den Bergdarstellungen dieser Zeit wirkt: Sie feiert einen Begriff von Natur, deren Erhabenheit in ihrer Unabhängigkeit vom Menschen besteht. Und sie befriedet den Schrecken, der darin liegt, zum ästhetischen und damit konsumierbaren, beherrschbaren Bild. Fundiert wird diese Haltung nicht zuletzt durch eine Fülle geschichts- und naturphilosophischer Konzepte, in denen das Gebirge die Projektionsfläche einer idealen, göttliche Prinzipien spiegelnden Ordnung bildet. So beschreibt beispielsweise Albrecht von Haller in seiner aus einem antiurbanen Impuls entstandenen Dichtung *Die Alpen* (1729) das Gebirge als Ausdruck einer arkadischen Harmonie. Immanuel Kant (1724–1804) und Friedrich Schiller (1759–1805) definieren die Erhabenheit der natürlichen Berglandschaft als Zustand der Freiheit. Zu nennen ist hier auch Jean-Jacques Rousseau mit seiner *Die neue Heliose* (1761), ebenso wie Ralph Waldo Emerson (1803–1882) und seine Verehrung der Natur als Spiegel der göttlichen Ordnung. Auch wenn heute selbst der Mount Everest zum Ziel eines Massenalpinismus geworden ist, der regelmäßig am Hillary Step für Stausituationen sorgt, und es insofern mit der Freiheit und unberührten Einsamkeit in den Bergen nicht mehr so weit her ist: Noch in jedem heute neu erschlossenen spektakulären Skigebiet mit seinen euphemistisch „Aufstiegshilfen" genannten Transportschneisen in die felsigen Flanken der Berge steckt ein letzter Rest dieser Sehnsucht nach menschenloser Erhabenheit.

Die fast schon obsessive Intensität, mit der sich Stephan Huber mit Bergen beschäftigt, hat einerseits mit ihrer oben geschilderten paradoxen, janusköpfigen Qualität zu tun, die sie zu einem ergiebigen Gegenstand für seine stets ambivalenten skulpturalen Untersuchungen macht. Andererseits spiegelt sich darin auch ganz direkt die Herkunft des Künstlers aus dem Allgäu. Der

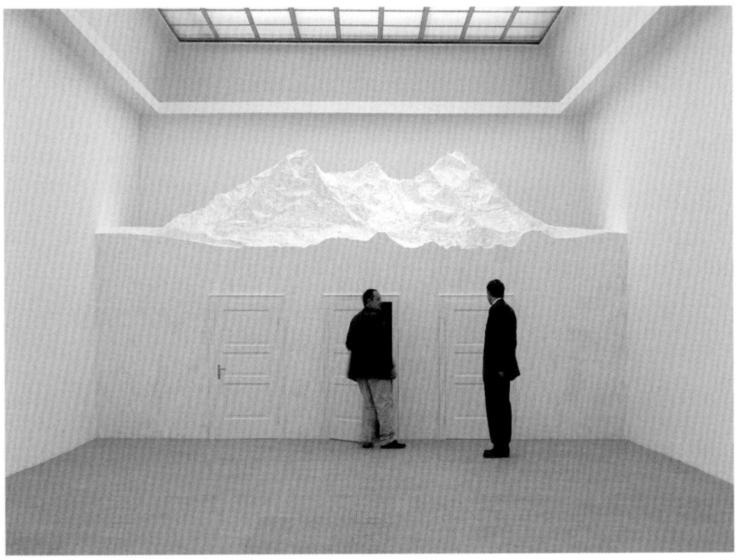

Stephan Huber und Stephan Berg vor *Saussures Herz* im Kunstverein Hannover
Stephan Huber and Stephan Berg in front of *Saussures Herz* in the Kunstverein Hannover

the other pacifying the immanent terror into an aesthetic, and thus consumable, controllable image. This attitude is founded not least in a wealth of historical and natural philosophical concepts in which mountains supply the projection surface for an ideal order reflecting divine principles. Thus Albrecht von Haller (1708–1777), for example, describes mountains as the expression of arcadian harmony in his anti-urban poem *The Alps* (1729). Immanuel Kant (1724–1804) and Friedrich Schiller (1759–1805) define the sublimity of the natural mountain landscape as a state of freedom. Jean-Jacques Rousseau (1712–1778) and his *The New Heloise* (1761) should also be mentioned in this context, along with Ralph Waldo Emerson (1803–1882) and his veneration of nature as a mirror of divine order. Nowadays, even Mount Everest has become the destination of mass mountaineering tourism, regularly causing queues at the Hillary Step, so that the freedom and untouched solitude of the mountains might seem within easier reach than ever: in every newly developed spectacular ski resort today, with its euphemistically named 'ascent aids' consisting of transport lifts penetrating the rocky flanks of the mountains, there is a last remnant of this longing for solitary sublimity.

The almost obsessive intensity with which Stephan Huber approaches mountains is linked on the one hand with the paradoxical, Janus-faced quality described above, making them a rich subject for his invariably ambivalent sculptural investigations. And on the other, it also directly reflects the artist's origins in the Allgäu region. The ever-present background of the snowy peaks there, 'their sublime grandeur', which at the same time restricts the view, combined with the sensual Catholicism of Bavaria and the Baroque aesthetics of

dort stets präsente Hintergrund der Schneegipfel, „ihre erhabene Größe, die zugleich den Blick beengt, verbunden mit dem sinnenfrohen Katholizismus Bayerns und der barocken Kulissenästhetik seines zweiten Lebensortes München, bilden gewissermaßen den „Wurzelgrund", aus dem sich dieses Lebenswerk speist. Dabei können die Berge, auf die sich Stephan Huber bezieht, sowohl fiktiv sein – beispielsweise der Berg aus Steven Spielbergs *Close Encounters of the Third Kind* (1977) –, wie auch präzise Nachbildungen realer Berggipfel. Allerdings bezieht sich die Präzision, die der Künstler dabei anstrebt, eher auf das Idealbild des jeweiligen Berges als auf seine topografische Wirklichkeit. Die aus Dentalgips geformten Gipfel sind entsprechend immer so angelegt, dass sie eine perfekte Schauseite bieten und damit ihren Status als bildhafte Idealisierungskulissen unterstreichen. Der Modellcharakter dieser aus Rigipssockeln herauswachsenden, wohnzimmertauglichen Bergskulpturen macht sie zu den beherrschbaren ästhetischen Konstrukten, die wiederum das Ergebnis einer über Jahrhunderte entwickelten kulturellen und touristischen Praxis sind.

Beispielhaft zeigt sich die Huber-typische Verschränkung aus biografischem Regionalismus, suggestiver Überwältigungsästhetik, bühnenhafter Konstruktion und ironischer Distanzierung an seiner 1997 für die Neue Messe in München entstandenen Arbeit *Gran Paradiso*, die auf einem riesigen Regalsystem die wichtigsten Alpengipfel als strahlend weiße Modelle vor der bei Föhn sichtbaren wirklichen Kette der Alpen und in einer gigantischen Vitrine die wichtigsten Alpenflüsse als Neonkarte präsentiert. Gleich in doppelter Hinsicht spielt Huber hier mit Größe und Maßstab der verhandelten Elemente: Die in Wirklichkeit eher kleinen Regale und Vitrinen erscheinen monströs übersteigert, während die real gewaltigen Berge und Flüsse zur überschaubaren Regalware werden. Analog zum Standort bei der Neuen Messe wird zur Ware auch das, was als realer Bestandteil unserer Landschaft eigentlich nicht handelbar ist. Andererseits folgt Huber damit exakt den Vernutzungsstrategien heutigen Konsumdenkens, in dem die Föhnkulisse der

the backdrop of his second home, Munich, form, as it were, the 'root bedrock that nourishes his life's work. The mountains Stephan Huber refers to can be fictitious – for example, the mountain from Steven Spielberg's *Close Encounters of the Third Kind* (1977) – as well as exact replicas of real mountain peaks. The precision the artist strives for, however, refers more to the ideal image of the mountain in question than to its topographical reality. Accordingly, the peaks moulded from dental stone are always designed to offer a perfect view from one angle, thereby underlining their status as backdrops for idealised images. The model character of these living-room-size mountain sculptures, emerging from plasterboard bases, makes them the controllable aesthetic constructs that are in turn the result of a cultural and touristic practice developed over centuries.

Huber's typical interweaving of biographical regionalism, suggestive overpowering aesthetics, stage-like construction and ironic distancing is exemplified by his 1997 work *Gran Paradiso* for the Neue Messe fairground in Munich. It displays the most important Alpine peaks on a huge shelf system, as gleaming white models in front of the real chain of the Alps visible when the *föhn,* the hot southerly wind from the Alps, is blowing, as well as the most important Alpine rivers like neon maps in a gigantic showcase. Huber plays with the size and scale of the negotiated elements in two respects: The shelves and showcases, which in reality are usually quite small, appear monstrously exaggerated, while the mountains and rivers, which in reality are enormous, become manageable shelf goods. Analogous to its location at the new fairground, what is a real component of our landscape and actually not tradable thus becomes merchandise. On the other hand, Huber follows precisely the strategies of modern consumerism, in which the *föhn* scenery of the Alps is seen primarily as an image-promoting – and thus sales-promoting – argument for the location of the new Munich trade fair. The blending of real and model-like mountain peaks, possible under the influence of the *föhn,* also strikingly

Alpen vor allem als ein image- und damit verkaufsförderndes Argument für den Handelsstandort der Münchner Messe gesehen wird. Die bei Föhn mögliche Verblendung aus realen und modellhaften Berggipfeln zeigt darüber hinaus eindrücklich, wie sehr wir die Realität längst schon vor allem in seiner Form als modellhaftes Bild genießen. In gewisser Weise entspricht so eine Postkarte vom Matterhorn viel eher unserer Erwartung von der Wirklichkeit dieses Berges als seine Realität, schon deswegen, weil sich dieser Berg nur selten in der verdichteten Prägnanz zeigt, die das Foto bietet. Die überschaubare Größe dieser Replikatgipfel zitiert ebenso eine verlorene Erhabenheit wie das strahlende Weiß der Bergimitate, welches das eisige Weiß zerklüfteter Gletscherfelder nur aufruft, um es zugleich wieder ein Stück weit zu dementieren.

Hubers Bergskulpturen sind in diesem Sinn stets Modelle eines Bildes der Natur, die selbst nur als Konstruktion erlebbar ist. Erhabenheit, so signalisiert der Künstler, verkörpert die Idee einer Absolutheit, die im Bild nur als „als ob“, als ironisches Zitat Wirklichkeit werden kann. Mit seinem skulpturalen Gipfeltreffen gelingt Huber eine fulminante Balance zwischen barocker Lust an Überwältigung und Entzauberung. Die Berge sind gleichzeitig Referenz auf die regionale biografische Herkunft des Künstlers und damit Reflexion künstlerischer Verortung, scheinbare bruchlose mimetische Vergegenwärtigung, autonome Skulptur und deren Kritik, und nicht zuletzt Illusionismus und dessen gleichzeitige Dekonstruktion. In ihnen atmet einerseits die Idee des Berges als Ideal- und unkritisierbare Urskulptur, die andererseits allein schon durch die Nüchternheit, mit der das Bergmassiv umstandslos in einem weißen Rigipssockel endet, wieder von jedem möglichen Pathos befreit wird. Die Nonchalance dieser Verbindung aus Werk und Podest täuscht auf den ersten Blick über den fundamentalen Effekt hinweg, der damit verbunden ist: Gewissermaßen löst Huber das jahrhundertealte Sockelproblem, indem er Berg und Sockel als untrennbare Einheit inszeniert. Dass jeder dieser Sockelberge und Bergsockel durch unter ihnen angebrachten

demonstrates how much we have long enjoyed reality principally in its form as a model-like image. In some respects, a postcard of the Matterhorn corresponds much more to our expectations of the reality of this mountain than to its actual appearance, if only because this mountain rarely displays itself in the condensed conciseness that the photograph offers. The manageable size of these replicate peaks cites a lost sublimity just as much as the radiant white of the mountain imitations, which invokes the icy whiteness of jagged glacier fields, only to partially deny it again at the same time.

Huber's mountain sculptures are in this sense always models of an image of nature, which itself can only be experienced as a construction. Sublimity, the artist signals, embodies the idea of an absoluteness that can only become reality in an image as an 'as if', as an ironic quotation. With his sculptural summit, Huber achieves a brilliant balance between the Baroque pleasure in overpowering and an act of disillusionment. The mountains are simultaneously a reference to the artist's regional biographical origins and thus a reflection of artistic localisation, a seemingly unbroken mimetic realisation, an autonomous sculpture, and its critique, and, not least, illusionism and at the same time, its deconstruction. The idea of the mountain as an ideal and primordial sculpture that is beyond criticism breathes in them, yet at the same time it is freed from any possible pathos by the very sobriety with which the mountain massif terminates abruptly in a white plasterboard base. At first glance, the nonchalance of this combination of work and pedestal belies the fundamental effect it has: in a sense, Huber solves the centuries-old pedestal problem by staging mountain and pedestal as an inseparable unit. The fact that each of these pedestal-mountains and mountain-pedestals is also movable, by means of rollers mounted underneath, is another nice ironic twist with which the artist declares the mountain – the epitome of the statically immovable – to be a mobile, always available 'negotiating mass', but without completely depriving it of its inner monumentality.

Rollen auch noch beweglich wird, ist eine weitere schöne ironische Volte, mit der der Künstler den Berg als Inbegriff des statisch Unverrückbaren einerseits zur mobilen, stets verfügbaren „Verhandlungsmasse“ deklariert, ohne ihm dabei aber andererseits seine innere Monumentalität völlig zu entziehen.

Diese Form der Brechung des Absoluten, der Relativierung des Reinen, findet sich durchgehend in Hubers Werk. Strukturell spiegelt sich darin immer auch der Kampf des Künstlers gegen das Fantasma einer autonomen Kunst mit ihren um sich selbst kreisenden Absolutheitsansprüchen. Stattdessen arbeitet Huber offensiv mit dem gesamten Potenzial, das die minimalgeprägte Zeit der 1970er-Jahre als Sündenfall empfand: Erzählung, Bühnenhaftigkeit, Illusion, Allegorie, Metapher, Symbol, Übertreibung, Emphase, Pathos und Psychoanalyse. So entsteht ein eigensinniges, strikt antiformalistisches Programm, das durchaus surreale Momente kennt und darüber hinaus das offene Paradox liebt, also diesen Zustand, in dem etwas zugleich als möglich und unmöglich erscheint, in dem alles, was sich zeigt, zur Kippfigur zwischen einem Noch-Nicht und Nicht-Mehr wird. Je komplexer die einzelnen Werkelemente dabei besetzt sind, umso größere ästhetische Kraft gewinnen sie für den Künstler. Immer gilt: Erst als paradoxe Bedeutungszwitter werden die einzelnen Werke gültig.

Auch die vierteilige Fotofolge *Shining* (2001) ordnet sich in diese Ambivalenzstrategie ein. Zu sehen ist das modifizierte Modell des Elternhauses des Künstlers, das auf einer riesigen Eisscholle inmitten bizarrer Eisberge schwimmt, deren Ausdehnung im wabernden Eisnebel verschwimmt. Das Haus in der Eiswüste ist ein deutlicher Verweis auf das völlig eingeschneite und dadurch von der Außenwelt abgeschnittene Overlook-Hotel in Stanley Kubricks Film *Shining* (1980). Allein schon durch die Verwendung des Filmtitels erscheint das heimelig wirkende Haus nicht als Fluchtalternative zu der menschenfeindlichen, eisigen Umgebungsatmosphäre, sondern

This form of refraction of the absolute, the relativisation of the pure, can be found throughout Huber's work. Structurally, it always reflects the artist's struggle against the phantasm of an autonomous art, with its claims to absoluteness that revolve around itself. Instead, Huber works offensively with the entire potential of what the Minimalist 1970s regarded as abhorrent: narrative, stagecraft, illusion, allegory, metaphor, symbol, exaggeration, emphasis, pathos, and psychoanalysis. The result is an obstinate, strictly anti-formalist programme that certainly has surreal moments and, moreover, loves the open paradox, that is, the state in which something appears to be possible and impossible at the same time, in which everything that appears becomes a tipping point between not-yet and no-more. The more complex the individual elements of the work are, the greater aesthetic power they acquire for the artist. For him, it is always the case that the individual works only become valid as paradoxical hermaphrodites of meaning.

The four-part photo series *Shining* (2001) likewise fits into this strategy of ambivalence. It depicts the modified model of the house of the artist's parents, floating on a huge ice floe amidst bizarre icebergs whose expanse blurs in the billowing ice fog. The house in the ice desert is a clear reference to the Overlook Hotel in Stanley Kubrick's film *The Shining* (1980), which is completely snowed in and thus cut off from the outside world. Through the use of the film title alone, the cosy-looking house does not seem an alternative escape to the hostile, icy surrounding atmosphere, but rather as a trap. The protection it seems to offer will probably not be forthcoming in reality. It is less an image of a longing for a cold memory that can no longer be revitalised, than a modified paraphrase of the elegy of an irretrievably failed hope in Caspar David Friedrich's (1774–1840) *Sea of Ice*. It is an image for an insecurity that begins outside and is far from ending inside. And at the same time, a self-ironic deconstruction of the interpretive offering set in motion visually and allusively. In the sequence of images, the audience easily recognises the

eher als Falle. Den Schutz, den es anzubieten scheint, wird es vermutlich in Wirklichkeit nicht leisten können. Es ist weniger das Sehnsuchtsbild für eine erkaltete, nicht mehr revitalisierbare Erinnerung als eine modifizierte Paraphrase der *Eismeer*-Elegie von Caspar David Friedrich über eine endgültig gescheiterte Hoffnung. Es ist ein Bild für eine Verunsicherung, die draußen beginnt und innen noch lange nicht endet. Und dabei auch eine selbstironische Dekonstruktion des selbst visuell und anspielungsreich in Gang gesetzten Interpretationsangebots. Im Ablauf der Bildfolge erkennt das Publikum unschwer den Bühnenillusionismus des Geschehens. Bild für Bild bröckelt die Inszenierung, werden Trockeneisnebel, gipsbekleisterte Styropor-Eisberge und Haus als modellhafte Bühnenkonstruktion kenntlich, die nicht auf perfekte Täuschung zielt, sondern ihren Mehrwert gerade aus dem Moment der „Ent-Täuschung", der offensiven Vorführung des Konstruierten als Konstrukt zieht.

Was immer auch in diesem Werk passiert: Nie fügt sich der allegorische Reigen aus spektakulären und stillen, aus hochdramatischen und reduziert introvertierten Werken zur konsistent erzählbaren Geschichte. Die Störung erweist sich als wichtiger als die Kongruenz. Die zwei Hauptquellen, aus denen Huber seine begehbaren Bilder schöpft, das „Reservoir des Alltags", wie er formuliert, und das aus dem Barock gespeiste Material einer allegorischen Bildsprachlichkeit fügen sich in seinen Werken zu einer Synthese der Widersprüchlichkeit. Hubers Erzählungen vertrauen einer Bildsprache, deren metaphorischer Duktus bewusst soweit paradox aufgeladen wird, dass er genau die Grenze semantischer, psychologischer, kunsthistorischer und soziologischer Komplexität erreicht, an der er sich, ohne zu ex- oder implodieren, selbst als permanente Frage präsentiert. Die dauernde Reibung der widersprüchlichen Elemente erzeugt einen Funkenflug, in dem die Vorstellung einer „ein-fach" zu benennenden, kausal entwickelbaren Welt verbrennt, zugunsten des Leuchtens der Funken selbst.

staged illusionism of the action. Frame by frame, the staging crumbles, dry ice fog, plastered Styrofoam icebergs, and house become recognisable as a model stage construction which does not aim for perfect deception, but draws its added value precisely from the moment of 'de-deception', the offensive presentation of the constructed as a construct.

Regardless of whatever occurs in this work: Never does the allegorical round dance of the spectacular and silent, of the highly dramatic and reduced introverted works add up to a coherent story waiting to be told. Disruption proves to be more important than congruence. The two main sources from which Huber draws for his images, the 'reservoir of everyday life', as he puts it, and the material of an allegorical visual language nourished by the Baroque, combine in his works to form a synthesis of contradictions. Huber's narratives trust a pictorial language whose metaphorical ductus is deliberately charged with paradox, to the extent that it reaches precisely the limit of semantic, psychological, art-historical and sociological complexity, at which it presents itself – without ex- or imploding – as a permanent question. The constant friction of the contradictory elements creates a flight of sparks, in which the idea of a causally developable world that can be 'simply' named burns out, in favour of the glow of the sparks themselves.

4 Berge, 3 Karten
2014
Rauminstallation / Room installation
Kunstmuseum Bonn

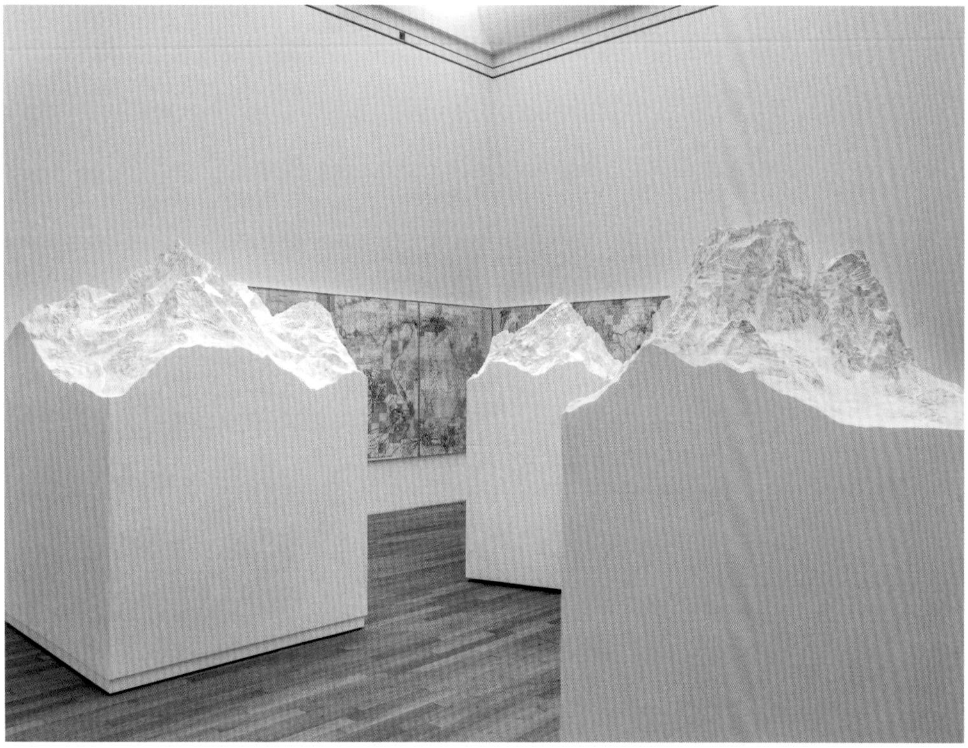

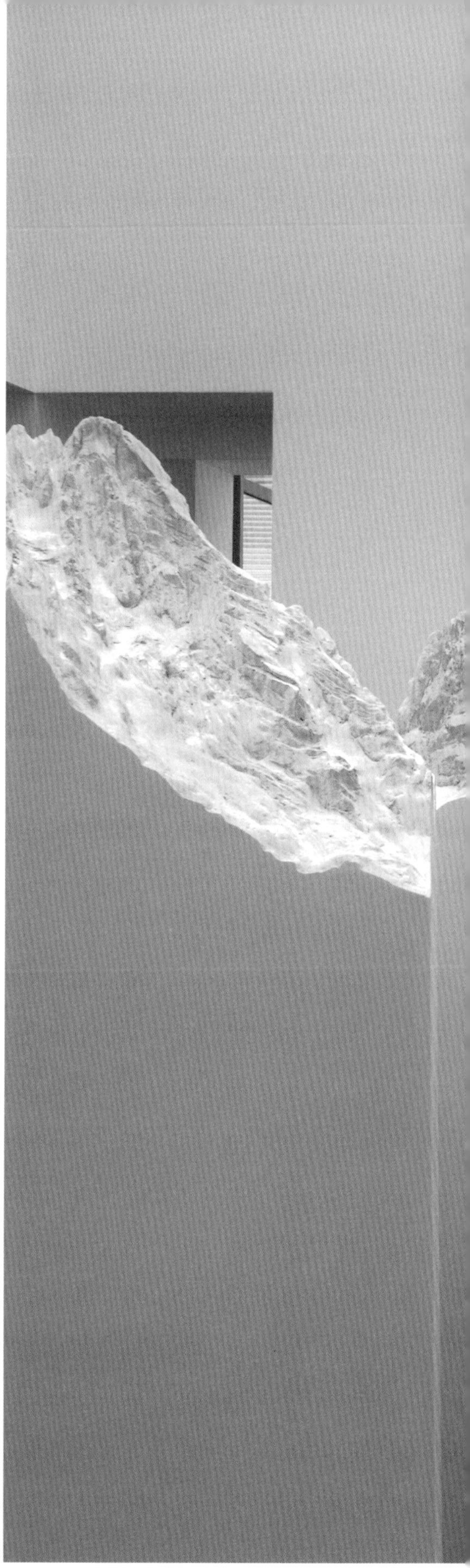

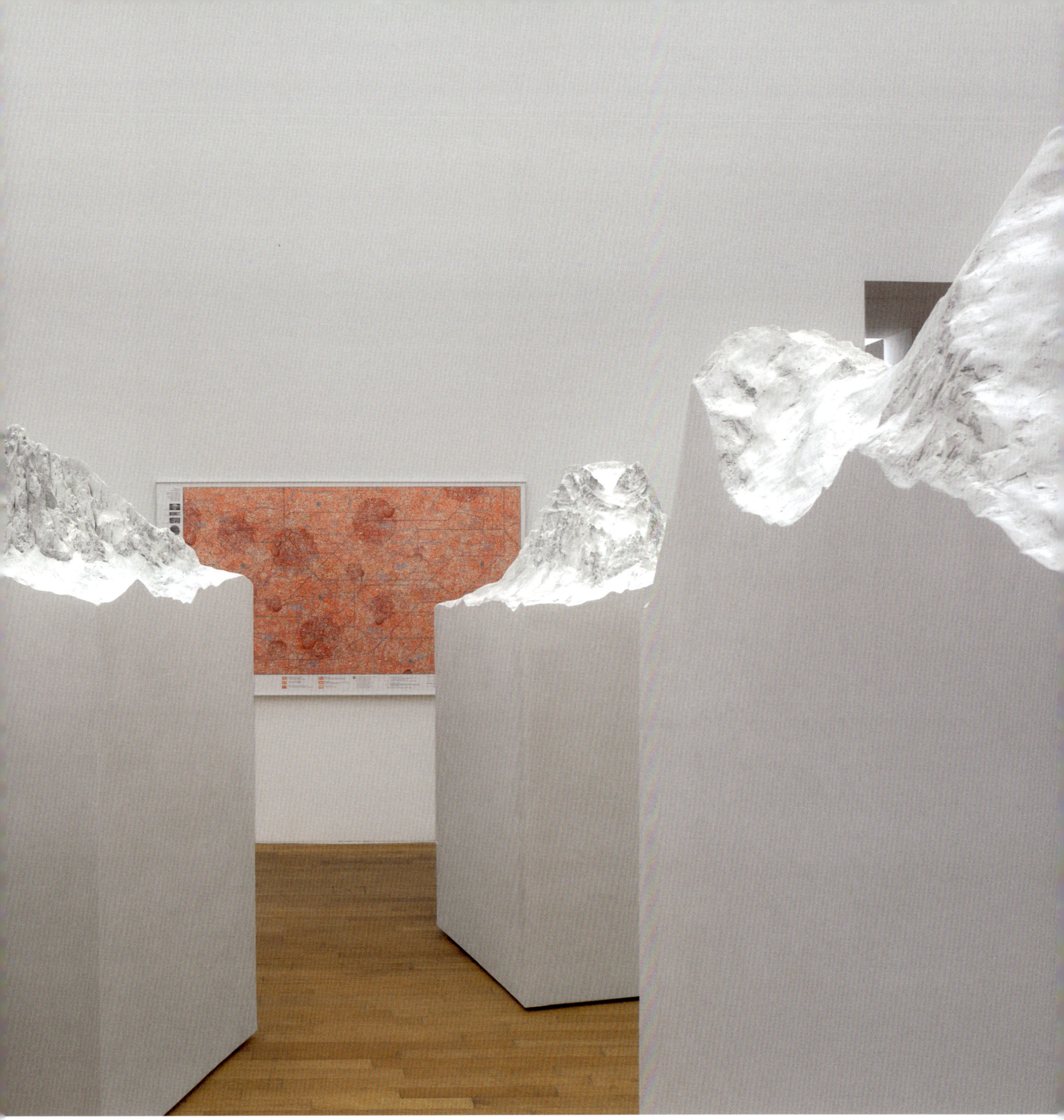

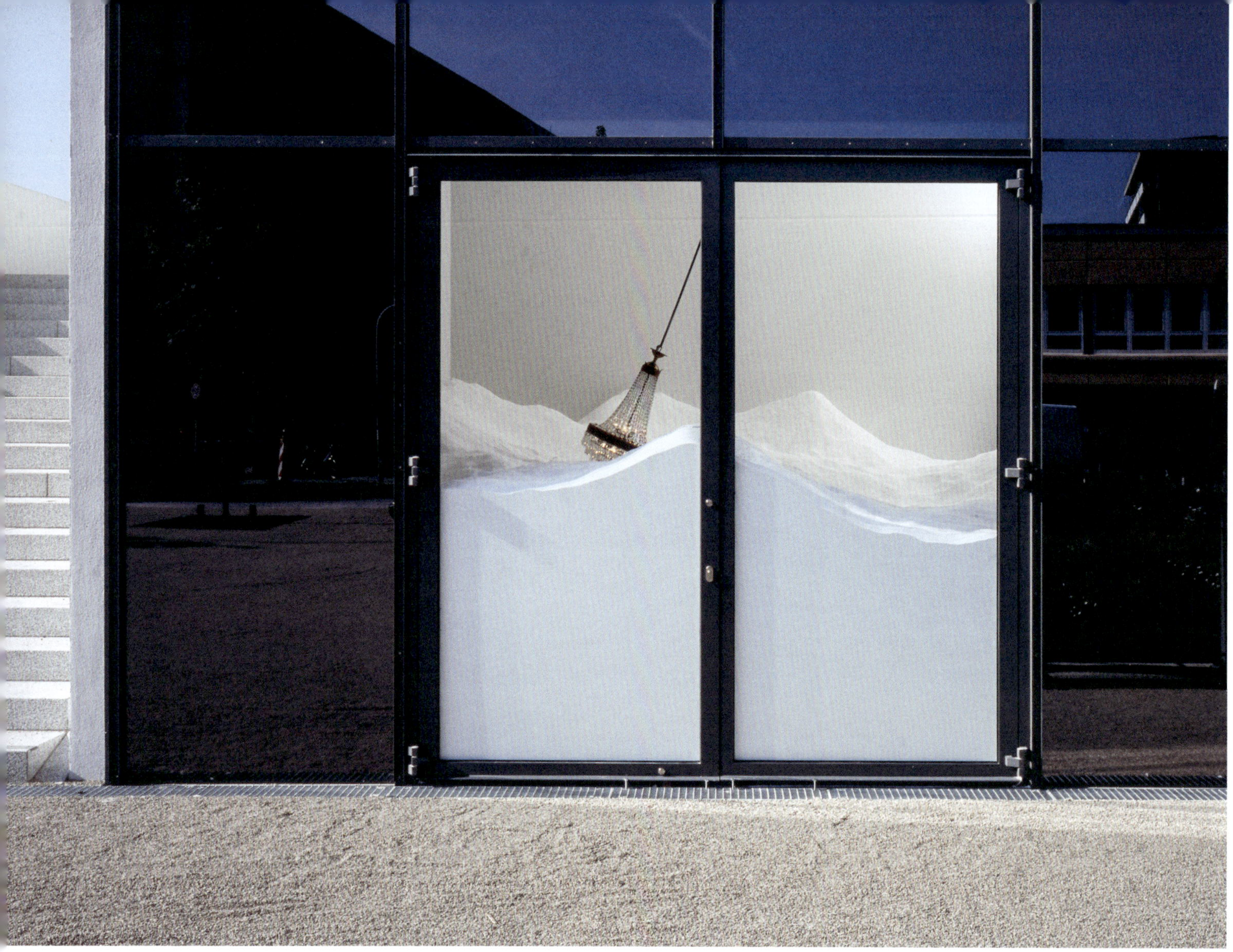

Kalte Kammer
2005
Kubus im Petuelpark,
München / Munich

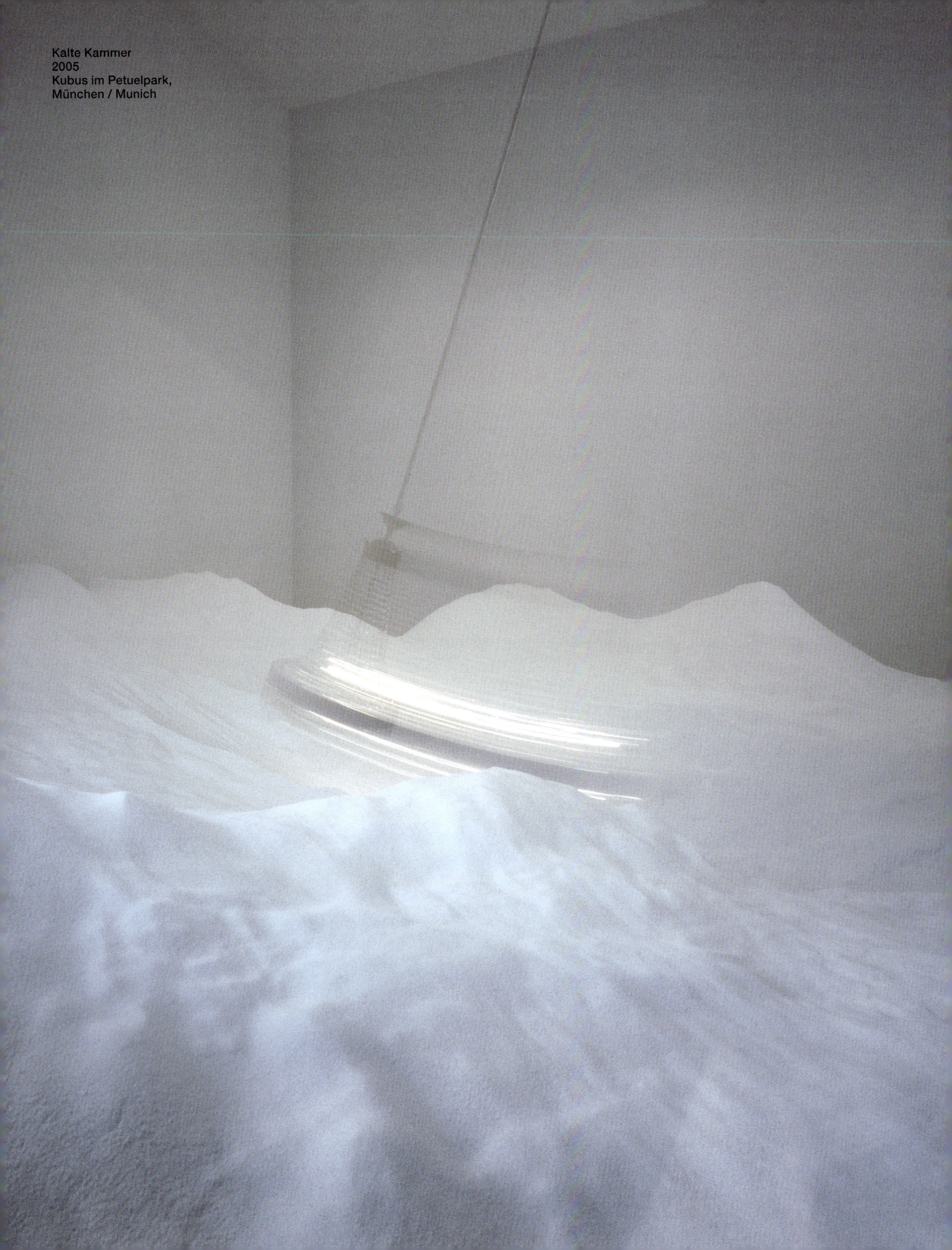

Zitronenstadel
2005

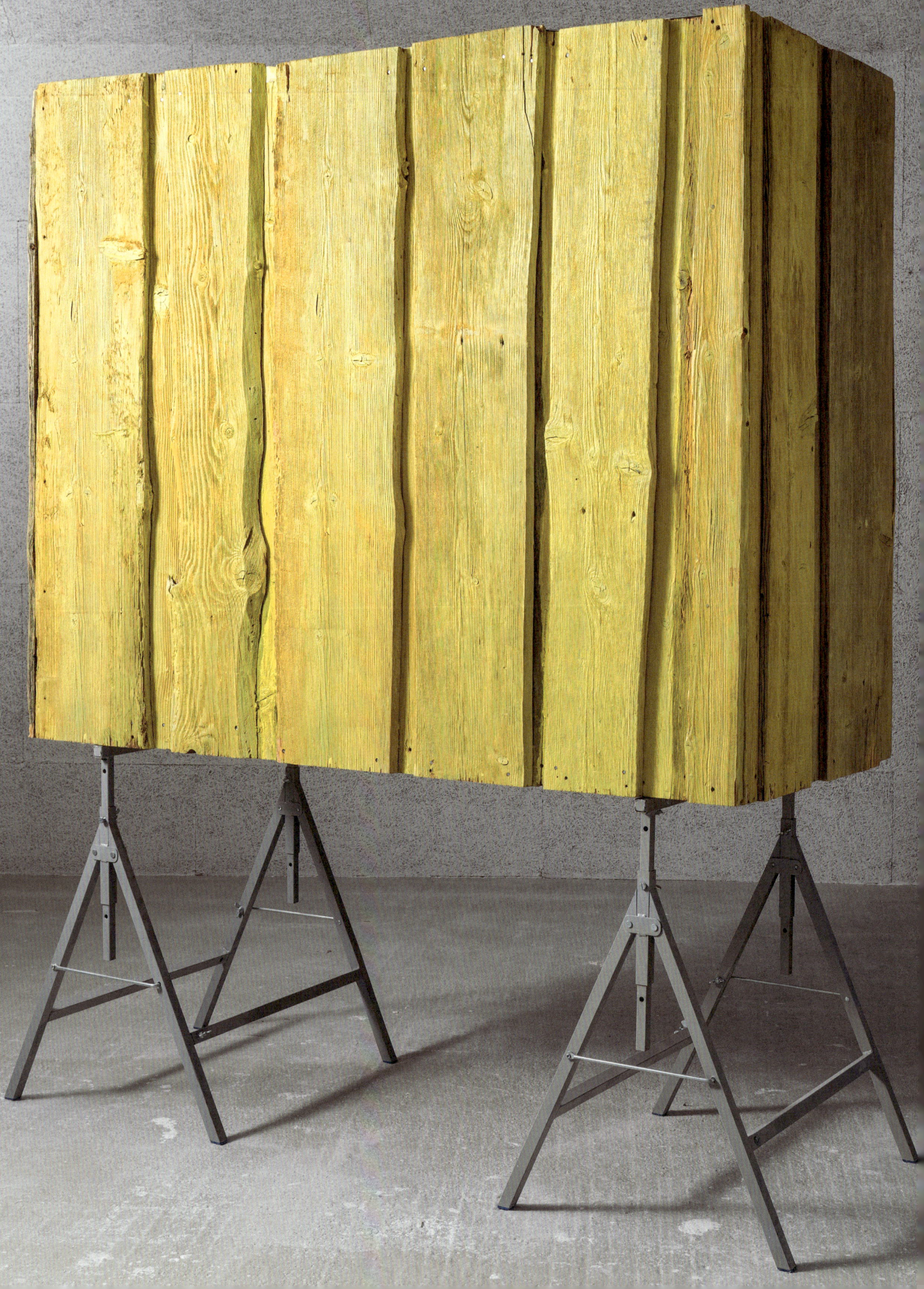

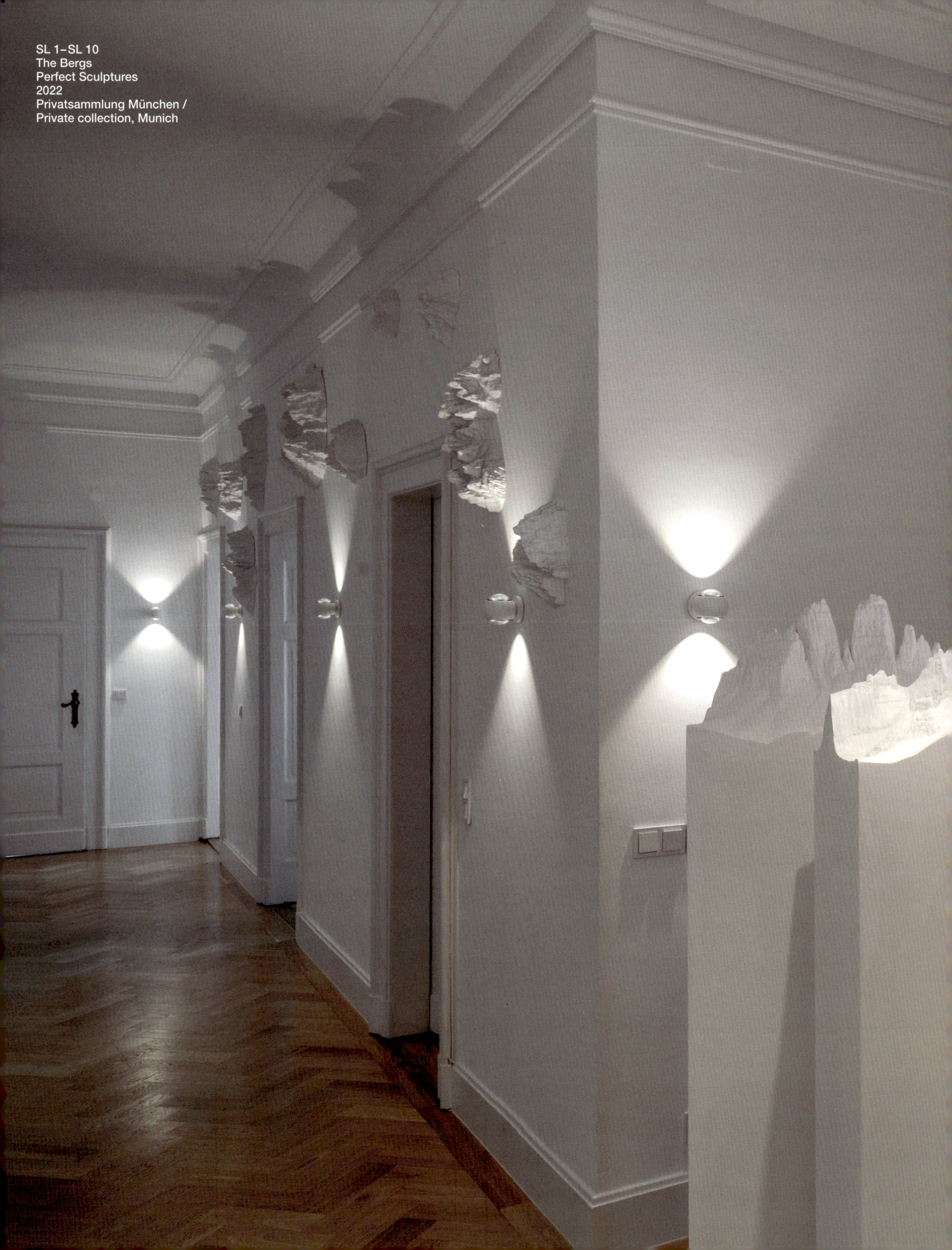

SL 1–SL 10
The Bergs
Perfect Sculptures
2022
Privatsammlung München /
Private collection, Munich

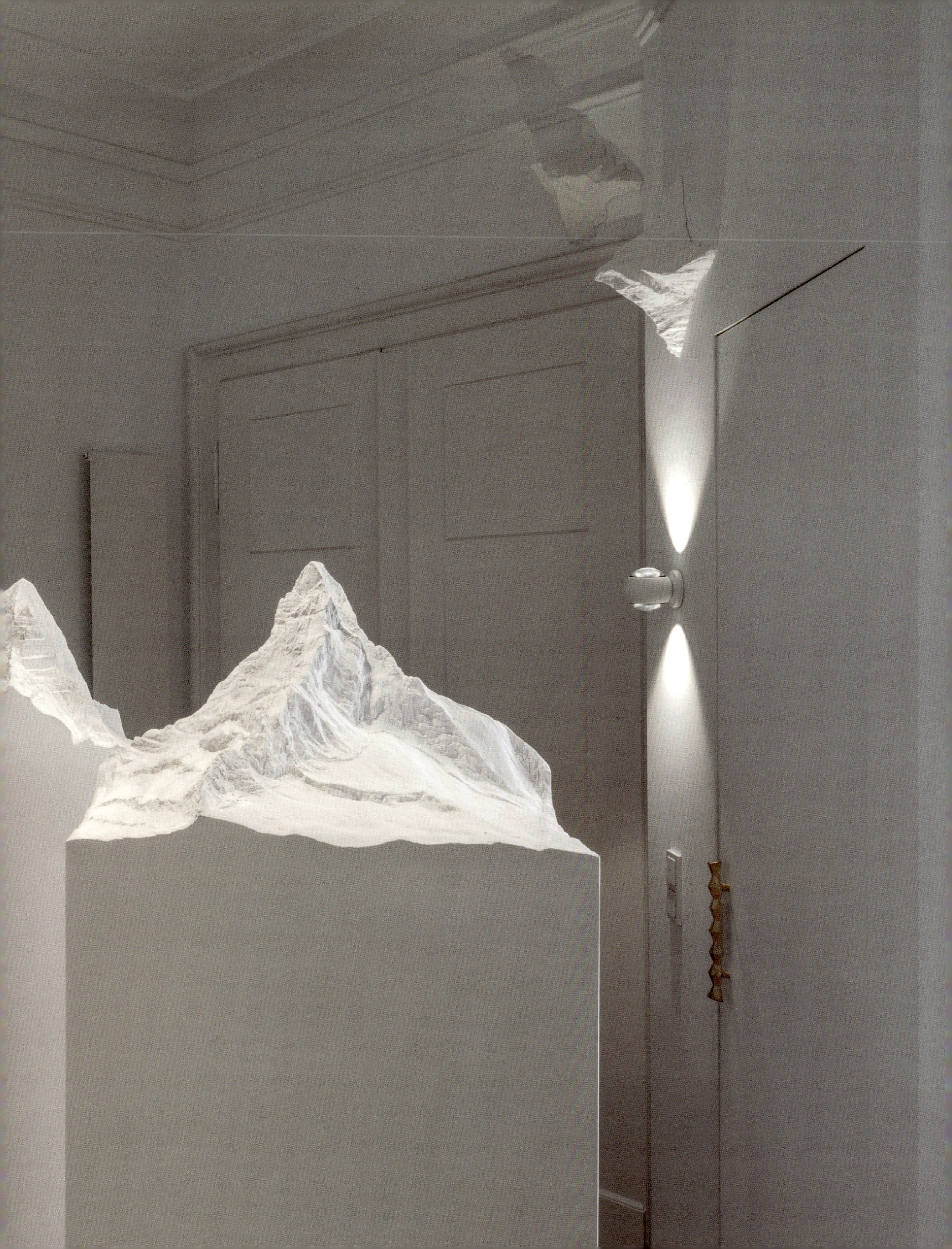

Perfect Sculptures
2014–2018

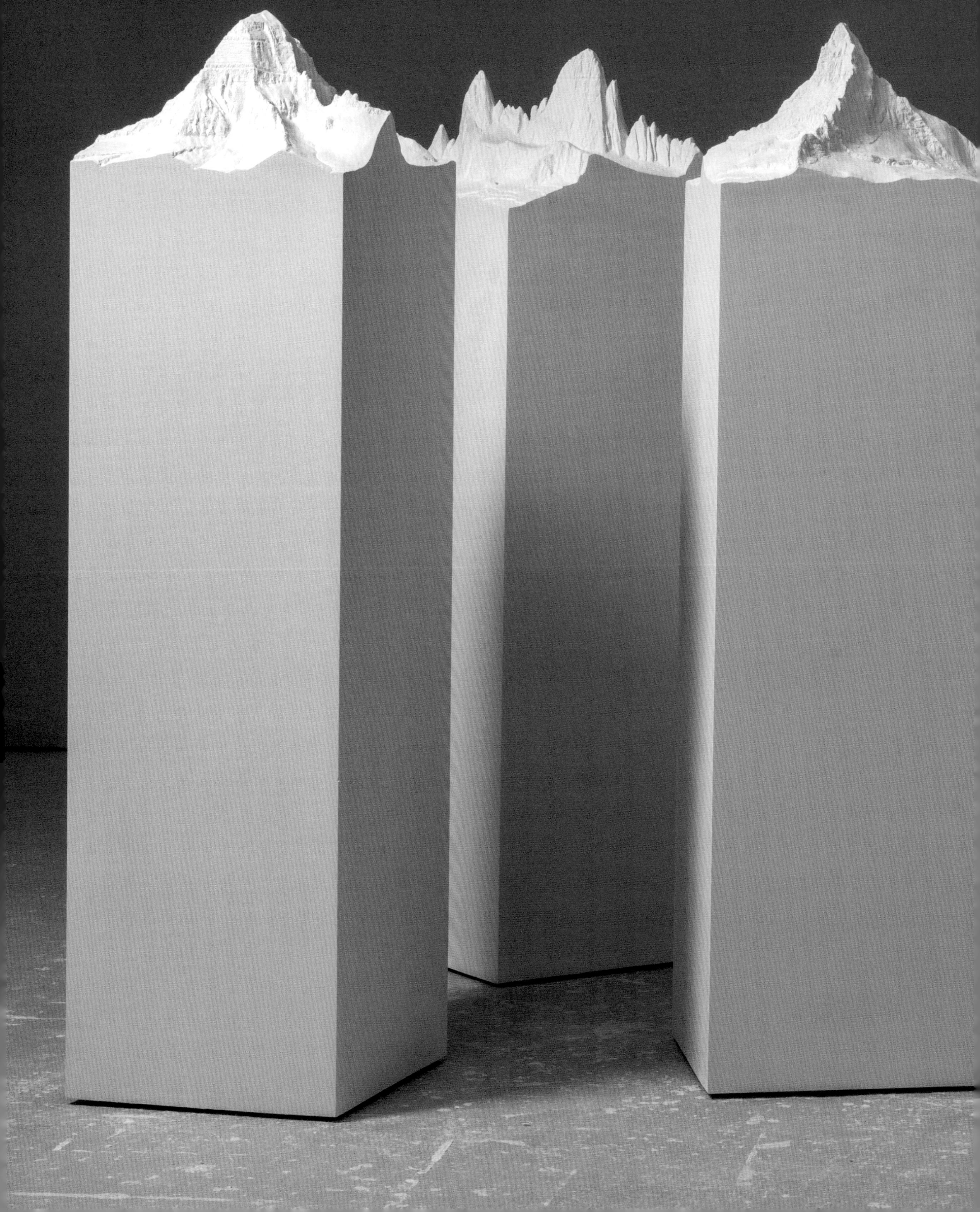

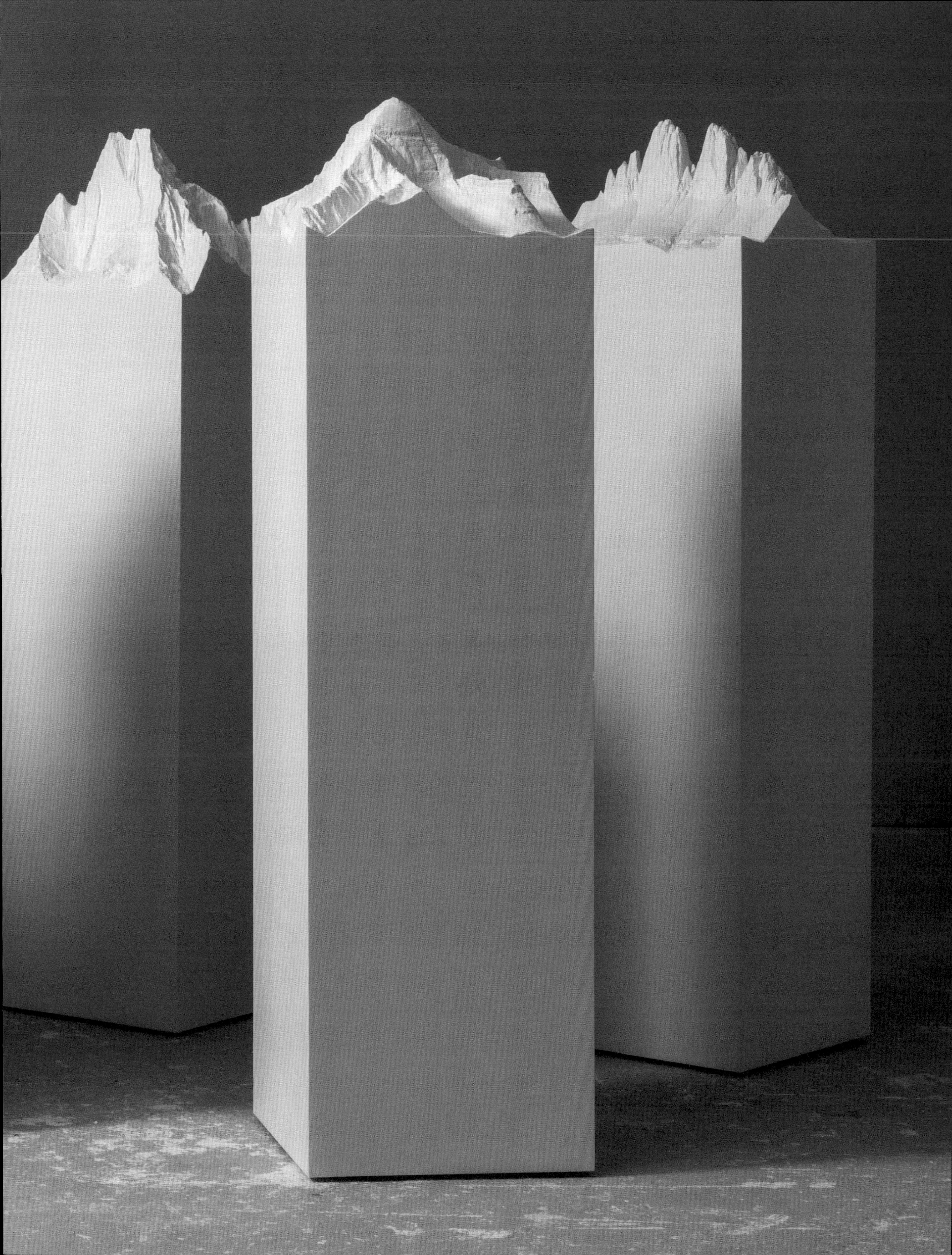

Matterpuchare, Assinash, Fitz Cime
2014/15

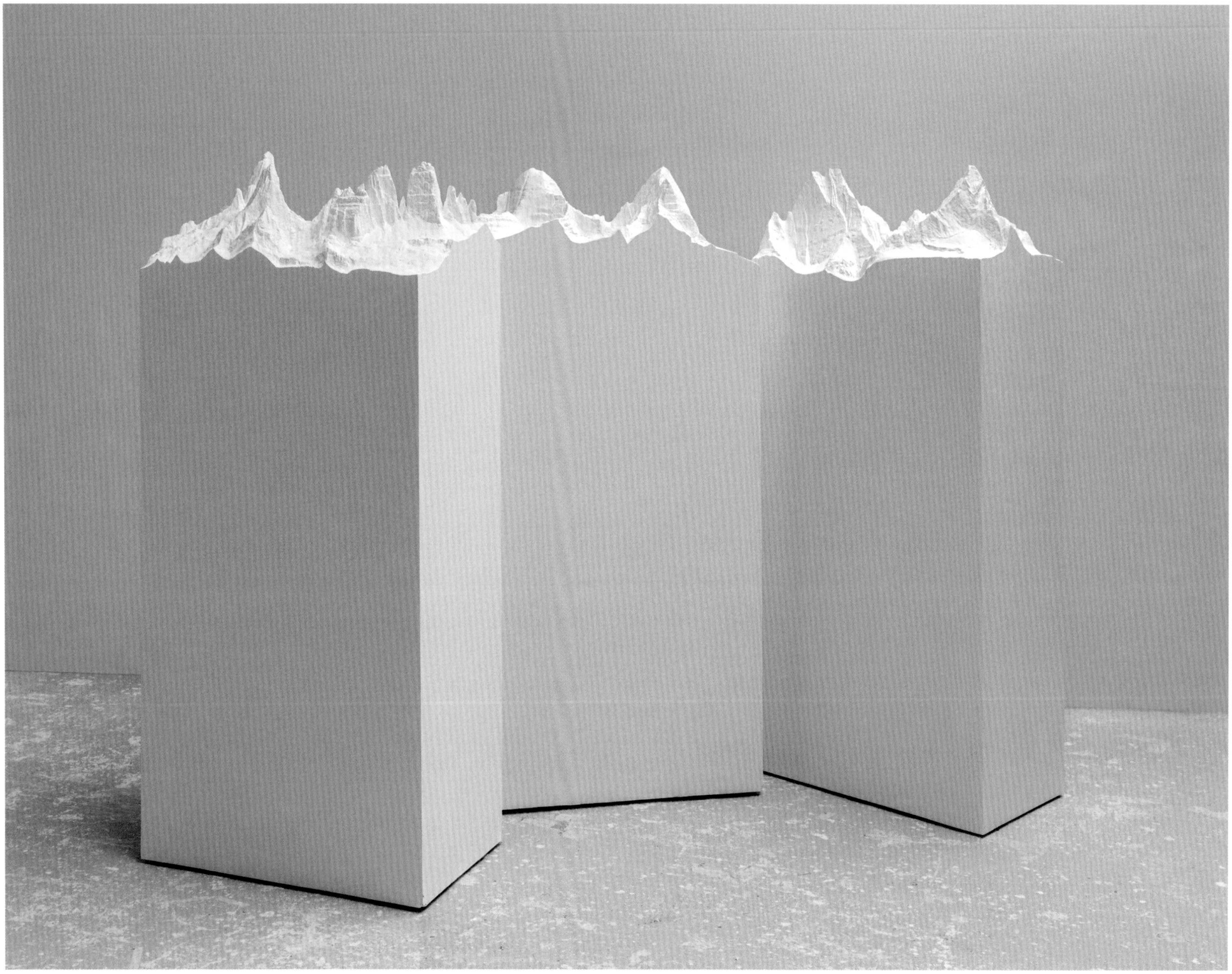

Matterpuchare
Detail
2014/15

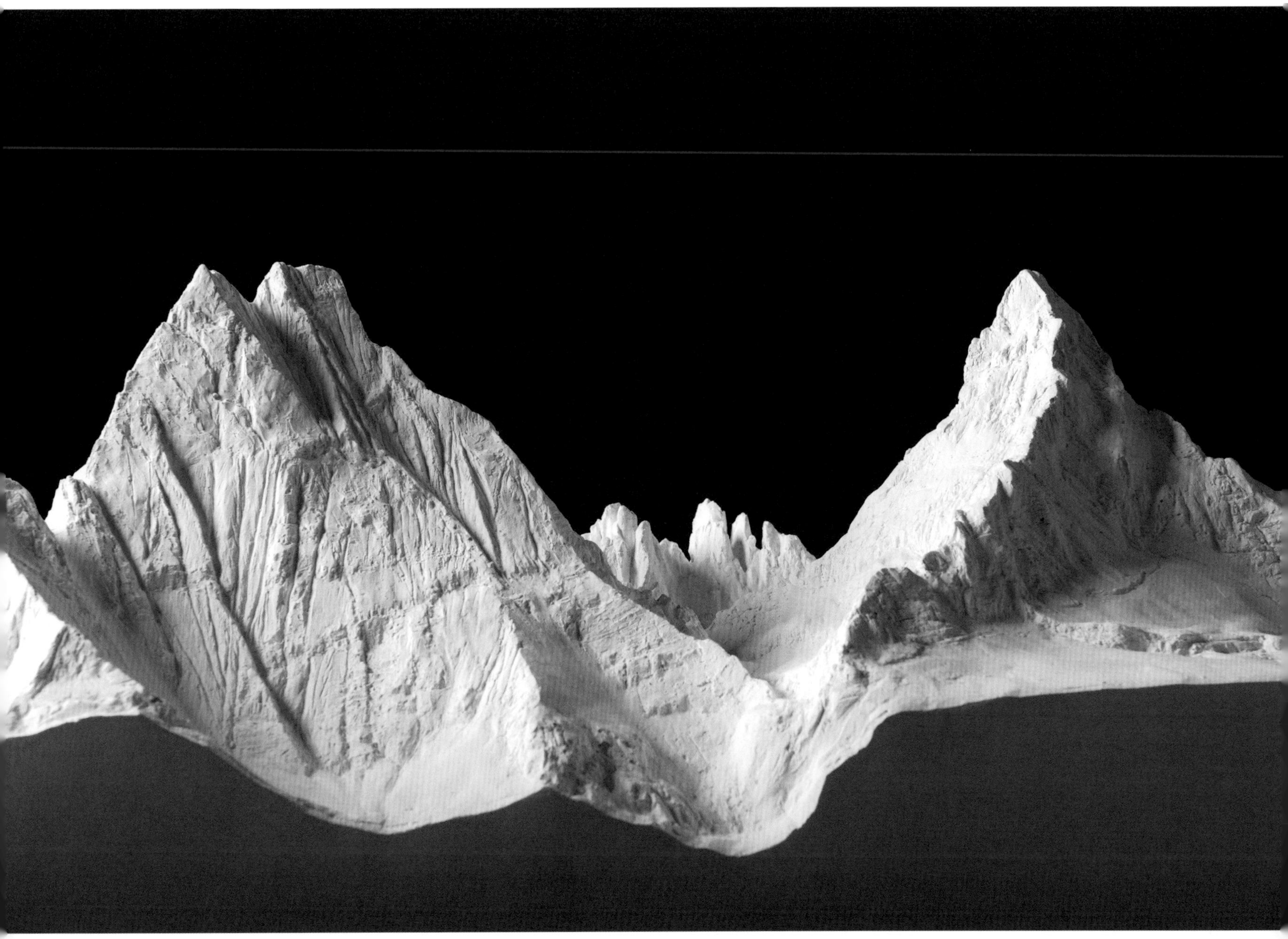

Fitz Cime
Detail
2014/15

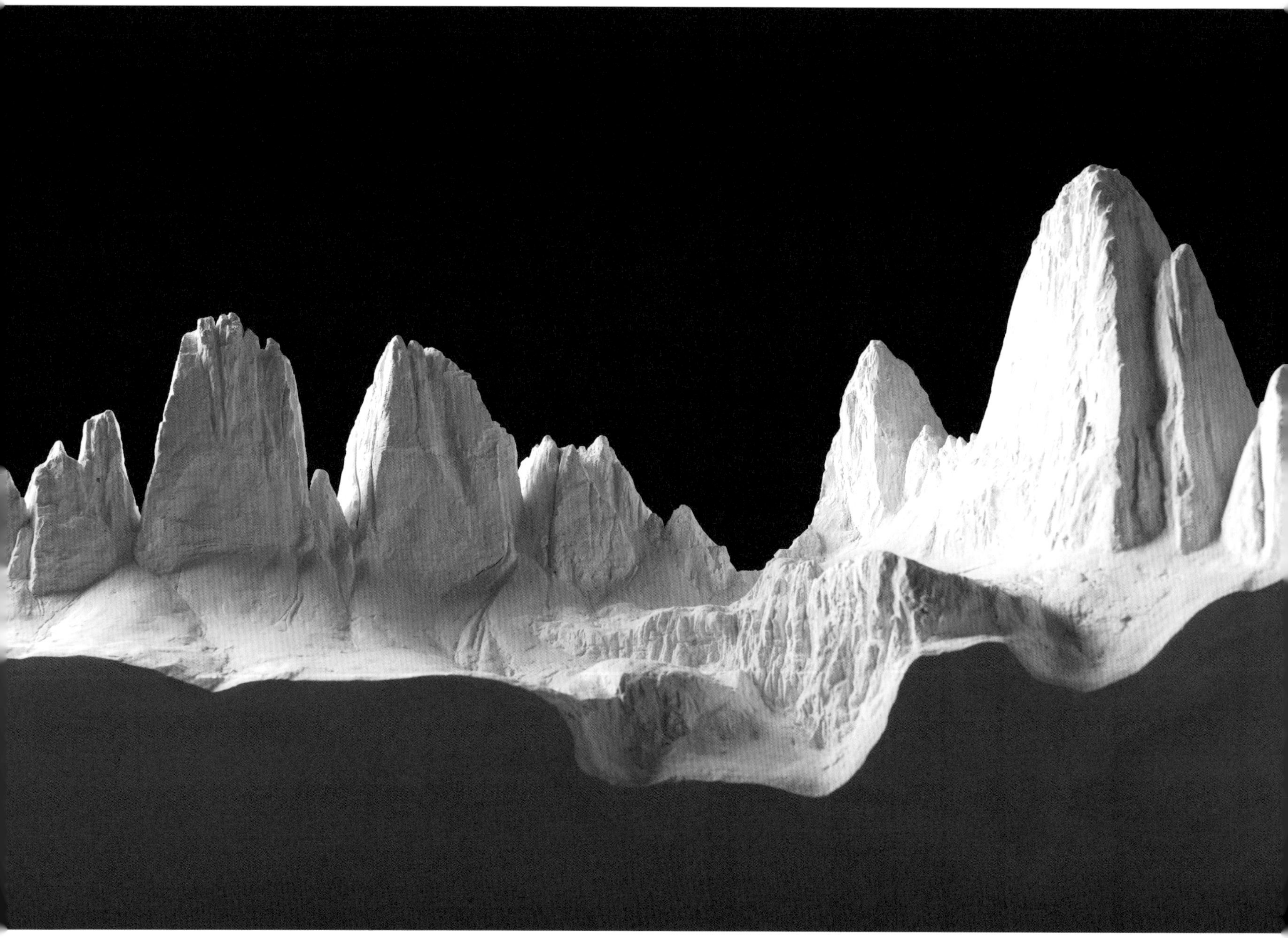

Assinash
Detail
2014/15

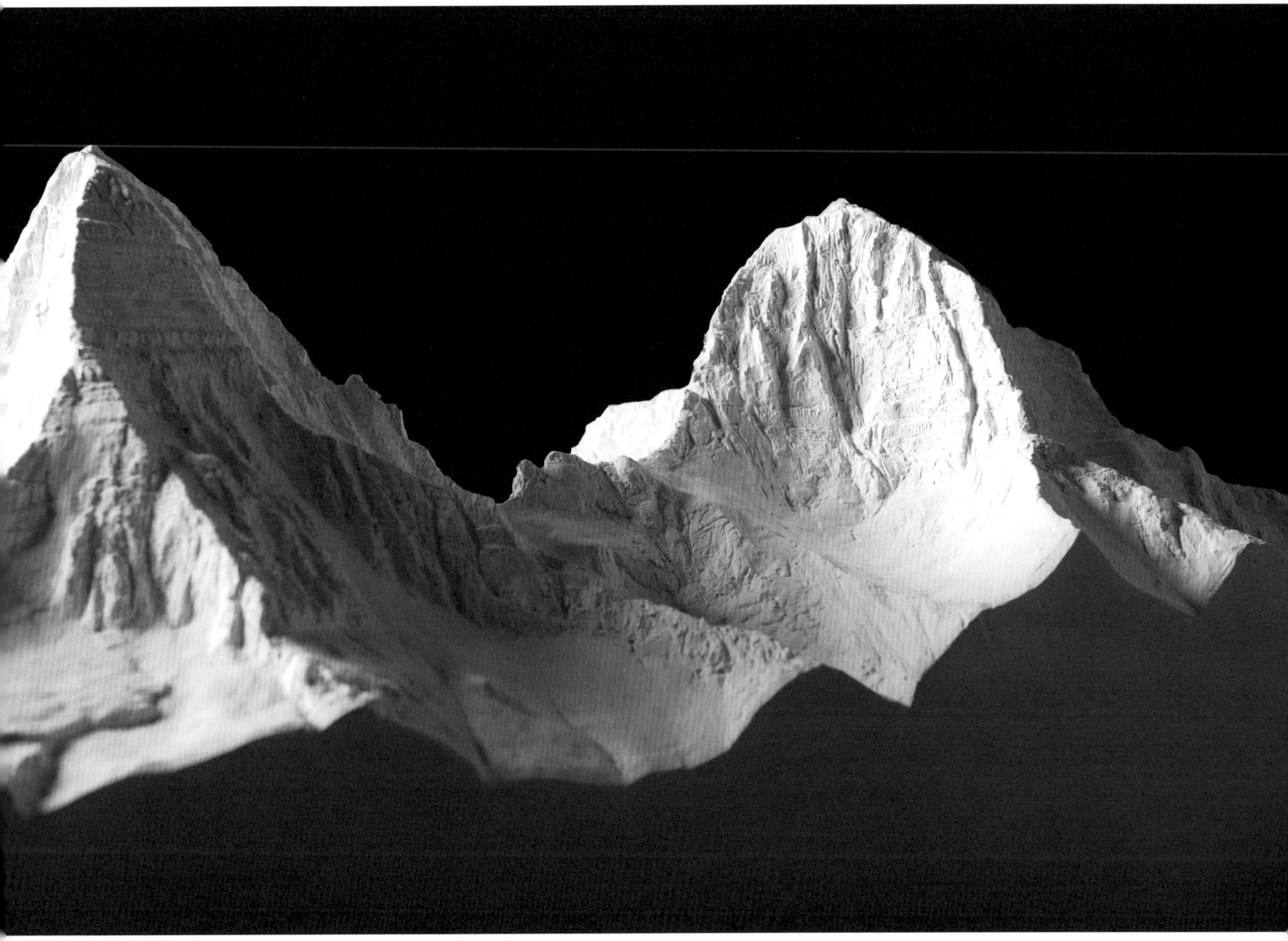

Südlich-biografisches Panorama
2016
Rauminstallation / Room installation
MMK Frankfurt

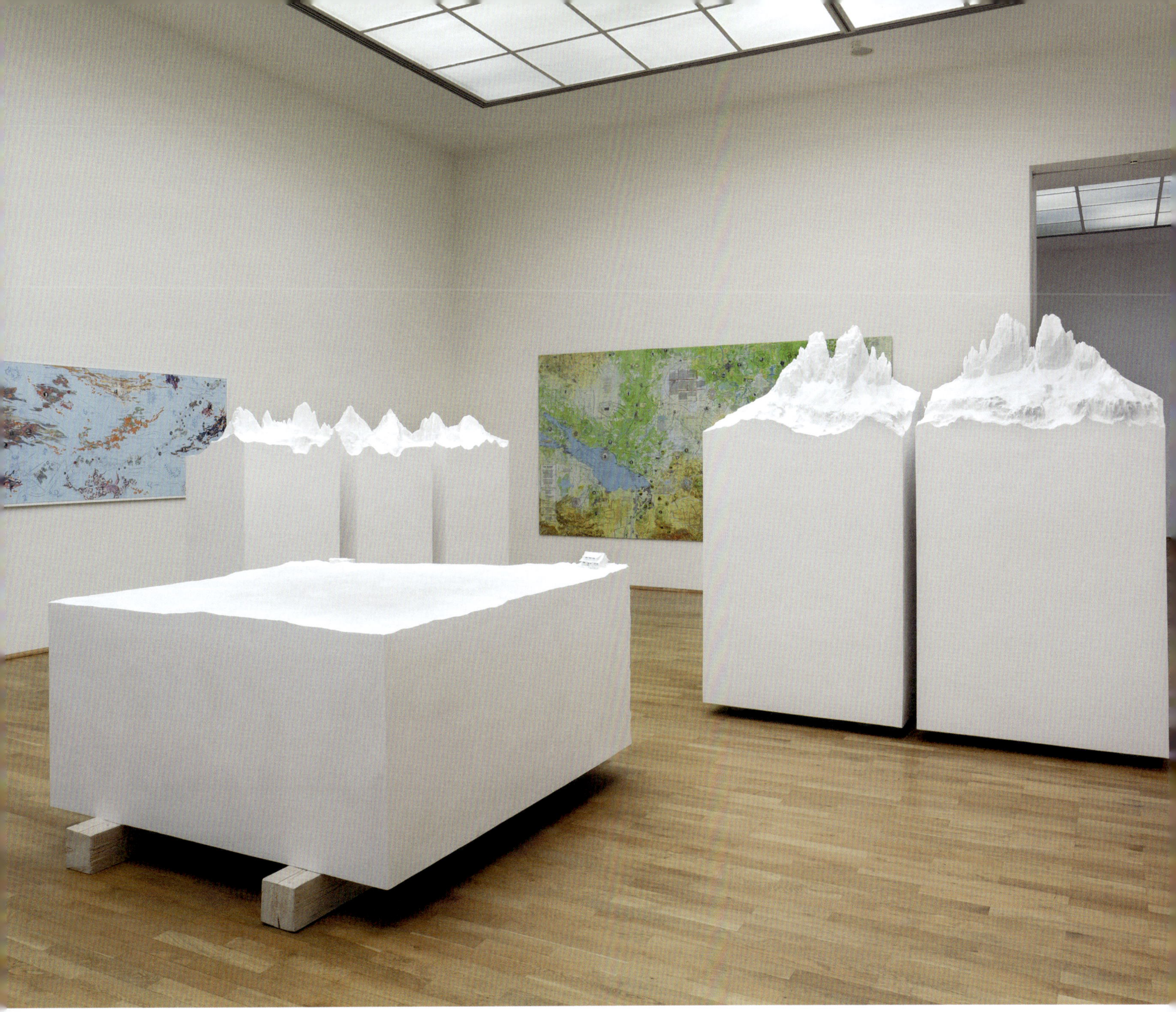

Family Affairs
2016

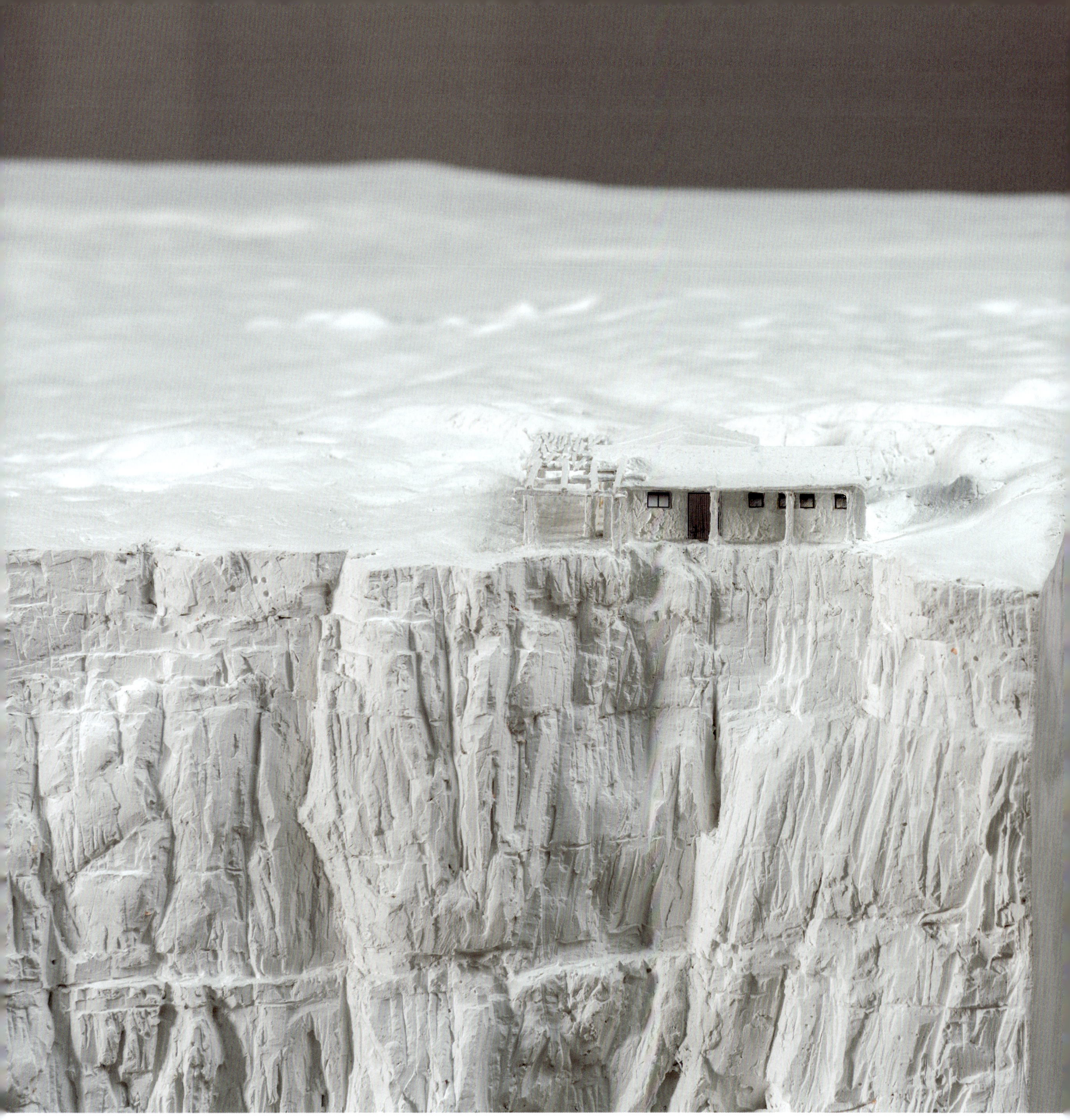

Family Affairs
2016

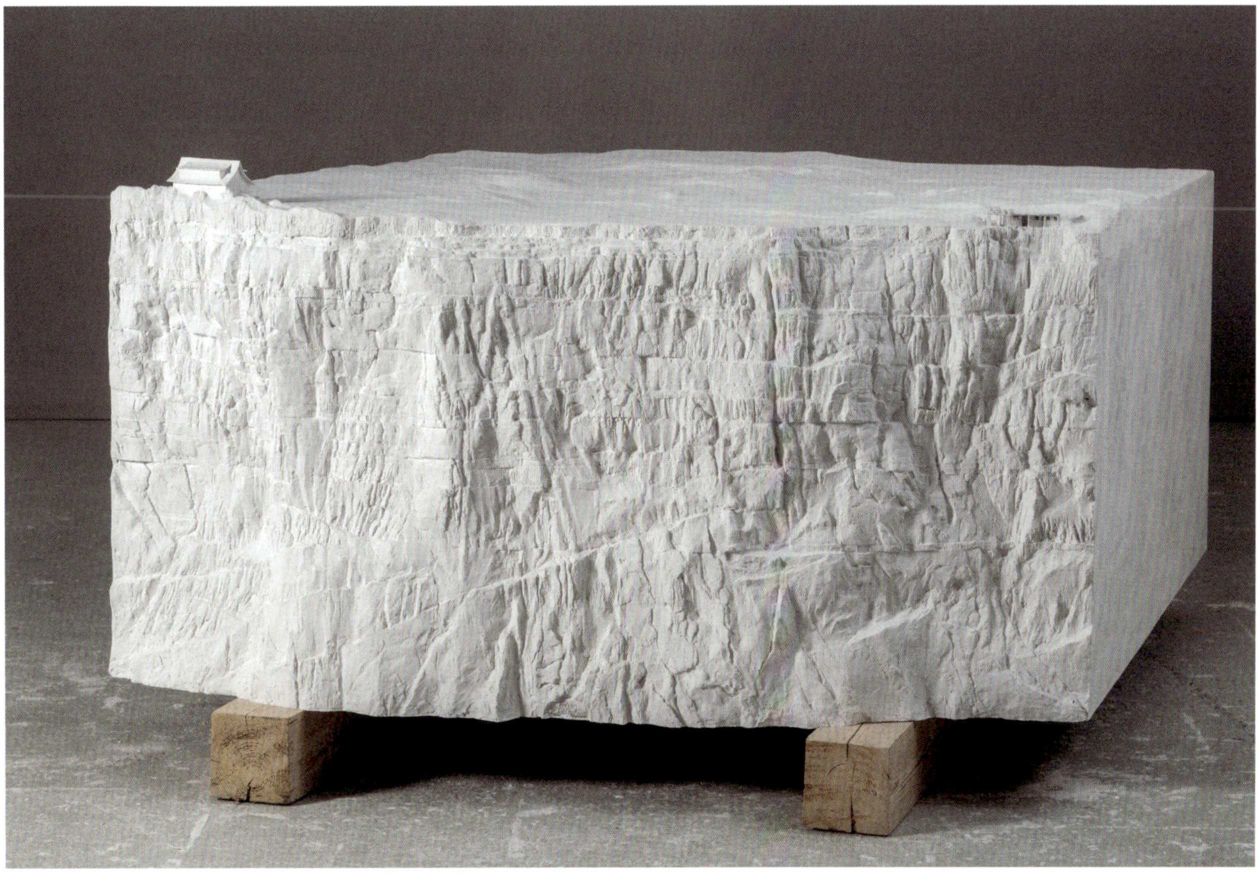

Rauminstallation
Room installation
2016
Kulturfabrik Lindenberg

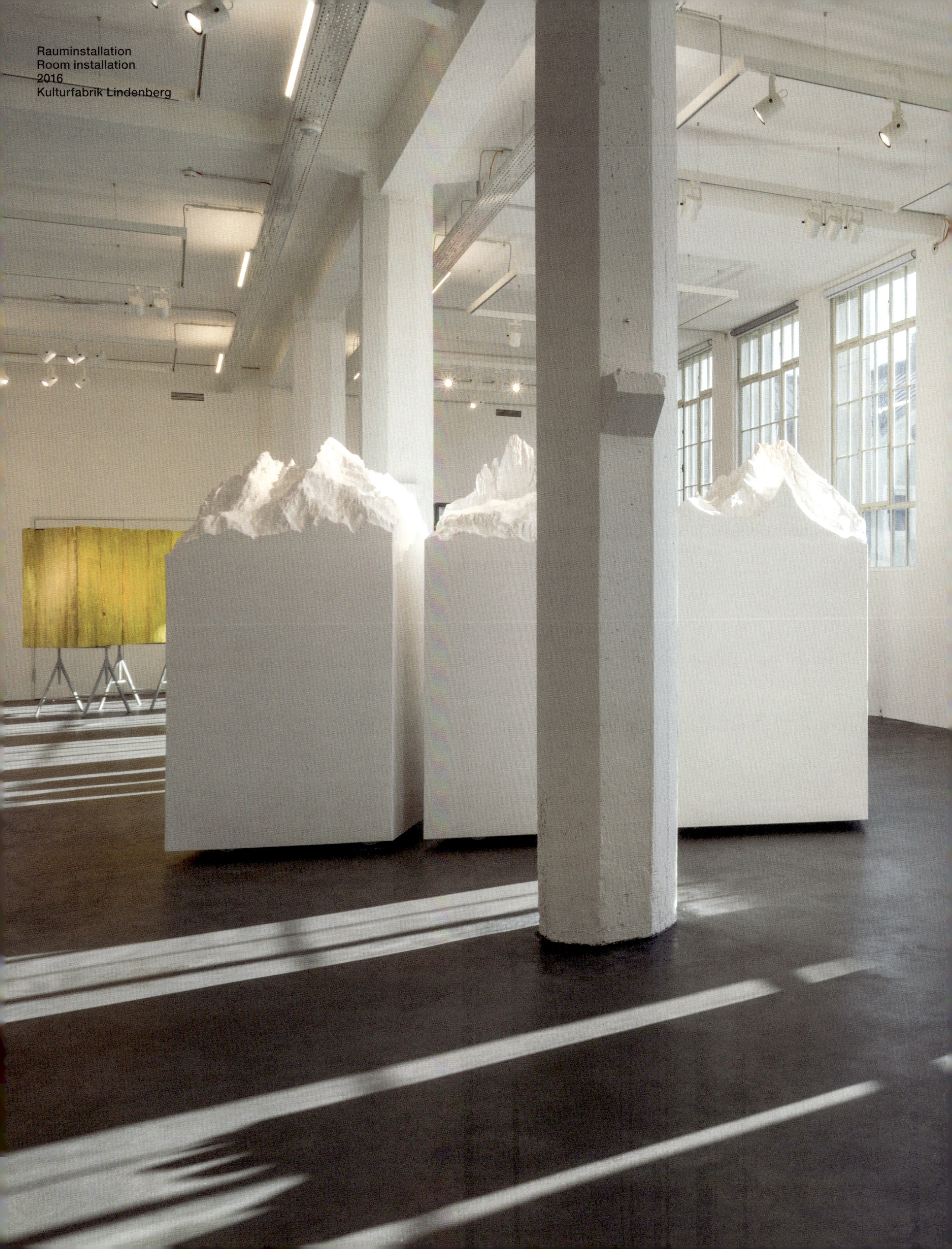

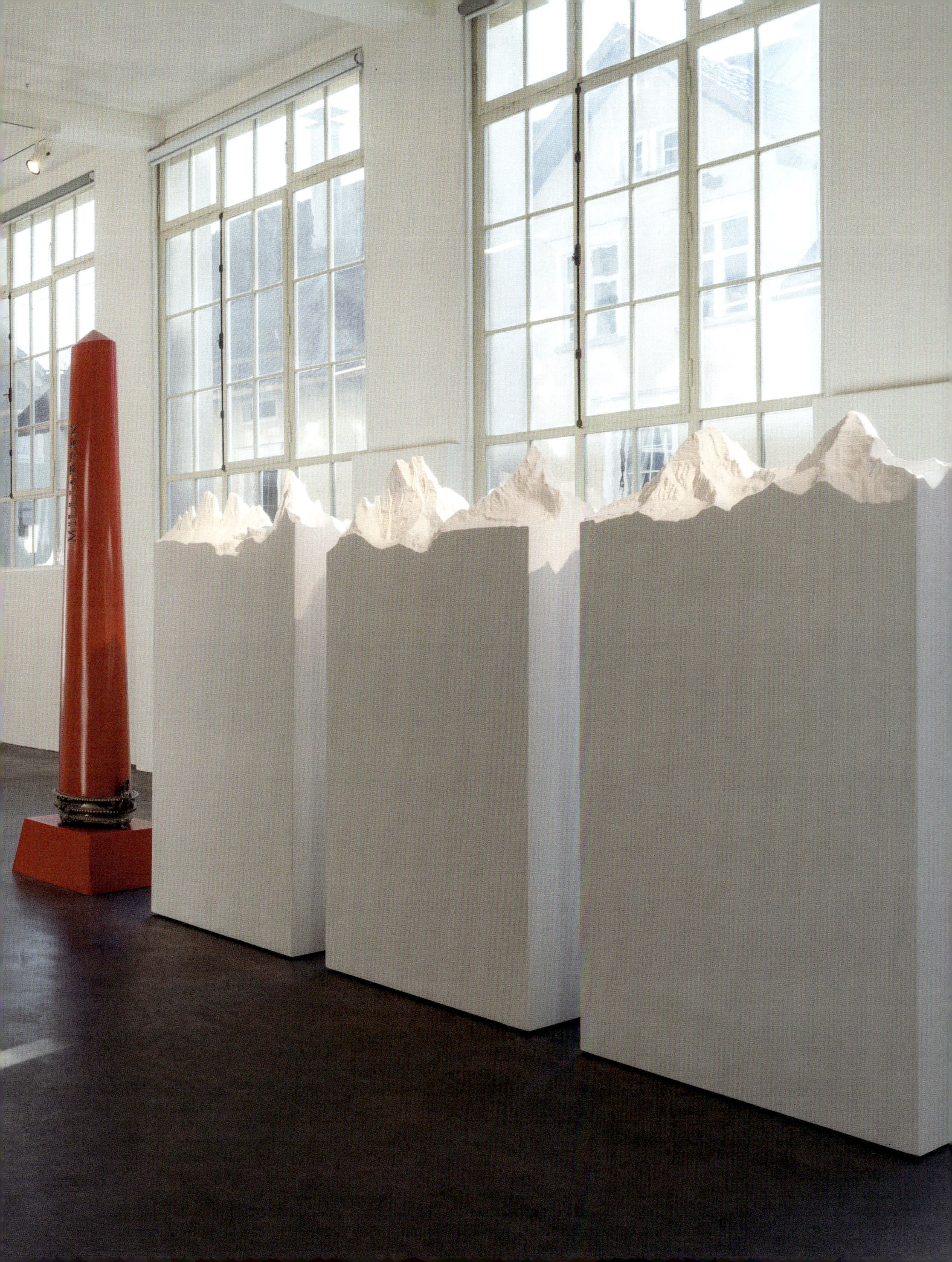
MILLIARDEN

Rekonstruktion eines
folgenschweren Streites
2016

Rekonstruktion des folgensc

(1)

Am frühen Nachmittag des 30.5.1882 geraten die Brüder Ewald und Cornelius Reich auf dem Hof des Fabrikgeländes ihrer Firma in einen folgenreichen Streit. Auslöser ist die unterschiedliche Bewertung des von Cornelius Reich eigenmächtig bei Carl Hanftstaengl in Auftrag gegebenen, sehr teuren neuen Signets der Firma Ottmar Reich. Ewald Reich spricht sich vehement gegen dessen Verwendung aus.Der dritte Bruder Anton Reich, der die immer lauter werdende Auseinandersetzung von seinem Bürofenster beobachtet hat, begibt sich kurzerhand in den Hof und will die streitenden Brüder trennen, kommt jedoch zu spät. Im Eifer des Gesprächs stößt Cornelius Ewald um, dieser fällt unglücklich auf eine gusseiserne, wahrscheinlich aus einer Transportkarre gefallenen Hutform. Blutend bleibt er schwer verletzt liegen. Fassungslos und verzweifelt läuft Cornelius davon. Ewald verbringt drei Wochen im Lindenberger Hospital, danach hält er sich für einen längeren Kuraufenthalt in Davos auf. Er erholt sich nie mehr gänzlich von diesem Sturz, leidet unter ständigen Kopfschmerzen und häufigen Ohnmachten.

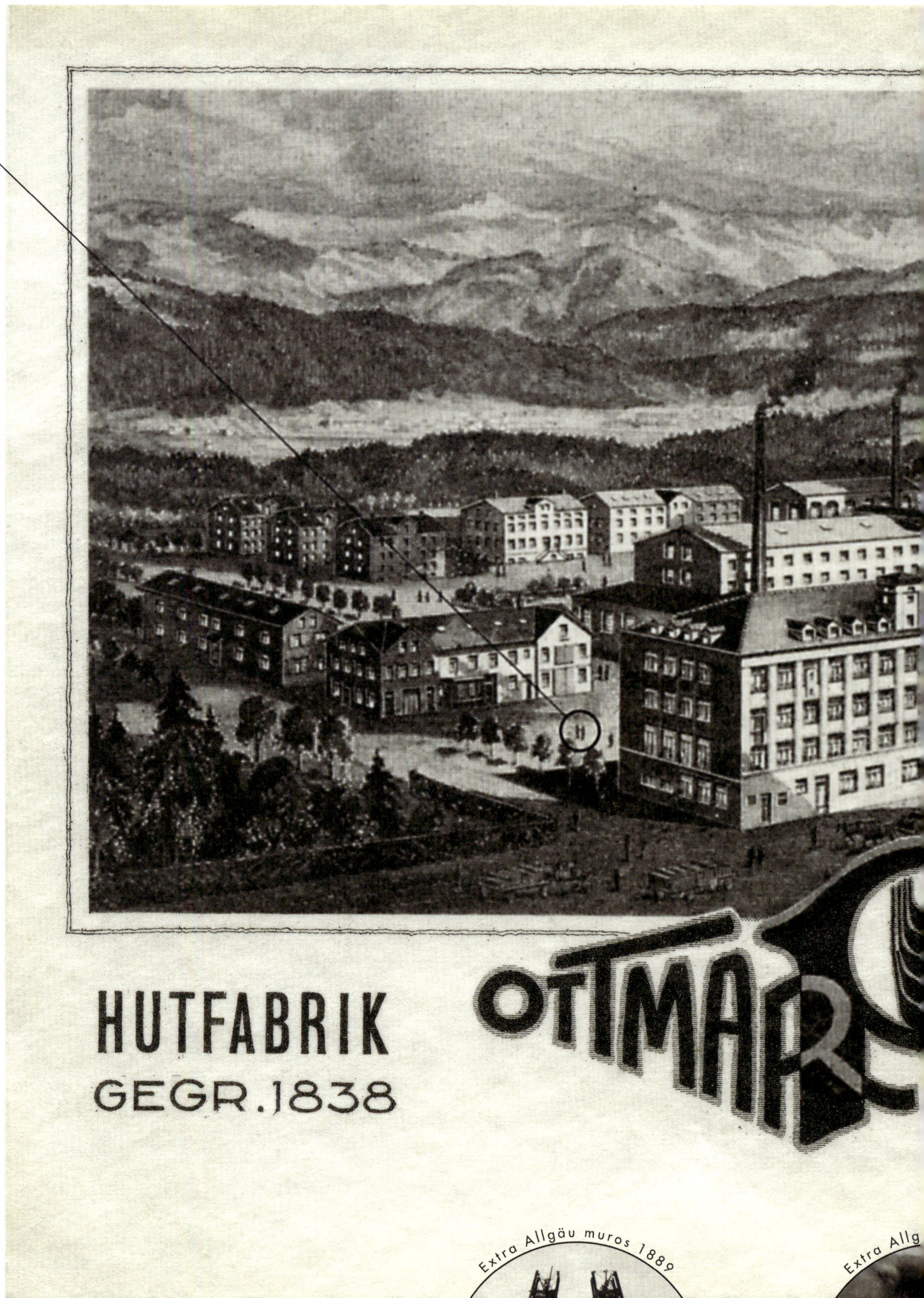

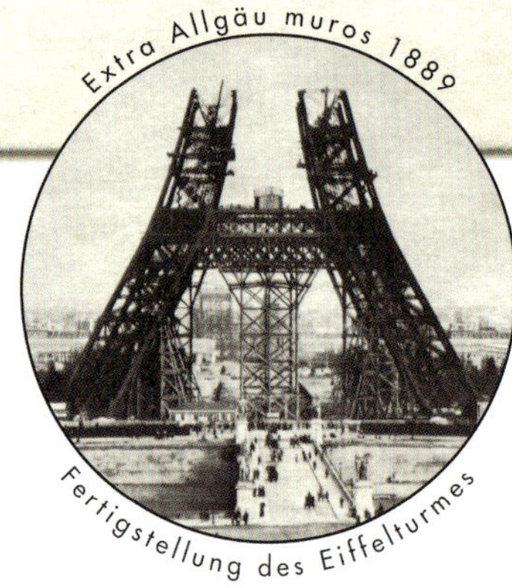

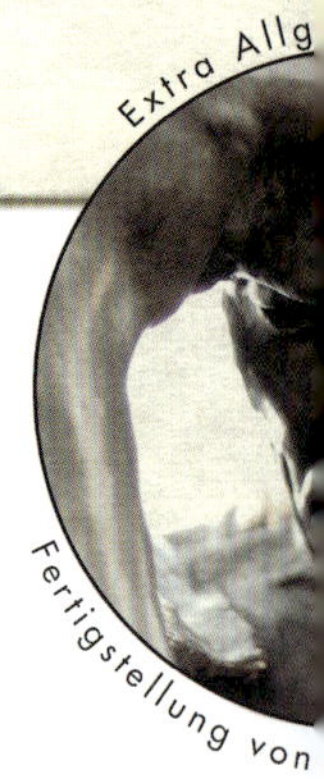

en Streites vom 30.5.1882

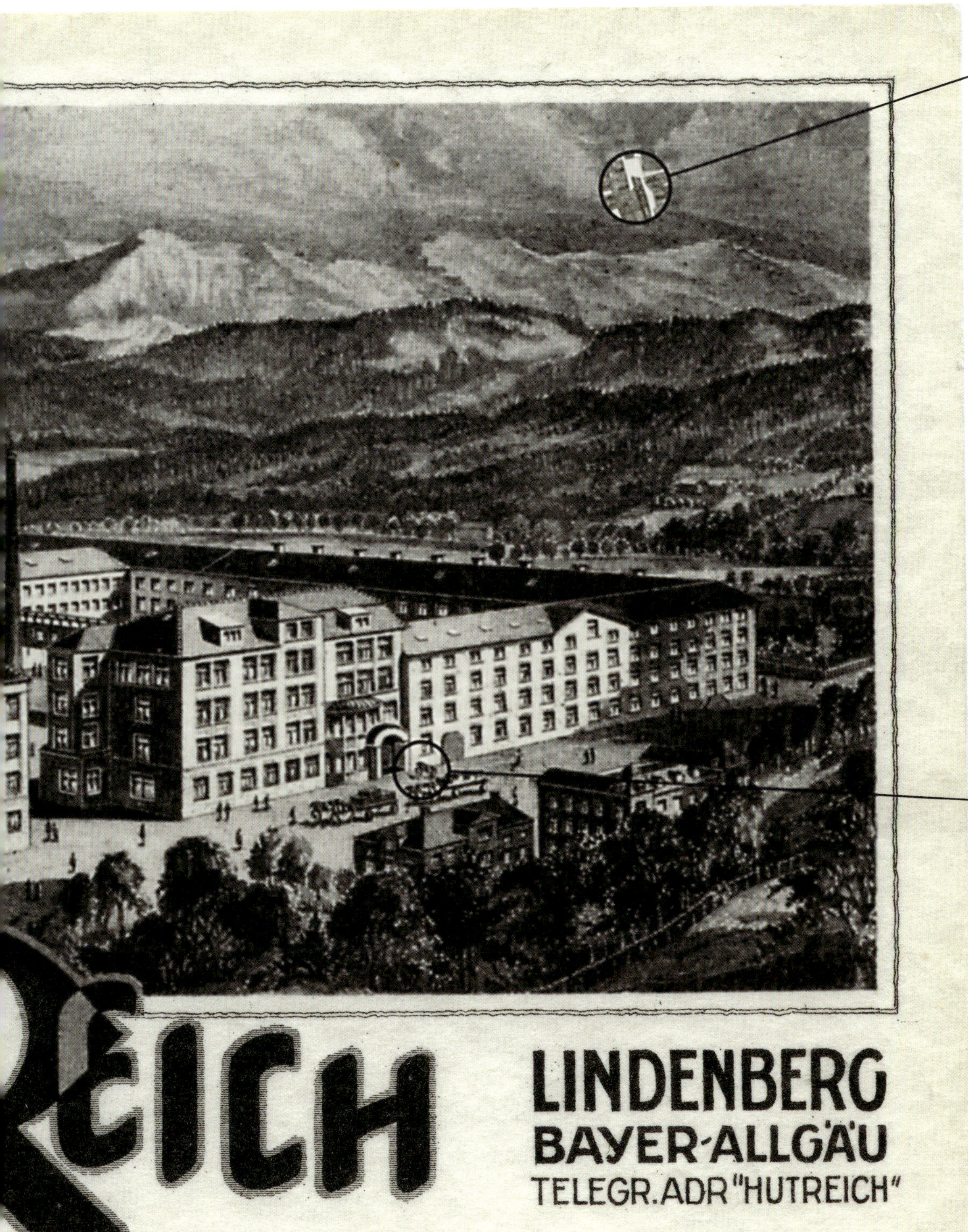

(2)

Nach zwei Wochen erreicht Cornelius Reich mittellos Mailand. Während der ersten Monate erhält er Unterkunft bei dem Strohlieferanten Gianlucca Monetti. Cornelius Reich beschließt in Mailand zu bleiben. Aus Scham reagiert er auf keinen Brief und bricht schließlich den Kontakt mit seiner Familie in Lindenberg ab. Dort haben mittlerweile Anton und Ewald Reich die alleinige Leitung der Firma Ottmar Reich übernommen.
Cornelius Reich baut mit Geschick und harter Hand den Pferdehandel „Reich und Monetti" auf und beliefert ganz Europa, sowie die amerikanische Ostküste mit seinen Lastpferden.
1889 verkauft er zwei seltene Murgeser, die aus einer Zwillingsgeburt stammen. Beide haben am Widerrist eine, erst auf den zweiten Blick erkennbare, identische graue Zeichnung, die einem Kreuz ähnelt .
Ein Pferd wird nach Amerika verschifft und wird für die damalige große Summe von 3500 Dollar an den Polizeichef von Boston, William Sorgot verkauft.
Am 1. Mai 1891 wird der Murgeser während einer Demonstration von sozialistischen Textilarbeitern schwer verletzt und erhält den Gnadenschuss von Sorgots Assistenten.

(3)

Der zweite Murgeser wird zusammen mit neun weiteren Pferden 1893 von dem Hörbranzer Pferdehändler Gottfried Messner, der Geschäftsbeziehungen mit der Mailänder Firma unterhält, an die Firma Ottmar Reich verkauft. Die rapide anwachsende Hutproduktion erfordert einen großen Fuhrpark, um die Versandware an die Bahnstation Röthenbach zu transportieren.
Am 27.2.1895 kommt es zum tragischen Unfall. Das Murgeser Pferd reißt sich vor dem Haupteingang der Hutfabrik los und versetzt dem in diesem Moment aus der Türe tretenden Ewald Reich einen tödlichen Tritt.
Im selben Jahr, am 11.9.1895, stirbt Cornelius Reich an einem Hirnschlag in Mailand. Ein Jahr zuvor wurde er von König Umberto dem I. in den Stand des Hofmarschall erhoben.

Rekonstruiert aus Briefen der Familie Reich, dem amtlichen Personenregister der Gemeinde Hörbranz, der Biblioteca Nazionale Braidense, Mailand und dem Stadtarchiv Lindenberg.

os 1895

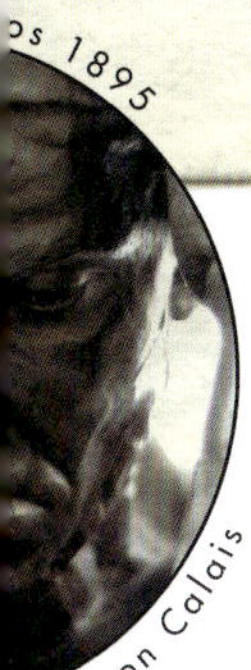

rger von Calais

Extra Allgäu muros 1882

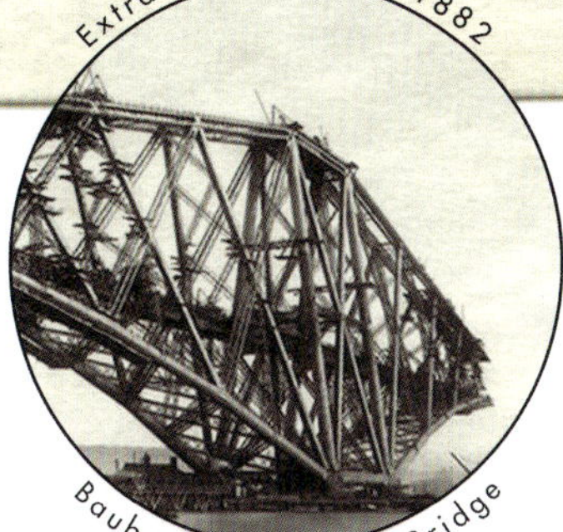

Baubeginn der Forth Bridge

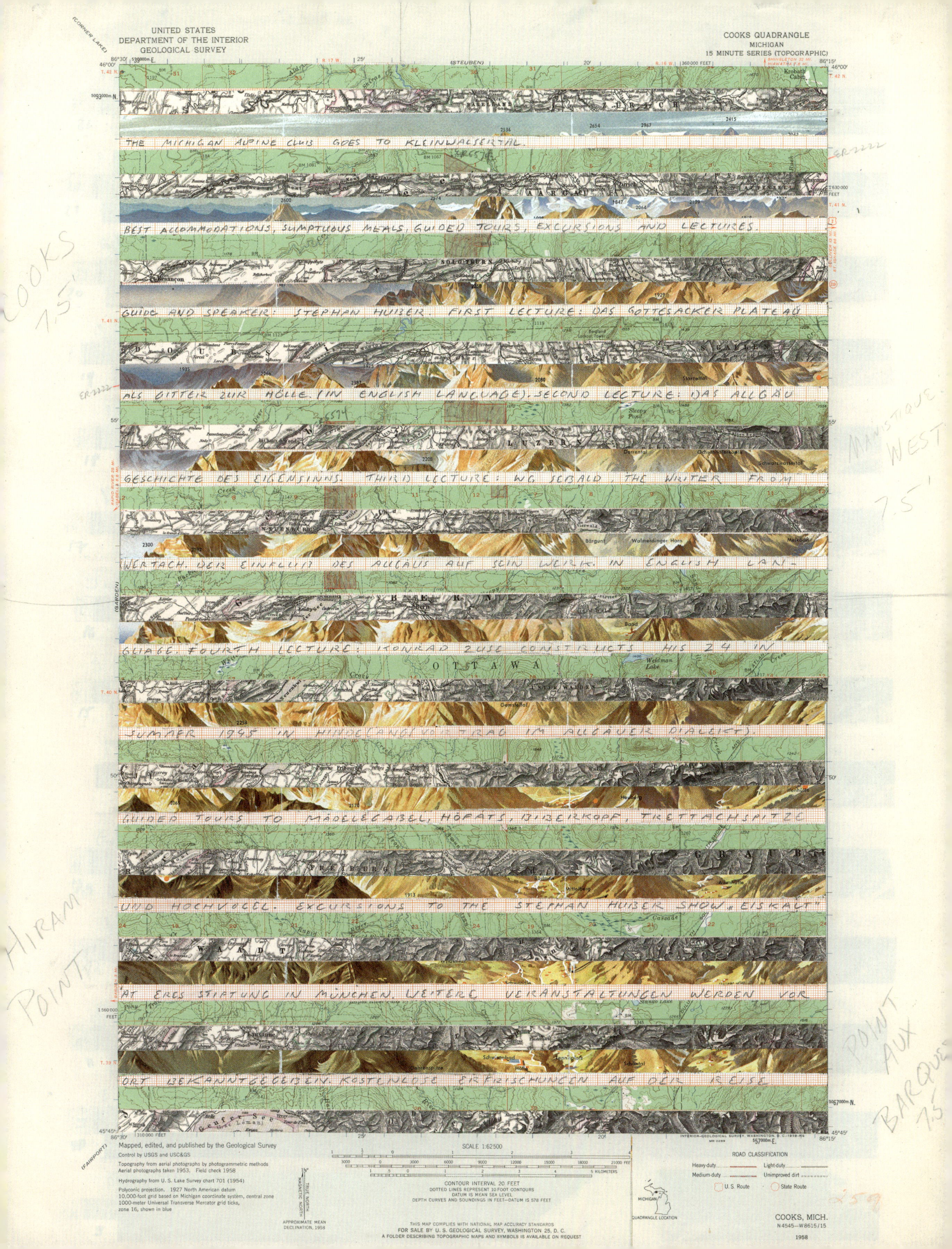
THE MICHIGAN ALPINE CLUB GOES TO KLEINWALSERTAL.
BEST ACCOMMODATIONS, SUMPTUOUS MEALS, GUIDED TOURS, EXCURSIONS AND LECTURES.
GUIDE AND SPEAKER: STEPHAN HUBER. FIRST LECTURE: DAS GOTTESACKER PLATEAU
ALS GITTER ZUR HÖLLE (IN ENGLISH LANGUAGE). SECOND LECTURE: DAS ALLGÄU
GESCHICHTE DES EIGENSINNS. THIRD LECTURE: W.G. SEBALD, THE WRITER FROM
WERTACH. DER EINFLUß DES ALLGÄUS AUF SEIN WERK. IN ENGLISH LAN-
GUAGE. FOURTH LECTURE: KONRAD ZUSE CONSTRUCTS HIS Z4 IN
SUMMER 1945 IN HINDELANG (VORTRAG IM ALLGÄUER DIALEKT).
GUIDED TOURS TO MÄDELEGABEL, HÖFATS, BIBERKOPF, TRETTACHSPITZE
UND HOCHVOGEL. EXCURSIONS TO THE STEPHAN HUBER SHOW "EISKALT"
AT EROS STIFTUNG IN MÜNCHEN. WEITERE VERANSTALTUNGEN WERDEN VOR
ORT BEKANNTGEGEBEN. KOSTENLOSE ERFRISCHUNGEN AUF DER REISE.

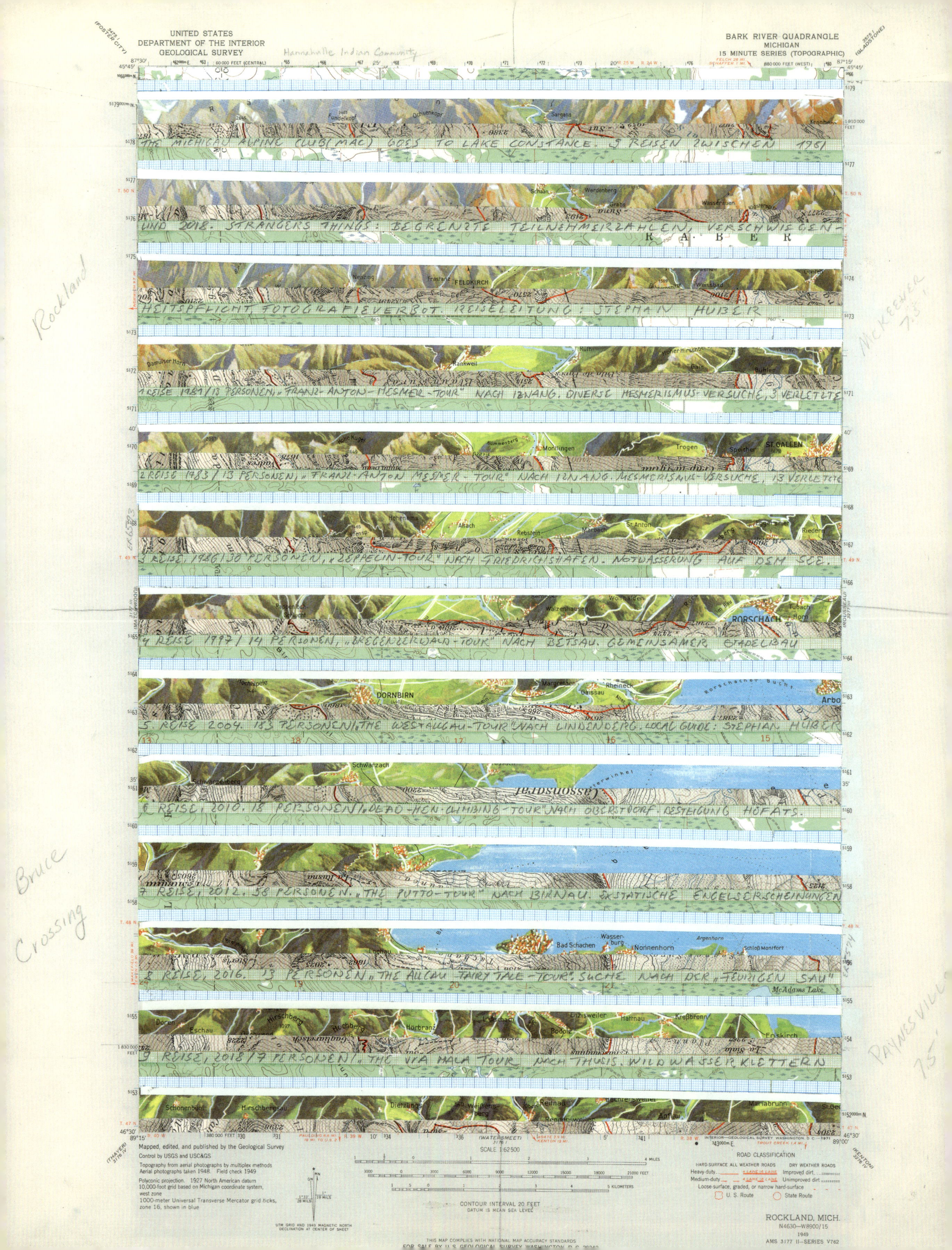
UNITED STATES
DEPARTMENT OF THE INTERIOR
GEOLOGICAL SURVEY
Hannahville Indian Community
BARK RIVER QUADRANGLE
MICHIGAN
15 MINUTE SERIES (TOPOGRAPHIC)
THE MICHIGAN ALPINE CLUB (MAC) GOES TO LAKE CONSTANCE. 9 REISEN ZWISCHEN 1981
UND 2018. STRANGERS THINGS: BEGRENZTE TEILNEHMERZAHLEN, VERSCHWIEGEN-
HEITSPFLICHT, FOTOGRAFIEVERBOT. REISELEITUNG: STEPHAN HUBER
1 REISE 1981 / 13 PERSONEN, „FRANZ-ANTON-MESMER-TOUR" NACH IZNANG. DIVERSE MESMERISMUS-VERSUCHE, 3 VERLETZTE
2 REISE 1983 / 13 PERSONEN, „FRANZ-ANTON MESMER-TOUR" NACH IZNANG. MESMERISMUS-VERSUCHE, 13 VERLETZTE
3 REISE, 1986 / 30 PERSONEN, „ZEPPELIN-TOUR" NACH FRIEDRICHSHAFEN. NOTWASSERUNG AUF DEM SEE.
4 REISE 1997 / 14 PERSONEN, „BREGENZERWALD-TOUR" NACH BETSAU. GEMEINSAMER STADELBAU
5. REISE 2004. 183 PERSONEN / „THE WESTALLGAU-TOUR" NACH LINDENBERG. LOCAL GUIDE: STEPHAN HUBER
6 REISE, 2010. 18 PERSONEN / „DEAD-HEN-CLIMBING-TOUR" NACH OBERSTDORF. BESTEIGUNG HÖFATS.
7 REISE, 2012. 58 PERSONEN. „THE PUTTO-TOUR" NACH BIRNAU. EKSTATISCHE ENGELSERSCHEINUNGEN
8 REISE, 2016. 13 PERSONEN „THE ALLGAU FAIRY TALE-TOUR". SUCHE NACH DER „FEURIGEN SAU"
9 REISE, 2018 / 7 PERSONEN / „THE VIA MALA TOUR" NACH THUSIS. WILDWASSERKLETTERN
Rockland
McKeever 7.5'
Bruce Crossing
Paynesville 7.5'
ROCKLAND, MICH.
N4630—W8900/15
1949
AMS 3177 II—SERIES V762
CONTOUR INTERVAL 20 FEET
DATUM IS MEAN SEA LEVEL
ROAD CLASSIFICATION
THIS MAP COMPLIES WITH NATIONAL MAP ACCURACY STANDARDS
FOR SALE BY U.S. GEOLOGICAL SURVEY, WASHINGTON, D.C. 20242

Lo & Behold, 17
2018

Perfect Sculptures
Strudel
2019
Charim Galerie,
Wien / Vienna

Rauminstallation
Room installation
2019
Kunstmuseum Lindau

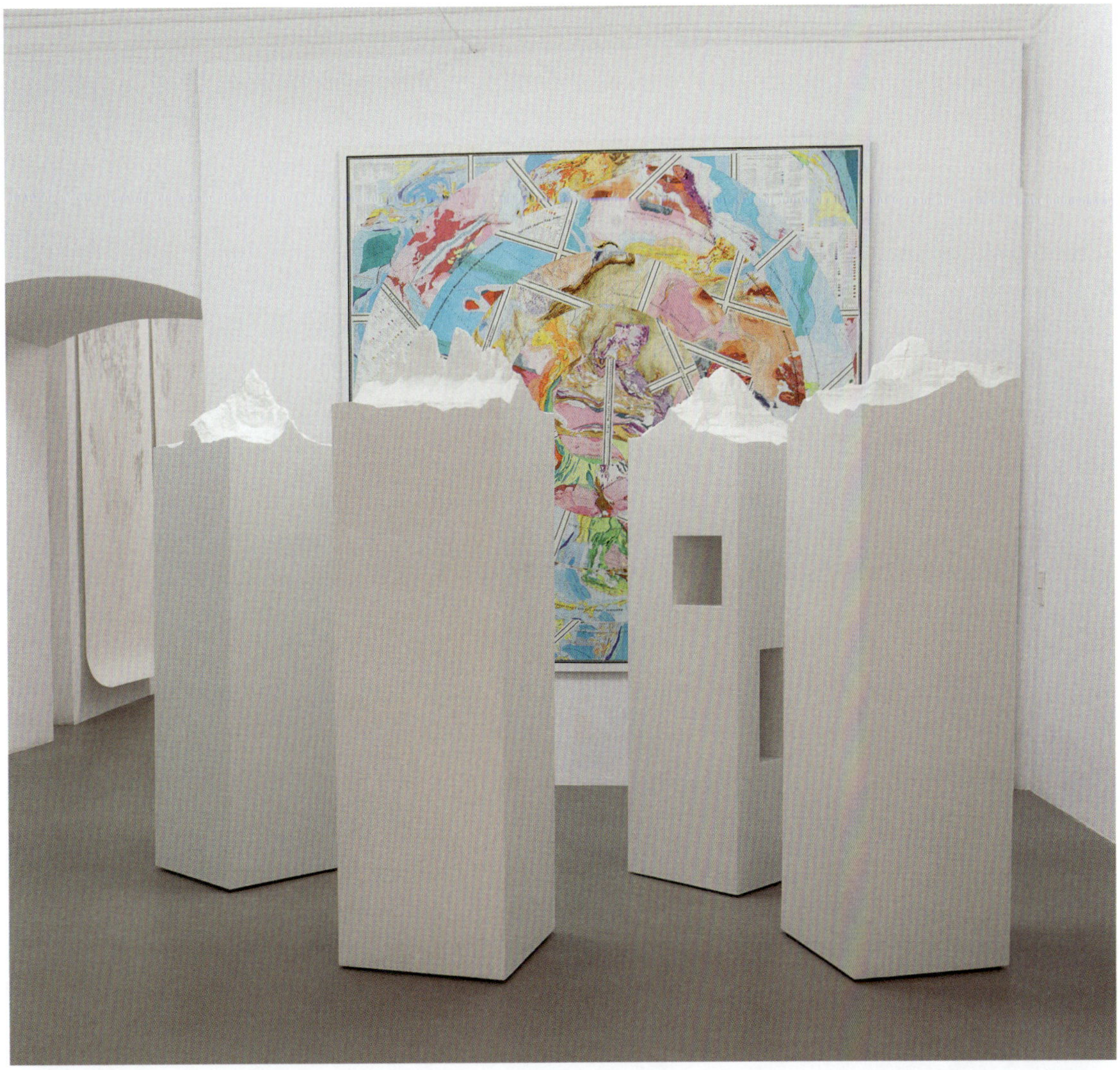

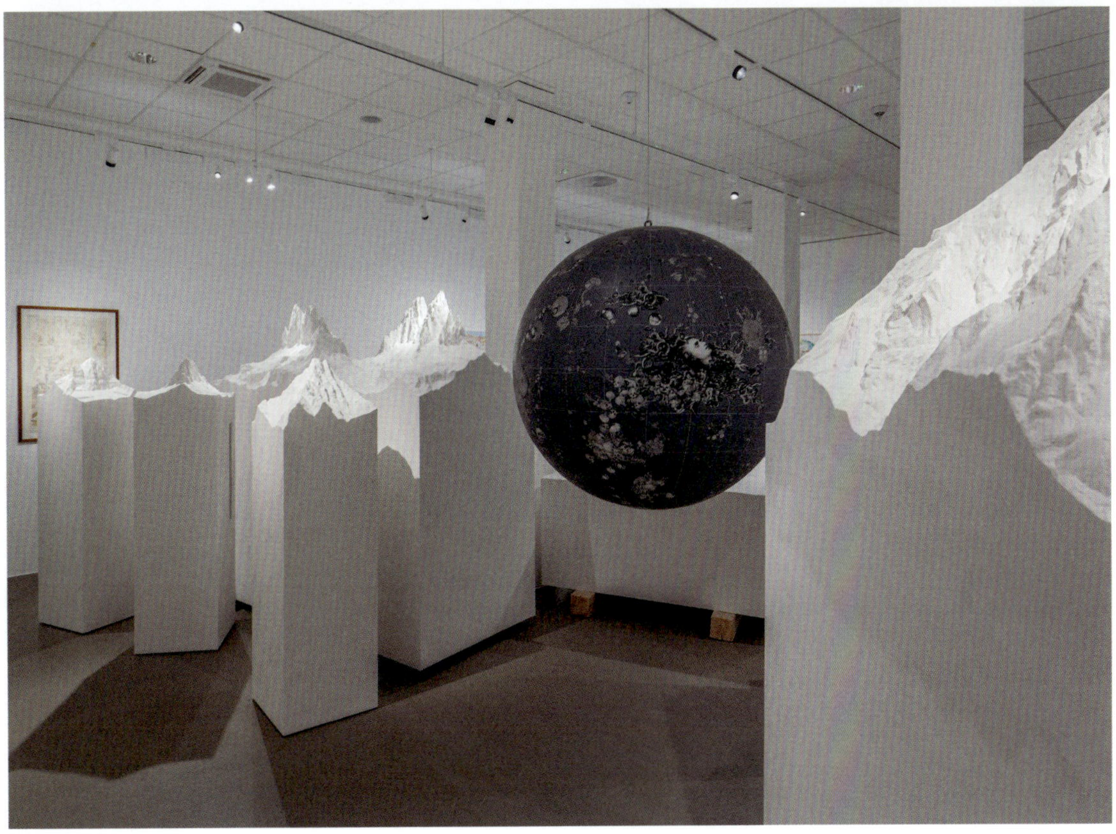

Island II (Osterinsel)
2021

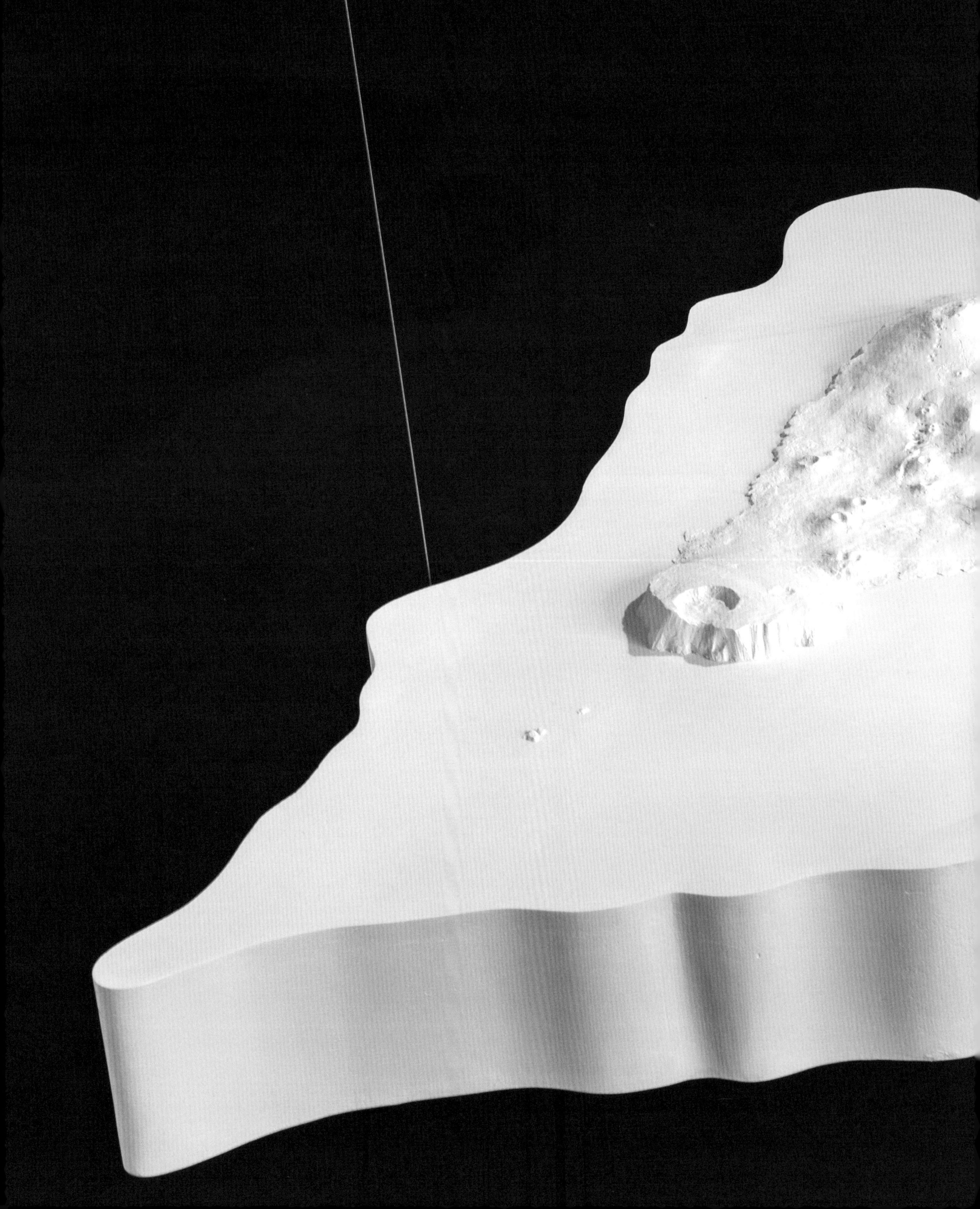

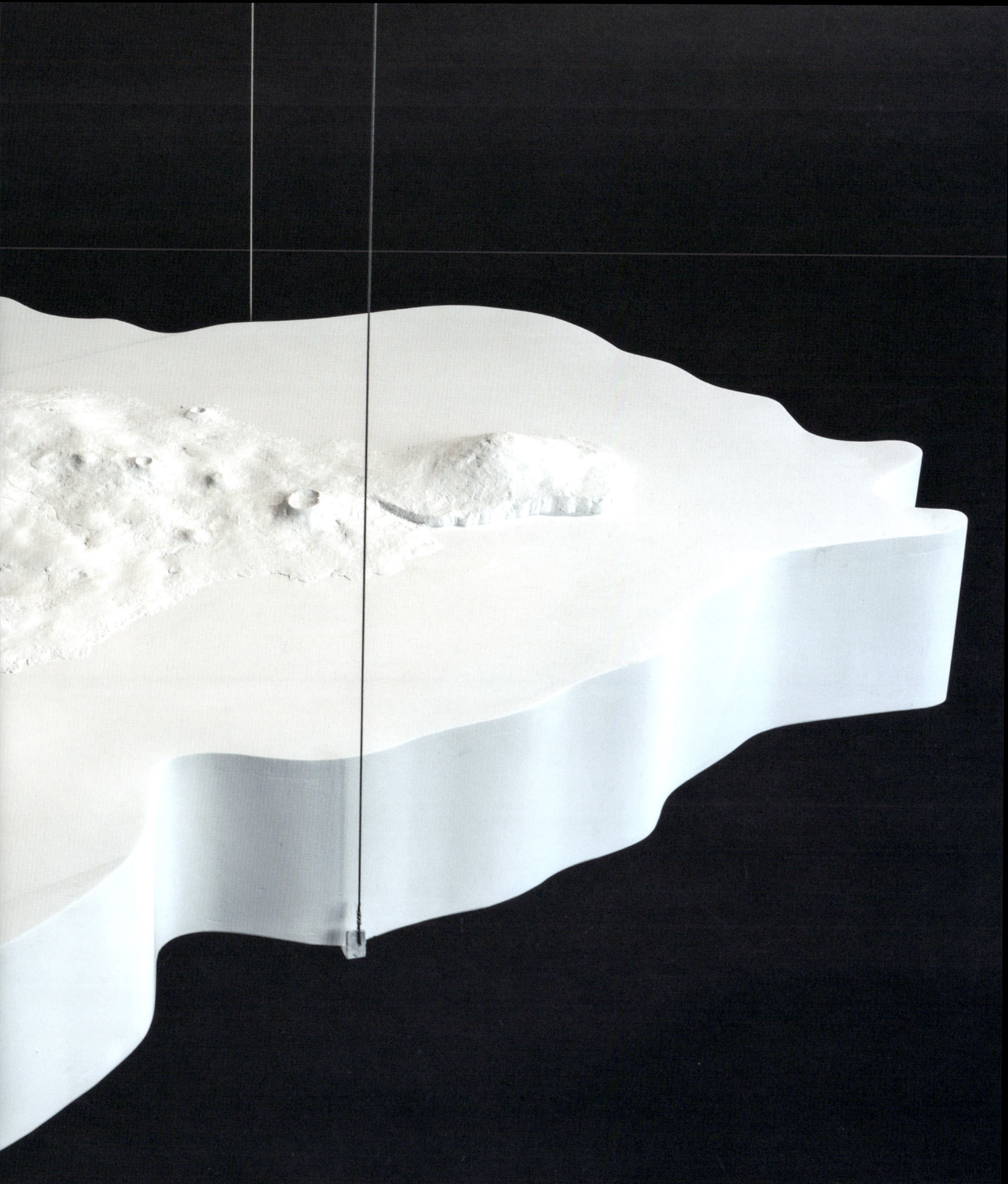

Rauminstallation
Room installation
2021
Galerie Max Weber Six Friedrich,
München / Munich

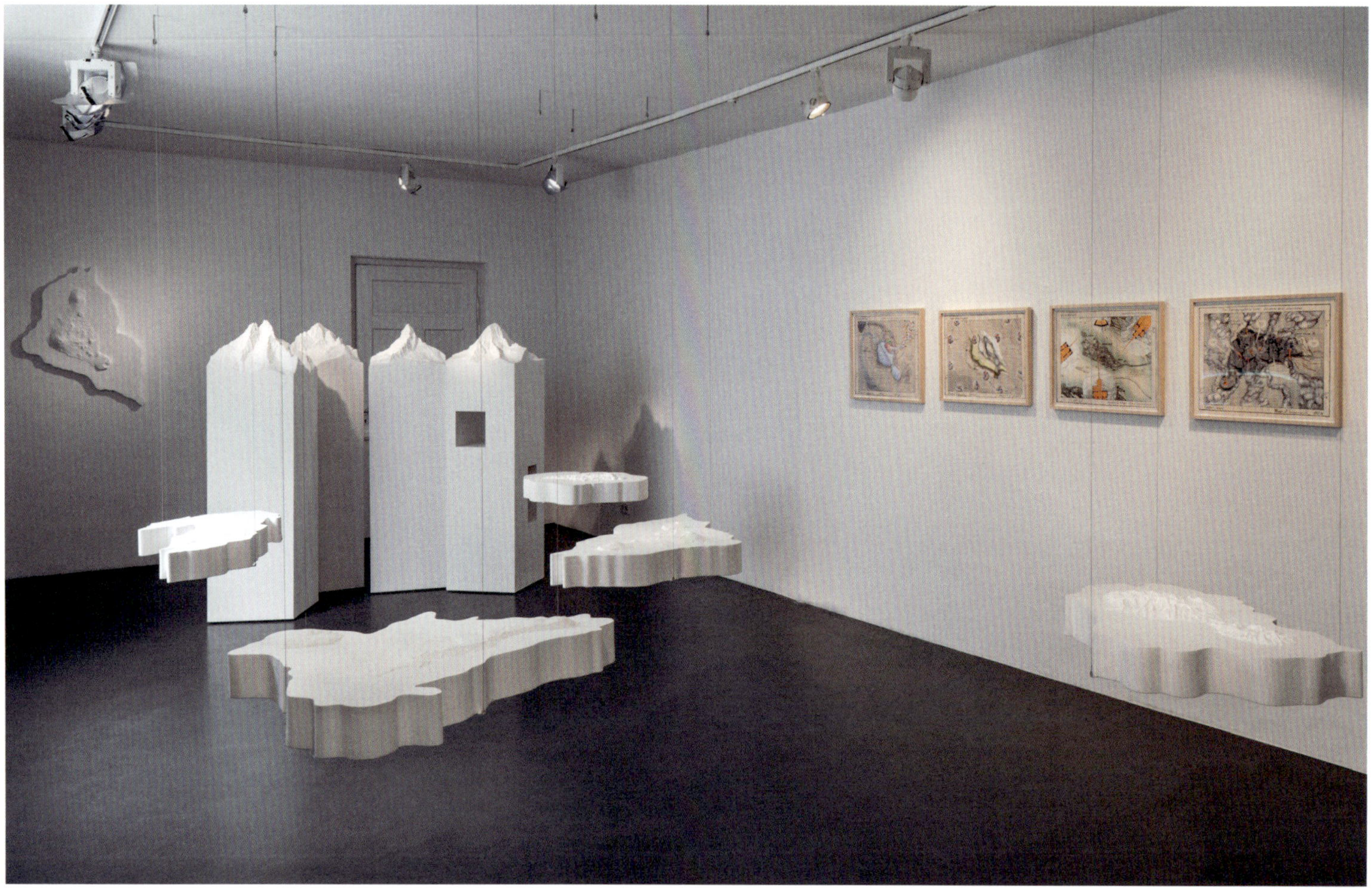

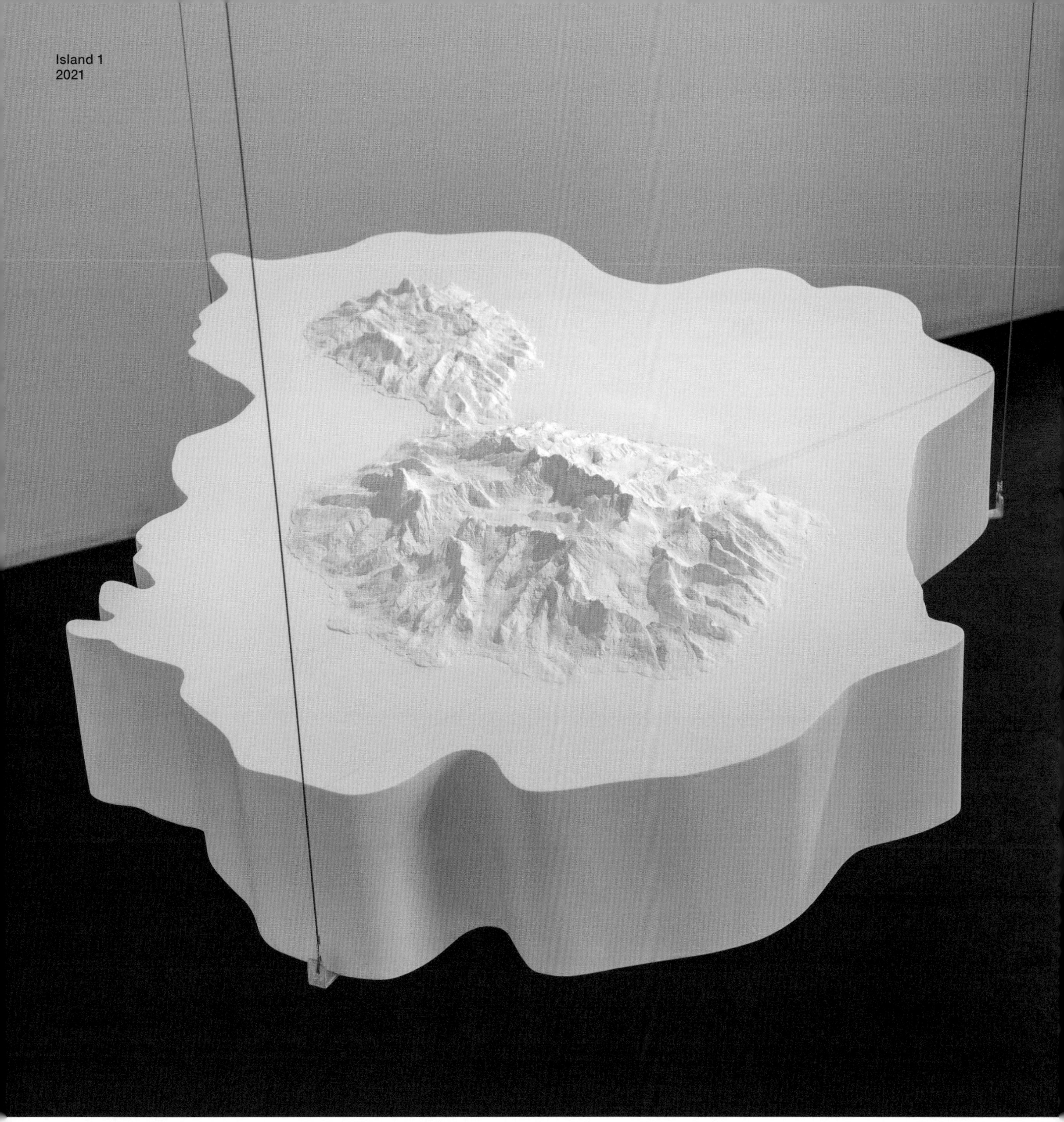

Island 1
2021

Montagna sospesa / Tre Cime
2022
CAS, München / Munich

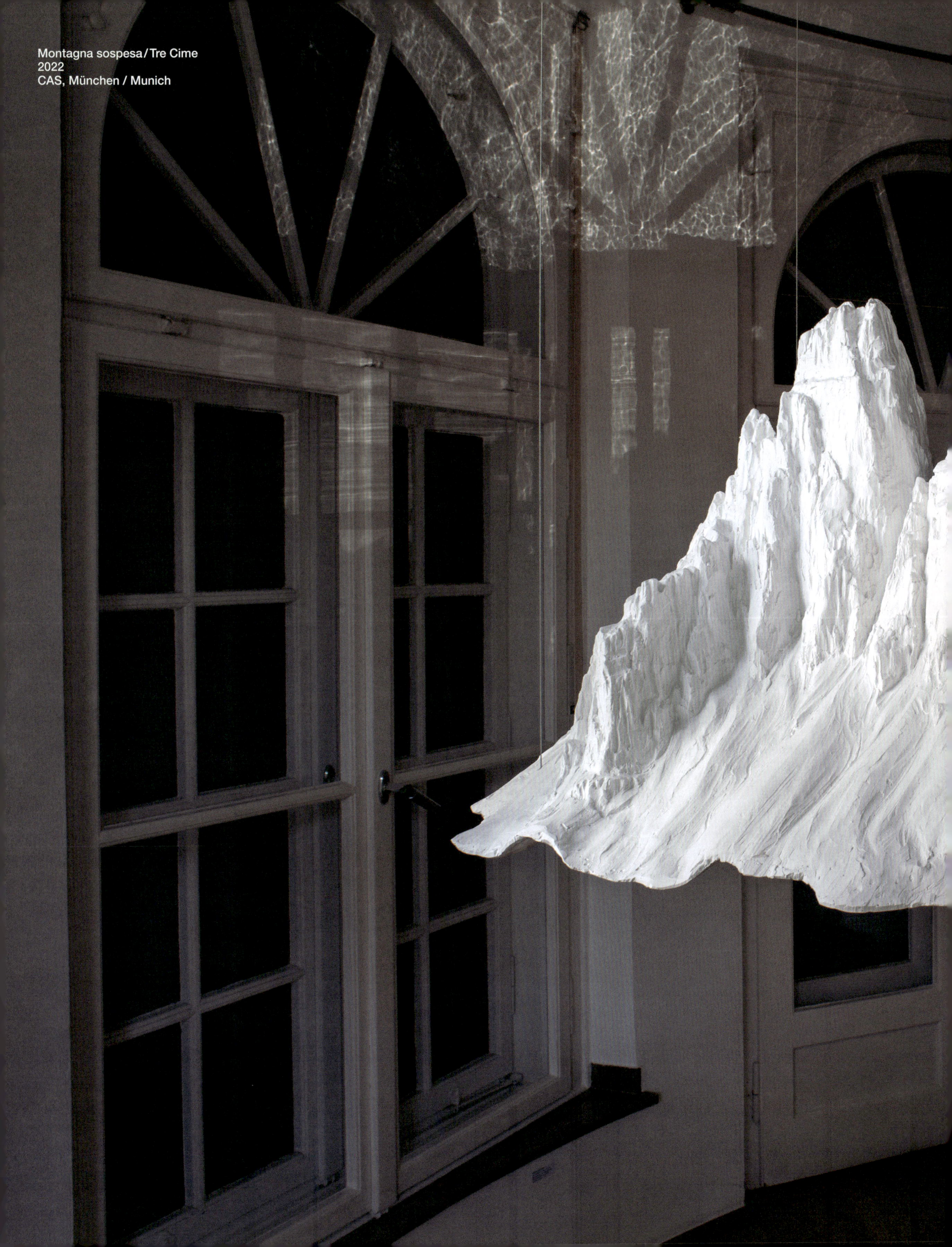

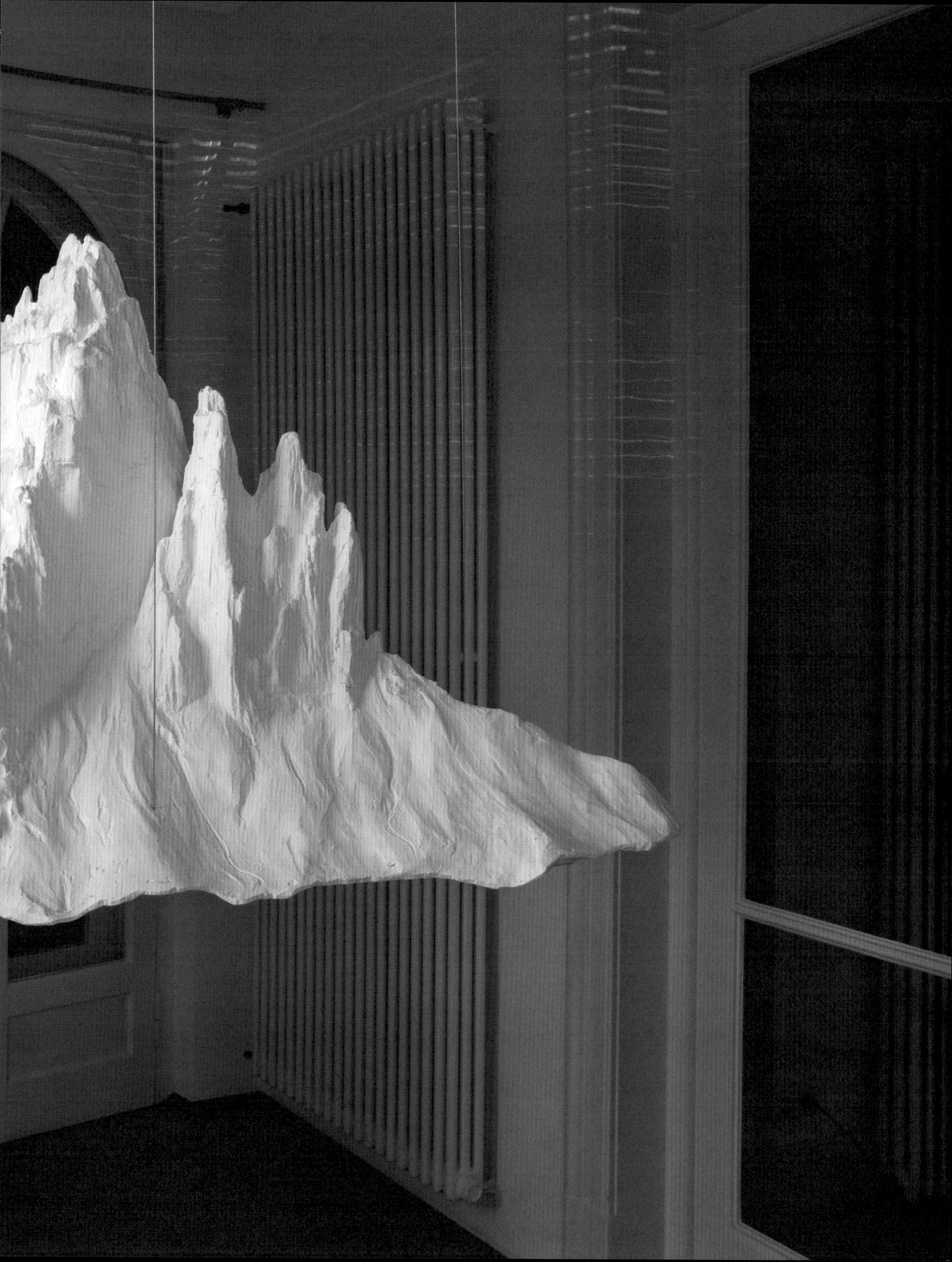

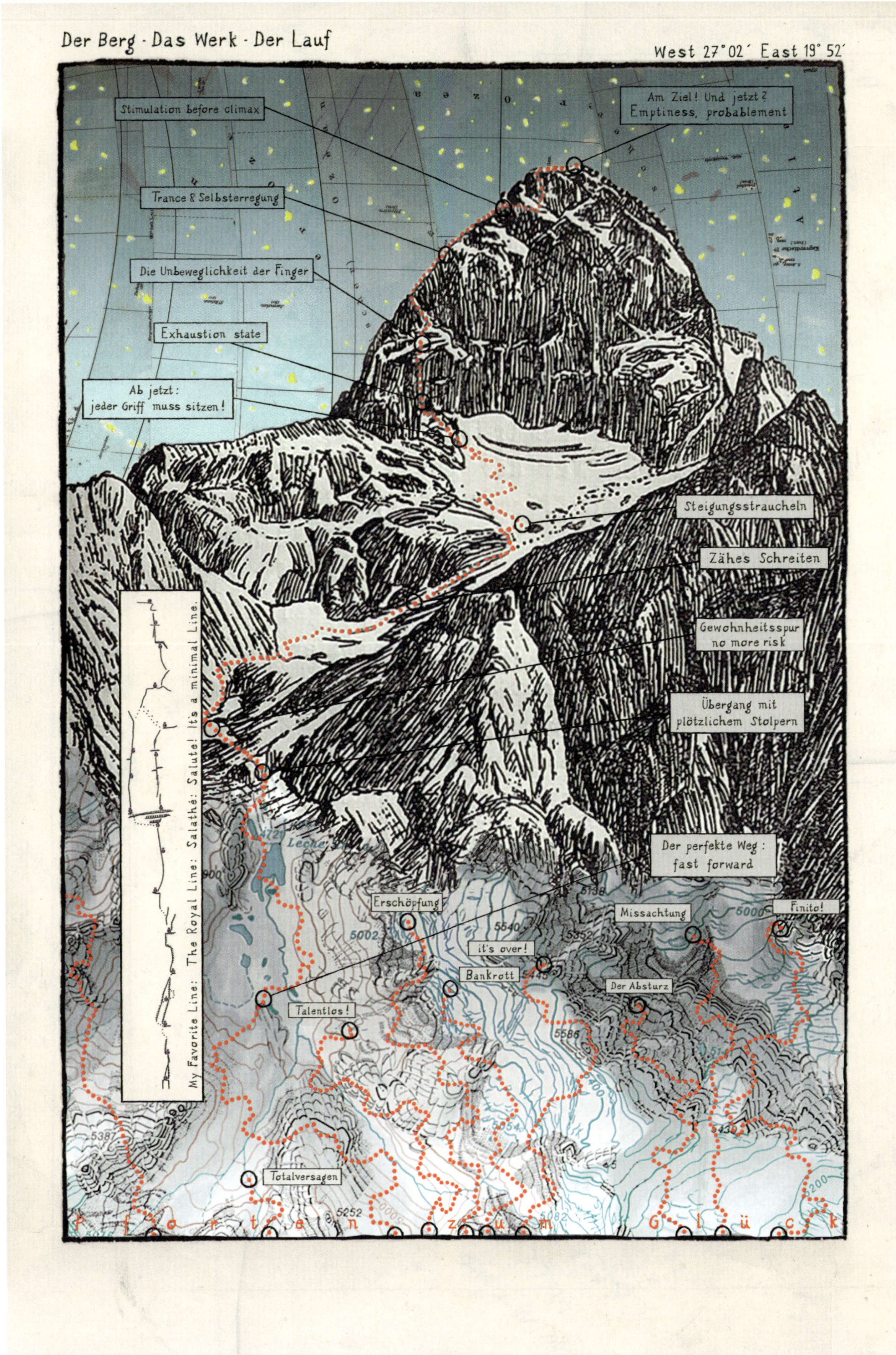
Der Berg · Das Werk · Der Lauf
West 27°02´ East 19°52´
Stimulation before climax
Am Ziel! Und jetzt?
Emptiness, probablement
Trance & Selbsterregung
Die Unbeweglichkeit der Finger
Exhaustion state
Ab jetzt:
jeder Griff muss sitzen!
Steigungsstraucheln
Zähes Schreiten
Gewohnheitsspur
no more risk
Übergang mit
plötzlichem Stolpern
My Favorite Line: The Royal Line: Salathé: Salute! It's a minimal Line.
Der perfekte Weg:
fast forward
Erschöpfung
Missachtung
Finito!
it's over!
Bankrott
Der Absturz
Talentlos!
Totalversagen
P f o r t e n z u m G l ü c k

Tunnel
2022

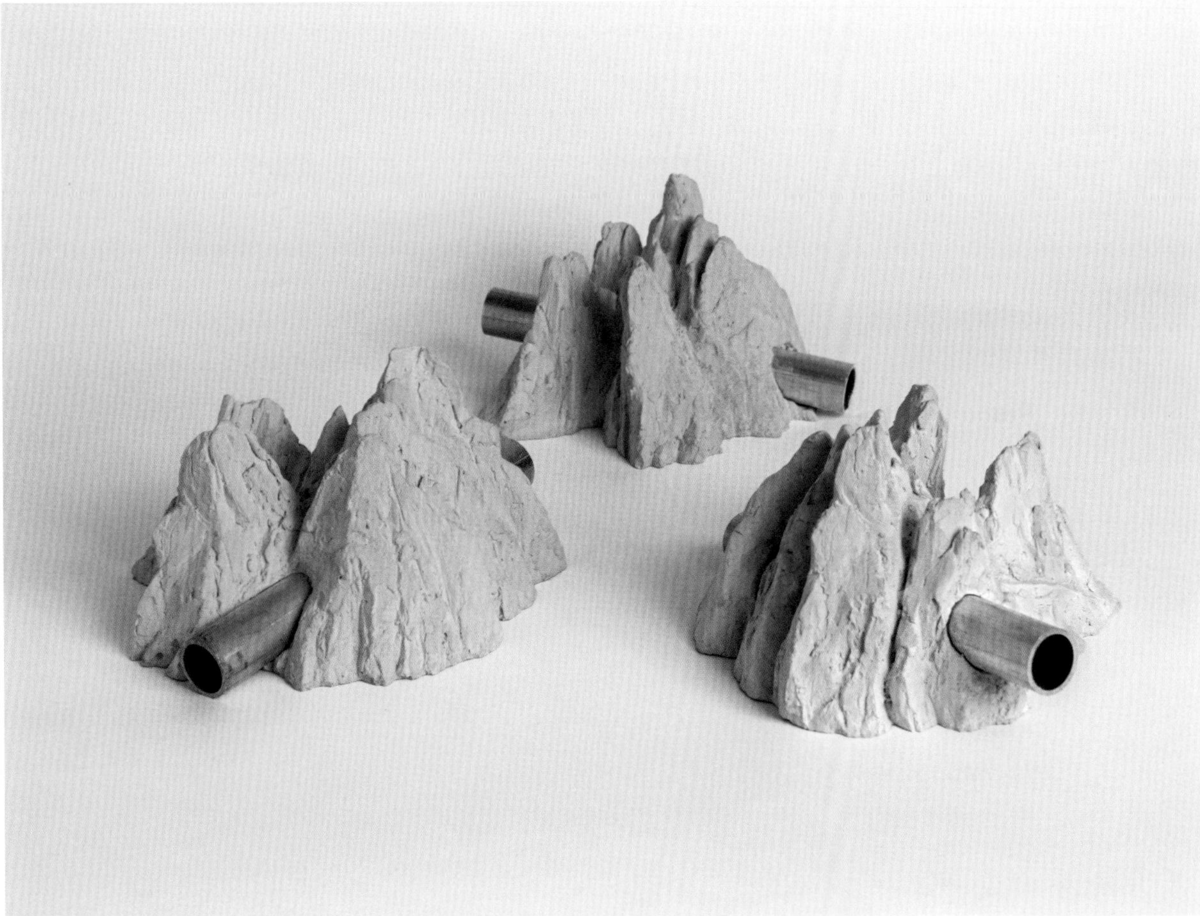

Anmerkungen
Notes

Verzeichnis der abgebildeten Werke:
Kommentare, Daten, Quellen
und Materialien zu den Arbeiten
List of Illustrated Works:
Comments, information, sources,
and materials regarding the works

Vorsatz / Endpaper 1

SL 1–SL 10, The Bergs I–III
2008–2022
Dentalgips, Rupfen
Verschiedene Maße; Bergkranz: Durchmesser 80 cm
SL 1–SL 10, The Bergs I–III
2008–2022
Dental plaster, hessian
Various dimensions; mountain peak: diameter 80 cm

Vorsatz / Endpaper 2

Blick ins Atelier mit Skulpturen aus den Jahren 1998–2023
Dentalgips, Rupfen, Aluminium, Gipskartonplatten, Holz, Wandglätter
Verschiedene Maße
View of studio with sculptures from 1998 to 2023
Dental plaster, hessian, aluminium, plasterboards, wood, finish filler
Various dimensions

Vorsatz / Endpaper 3

Im Lager
Detail
1997/2010
Pigmentprint auf Fourdrinier-Zeichenpapier
48 × 32 cm
Auflage: 3 + 1 AP
Im Lager (In the Storeroom)
Detail
1997/2010
Pigment print on Fourdrinier drawing paper
48 × 32 cm
Edition: 3 + 1 artist proof

15–17

Die Alpen
1992
Glas, Glassmalten (Mosaik), Edelstahl, Wassertechnik
Gesamthöhe (inklusive Hängeseile) 13 Meter
Mosaiktafel: 330 × 250 cm
Glasplatte: 360 × 360 cm
Trog: Länge 400 cm
Flughafen München, Terminal 1, Knoten A
Die Vorlage für das Mosaik ist eine Fotografie meines Bruders Johannes. Sie zeigt den Biberkopf im Kleinen Walsertal. Mein Bruder, der 2022 verstarb, hinterließ ein umfangreiches Konvolut an Fotografien aus den Allgäuer Alpen und den angrenzenden Gebieten.
Die Alpen (The Alps)
1992
Glass, smalti (mosaic), stainless steel, water equipment
Total height (including suspension rope) 13 metres
Mosaic panel: 330 × 250 cm
Glass plate: 360 × 360 cm
Trough: length 400 cm
Munich Airport, terminal 1, hall A
The source for the mosaic is a photograph by my brother Johannes. It depicts the Biberkopf mountain in the Kleiner Walsertal. My brother, who died in 2022, left an extensive collection of photographs of the Allgäu Alps and surrounding areas.

19–23

Die Wahrheit bin ich
1994
Beitrag zur Gruppenausstellung *Scharf im Schauen*, Haus der Kunst, München
Mixed Media
Ca. 500 × 500 × 400 cm
Im Besitz des Künstlers
Aus dem Bergregal sind, in an- und abschwellenden Lautstärken, Wortfetzen zu hören:

Die folgende Bildstrecke zeigt Fotografien aus privaten Umfeldern, aus wohnungsähnlichen Situationen und Momentaufnahmen aus meinem Atelier und Lager.
The following sequence shows photographs from private contexts, from situations resembling apartments, and spontaneous pictures from my studio and warehouse.

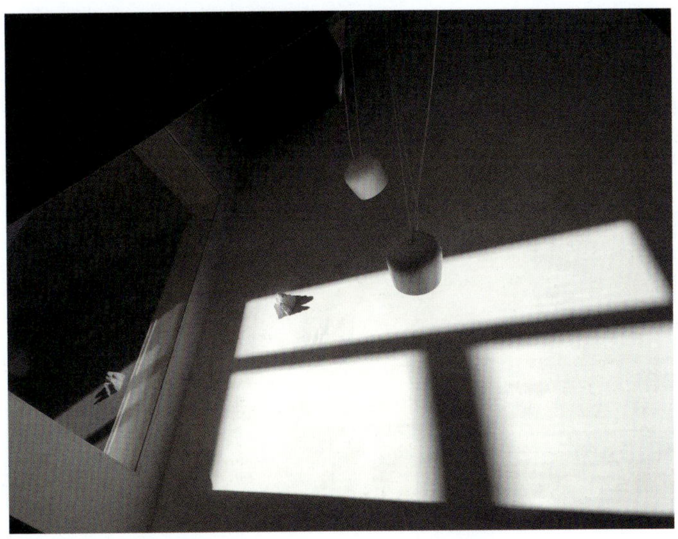

Privatsammlung, Brüssel, Belgien
Private collection, Brussels, Belgium

„...: ich klammere mich ... nein ... kein ... wenn das Eis bri ... weiter ... gibt kein ... ich bin vollko ... bricht ... in die gläserne Schicht ... der peitschende .... bricht ... ich ... spüre nicht ... ist das ... der Donner ... der ... bricht ... ist ... das ... finger ... meine fing ... taub ... gähnende ... bricht ... ich bin vollkomm ... erfro ... bricht ... ammere mich ... an ... den ... nass ... rutsche ... utsche ... bi ...“
Sprecherin: Silvie Sperlich
Die Wahrheit bin ich (I am the Truth)
1994
Exhibited at the group show *Scharf im Schauen*, Haus der Kunst, Munich
Mixed media
ca. 500 × 500 × 400 cm
In the artist's possession
Fragments of words, in increasing and decreasing volume, are emitted by the shelves of mountains:
'...: I clasp myself ... no ... none ... when the ice bre- ... further ... give no ... I am comple– ... breaks ... in the glass layer ... the whipping ... breaks ... I ... feel nothing ... is the ... the thunder ... the ... breaks ... is ... the ... finger ... my fing- ... numb ... yawning ... breaks ... I am comple– ... fro- ... breaks ... -asp myself ... on ... the ... wet ... slip ... -lip ... bi ... '
Speaker: Silvie Sperlich

25

Das rote Bergbuch
1979
Historisches Fotoalbum, Polyester, Acrylfarbe
22 × 17 × 7 cm
Sammlung des Künstlers
Das rote Bergbuch
(The Red Mountain Book)
1979
Historical photo album, polyester, acrylic paint
22 × 17 × 7 cm
Collection of the artist

Berg und Steinbuch
1980
Buch, Stein, Polyester, Acryllack
21 × 15 × 5 cm
Sammlung des Künstlers
Berg und Steinbuch
(Mountain and Stone Book)
1980
Book, stone, polyester, acrylic varnish
21 × 15 × 5 cm
Collection of the artist

Das Kletterbuch
1980
Buch, Schnur
30 × 15 × 20 cm
Sammlung des Künstlers
Das Kletterbuch (The Climbing Book)
1980
Book, rope
30 × 15 × 20 cm
Collection of the artist

26

Heimat
1993
Siebdruck auf Papier
86 × 39 cm
Auflage: 8 + 2 AP
Heimat (Homeland)
1993
Silkscreen on paper
86 × 39 cm
Edition: 8 + 2 artist proofs

27

Gotthard
1993
Siebdruck auf Papier
86 × 39 cm
Auflage: 8 + 2 AP
Gotthard
1993
Silkscreen on paper
86 × 39 cm
Edition: 8 + 2 artist proofs

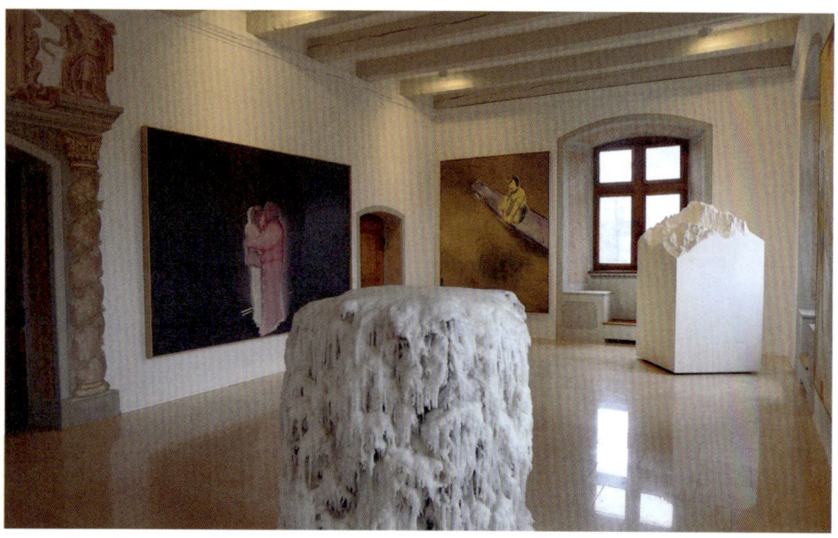

Sigg Collection, Mauensee, Schweiz / Switzerland

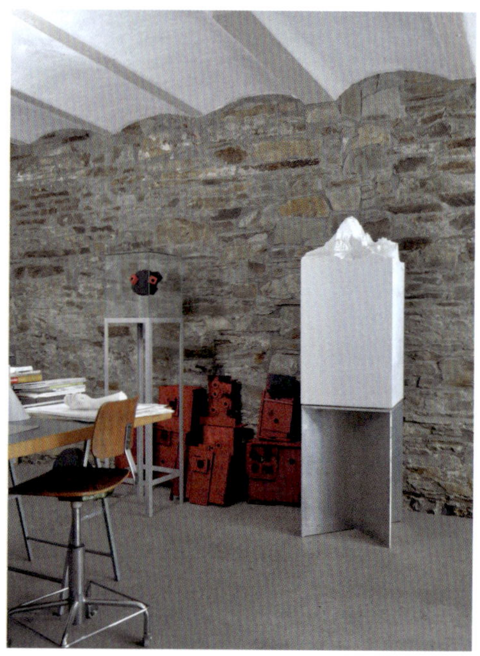

Privatsammlung, Burbach, Deutschland
Private collection, Burbach, Germany

Tautologisches Konstrukt
1993
Siebdruck auf Fotografie
60,5 × 46 cm
Auflage: 11 + 2 AP
Erstellt für den Kunstraum München. Der Text ist einer alten Postkarte entnommen und lautet:
„Herzliche Grüße aus dem Krieg, es geht mir bis jetzt sehr gut."
Die Unterschrift ist unleserlich.
Tautologisches Konstrukt (Tautological Construct)
1993
Silkscreen on photograph
60.5 × 46 cm
Edition: 11 + 2 artist proofs
Created for the Kunstraum München museum. The text is taken from an old postcard and states:
'Warmest regards from the war; I have been doing very well till now.'
The signature is illegible.

28

Wasser & Stein
1992
Zweiteilig
Teil 1: Sandstein, Siebdruck auf Marmor, Leuchtkasten mit Großbild-Diapositiv
Länge 280 cm
Privatsammlung München
Wasser & Stein (Water and Stone)
1992
Two parts
Part 1: Sandstone, silkscreen on marble, lightbox with large-image slide
Length 280 cm
Private collection, Munich

29

Wasser & Stein
1992
Zweiteilig
Teil 2: Sandstein, Siebdruck auf Glas, Blauglasscheiben, Leuchtkasten mit Großbild-Diapositiv
Länge 280 cm
Privatsammlung München
Wasser & Stein (Water and Stone)
1992
Two parts
Part 2: Sandstone, silkscreen on glass, blue glass pane, lightbox with large-image slide
Length 280 cm
Private collection, Munich

30/31

Südkreuz
1992
Aluminium, Eisenblech, Siebdruckplatten, Beton, Gummi
490 × 260 × 140 cm
Aufgrund von Transportschäden wurde die Arbeit zerstört.
Südkreuz (Southern Cross)
1992
Aluminium, iron sheet, silkscreen plates, cement, rubber
490 × 260 × 140 cm
Due to damage occurred during transport the work was destroyed.

32–35

Nobile
1997
11 Leuchtkästen
Aluminium, Glas, Diatrans-Folien, Leuchtmittel
Je 67 × 14 × 10 cm
Sammlung Landesbank Baden-Württemberg, Stuttgart
Die Vorlagen für die fiktive Expedition entstammen alten Postkarten, Büchern und Fotografien. Die Collagen sind sowohl analog wie digital erstellt.
Die Leuchtkästen finden sich in einem unterirdischen Verbindungstrakt zwischen zwei Verwaltungsgebäuden der Landesbank Baden-Württemberg.
Nobile
1997
11 lightboxes
Aluminium, glass, Diatrans foils, lighting
Each 67 × 14 × 10 cm
Collection of the Landesbank Baden-Württemberg, Stuttgart
The sources for this fictional expedition were old postcards, books and photographs. The collages were made both in analogue as well as digital manner.
The lightboxes are located in an underground corridor connecting two administration buildings of the Landesbank Baden-Württemberg.

36–39

Gran Paradiso
1997
Stahl, GFK, Glas, Neon
Vitrine: 1570 × 270 × 570 cm
Regal: 1250 × 2100 × 1270 cm
Neue Messe München, Vorfeld Haupteingang
In der Vitrine finden sich – horizontal geordnet und gehängt – die zwölf großen, aus Neon nachgeformten Alpenflüsse: Adda (mit Lago di Como), Mincio (mit Lago di Garda), Po, Adige, Rhône (mit Lac Léman), Ticino (mit Lago Maggiore), Inn, Rhein (mit Bodensee), Donau, Isar, Mur, Drau
Im Regal präsentieren sich insgesamt 29 Alpengipfel, die auf der folgenden Doppelseite einzeln vorgestellt werden. Die unterschiedlichen Größen und Höhen der Berge wurden zugunsten eines stimmigen Gesamtbildes verändert.
Gran Paradiso
1997
Steel GFK, glass, neon
Display case: 1570 × 270 × 570 cm
Shelves: 1250 × 2100 × 1270 cm
Neue Messe München, area in front of the main entrance
The display case contains the twelve major Alpine rivers, modelled in neon, arranged vertically and hung:
Adda (with Lago di Como), Mincio (with Lago di Garda), Po, Adige, Rhône (with Lac Léman), Ticino (with Lago Maggiore), Inn, Rhine (with Lake Constance), Danube, Isar, Mur, Drave
The shelves present a total of 29 Alpine peaks, which are individually presented on the following double pages. The different sizes and heights of the mountains were modified in favour of a harmonious overall image.

38

Von oben nach unten und von links nach rechts
From top to bottom and from left to right:

Aiguille Verte, Bietschhorn, Civetta
Eiger/Mönch/Jungfrau
Gran Zebru, Großglockner, Habicht
Schreckhorn/Lauteraarhorn, Marmolada
Pelmo, Piz Badile, Bernina
Tre Cime, Watzmann, Weisshorn

39

Von oben nach unten und von links nach rechts
From top to bottom and from left to right:

Dent Blanche, Dom/Täschhorn
Grand Combin, Grandes Jorasses
Hochgall, Hochvogel, Laliderer
Matterhorn, Mont Blanc
Piz Linard, Sasso Lungo, Tödi
Wetterhorn, Zugspitze

41

Rauminstallation
1998
Einzelausstellung *Bauhütte / XX. Jahrhundert*, Galerie Six Friedrich Lisa Ungar, München
Room installation
1998
Solo show *Bauhütte / XX. Jahrhundert*, Galerie Six Friedrich Lisa Ungar, Munich

Civetta
1997
Dentalgips, Rupfen, Aluminium, Gipskartonplatten, Holz
158 × 164 × 240 cm
Auflage: 3
Civetta
1997
Dental plaster, hessian, aluminium, plasterboards, wood
158 × 164 × 240 cm
Edition: 3

Weisshorn
1997
Dentalgips, Rupfen, Aluminium, Gipskartonplatten, Holz
205 × 165 × 240 cm
Auflage: 3
Weisshorn
1997
Dental plaster, hessian, aluminium, plasterboards, wood
205 × 165 × 240 cm
Edition: 3

Mont Blanc
1997
Relief
Dentalgips, Rupfen, Aluminium, Holz
289 × 194 × 75 cm
Mont Blanc
1997
Relief
Dental plaster, hessian, aluminium, wood
289 × 194 × 75 cm

Trägerstaffel
(→ 46)

42–45

Polarium (3. Expedition)
1998
Einzelausstellung *Bauhütte / XX. Jahrhundert*, Galerie Six Friedrich Lisa Ungar, München
7 Leuchtkästen
Glas, Diatrans-Folien, Aluminium, Leuchtmittel
Je 90 × 15 × 19 cm
Auflage: 3
Sammlung Bundesministerium der Finanzen, Berlin
Die Vorlagen für die fiktive Expedition entstammen alten Postkarten, Büchern und Fotografien. Die meisten Bildfragmente sind aus Fotografien der Shackleton-Expedition (1914–1916) entnommen. Die Bilder wurden sowohl analog als auch digital collagiert. Die 3. Auflage wurde in Form von Einzelkästen produziert.
Polarium (3d Expedition)
1998
Solo show *Bauhütte / XX. Jahrhundert*, Galerie Six Friedrich Lisa Ungar, Munich
7 lightboxes
Glass, Diatrans foils, aluminium, lighting
Each 90 × 15 × 19 cm
Edition: 3
Collection Bundesministerium der Finanzen, Berlin
The sources for the fictional expedition are old postcards, books and photographs. Most of the fragments of images were taken from photographs of the Shackleton expedition (1914–1916).

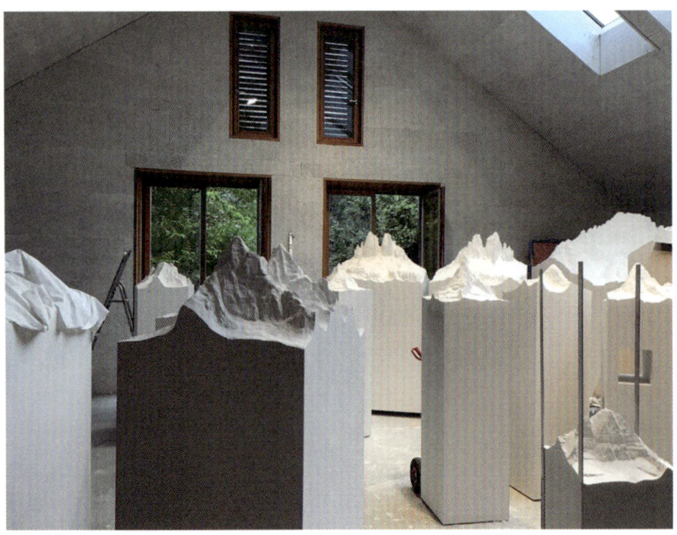

Atelier, 2020 / Studio, 2020

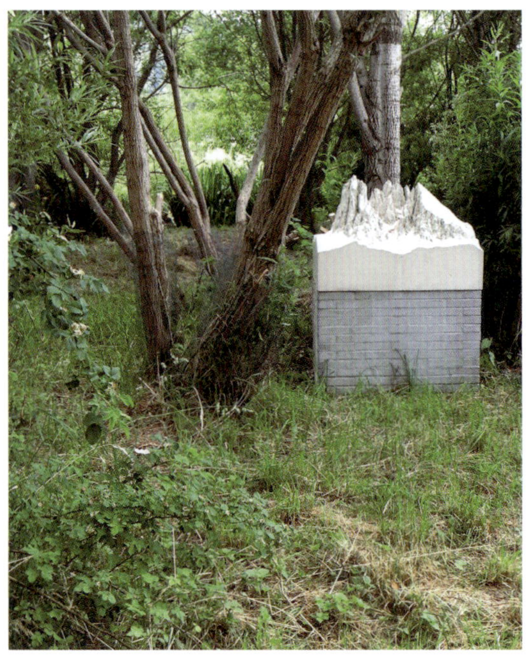

Privatbesitz, Allgäu, Deutschland
Private ownership, Allgäu, Germany

The images were collaged both with analogue as well as digital processes. The third edition was produced in the form of individual boxes.

46

Trägerstaffel
1998
Kiton-Anzug, Stickereien, Eisenstange, Drahtseil
Im Besitz des Künstlers
Der schwarze Luxusanzug ist mit 42 Namen von Sherpas, die als Träger und Helfer den Mount Everest bestiegen haben, bestickt.
Trägerstaffel (Porter Squad)
1998
Suit from Kiton, embroidery, iron rod, wire cable
In the artist's possession
The black luxury suit is embroidered with the names of 42 Sherpas who have climbed Mount Everest as porters and assistants.

47

Civetta und Weisshorn
1998
Doppelausstellung *Andrea Santarlasci Stephan Huber*, Galleria La Nuova Pesa, Rom
Civetta and Weisshorn
1998
Double exhibition *Andrea Santarlasci Stephan Huber*, Galleria La Nuova Pesa, Rome

Vorne
In front:

Civetta
1997
Dentalgips, Rupfen, Aluminium, Holz
Grundfläche 158 × 164 cm, Höhe 103 cm
Auflage: 3 mit verschiedenen Höhen
Civetta
1997
Dental plaster, hessian, aluminium, wood
Area 158 × 164 cm, height 103 cm
Edition: 3 with varying heights

Hinten
In the back:

Weisshorn
1997
(→ 41)

48

Weisshorn
1998
Doppelausstellung *Raffaela Nappo Stephan Huber*, Villa Comunale, Neapel
Weisshorn
1998
Double exhibition *Raffaela Nappo Stephan Huber*, Villa Comunale, Naples

Weisshorn
1997
(→ 41)

49

Gott als Berg denken
1999
Rauminstallation Heilig-Geist-Kirche, Landshut
Beitrag zur Gruppenausstellung *Schöpfung* des Diözesanmuseums Freising (Karmelitenkirche München, Diözesanmuseum Freising, Heilig-Geist-Kirche Landshut)
Alle Berge: Dentalgips, Rupfen, Aluminium, Gipskartonplatten, Holz
Gott als Berg denken (Think of God as a Mountain)
1999
Room installation Heilig-Geist-Kirche, Landshut

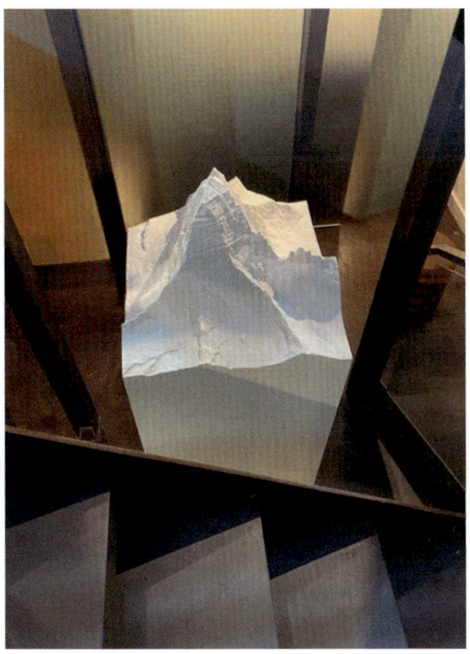

Privatbesitz, Telluride, USA
Private ownership, Telluride, USA

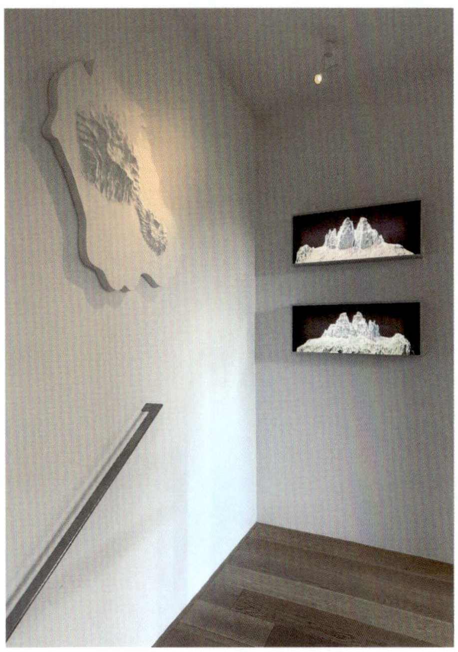

Privatsammlung, Starnberg, Deutschland
Private collection, Starnberg, Germany

Exhibited at the group show *Schöpfung* at the Diözesanmuseum Freising (Carmelite church Munich, Diözesanmuseum Freising, Heilig-Geist-Kirche, Landshut)
All mountains: dental plaster, hessian, aluminium, plasterboards, wood

Von links nach rechts
From left to right:

Spielberg
1996
185 × 165 × 230 cm
Unikat
Im Besitz des Künstlers
Spielberg
1996
185 × 165 × 230 cm
Unique work
In the artist's possession

Weisshorn
(→ 41)

Civetta
1997
158 × 164 × 225 cm
Auflage: 3
Civetta
1997
158 × 164 × 225 cm
Edition: 3

Sasso Lungo
1996/97
167 × 164 × 220 cm
Auflage: 3
Sasso Lungo
1996/97
167 × 164 × 2
Edition: 3

In der Apsis zu sehen
Visible in the apse:

Pia Stadtbäumer, *Arme*, 1995

50

Gran Paradiso II
1998
Rauminstallation
Montblanc Kulturstiftung, Hamburg
Dentalgips, Rupfen, Aluminium, Gipskartonplatten, Holz, Neon, Elektrik
Sammlung Hamburger Kunsthalle
Gran Paradiso II
1998
Room installation
Montblanc Kulturstiftung, Hamburg
Dental plaster, hessian, aluminium, plasterboards, wood, neon, electronics
Collection of the Hamburger Kunsthalle

Berge
Mountains:

Civetta
(→ 49)

Weisshorn
(→ 41)

Mont Blanc
1996/97
289 × 194 × 235 cm
Auflage: 3
Mont Blanc
1996/97
289 × 194 × 235 cm
Edition: 3

Flussläufe
River courses:

Rhein, Po und Rhône
Neon-Einzelstücke
Gesamtlänge jeweils ca. 30 Meter
Rhein, Po and Rhône
Individual neon works
Total length each ca. 30 metres

52/53

Gran Paradiso II
1999
Rauminstallation
Hamburger Kunsthalle
(→ 50)
Sammlung Hamburger Kunsthalle
In der Hamburger Kunsthalle wurde die ursprünglich in der Montblanc Kulturstiftung präsentierte Arbeit in neuer Form aufgebaut. Alle „Neonflüsse" waren nun zweigeteilt und liefen auf einen Raumeckpunkt des Fußbodens zu.
Gran Paradiso II
1999
Room installation
Hamburger Kunsthalle
(→ 50)
Collection of the Hamburger Kunsthalle
The work originally presented in the Montblanc Kulturstiftung was displayed in a new arrangement in the Hamburger Kunsthalle. All of the 'neon rivers' were now divided in two and led to a corner on the floor of the room.

54–56

Depositopo
1999
Rauminstallation
Arsenale, Biennale di Venezia, Venedig
Dentalgips, Rupfen, Aluminium, Gipskartonplatten, Holz, Neon, Elektrik
Depositopo
1999
Room installation
Arsenale, Venice Biennale, Venice
Dental plaster, hessian, aluminium, plasterboards, wood, neon, electronics

Berge
Mountains:

Weisshorn
(→ 41)
Civetta
(→ 49)
Sasso Lungo
(→ 49)
Spielberg
(→ 49)
Mont Blanc, französische Seite
Mont Blanc, French side
(→ 50)
Mont Blanc, italienische Seite
Mont Blanc, Italian side
(→ 50)

Flusslauf
River courses:

Po
Neon-Einzelstücke
Gesamtlänge ca. 120 Meter
Die große Halle im Arsenale war bis zu diesem Zeitpunkt nie genutzt worden und angefüllt mit hauptsächlich maritimem Müll, den ich nur an einigen Stellen zur Seite geräumt habe, um Skulpturen und Neonstücke installieren zu können. Die Nachbildung des Flusslaufes Po schwebte auf dünnen Aluminiumstäben zwischen und über dem Müll.
Po
Individual pieces of neon
Total length ca. 120 metres
The large hall in the Arsenale had never been used up to then and was filled with junk, mainly marine debris. I cleared only a few spots to install sculptures

and neon pieces. The reproduction of the course of the river Po floated on thin aluminium rods between and above the junk.

57

Großes Panorama
2006
Offsetdruck auf Papier
88 × 52 cm
Auflage: 800, signiert, nicht nummeriert
Sonderedition: 24, nummeriert, signiert und vom Künstler verlegt
Auftraggeber: Siemens AG
Großes Panorama (Great Panorama)
2006
Offset print on paper
88 × 52 cm
Edition: 800, signed, not numbered
Special edition: 24, numbered, signed and published by the artist
Commissioned by: Siemens AG

59

For Louis
2000
Dentalgips, Rupfen, Edelstahl
Ca. 60 × 40 × 40 cm
Auflage: 12 + AP
For Louis
2000
Dental plaster, hessian, stainless steel
Ca. 60 × 40 × 40 cm
Edition: 12 + artist proofs

Sasso Lungo auf einem Hutständer ist eine Jahresgabe von 2001 für den Schleswig-Holsteinischen Kunstverein, Kiel.
Sasso Lungo on a hat stand is an annual special edition for the Schleswig-Holsteinischer Kunstverein, Kiel.

Krone
2000
Dentalgips, Rupfen, Schnur
60 × 40 × 40 cm
Auflage: 100
Sonderedition für *Die Welt*, kuratiert von Harald Szeemann anlässlich der Biennale di Venezia, 1999.
Krone
2000
Dental plaster, hessian, rope
60 × 40 × 40 cm
Edition: 100
Special edition for the *Die Welt*, curated by Harald Szeemann on the occasion of the Venice Biennale, 1999

60–63

Saussures Herz
2000/01
Einzelausstellung *8,5 Zi.-Whg. f. Künstler, 49J.*, Lenbachhaus, München
Dentalgips, Rupfen, Aluminium, Gipskartonplatten, Holz, Edelstahl, Glas, Silikon, Luftpumpe mit Motor
Ca. 700 × 200 × 350 cm
Sammlung Museum der bildenden Künste, Leipzig
Die Länge variiert je nach Ausstellungsraum, da die Skulptur immer als eine Raumtrennung eingebaut ist. Die unter dem Bergmassiv Eiger, Mönch und Jungfrau gelegene, an einen Aufzug erinnernde Edelstahlkabine ist lediglich durch die mittlere der drei kleinen Türen betretbar. Im Innenraum pulsiert in einer beleuchteten Vitrine ein aus Silikon gefertigtes anatomisches Herzmodell. Ein maschinelles Pumpgeräusch ist zu hören. Der Titel bezieht sich auf Horace Bénédict de Saussure, den Genfer Naturforscher und Bergsteiger.
Saussures Herz (Saussure's Heart)
2000/01
Solo show *8,5 Zi.-Whg. f. Künstler, 49J.*, Lenbachhaus, Munich
Dental plaster, hessian, aluminium, plasterboards, wood, stainless steel, glass, silicon, air pump with motor
ca. 700 × 200 × 350 cm
Collection of the Museum der bildenden Künste, Leipzig

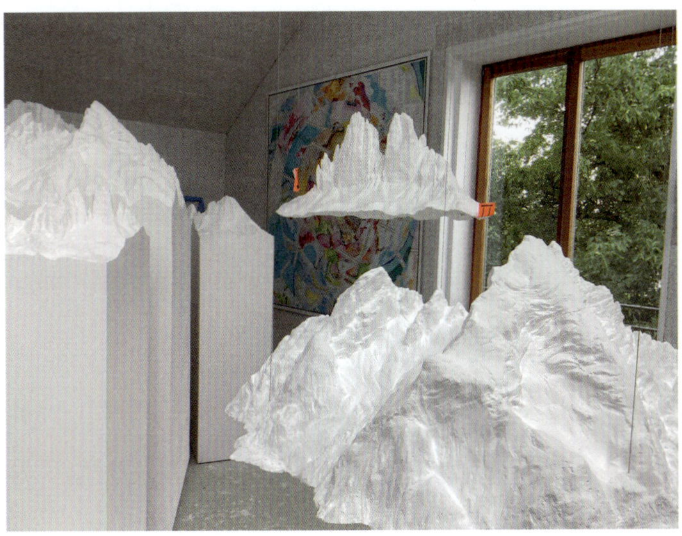

Atelier, 2023 / Studio, 2023

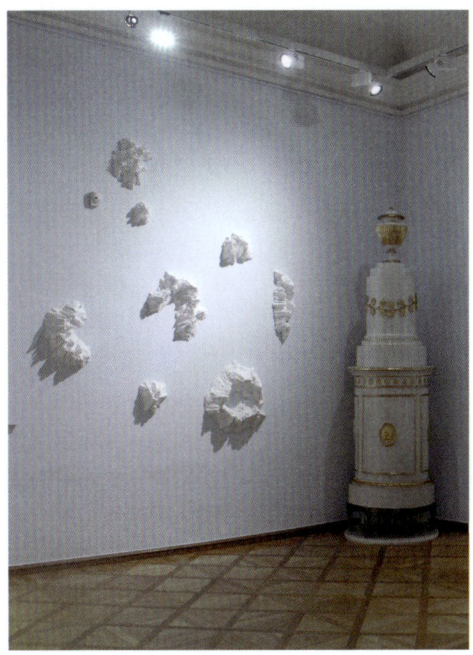

Residenzgalerie, Salzburg, Österreich / Austria

The length varies according to the exhibition room, since the sculpture is always installed as a room separator. The stainless steel cabin lying under the mountain range of the Eiger, Mönch and Jungfrau recalls a lift and can only be accessed through the middle of the three small doors. Inside, an anatomical model of a heart made of silicon pulsates in a lighted display case. One can hear the mechanical sound of a pump. The title refers to Horace Bénédict de Saussure, the natural explorer and mountain climber from Geneva.

64

Saussures Herz
(→ 60–63)
Sammlung Museum der bildenden Künste, Leipzig
Saussures Herz (Saussure's Heart)
Details
(→ 60–63)
Collection of the Museum der bildenden Künste, Leipzig

66

Ernstes Spiel
2006
Bleistift und Tusche auf topografischer Karte
69 × 63 cm
Privatsammlung Berlin
Ernstes Spiel (Serious Game)
2006
Pencil and ink on topographical map
69 × 63 cm
Private collection, Berlin

67

Hier und Jetzt
2006
Bleistift und Tusche auf topografischer Karte
69 × 63 cm
Sammlung Eres-Stiftung, München
Hier und Jetzt (Here and Now)
2006
Pencil and ink on topographical map
69 × 63 cm
Collection of the Eres Stiftung, Munich

68

Mein Ausflug zum Spiral Jetty im Jahr 1957
2003
Digital bearbeitete Fotografie
22 × 16 cm
Sammlung des Künstlers
Mein Ausflug zum Spiral Jetty im Jahr 1957 (My Excursion to Spiral Jetty in 1957)
2003
Digitally processed photograph
22 x 16 cm
Collection of the artist

Mein zufälliges dabei sein bei Asphalt Rundown im Jahr 1958
2003
Digital bearbeitete Fotografie
22 × 16 cm
Sammlung des Künstlers
Mein zufälliges dabei sein bei Asphalt Rundown im Jahr 1958 (My Accidental Witnessing of Asphalt Rundown in 1958)
2003
Digitally processed photograph
22 x 16 cm
Collection of the artist

70/71

Shit Happens
2001
Videoskulptur
Video, Loop, Soundsystem, Elektrik, Gipskartonplatten, Holz
Türe: Höhe ca. 75 cm
Auflage: 3
Beim Öffnen der Türe ist in einem rund zwei Meter tiefen trapezförmigen Raum das Video einer Lawine zu sehen, die mit dröhnendem Geräusch direkt auf den Betrachter zurast, dabei eine Hütte zertrümmert und sich in weißem Gestöber auflöst.
Shit Happens
2001
Video sculpture
Video, loop, sound system, electronics, plasterboards, wood
Doors: height ca. 75 cm
Edition: 3
Opening the door reveals an approximately two metre-deep, trapezoid space, in which a video loop displays an avalanche that advances directly toward the viewer with a menacing sound, destroying a hut and dissolving into a white flurry.

73

Shining
2004
2 Leuchtkästen
Großbild-Diapositive
Je 65 × 65 × 8 cm
Auflage: 4 + 1 AP
Shining zeigt das Modell meines Elternhauses in einer weißen Eislandschaft. In der Leuchtkastenversion dieses Titels ist der Fotoset mit der gesamten Kulisse sichtbar. Für das kleine Katalogbuch im Münchner Center for Advanced Studies der LMU München schrieb ich 2022 dazu folgenden Text:
„*Shining* entstand im Jahr 1999. Damals begann ich mich näher mit meiner Biografie im bundesrepublikanischen Nachkriegskontext zu beschäftigen. Es öffnete sich ein Reservoir voll ‚mitteilenswerter Erfahrung' (Adorno). Den fiktionalen Zeitpunkt der Aufnahme legte ich ins Jahr 1956, also vier Jahre nach meiner Geburt und ein Jahr nach dem Bau dieses Hauses im Allgäu. Meine kunstinteressierte Mutter war betroffen, als sie die Abbildungen von *Shining* in einem Katalog sah. Ich glaube, sie empfand diese Arbeit als einen verletzenden Angriff auf die Familie, zumindest als Angriff gegen ihr ständiges Bemühen um ein wohltemperiertes Wohnklima. Als Mutter und Ehefrau war sie damals eine Geborgenheitserschafferin mit der Aufgabe, neun Jahre nach der Niederschlagung des Nationalsozialismus eine weiche, geschichtsvergessene Familientextur herzustellen. Ungläubig nahm sie deshalb meinen Hinweis zur Kenntnis, bei *Shining* ginge es nicht um die Familie Huber, in der ich mich in meiner frühesten Kindheit als durchaus geborgen empfand. Nein, ich versicherte meiner Mutter, dass mich viel genereller die seelische Befindlichkeit von 1956 interessiere und dass ich ein Psychobild, eine Metapher für die Kälte der Nachkriegszeit suche. Ich erklärte ihr, dass es das allgemeine sedierte Geschichtsempfinden mit der Absenz des Holocaust sei, das mich interessiere, die Gesprächsverweigerung die jüngste Vergangenheit betreffend, die

Nazilehrer und traumatisierten Kriegsväter, letztlich das gesamte psycho-soziologische Umfeld meiner Kindheit. Dass ich auf der Folie der eigenen Biografie kollektive Geschichte erarbeitet hatte, störte meine Mutter. Einerseits, weil sie persönlich darin involviert war, andererseits war Kunst für sie immer Kanon jenseits der Selbstbespiegelung. Für mich war das Biografische jedoch der ‚Palast der Erinnerung' (Lars Gustafsson) und damit die eigentliche Befreiung aus dem innovationsaffinen Kanon der zeitgenössischen Kunst. Selbst wenn mich meine Zeitreise mit meinem Elternhaus auf diese Eisbühne ins Jahr 1956 beamte, so befand man sich immer noch elf Jahre entfernt von der Veröffentlichung des Buches *Die Unfähigkeit zu trauern* von Margarete und Alexander Mitscherlich."

Shining
2004
2 lightboxes
Large image slide
Each 65 × 65 × 8 cm
Edition: 4 + 1 artist proof

Shining depicts the model of my parents' house in an icy white landscape. The lightbox version of this work displays the set of photos with the entire scenery. I wrote the following text for the small catalogue at the Munich Center for Advanced Studies of the Ludwig Maximilians Universität in 2022:

'*Shining* was created in 1999. That was when I began to explore my biography more intensely within the context of the Federal Republic of Germany. A reservoir of 'experience worth communicating' (Adorno) opened up. I situated the fictional time when the photograph was taken in 1956, that is, four years after my birth and one year after the construction of the house in the Allgäu. My mother, who is interested in art, was disconcerted when she saw the pictures of *Shining* in a catalogue. I think she regarded this work as a scathing attack on the family, at least as an attack on her continuous efforts to maintain an even-tempered living climate. As mother and wife she was at that time a creator of comfort, tasked with generating a soft, history-denying family texture nine years after the defeat of Nazism. She did not believe me when I explained that *Shining* was not about the Huber family, in which I did indeed feel protected during my earliest childhood. No, I assured my mother, I was much more interested in the general psychological state of mind around 1956. I was seeking a psycho-image, a metaphor, for the coldness of the post-war years. I explained that I was interested in the widespread, sedated sensibility for history with the absence of the Holocaust, the refusal to talk about the recent past, the Nazi teachers and the traumatised war fathers, and ultimately the entire psycho-social environment of my childhood. That I addressed collective history through the material of my own biography disturbed my mother. On the one hand, because she was personally involved in it, and on the other, because art for her was always a canon beyond self-reflection. For me, by contrast, my biography provided a 'palace of memory' (Lars Gustafsson) and consequently a true liberation from the innovation-driven canon of contemporary art. Even if my time travel with my parents' house beamed me to this icy stage in 1956, it was still eleven years before the publication of the book *Inability of Mourning* by Margarete and Alexander Mitscherlich.'

74–77

Shining
2001
4 Fotografien
Lambdaprints auf Ilfordpapier, Pigmentprint auf Baumwolle-Velinpapier
Auflage: 7 + 2 AP
75 × 43 cm
42 × 59 cm

Die Größenvariation innerhalb der Auflage liegt im nachträglichen Austausch der schlecht alternden Lambdaprints durch haltbare Pigmentprints auf säurefreiem Papier begründet. Auf Wunsch der Besitzer ändere ich, unter Beibehaltung der Auflagennummer, auch die Größe des Ausdrucks.

Shining
2001
4 photographs
Lambda prints on Ilford paper, pigment print on cotton vellum paper
Edition: 7 + 2 artist proofs
75 × 43 cm
42 × 59 cm

The variation in sizes within the edition resulted from the later substitution of the Lambda prints, which age badly, by more stable pigment prints on acid-free paper. If requested by the owner, I can modify the size of print, while maintaining the edition number.

78/79

Ohne Titel
1998
Bleistift, Tusche, Farbstift auf DAV-Landkarte Hochvogel
22 × 31 cm
Privatsammlung Ulm

Ohne Titel (Untitled)
1998
Pencil, ink, coloured pen on DAV map 'Hochvogel'
22 × 31 cm
Private collection, Ulm

80–83

Lager A–E
2003/2019
5 Leuchtkästen
Großbild-Diapositive
Je 50 × 50 cm
Auflage: 4 + 2 AP
Privatsammlung München

Lager A–E (Storeroom A–E)
2003/2019
5 lightboxes
Large image slide
Each 50 × 50 cm
Edition: 4 + 2 artist proofs
Private collection, Munich

84–103

Im Gespräch zwischen Reinhold Messner und mir tauchen Namen, Berge und Museen auf, die im Folgenden in alphabetischer Reihenfolge für den nicht bergaffinen Leser kurz beschrieben werden.

The conversation between Reinhold Messner and myself refers to various people, mountains and museums that might be unfamiliar to those who are not fans of mountains. They are briefly explained below in alphabetical order.

Bauer, Paul (1896–1990)
Der Deutsche war verantwortlich für die nationalsozialistische Gleichschaltung des Bergsteigens.
Bauer, Paul (1896–1990)
This German climber was responsible for enforcing conformity to Nazi ideology in German mountaineering.

Bonatti, Walter (1930–2011)
Der Italiener galt als einer der begabtesten Bergsteiger seiner Zeit. Er verfasste 20 Bücher.
Bonatti, Walter (1930–2011)
The Italian mountaineer was regarded as one of the most talented climbers of his time. He wrote 20 books.

Bridwell, Jim (1944–2018)
Der Amerikaner war Protagonist des Bigwall- und Freikletterns im Yosemite-Park.
Bridwell, Jim (1944–2018)
The American pioneer of big wall and free climbing in Yosemite National Park.

Buhl, Hermann (1924–1957)
Der Österreicher war Erstbesteiger des Nanga Parbat. Als Geschäftsführer der Hutfabrik Ottmar Reich stattete mein Vater Hermann Buhl für seine Expedition am Broad Peak mit Mützen und Hüten aus. Davon zeugt ein Buch mit einer Buhlschen Widmung, die meinem Vater galt und mich als Kind faszinierte.
Buhl, Hermann (1924–1957)
The Austrian mountaineer was the first to climb Nanga Parbat. My father, the managing director of the hat manufacturer Hutfabrik Ottmar Reich, equipped Hermann Buhl with caps and hats for his expedition to Broad Peak. This is corroborated by a book with a dedication from Buhl to my father, which fascinated me as a child.

El Capitan
Die tausend Meter hohe Felswand im Yosemite-Park/USA birgt einige der schwierigsten Kletterrouten der Welt.
El Capitan
The 1,000-metre high rock face in Yosemite National Park (United States) represents one of the most difficult climbing routes in the world.

Herrligkoffer, Karl Maria (1916–1991)
Der deutsche Arzt war Expeditionsleiter im Himalaya und Karakorum.
Herrligkoffer, Karl Maria (1916–1991)
The German physician led expeditions to the Himalayas and the Karakoram Mountains.

Herzog, Maurice (1919–2012)
Der französische Bergsteiger war später Minister im Kabinett von Charles de Gaulle. Herzogs Buch *Annapurna* (1951) erreichte eine Millionenauflage.
Herzog, Maurice (1919–2012)
The French mountaineer was later minister in Charles de Gaulle's cabinet. His book *Annapurna* (1951) was a bestseller.

Hill, Lynn (*1961)
Die herausragende amerikanische Sportkletterin kletterte die Route *The Nose* am El Capitan erstmals frei – eine Pionierleistung.
Hill, Lynn (*1961)
The excellent US-American sports climber ascended the 'Nose' route on El Capitan solo for the first time – a pioneering achievement.

Hillary, Edmund (1919–2008)
Dem neuseeländischen Bergsteiger gelang zusammen mit dem nepalesischen Sherpa Tenzing Norgay 1953 die Erstbesteigung des Mount Everest.
Hillary, Edmund (1919–2008)
The mountaineer from New Zealand was the first to climb Mount Everest in 1953 together with the Nepalese Sherpa Tenzing Norgay.

Lachenal, Louis (1921–1955)
Die Franzosen Lachenal und Maurice Herzog waren die Ersten, die 1950 auf dem Gipfel eines Achttausenders standen.
Lachenal, Louis (1921–1955)
The Frenchmen Lachenal and Maurice Herzog were the first to ascend to the peak of an eight-thousander in 1950.

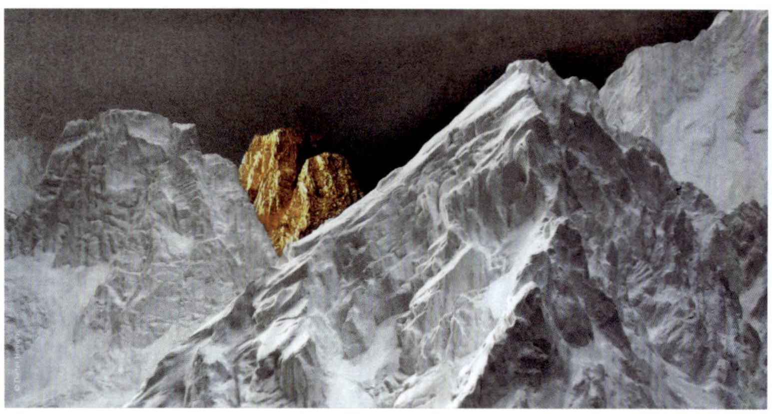

Atelier, 2005
Studio, 2005

Mallory, George (1886–1924)
Der Brite war ein Wegbereiter des Bergsteigens am Mount Everest.
Mallory, George (1886–1924)
The British alpinist was a pioneer of mountaineering on Mount Everest.

Merkl, Willy (1900–1934)
Der Deutsche wurde zur deutschen Heldenfigur des sogenannten „deutschen Schicksalsberges“ Nanga Parbat hochstilisiert. Dort starb er 1934 zusammen mit zehn anderen Bergsteigern.
Merkl, Willy (1900–1934)
The German climber was elevated into a German hero of the so-called 'fateful' German mountain Nanga Parbat. He died there in 1934 with ten other climbers.

MMM: Messner Mountain Museum
In unserem Gespräch werden immer wieder drei von sechs Messner Mountain Museen erwähnt
MMM: Messner Mountain Museum
Our conversation mentions three of the six Messner Mountain Museums:

MMM Firmian
Das Museum auf Schloss Sigmundskron in Bozen ist das Herzstück der Messner Mountain Museen und thematisiert die Auseinandersetzung Mensch und Berg.
MMM Firmian
The museum at Sigmundskron castle in Bozen/Bolzano is the hub of the Messner Mountain Museums, presenting the encounter between human and mountain.

MMM Corones auf dem Kronplatz bei St. Vigil
Erbaut von Zaha Hadid, widmet sich das Museum der Königsdisziplin des Bergsteigens, dem traditionellen Alpinismus.
MMM Corones at the Kronplatz near St. Vigil
Built by Zaha Hadid, the museum is dedicated to the supreme discipline of mountaineering, traditional alpinism.

Das MMM Dolomites
Das Museum auf dem Monte Rite bei Cibiana di Cadore erzählt die Geschichte der Dolomiten.
MMM Dolomites
The museum on Monte Rite near Cibiana di Cadore tells the story of the Dolomites.

Mummery, Albert (1855–1895)
Der britische Ökonom war einer der führenden Bergsteiger seiner Zeit, bevor er am Nanga Parbat verscholl.
Mummery, Albert (1855–1895)
The British economist was one of the leading alpinists of his time, before he disappeared on Nanga Parbat.

Preuß, Paul (1886–1913)
Dem österreichischen Bergsteiger gelangen 300 Besteigungen im Alleingang ohne Hilfsmittel. Er gilt als einer der geistigen Väter des Freikletterns und sicherte das Bergsteigen durch Bücher und Vorträge intellektuell ab.
Preuß, Paul (1886–1913)
The Austrian climber made 300 ascents alone without aids. He is regarded as one of the spiritual fathers of free climbing and gave mountaineering with intellectual recognition.

Robbins, Royal (1935–2017)
Der amerikanische Pionier des Big-Wall-Kletterns kletterte am El Capitan die damals schwierigsten Routen der Welt. Er schrieb zwei einflussreiche Bücher über das Felsklettern.
Robbins, Royal (1935–2017)
The US-American pioneer of big wall climbing ascended El Capitan via the most difficult routes in the world. He wrote two highly influential books on rock climbing.

Roberts, Colonel James (1916–1997)
Der britische Bergsteiger war Militärattaché in Kathmandu. Er gilt als der Begründer des Trekkings in Nepal.
Roberts, Colonel James (1916–1997)
The British mountaineer was military attaché in Kathmandu. He is regarded as the founder of trekking in Nepal.

Scott, Doug (1941–2020)
Der Brite zählt zu den erfolgreichsten und besten Höhenbergsteigern aller Zeiten.
Scott, Doug (1941–2020)
The British alpinist numbers among the most successful and best extreme mountain climbers of all times.

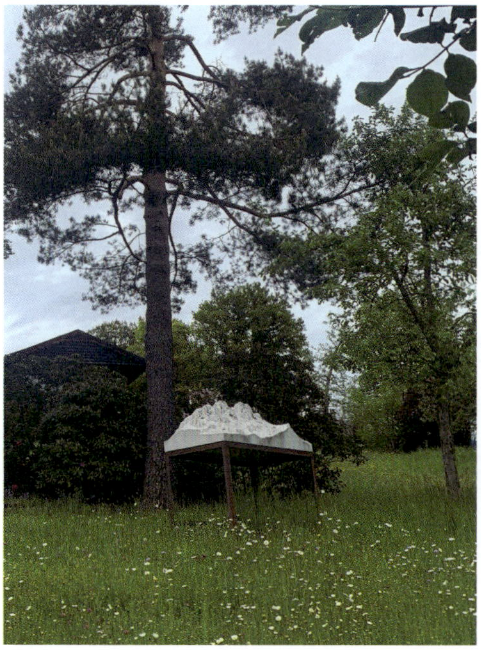

Privatsammlung, Chiemsee, Deutschland
Private collection, Chiemsee, Germany

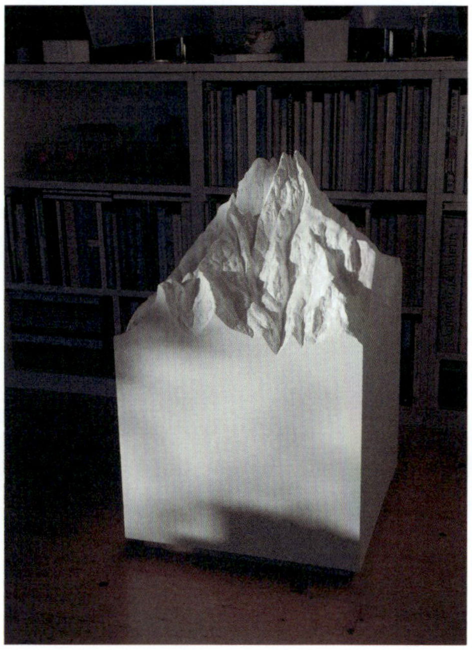

Privatsammlung, Ulm, Deutschland
Private collection, Ulm, Germany

Terray, Lionel (1921–1965)
Der französische Bergsteiger verzeichnete zahlreiche erfolgreiche Erstbesteigungen und schrieb das berühmte Bergbuch *Die Eroberung des Unnützen*.
Terray, Lionel (1921–1965)
The French climber completed numerous successful first ascents and wrote the famous mountaineering book *Conquistadors of the Useless*.

Whymper, Edward (1840–1911)
Der englische Erstbesteiger des Matterhorns war Bergführer, Schriftsteller und Zeichner.
Whymper, Edward (1840–1911)
The English mountaineer, writer and draughtsman was the first to ascend the Matterhorn.

Zurbriggen, Matthias (1856–1917)
Dem Schweizer Bergführer gelangen viele Erstbesteigungen und Höhenrekorde. Nach dem Ende seiner Karriere stürzte er sozial ab, wurde Landstreicher und wählte in Genf den Freitod.
Zurbriggen, Matthias (1856–1917)
The Swiss climber made many first ascents and set a number of altitude records. After the end of his career he fell into social decline, became a tramp, and committed suicide in Geneva.

105–111

In die Berge schreien
2005/06
Rauminstallation
Dentalgips, Rupfen, Aluminium, Holz, Glas, Silikon, Soundsystem
Mont Blanc stehend:
289 × 194 × 235 cm
Mont Blanc gekippt:
289 × 150 × 194 cm
MMM Firmian auf Schloss Sigmundskron, Bozen
Neben dem stehenden Mont Blanc befindet sich der im 90-Grad-Winkel gekippte, obere Teil des Mont Blancs, auf dessen senkrechter Seite eine in die Fläche eingelassene Vitrine mit einem anatomischen Silikonherz zu sehen ist. Daraus ertönen die von mir geschriebenen und von einem Schauspieler vertonten fiktiven Tagebucheintragungen von Horace Bénédict de Saussure, dem Genfer Naturforscher, der maßgeblich die Besteigung des Mont Blancs vorantrieb.
In die Berge schreien
(Screaming in the Mountains)
2005/06
Room installation
Dental plaster, hessian, aluminium, wood, glass, silicone, sound system
Mont Blanc vertical:
289 × 194 × 235 cm
Mont Blanc horizontal:
289 × 150 × 194 cm
MMM Firmian at Schloss Sigmundskron, Bolzano
Next to the standing, vertical Mont Blanc is another mountain, the upper part of Mont Blanc, tilted at 90 degrees. A display case is inserted into its vertical side with an anatomic model of a silicone heart. The fictional diary entries of Horace Bénédict de Saussure, the Geneva natural scientist and promoter of the ascent of Mont Blanc, are sounded by the heart. They were written by me and are read by an actor.

Tagebuchaufzeichnungen des Horace Bénédict de Saussure
Diary entries of Horace Bénédict de Saussure:

Eintrag vom 14.5.1765
„Ich muss hoch. Ich will hoch. Ich werde es schaffen. Der Mont Blanc ist bei mir eine Krankheit geworden. Ich kann den Berg nicht mehr anblicken, ohne von schmerzhaftem Verlangen nach ihm ergriffen zu werden. Ich bin Berggläubiger geworden. Ein Felsbegehrer. Ein Schneesüchtiger."
Entry of 14 May 1765
'I have to go up. I want to go up. I will make it. Mont Blanc has become a disease with me. I can no longer look at the mountain without being seized by a painful desire for it. I have become a mountain believer. A desirer of rock. A snow addict.'

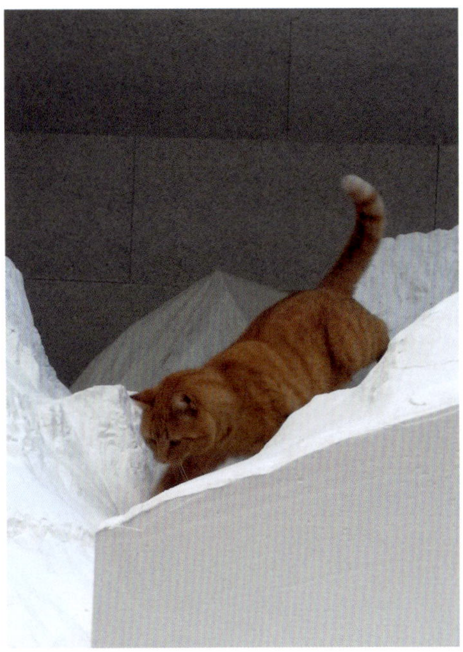

Atelier, 2019 / Studio, 2019

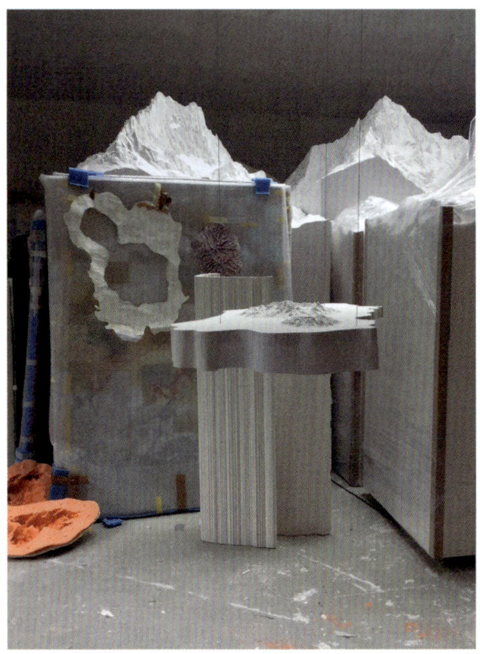

Atelier, 2020 / Studio, 2020

Eintrag vom 17.5.1765
„Ich werde ihn besteigen. Ich werde der Erste sein. Dies wird alle meine wissenschaftlichen Untersuchungen in den Schatten stellen. Meine Freunde in Europa werden überrascht sein. Noch niemals war ein Mensch höher."
Entry of 17 May 1765
'I will climb it. I will be the first. This will eclipse all my scientific research. My friends in Europe will be surprised. No man has ever been higher.'

Eintrag vom 1.8.1786
„Henri erzählte, Balmat und Piccard, der Kristallsucher und der Wunderdoktor, werden nächste Woche den Mont Blanc besteigen. Soll ich das glauben? Kann ich ihnen noch zuvorkommen? Ich bin fassungslos. Meine Idee. Meine Vision."
Entry of 1 August 1786
'Henri told me that Balmat and Piccard, the crystal seeker and the miracle doctor, will climb Mont Blanc next week. Should I believe that? Can I still beat them to it? I am stunned. My idea. My vision.'

Eintrag vom 7.8.1786
„Unglaublich. Balmat und Piccard auf dem Gipfel. Diese einfachen Gemüter. Dennoch großen Respekt. Aber sie sind sich der Tragweite ihres Erfolges sicher nicht bewusst. Ich habe es geahnt. Es ist möglich. Ich habe sie dazu gebracht. Ich werde es auch tun. Ich werde die Besteigung verankern in den intellektuellen Kreisen Europas. Es wird keine körperliche Leistung, sondern die Kraft einer Idee. Mein Punkt außerhalb der Welt, von der ich sie bewegen kann. Wir werden nicht mehr flächig denken, sondern vertikal."
Entry of 7 August 1786
'Incredible. Balmat and Piccard on the summit. These simple minds. Still, great respect. But I'm sure they do not realise the magnitude of their success. I suspected it. It is possible. I made them do it. I will do it too. I will establish the climb in the intellectual circles of Europe. It will not be a physical feat, but the power of an idea. My spot outside the world from which I can move it. We will no longer think flatly, but vertically.'

Eintrag vom 1.12.1786
„Hässliche Intrigen zwischen Balmat und Piccard. Sie versuchen sich gegenseitig die Besteigung streitig zu machen. Sie sind wieder in den Niederungen angelangt. Sie haben die Größe ihrer Besteigung nie verstanden, weil sie körperlich denken. Was ist ein Muskel gegen eine Idee? Es ist deprimierend. Nächstes Frühjahr werde ich meine Vision verwirklichen."
Entry of 1 December 1786
'Ugly intrigues between Balmat and Piccard. They try to dispute each other's ascent. They are back in the lowlands. They have never understood the greatness of their ascent because they think physically. What is a muscle against an idea? It is depressing. Next spring I will realise my vision.'

Eintrag vom 1.5.1787
„Ende Juli werde ich den Mont Blanc besteigen. Ich habe Balmat als einen der Führer engagiert. Ideen brauchen starke Helfer."
Entry of 1 May 1787
'At the end of July I will climb Mont Blanc. I have engaged Balmat as one of the guides. Ideas need strong helpers.'

Eintrag vom 6.6.1787
„Noch fünf Wochen, dann wird meine Vision wahr. Erhabenheit wird triumphieren. Hatte gestern einen Traum, dass ich auf dem Gipfel stehe und sich mir die Welt nur aus sich selbst erklärt. Alles war von oben einsichtig. Alles hing in klaren Strukturen zusammen. Im Traum erschien mir mein Urenkel, der alles in Sprache fassen konnte, was ich erahnte. Ich war eins mit der Gegenwart, Vergangenheit und Zukunft. Ich konnte wie durch ein Fenster in die Salons von London und Paris sehen und sah die Menschen über mich sprechen. Chamonix war plötzlich zum Zentrum der Welt geworden."
Entry of 6 June 1787
'Five more weeks and my vision will come true. Sublimity will triumph. Had a dream yesterday that I was standing on the summit and the world explained itself to me solely from itself. Everything was clear from above. Everything was linked together in clear structures. In the dream, my great-grandson appeared to me, who was able to put into language everything that I had surmised. I was one with the present, the past, and the future. I could see in the salons of London and Paris as if through a window, I saw people talking about me. Chamonix had suddenly become the centre of the world.'

Eintrag vom 2.8.1787
„Wir sind auf dem Gipfel. Welch ein Ausblick. Mein Körper zittert vor Erregen. Meine Gedanken vibrieren vor Klarheit. Niemals zuvor fühlte ich mich so demütig und gleichzeitig so erhaben. Ich bin Teil des Universums. Der Mittler zwischen der Erde und der Unendlichkeit. Jahre der Arbeit haben mir dieses Gefühl nicht gegeben. Der Weg zurück in die Niederungen wird schwer werden."
Sprecher: Joseph Baum
Entry of 2 August 1787
'We are on the summit. What a view. My body trembles with excitement. My thoughts vibrate with clarity. Never before have I felt so humble and at the same time so exalted. I am part of the universe. The mediator between the earth and infinity. Years of work have not given me this feeling. The road back to the lowlands will be hard.'
Speaker: Joseph Baum

Region RM
2005/06
Lambdaprint auf Fotopapier
396 × 215 cm
Sammlung MMM, Messner Mountain Museum
An einer Wand des Raumes erstreckt sich eine große Landkarte. *Region RM* ist eine Collage aus verschiedenen geologischen, topografischen, militärischen und schulischen Karten mit fotografischen Fragmenten und anatomischen Darstellungen. Sie bildet die Einzugsbereiche von Reinhold Messners Bergmuseen ab.
Region RM
2005/06
Lambda print on photographic paper
396 × 215 cm
Collection of the MMM, Messner Mountain Museum
A large map stretches across one wall of the room. Region RM is a collage of various geological, topographical, military and school maps with photographic fragments and anatomical representations. It maps the drainage areas of Reinhold Messner's mountain museums.

113

Perfect Sculpture 6 (Tre Cime)
2016
Dentalgips, Rupfen, Holz, Gipskartonplatten, Wandglätter
48 × 48 × 180 cm
MMM Corones, Kronplatz bei St. Vigil
Sammlung MMM, Messner Mountain Museum
Perfect Sculpture 6 (Tre Cime)
2016
Dental plaster, hessian, wood, plasterboards, finish filler
48 × 48 × 180 cm
MMM Corones, Kronplatz near St. Vigil
Collection of the MMM, Messner Mountain Museum

114–116

3 Berge und 15 Bücher
2015
MMM Corones, Kronplatz bei St. Vigil
Sammlung MMM, Messner Mountain Museum
3 Berge und 15 Bücher (Three Mountains and Fifteen Books)
2015
MMM Corones, Kronplatz near St. Vigil
Collection MMM, Messner Mountain Museum

El Capitan
2014
Dentalgips, Rupfen, Aluminium, Holz, Gipskartonplatten, Wandglätter, Papier
120 × 120 × 230 cm
El Capitan
2014
Dental plaster, hessian, aluminium, wood, plasterboards, finish filler, paper
120 × 120 × 230 cm

Civetta
1998
Dentalgips, Rupfen, Aluminium, Holz, Gipskartonplatten, Wandglätter, Papier
110 × 110 × 225 cm
Civetta
1998
Dental plaster, hessian, aluminium, wood, plasterboards, finish filler, paper
110 × 110 × 225 cm

Pelmo
1998
Dentalgips, Rupfen, Aluminium, Holz, Gipskartonplatten, Wandglätter, Papier
110 × 110 × 225 cm
In den Bergsockeln finden sich Vertiefungen für Bücher. Alle Buchexemplare haben fiktionale Titel und erschienen in fiktionalen Verlagen.
Pelmo
1998
Dental plaster, hessian, aluminium, wood, plasterboards, finish filler, paper
110 × 110 × 225 cm
There are recesses for books in the mountains' pedestals. All of the copies have fictional titles and were published by fictional publishers.

Buchtitel in der Vertiefung der Civetta
Book titles in the recess of the Civetta:

Stephan Huber Reinhold Messner, *King of the Mountains 1. Ein Psychogramm*, Labyrinth Verlag
Stephan Huber Reinhold Messner, *King of the Mountains 2. Ein Psychogramm*, Labyrinth Verlag
Reinhold Messner, *Schiefer Tod*, Edition Second Step
Huber/Saussure, *Balmat im Felsendom*, Labyrinth Verlag
Stephan Huber, *Monti Sacri I. Ikonografie & Obsession*, Edition Sublime
Stephan Huber & Reinhold Messner, *King of the Mountains 1. A Psychological Study*, Labyrinth Verlag
Stephan Huber & Reinhold Messner, *King of the Mountains 2. A Psychological Study*, Labyrinth Verlag
Reinhold Messner, *Steep Death*, Edition Second Step
Huber/Saussure, *Balmat in the Felsendom*, Labyrinth Verlag
Stephan Huber, *Monti Sacri I, Iconography & Obsession*, Edition Sublime

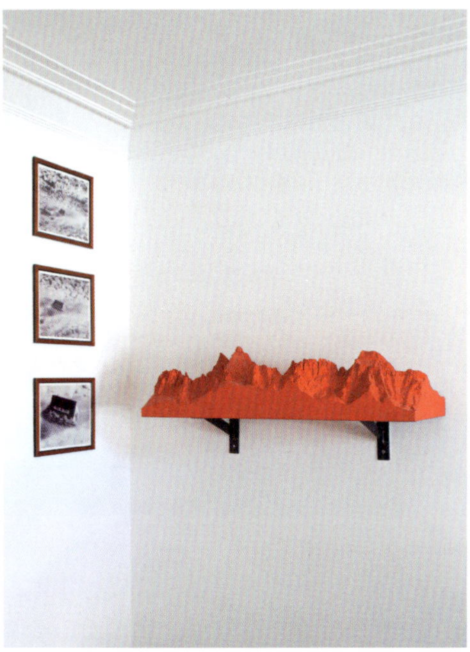

Privatsammlung, München, Deutschland
Private collection, Munich, Germany

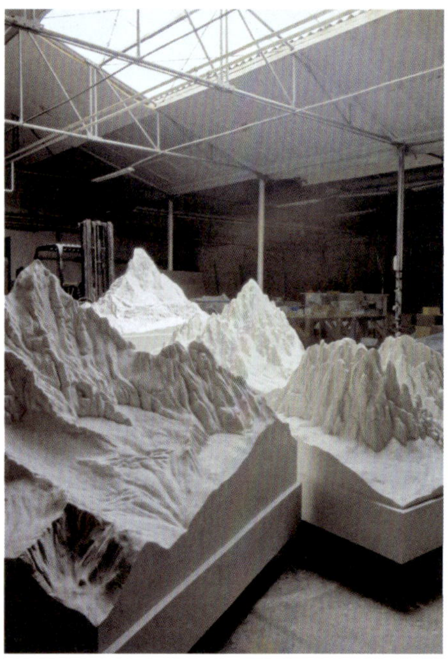

Atelier, 1999 / Studio, 1999

Buchtitel in den Vertiefungen des Pelmo
Book titles in the recess of the Pelmo:

Buchnische 1:
Stephan Huber, *Soziales Milieu im Höllengebirge*, Labyrinth Verlag
Stephan Huber, *Tod im Tiefland. Eine Studie über die Verdrängung*, Verlag Second Step
Huber/Huber, *Bella Vista pure form. Manolo Il Mago*, Edition Sublime
Reinhold Messner, *Free Solo*, Edition Second Step
Buchnische 2:
R. Messner, *Spigollo giallo I*, pure form
R. Messner, *Spigollo giallo II*, pure form
Huber Jardine Messner, *Seperate Reality*, Edition Sublime
Stephan Huber, *Nordwand Südkreuz*, Labyrinth Verlag
Book niche 1:
Stephan Huber, *Social Milieu in the Höllengebirge*, Labyrinth Verlag
Stephan Huber, *Death in the Lowlands. A Study of Repression*, Verlag Second Step
Huber/Huber, *Bella Vista, Pure Form. Manolo Il Mago*, Edition Sublime
Reinhold Messner, *Free Solo*, Edition Second Step
Book niche 2:
R. Messner, *Spigollo giallo I, Pure Form*
R. Messner, *Spigollo giallo II, Pure Form*
Huber Jardine Messner, *Separate Reality*, Edition Sublime
Stephan Huber, *Nordwand Südkreuz*, Labyrinth Verlag

Buchtitel in der Vertiefung des El Capitan
Book titles in the recess of the El Capitan:

Waren Harding, *The Nose*, Wilderness Books
Huber/Huber, *Am Limit*, Edition Second Step
Royal Robbins, *Salathé Wall*, Labyrinth Verlag
Jim Bridwell, *The Anarchism*, The Mountaineers Publisher
Lynn Hill, *It goes, boys*, Edition Second Step
Warren Harding, *The Nose*, Wilderness Books
Huber/Huber, *At the Limit*, Edition Second Step
Royal Robbins, *Salathé Wall*, Labyrinth Verlag
Jim Bridwell, *The Anarchism*, The Mountaineers' Publisher
Lynn Hill, *It Goes, Boys*, Edition Second Step

118–123

Bergederweltremix
2015
Fünfteilig
Lamdaprint auf Fotopapier auf Aludibond
850 × 202 cm
MMM Corones, Kronplatz bei St. Vigil
Sammlung MMM, Messner Mountain Museum
Collage aus verschiedenen topografischen Landkarten und Fotografien. Alle wichtigen Gebirge der Welt sind kartografisch zusammengefügt. Erläuterungen zu Personen oder Ereignissen befinden sich im oberen Teil der Karte, die aus geologischen Kartenfragmenten gestaltet ist. Im unteren Teil verknüpft eine Zeitschiene die politischen, kulturellen und alpinen Ereignisse durch fünf Jahrhunderte.
Bergederweltremix
(Mountains of the World Remix)
2015
Five parts
Lambda print on photographic paperon Aludibond
850 × 202 cm
MMM Corones, Kronplatz near St. Vigil
Collection of the MMM, Messner Mountain Museum
Collage of various topographic maps and photographs. All the important mountain ranges of the world are mapped together. Explanations about people or events are in the upper part of the map, which is made up of geological map fragments. In the lower part there is a timeline linking political, cultural, and alpine events through five centuries.

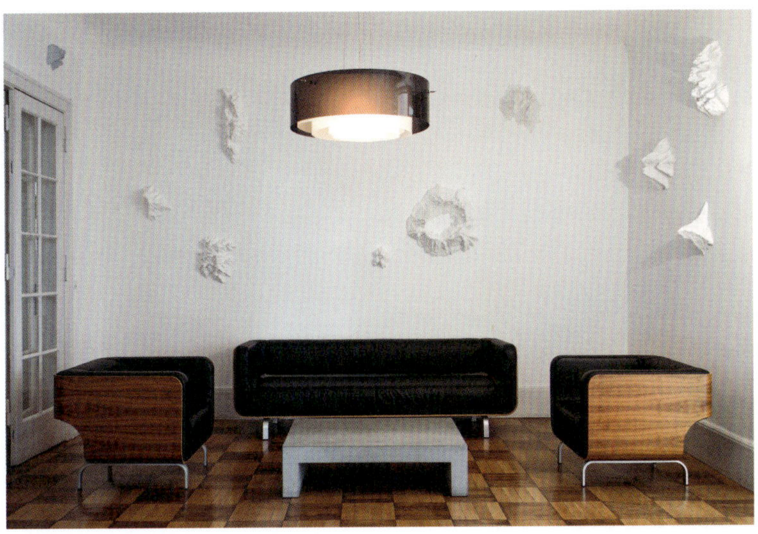

CAS, München, Deutschland
CAS, Munich, Germany

131

Rauminstallation
2002
MMM Dolomites, Monte Rite,
Cibiana di Cadore
Room installation
2002
MMM Dolomites, Monte Rite,
Cibiana di Cadore

Pelmo
1998
(→ 114–116)

Civetta
1998
(→ 114–116)

Antelao
1998
Dentalgips, Rupfen, Aluminium, Holz,
Gipskartonplatten, Wandglätter
110 × 110 × 225 cm
Auflage: 3; davon eine Auflage ohne
Gipskartonsockel mit den Maßen
110 × 110 × 95 cm
Antelao
1998
Dental plaster, hessian, aluminium,
wood, plasterboards, finish filler
110 × 110 × 225 cm
Edition: 3; one of them without plaster-board pedestal with the dimensions
110 × 110 × 95 cm

Buchtitel in der Vertiefung
Book titles in the recess:
Huber/Inoue/Messner, *Die Eiswand*,
Labyrinth Verlag
Stephan Huber & Peter Rosegger, *Sturm über dem Allgäu*, Labyrinth Verlag
Reinhold Messner, *Vertical Limit*,
Edition Second Step
Reinhold Messner, *Die Kunst des Kletterns I*, pure form
Reinhold Messner, *Free Solo*,
Edition Second Step
Huber/Inoue/Messner, *The Ice Wall*,
Labyrinth Verlag
Stephan Huber & Peter Rosegger,
***Storm Over the Allgäu*, Labyrinth Verlag**
Reinhold Messner, *Vertical Limit*,
Edition Second Step
Reinhold Messner, *The Art of Climbing I*, Pure Form
Reinhold Messner, *Free Solo*,
Edition Second Step

Im Hintergrund
In the background:

Tre Cime
2001
Leuchtkästen, Version A
Sammlung MMM, Messner
Mountain Museum
Tre Cime
2001
Lightbox, version A
Collection of the MMM,
Messner Mountain Museum
(→ 154/155)

132/133

Panorama Nr. 2
1999
Aus einer Serie von sechs Panoramen
Dentalgips, Rupfen, Eisen, Acryl,
Tusche
130 × 40 × 40 cm
Beschriftung: Yasushi 1907, Adalbert 1805, Bert 1898, Lars 1936, Thomas ca. 1930, Arno 1914, Italo 1923, Lewis 1832, Cesare 1908.
Die Vornamen und Geburtsdaten gehören (von links nach rechts) zu Inoue, Stifter, Brecht, Gustafsson, Pynchon, Schmidt, Calvino, Carroll und Pavese.
Sammlung Kunsthalle Hamburg
In insgesamt sechs Panoramen habe ich verschiedene Berge aus verschiedenen Regionen zu scheinbar zusammengehörigen Massiven verknüpft. Auf den jeweiligen Vorderfronten sind den einzelnen Bergen Namen mit Jahreszahlen zugeordnet. Sie stehen für meine damaligen „Heroen“ aus dem kulturellen Kontext:
Panorama 1: Die Bildenden Künstler 1; Panorama 2: Die Literaten; Panorama 3:

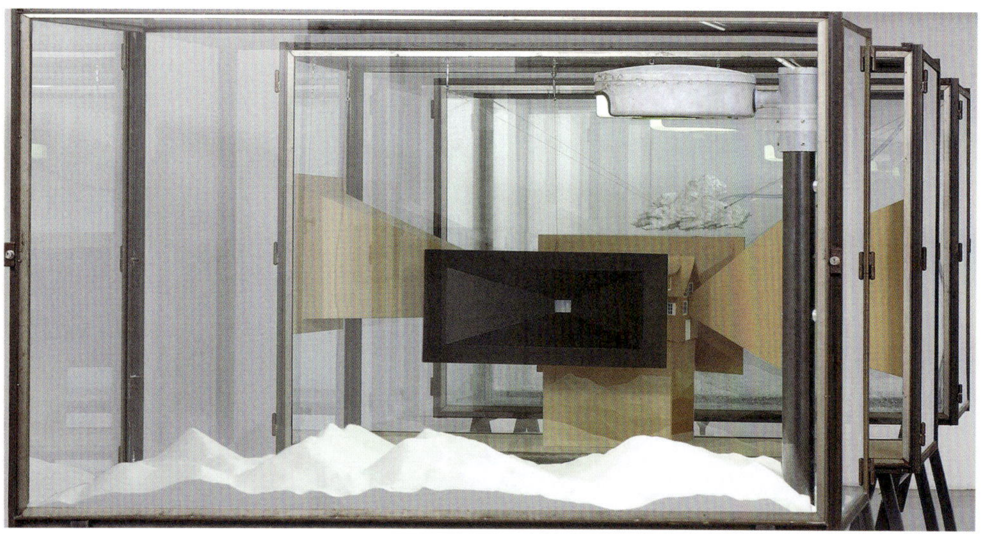

Sammlung Tiroler Landesmuseum, Innsbruck, Österreich
Collection of the Tiroler Landesmuseum, Innsbruck, Austria

Die Münchner Maler und Architekten; Panorama 4: Die Bildenden Künstler 2; Panorama 5: Lebensdaten von Marcel Duchamp; Panorama 6: keine Beschriftung.
Panorama Nr. 2 (Panorama No. 2)
1999
From a series of six panoramas
Dental plaster, hessian, iron, acrylic, ink
130 × 40 × 40 cm
Labels: Yasushi 1907, Bert 1898, Lars 1936, Thomas ca. 1930, Arno 1914, Italo 1923, Lewis 1832, Cesare 1908. The first names and dates of birth belong to Inoue, Stifter, Brecht, Gustafsson, Pynchon, Schmidt, Calvino, Carroll, and Pavese (from left to right).
Collection of the Kunsthalle Hamburg
In a total of six panoramas, I have connected various mountains from different regions to form ranges that appear to belong together. Names with dates are assigned to the individual mountains on the respective fronts. They stand for my 'heroes' from the cultural context at the time: Panorama 1: The visual artists I; Panorama 2: The literary figures; Panorama 3: The Munich painters and architects; Panorama 4: The visual artists II; Panorama 5: Biographical data of Marcel Duchamp; Panorama 6: no inscription.

134/135

Panorama Nr. 4
1999
Aus einer Serie von sechs Panoramen
139 × 42 × 40 cm
Beschriftung: Paolo ca. 1400, James 1860, Georges 1593, Veit 1445, Albrecht 1480, Simone 1284, Guilio 1499, Melozzo 1438, Jacopo 1494. Die Vornamen und Geburtsdaten gehören (von links nach rechts) zu Uccello, Ensor, de la Tour, Stoß, Altdorfer, Martini, Romano, da Forli, Pontormo
Privatsammlung München
Panorama Nr. 4. (Panorama No. 4)
1999
From a series of six panoramas
139 × 42 × 40 cm
Labels: Paolo ca. 1400, James 1860, Georges 1593, Veit 1445, Albrecht 1480, Simone 1284, Guilio 1499, Melozzo 1438, Jacopo 1494. The first names and dates of birth belong (from left to right) to Uccello, Ensor, de la Tour, Stoß, Altdorfer, Martini, Romano, da Forli, Pontormo.
Private collection, Munich

136–141

Expedition Nr. 3
2005
10 Leuchtkästen mit 20 verschiedenen Abbildungen
Aluminium, Glas, Großbild-Diapositive, Drahtseile, Leuchtmittel, Dimmer
Je 90 × 19 × 20 cm
Auflage: 3 (mit leichten Variationen)
Privatsammlung München
Expedition Nr. 3. (Expedition No. 3)
2005
10 lightboxes with 20 different images
Aluminium, glass, large image slide, wire cable, lighting, dimmer
Each 90 × 19 × 20 cm
Edition: 3 (with slight variations)
Private collection, Munich

142

Rauminstallation
2005
49 Nord 6 Est Frac Lorraine, Metz
Beitrag zur Gruppenausstellung *Quand les Latitudes deviennent Suisses*
Room installation
2005
49 Nord 6 Est Frac Lorraine, Metz
Exhibited at the group show *Quand les Latitudes deviennent Suisses*

Berge
Mountains:

Antelao
1998
(→ 131)

Weisshorn
1998
(→ 41)

Pelmo
1998
(→ 114–116)

Videoskulptur
Video sculpture:

Shit happens
2001
(→ 70/71)

143

Doppelberg
2013
Dentalgips, Rupfen, Aluminium, Holz, Gipskartonplatten, Wandglätter, Lasträder
111 × 111 × 219 cm
Im Besitz des Künstlers
Zwei identische Skulpturen von den Tre Cime stehen parallel zueinander. Eine der beiden ist um 180 Grad gedreht.
Doppelberg
2013
Dental plaster, hessian, aluminium, wood, plasterboards, finish filler, load wheels
111 × 111 × 219 cm
In the artist's possession
Two identical sculptures of the Tre Cime stand next to one another. One of them is rotated through 180 degrees.

144

Antelao/Berlin
2011/2016
Versuchsanordnung für einen neuen Sockel
Dentalgips, Rupfen, Aluminium, Stahl
110 × 110 × 90 cm
Privatbesitz Berlin
Antelao/Berlin
2011/2016
Experimental design for a new pedestal
Dental plaster, hessian, aluminium, steel
110 × 110 × 90 cm
Private collection, Berlin

145

Watzmann
Detail
2013
Dentalgips, Rupfen, Aluminium, Holz, Gipskartonplatten, Wandglätter
110 × 110 × 225 cm

Auflage: 3
Watzmann
Detail
2013
Dental plaster, hessian, aluminium, wood, plasterboards, finish filler
110 × 110 × 225 cm
Edition: 3

146–148

L'Allgäu probablement und Hochvogel
2012/13
Foyer Verwaltungsgebäude der Löwenbrauerei Meckatz/Heimenkirch im Allgäu
Sammlung Löwenbrauerei, Meckatz, Heimenkirch
L'Allgäu probablement and Hochvogel (The Allgäu Probably and Hochvogel)
2012/2013
Lobby of the administrative building of the Löwenbrauerei brewery Meckatz/Heimenkirch im Allgäu
Collection of the Löwenbrauerei, Meckatz, Heimenkirch

Hochvogel, 2012
Dentalgips, Rupfen, Aluminium, Holz, Gipskartonplatten, Wandglätter, Lastrollen
110 × 110 × 220 cm
Hochvogel, 2012
Dental plaster, hessian, aluminium, wood, plasterboards, finish filler, rollers
110 × 110 × 220 cm

L'Allgäu probablement
Pigmentprint auf Fourdrinier-Zeichenpapier auf Aludibond
400 × 207 × 2 cm
Der Hochvogel als einer der Allgäuer Hauptberge ist vor eine Landkarte platziert, die das – geografisch erweiterte – Allgäu zeigt und dabei die diese Region prägenden Personen vor Augen führt. Ihre Porträts sind umgeben mit aureolenartigen Energiefeldern und eingebettet in eine historische, soziologische und psychologische Erzählung, ein Jahrhunderte überspannendes Narrativ zwischen High and Low, zwischen Ernst und Ironie, zwischen Geschichte und Sagen.
Eine zweite, leicht veränderte Version der Landkarte befindet sich in einer Privatsammlung in Brüssel.
L'Allgäu probablement (The Allgäu Probably)
Pigment print on Fourdrinier drawing paper on Aludibond
400 × 207 × 2 cm
The Hochvogel, as one of the main mountains of the Allgäu, is placed in front of a map that shows the geographically expanded Allgäu, thereby bringing the people who formed this region to mind. Their portraits are surrounded by aureole-like energy fields and embedded in a historical, sociological, and psychological narrative. A narrative that spans centuries between high and low, seriousness and irony, history and legend.
A second, slightly altered version of the map is in a private collection in Brussels.

150

Shiny Marmolada I & II
2015
2 Leuchtkästen
Großbild-Diapositive
Je 130 × 75 cm
Auflage: 3 + 1 AP
Shiny Marmolada I & II
2015
2 lightboxes
Large image slide
Each 130 × 75 cm
Edition: 3 + 1 artist proof

151

Expedition I & IV
2010
Collagierte Zeichnung
Buchillustration und Landkartenfragment, Bleistift, Tusche, Pigmentstift
60 × 27,5 cm
Im Besitz des Künstlers
Expedition I & IV
2010
Collaged drawing
Book illustration and map fragment, pencil, ink, pigment pencil
60 × 27.5 cm
In the artist's possession

152/153

Expedition VIII
2010
Collagierte Zeichnung
Buchillustration und Landkartenfragment, Bleistift, Tusche, Pigmentstift
60 × 27,5 cm
Im Besitz des Künstlers
Expedition VIII
2010
Collaged drawing
Book illustration and fragment of map, pencil, ink, pigment pencil
60 × 27.5 cm
In the artist's possession

154/155

Tre Cime
2012
Version A: 4 Leuchtkästen
Großbild-Diapositive
Je 72 × 52 × 10 cm
Auflage: 7 + 2 AP
Version B: 4 Leuchtkästen
Großbild-Diapositive
Je 100 × 45 × 10 cm
Auflage: 3 + 1 AP
Version C: 5 zweiteilige Unikate
Verschiedene Größen mit variierten Ausschnitten
Tre Cime
2012
Version A: 4 lightboxes
Large image slide
Each 72 × 52 × 10 cm
Edition: 7 + 2 artist proofs
Version B: 4 lightboxes
Large image slide
Each 100 × 45 × 10 cm
Edition: 3 + 1 artist proof
Version C: 5 two-part unique works
Varying dimensions with different cut-outs

156/157

Großes Panorama II
2021
Leuchtkasten
Großbild-Diapositiv
100 × 40 × 10 cm
Auflage: 4 × 1 AP
Großes Panorama II (Large Panorama II)
2021

Lightbox
Large image slide
100 × 40 × 10 cm
Edition: 4 × 1 artist proof

158/159

Pelmo
2006
3 Leuchtkästen
Großbild-Diapositive
Je 51 × 61 × 10 cm
Auflage: 5 + 1 AP
Pelmo
2006
3 lightboxes
Large image slide
Each 51 × 61 × 10 cm
Edition: 5 + 1 artist proof

161/162

Expedition Nr. 17
2008
Zwei Blätter
Siebdruck auf Papier
Je 87,5 × 64 cm
Auflage: 15
Die digital bearbeiteten, historischen Fotografien sind durch fiktionale Texte neu interpretiert.
Expedition Nr. 17 (Expedition No. 17)
2008
Two sheets
Silkscreen on paper
Each 87.5 × 64 cm
Edition: 15
The digitally processed historical photographs have been reinterpreted via fictional texts.

163/164

Expedition Nr. 16
2008
Zwei Blätter
Siebdruck auf Papier
Je 87,5 × 64 cm
Auflage: 15
Die digital bearbeiteten, historischen Fotografien sind durch fiktionale Texte neu interpretiert.
Expedition Nr. 16 (Expedition No. 16)
2008
Two sheets
Silkscreen on paper
Each 87.5 × 64 cm
Edition: 15
The digitally processed historical photographs have been reinterpreted via fictional texts.

165

Zugang Atelier Stephan Huber
2008
Siebdruck auf Papier
87,5 × 64 cm
Auflage: 15
Die digital bearbeitete, historische Fotografie ist durch einen fiktionalen Text neu interpretiert.
Zugang Atelier Stephan Huber (Access to the Studio of Stephan Huber)
2008
Silkscreen on paper
87.5 × 64 cm
Edition: 15
The digitally processed historical photographs have been reinterpreted via fictional texts.

166

Atelier Stephan Huber mit Wohnhütte
2008
Siebdruck auf Papier
87,5 × 64 cm
Auflage: 15
Die digital bearbeitete, historische Fotografie ist durch einen fiktionalen Text neu interpretiert.
Atelier Stephan Huber mit Wohnhütte (Stephan Huber's Studio with Hut)
2008
Silkscreen on paper

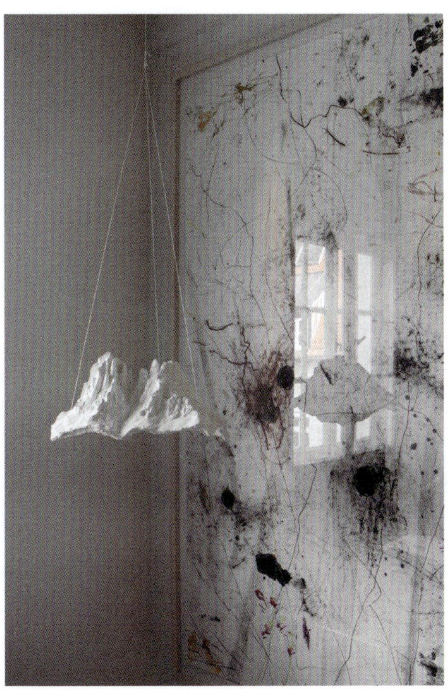

Privatsammlung, München, Deutschland; an der Wand eine Zeichnung von Hubert Scheibl
Private collection, Munich, Germany; on the wall, a drawing by Hubert Scheibl

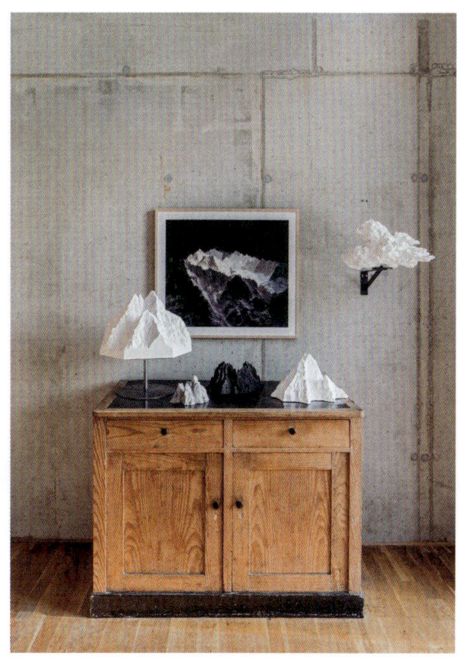

Privatbesitz, Allgäu, Deutschland
Private ownership, Allgäu, Germany

87.5 × 64 cm
Edition: 15
The digitally processed historical photographs have been reinterpreted via fictional texts.

176/177

4 Berge, 3 Karten
2014
Rauminstallation
Kunstmuseum Bonn
Sammlung Kunstmuseum Bonn
4 Berge, 3 Karten (Four Mountains, Three Maps)
2014
Room installation
Kunstmuseum Bonn
Collection of the Kunstmuseum Bonn

Berge
Mountains:

Weisshorn
1998
(→ 41)

Pelmo
1998
(→ 114–116)

Antelao
1997/98
(→ 131)

Sasso Lungo
1997/98
Dentalgips, Rupfen, Aluminium, Holz, Gipskartonplatten, Wandglätter, Lastrollen
110 × 110 × 225 cm
Sasso Lungo
1997/98
Dental plaster, hessian, aluminium, wood, plasterboards, finish filler, rollers
110 × 110 × 225 cm

Landkarten
Maps:

Pigmentprinte auf Fourdrinier-Zeichenpapier auf Aludibond
Pigment prints on Fourdrinier drawing paper on Aludibond

Geografie der Liebe
2010
Fünfteilig
650 × 180 cm
Geografie der Liebe (Geography of Love)
2010
Five parts
650 × 180 cm

La Ville Sentimentale
2013
220 × 123 cm
La Ville Sentimentale (The Sentimental Villa)
2013
220 × 123 cm

Alte Welt/Neue Welt
2009
Dreiteilig
385 × 185 cm
Alte Welt/Neue Welt (Old World / New World)
2009
Three parts
385 × 185 cm

178/179

Kalte Kammer
2005
Kubus im Petuelpark, München, Außenstelle des Lenbachhaus München von 2005 bis 2006
Teil des Kunstprojekt Petuelpark
Marmormehl, Holz, Kronleuchter, Motor
Ca. 500 × 500 cm
Kalte Kammer (Cold Chamber)
2005
Kubus in the Petuelpark, Munich, satellite pavilion of the Lenbachhaus Munich from 2005 to 2006
Part of the Kunstprojekt Petuelpark project
Marble powder, wood, chandelier, motor
ca. 500 × 500 cm

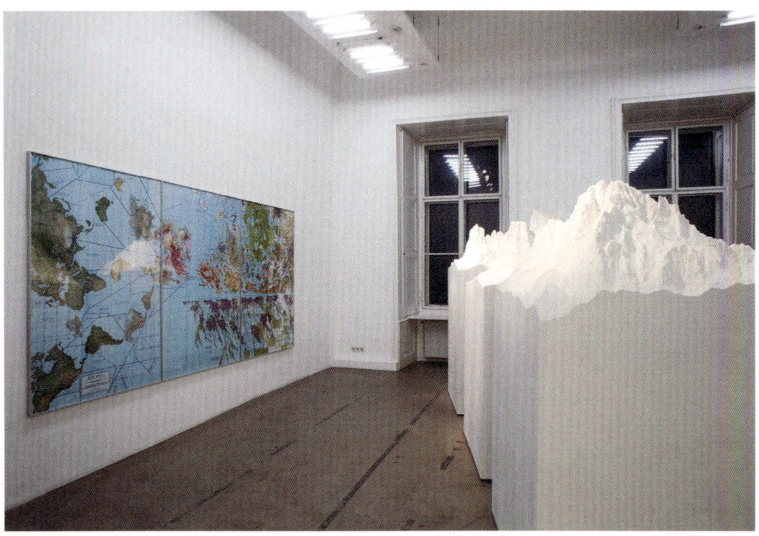

Charim Galerie, Wien, Österreich
Charim Galerie, Vienna, Austria

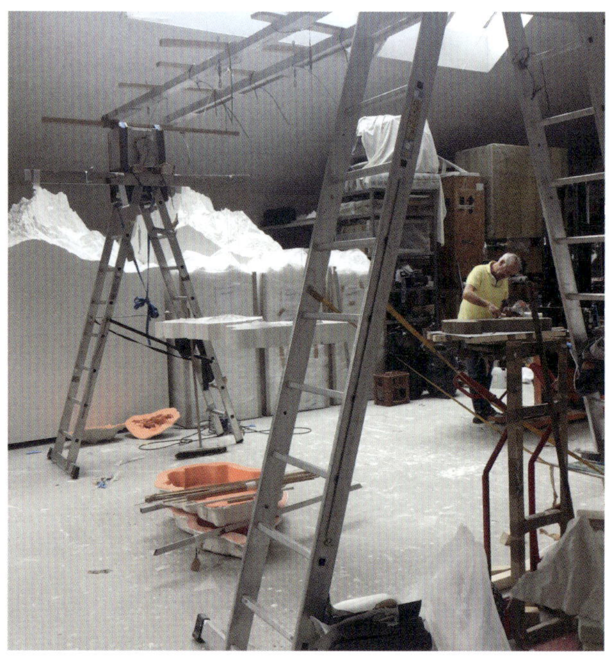

Atelier, 2019 / Studio, 2019

180/181

Zitronenstadel
2005
Holzbretter aus Abbruchscheune, Pigment, Werkstattböcke, Soundsystem, Loop
Kiste: 164 × 80 × 132 cm
Böcke: Höhe 90 cm
Im Besitz des Künstlers
Auf der Wiese vor meinem Allgäuer Elternhaus stand ein leuchtend gelb angemalter Heustadel, der im Volksmund Zitronenstadel hieß. Beim Blick aus dem elterlichen Haus, über den Stadel hinweg, war der imposante Höhenzug der Allgäuer Berge zu sehen. Aus der gelben Bretterkiste ertönt gedämpft ein gesprochener Text, der sich nach vierminütiger Pause wiederholt. Es sind die ersten Zeilen von *Also sprach Zarathustra* (1883) von Friedrich Nietzsche. Der Text wurde von meiner Nachbarbäuerin Waltraud Mair in den Allgäuer Dialekt übersetzt und von meinem Nachbarbauern Hubert Gast eingesprochen.
Zitronenstadel (Lemon Barn)
2005
Wood boards from a derelict barn, pigment, workshop trestles, sound system, loop
Box: 164 × 80 × 132 cm
Trestles: height 90 cm
In the artist's possession
On the meadow in front of my parents' house in the Allgäu there was a hay barn painted bright yellow, popularly known as the 'Zitronenstadel' (Lemon Barn). One could look out of my parents' house, across the barn, and see the imposing range of the Allgäu mountains. From the yellow box of boards sounds a spoken text, which is repeated after a four-minute break. It recites the first lines of *Thus Spoke Zarathustra* (1883) by Friedrich Nietzsche. The text was translated into the Allgäu dialect by my neighbour, the farmer Waltraud Mair, and recorded by my other neighbour, the farmer Hubert Gast.

Auszug aus dem gesprochenen Text
Excerpt from the spoken text:

„Zarathustra isch alloi s'Gebirg nag'stiege und neamad isch ihm verkomme.
Wo er aber ins Holz komme isch, isch z'mol a alter Ma vor ihm g'stande, wo sei heilige Hitte verlau hot, weil er im Holz Wuzla sammle wollt. Und also hot der Alte zum Zarathustra g'set: it fremd isch mir dea Wanderer, vor manchem Johr isch er do vorbei gange. Zarathustra hot er g'heiße, aber er hat sich verwandlet.
Damals hosch du die Äsche auf de Berg trage: Willst du heit die Fuier in d'Täler na trage?
Fürchtscht du di it vor Brandstifters Straufa? ..."
"Zarathustra isch alloi s'Gebirg nag'stiege und neamad isch ihm verkomme.
Wo er aber ins wood komme isch, isch z'mol a alter Ma vor ihm g'stande, wo sei heilige Hitte verlau hot, weil er im wood Wuzla sammle wollt. Und also hot der Alte zum Zarathustra g'set: it fremd isch mir dea Wanderer, vor manchem Johr isch er do vorbei gange. Zarathustra hot er g'heiße, aber er hat sich verwandlet.
Damals hosch du die Äsche auf de Berg trage: Willst du heit die Fuier in d'Täler na trage?
Fürchtscht du di it vor Brandstifters Straufa? ...'

Auszug aus dem Originaltext von Friedrich Nietzsche
Excerpt from the original text by Friedrich Nietzsche:

„Zarathustra stieg allein das Gebirge abwärts und Niemand begegnete ihm. Als er aber in die Wälder kam, stand auf einmal ein Greis vor ihm, der seine heilige Hütte verlassen hatte, um Wurzeln im Walde zu suchen. Und also sprach der Greis zu Zarathustra: Nicht fremd ist mir dieser Wanderer, vor manchem Jahre ging er hier vorbei. Zarathustra hieß er; aber er hat sich verwandelt. Damals trugst du deine Asche zu Berge: Willst du heute dein Feuer in die Thäler tragen? Fürchtest du nicht vor des Brandstifters Strafen? ..."

Zarathustra went down the mountain alone, no one meeting him. When he entered the forest, however, there suddenly stood before him an old man, who had left his holy hut to seek roots. And thus spake the old man to Zarathustra: 'No stranger to me is this wanderer: many years ago passed he by. Zarathustra he was called; but he hath altered. Then thou carriedst thine ashes into the mountains: wilt thou now carry thy fire into the valleys? Fearest thou not the incendiary's doom?...'

S. 182/183

SL 1–SL 10
2008–2022
(→ Vorsatz / Endpaper 1)

The Bergs I–III
2022
(→ Vorsatz / Endpaper 1)

Perfect Sculptures 1, 3, 6
(→ 184)
Privatsammlung München
Private collection, Munich

184/185

Perfect Sculptures
2014–2018
Dentalgips, Rupfen, Holz, Gipskartonplatten, Wandglätter
Je Berg: Grundfläche 48 × 48 cm, Höhe ca. 180 cm
Von links nach rechts:
Perfect Sculpture 1 (Assiniboine), Perfect Sculpture 2 (Fitz Roy), Perfect Sculpture 3 (Matterhorn), Perfect Sculpture 4 (Machapuchare), Perfect Sculpture 5 (Kailash), Perfect Sculpture 6 (Tre Cime)
Auflage: je 5
Die *Serie Perfect Sculptures* wird weitergeführt.
Perfect Sculptures
2014–2018
Dental plaster, hessian, wood, plasterboards, finish filler
Each mountain: area 48 × 48 cm, height ca. 180 cm
From left to right:
Perfect Sculpture 1 (Assiniboine), Perfect Sculpture 2 (Fitz Roy), Perfect Sculpture 3 (Matterhorn), Perfect Sculpture 4 (Machapuchare), Perfect Sculpture 5 (Kailash), Perfect Sculpture 6 (Tre Cime)
Edition: each one of 5
The series *Perfect Sculptures* will be continued.

186

Matterpuchare, Assinash, Fitz Cime
2014/15
Dentalgips, Rupfen, Holz, Gipskartonplatten, Wandglätter
Je 81 × 49 × 185 cm
Auflage: je 3
Von links nach rechts:
Matterpuchare (Machapuchare und Matterhorn), Assinash (Assiniboine und Kailash), Fitz Cime (Tre Cime und Fitz Roy)
Die in verschiedenen Erdteilen liegenden, maßstäblich vollkommen unterschiedlichen Berge sind so miteinander kombiniert und modelliert, dass sie zusammengehörig erscheinen.
Matterpuchare, Assinash, Fitz Cime
2015
Dental plaster, hessian, wood, plasterboards, finish filler
Each 81 × 49 × 185 cm
Edition: each one of 3
From left to right:
Matterpuchare (Machapuchare and Matterhorn), Assinash (Assiniboine and Kailash), Fitz Cime (Tre Cime and Fitz Roy)
The pairs of different mountains, located in different parts of the world and utterly different in scale, have been joined with one another and so modelled that they appear to belong together.

187

Matterpuchare
Detail
2014/15
(→ 186)

188

Fitz Cime
Detail
2014/15
(→ 186)

189

Assinash
Detail
2014/15
(→ 186)

191

Südlich-biografisches Panorama
2016
Rauminstallation
Verschiedene Arbeiten
MMK Frankfurt
Südlich-biografisches Panorama (Southern Biographical Panorama)
2016
Room installation
Various works
MMK Frankfurt

192–195

Family Affairs
2016
Dentalgips, Rupfen, Holz, Gipskartonplatten, Wandglätter, Pappe, Bleistift
205 × 160 × 100 cm
Im Besitz des Künstlers
An der Kante der Felswand stehen zwei Modellhäuser: mein Elternhaus mit Fenstern auf die Ebene und das letzte Refugium der Manson-Family mit Fenstern zum Abgrund.
Family Affairs
2016
Dental plaster, hessian, wood, plasterboards, finish filler, cardboard, pencil
205 × 160 × 100 cm
In the artist's possession
Two model houses are perched on the edge of the cliff: my parents' home with windows looking out on the plain and the last refuge of the Manson family with windows toward the abyss.

196/197

Rauminstallation
2016
Einzelausstellung *Zarathustra im Zitronenstadel*, Kulturfabrik Lindenberg
Die Kulturfabrik war ursprünglich ein Fabrikraum der Hutfabrik Ottmar Reich, die mein Vater als Geschäftsführer geleitet hatte. Sie wurde in den 1980er-Jahren wegen Unrentabilität geschlossen. In den erhalten gebliebenen, denkmalgeschützten Gebäuden befindet sich mittlerweile ein Hutmuseum und der oben genannte Ausstellungsraum. Die Ausstellung an meinem Kindheitsort war retrospektiv angelegt, mit der Betonung auf narrativ biografischen Arbeiten und den Bergskulpturen, die letztlich ihren Ursprung in der visuell alpinen Prägung meiner frühen Lebensjahre hatten.
Room installation
2016
Solo show *Zarathustra im Zitronenstadel* (Zarathustra in the Lemon Barn), Kulturfabrik Lindenberg
The Kulturfabrik was originally a factory of the Hutfabrik Ottmar Reich, at which my father was managing director. It was closed in the 1980s since it was no longer profitable. The surviving, heritage-listed buildings today house a hat museum and the above-named exhibition space. The exhibition at my childhood site was planned as a retrospective, emphasising biographical works and the mountain sculptures, which ultimately have their origin in the visual alpine surroundings of my early childhood.

198/199

Rekonstruktion eines folgenschweren Streites
2016
Pigmentprint auf Baumwolle-Velinpapier
100 × 90 cm
Sammlung Hutmuseum, Lindenberg
Eine alte Postkarte zeigt die mit meiner Familie verflochtene Hutfabrik Ottmar Reich in Lindenberg, nobilitiert durch die imposante Allgäuer Alpenkulisse. Drei neue Szenen, die die fiktionale Geschichte von tragischen Unfällen erzählen, habe ich in die stark vergrößerte Grafik einmontiert. Es gibt eine weitere Version in der Sammlung des Künstlers.

Rekonstruktion eines folgenschweren Streites (Reconstruction of an Argument with Serious Consequences)
2016
Pigment print on cotton vellum paper
100 × 90 cm
Collection of the Hutmuseum, Lindenberg
An old postcard shows the Hutfabrik Ottmar Reich in Lindenberg, ennobled by the striking Allgäu alpine scenery. This factory is closely associated with my family. I have inserted three new scenes, which narrate the fictional story of tragic accidents, in the greatly expanded graphic. A further version exists in the collection of the artist.

1.
In the afternoon of 30 May 1882 the brothers Ewald and Cornelius Reich got into a fateful argument in the courtyard of the factory at their company. It was triggered by their different opinions of the very expensive signets for the Ottmar Reich company, which had been ordered by Cornelius Reich on his own authority from Carl Hanftstaengel. Ewald Reich vehemently argued against using them. The third brother, Anton Reich, who noticed that the dispute was becoming increasingly louder from his office window, quickly went down to the courtyard to separate the quarrelling brothers, but arrived too late. In the heat of the argument Cornelius pushed Ewald, who unfortunately fell on a cast iron hat form that had probably fallen off a transport wagon. He was seriously injured and remained on the ground bleeding. Stunned and desperate, Cornelius ran away. Ewald spent three weeks at Lindenberg hospital, afterwards staying for a long time at Davos, taking the cure. He never recuperated entirely from the fall and suffered constantly from headaches and bouts of fainting.

2.
Two weeks later Cornelius Reich arrived in Milan, destitute. During his first months there he was taken in by the straw merchant Gianlucca Monetti. Cornelius Reich decide to remain in Milan. Driven by shame, he did not answer any letters and broke off contact with his family in Lindenberg. There Ewald and Anton assumed the sole management of the company Ottmar Reich.
With skill and hard work Cornelius Reich built up the horse transport company 'Reich and Monetti', supplying transport horses to all over Europe, as well as the East coast of the United States.
In 1889 he sold two rare Murgese horses that had been born as twins. Both had a grey sign that resembled a cross on their withers, recognisable only when one looked closely.
One horse was shipped to the United States and sold to the police chief of Boston, William Sorgot, for the then high sum of US$ 3,500.
On 1 May 1891 the Murgese was severely injured during a demonstration by socialist textile workers, receiving its coup de grâce from Sorgot's assistants.

3.
The second Murgese was sold together with nine other horses to the Ottmar Reich company in 1893 by the horse trader Gottfried Messner from Hörbranz, who had business relations with the Milan company. The rapidly expanding hat production required a large number of horses to transport the wares to the train station in Röthenbach.
On 27 February 1895 a tragic accident occurred when the Murgese escaped in front of the entrance to the hat factory and fatally kicked Ewald Reich, who at that moment was coming out of the door.
In that same year, on 11 September 1895, Cornelius Reich died from a stroke in Milan. The previous year he had been elevated to the post of Lord Great Chamberlain by the Italian king Umberto I.

Reconstructed from letters from the Reich family, the official personal record of the town of Hörbanz, the Biblioteca Nazionale Braidense, Milan, and the municipal archive Lindenberg.

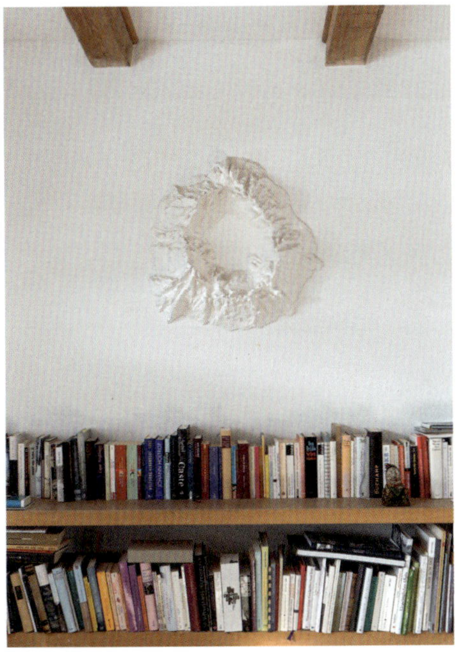

Privatbesitz, Allgäu, Deutschland
Private ownership, Allgäu, Germany

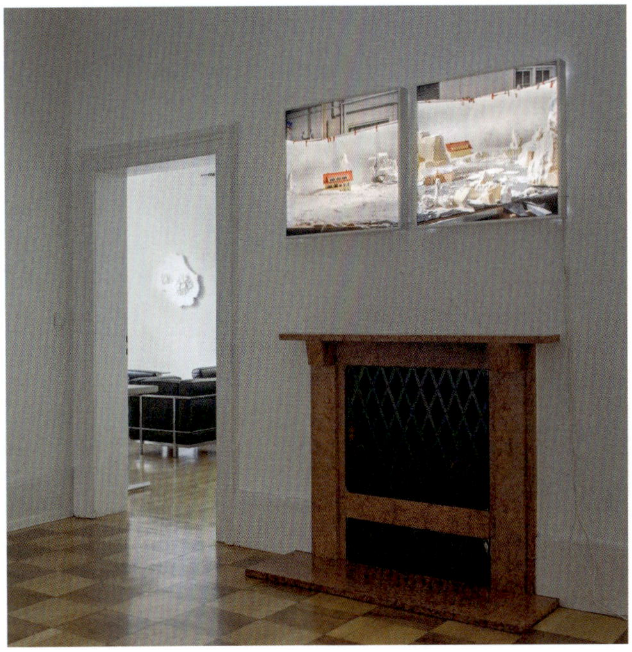

CAS, München, Deutschland
CAS, Munich, Germany

201

Lo & Behold, 12
2018
Pigmentprint auf Fourdrinier-Zeichenpapier
43 × 53 cm
Auflage: 6 + 1 AP
Eine Collage mit Fragmenten einer topografischen Karte von Michigan kündigt in Form eines handschriftlichen Eintrages eine fiktive Reise an, auf der ich den Michigan Alpine Club durch das „Kleine Walsertal" führen werde:

Lo & Behold, 12
2018
Pigment print on Fourdrinier drawing paper
43 × 53 cm
Edition: 6 + 1 artist proof
A collage with fragments of a topographical map of Michigan announces, in the form of a handwritten entry, a fictional trip in which I guide the Michigan Alpine Club through the 'Kleiner Walsertal':

The Michigan Alpine Club goes to Kleinwalsertal. Best accomodations, sumptuous meals, guided tours, excursions and lectures. Guide and speaker: Stephan Huber. First lecture: Das Gottesacker Plateau als Gitter zur Hölle (in English language). Second lecture: Das Allgäu. Geschichte des Eigensinns. Third lecture: WG Sebald, the writer from Wertach. Der Einfluß des Allgäus auf sein Werk (in English language). Fourth lecture: Konrad Zuse constructs his Z4 in Summer 1945 in Hindelang (Vortrag im Allgäuer Dialekt). Guided tours to Mädelegabel, Höfats, Biberkopf, Trettachspitze und Hochvogel. Excursions to the Stephan Huber Show "Eiskalt" at Eres-Stiftung in München. Weitere Veranstaltungen werden vor Ort bekanntgegeben. Kostenlose Erfrischungen auf der Reise.

202

Lo & Behold, 17
2018
Pigmentprint auf Fourdrinier-Zeichenpapier
43 × 53 cm
Auflage: 6 + 1 AP
Eine Collage mit Fragmenten einer topografischen Karte von Michigan erzählt in Form eines handschriftlichen Eintrags von den fiktiven Reisen, die ich mit dem Michigan Alpine Club um den Bodensee unternommen habe:

Lo & Behold, 17
2018
Pigment print on Fourdrinier drawing paper
43 × 53 cm
Edition: 6 + 1 artist proof
A collage with fragments of a topographical map of Michigan announces, in the form of a handwritten entry, a fictional trip which I took with the Michigan Alpine Club around Lake Constance:

The Michigan Alpine Club (MAC) goes to Lake Constance. 9 Reisen zwischen 1981 und 2018. Strangers things. Begrenzte Teilnehmerzahlen, Verschwiegenheitspflicht, Fotografierverbot. Reiseleitung: Stephan Huber. 1 Reise 1981/13 Personen „Franz-Anton-Messmer Tour" nach Iznang. Diverse Messmerismus-Versuche, 3 Verletzte. 2 Reise 1983/13 Personen: „Franz-Anton Messmer-Tour nach Iznang. Messmerismus-Versuche, 13 Verletzte. 3 Reise 1986/30 Personen, „Zeppelin-Tour" nach Friedrichshafen. Notwasserung auf dem See. 4 Reise 1997/14 Personen, „Bregenzerwald-Tour" nach Betsau. Gemeinsamer Stadelbau. 5. Reise 2004. 183 Personen „The Westallgäu-Tour" nach Lindenberg. Local guide: Stephan Huber. 6 Reise. 2010. 18 Personen „Dead-Men-Climbing-Tour" nach Oberstdorf. Besteigung Höfats. 7 Reise, 2012. 58 Personen. „The Putto-Tour" nach Birnau. Exstatische Engelserscheinungen. 8 Reise, 2016. 13 Personen „The Allgäu Fairy Tale-Tour". Suche nach der „Feurigen Sau". 9 Reise, 2018/ 7 Personen/„The Via Mala Tour" nach Thusis. Wildwasserklettern.

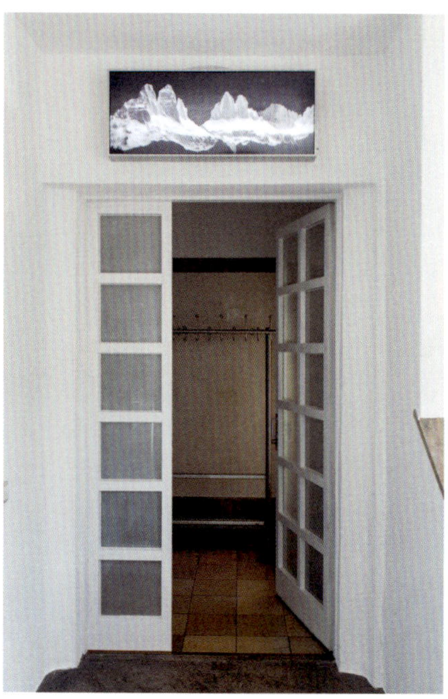

CAS, München, Deutschland
CAS, Munich, Germany

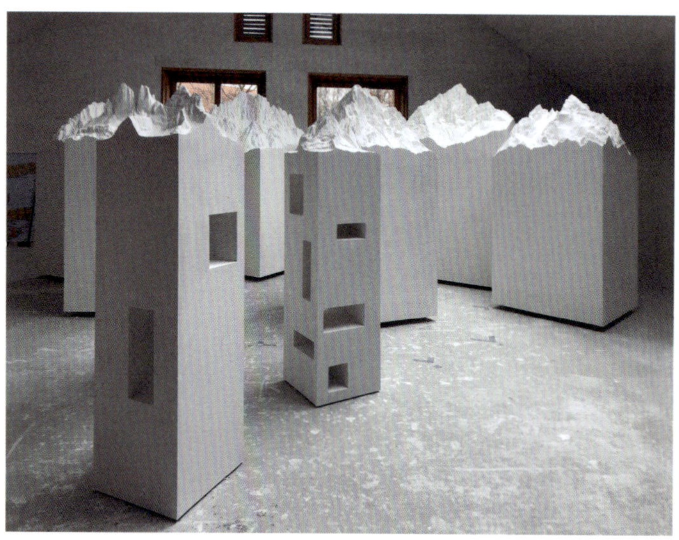

Atelier, 2020 / Studio, 2020

204/205

Oben
Above:

Perfect Sculptures
und Strudel
2019
Doppelausstellung *Elke Härtel*
Stephan Huber, Charim Galerie, Wien
Perfect Sculptures
und Strudel
(Perfect Sculptures and Strudel)
2019
Double exhibition *Elke Härtel*
Stephan Huber, Charim Galerie, Vienna

Perfect Sculptures 1, 3, 5, 6
(→ 184/185)

Strudel
2019
Zweiteilig
Pigmentprint auf Fourdrinier-
Zeichenpapier auf Aludibond
Je 130 × 260 cm
Auflage: 2
Sammlung Vita Sanatio/Art &
Living – Switzerland
Sammlung des Künstlers
Strudel
2019
Two parts
Pigment print on Fourdrinier drawing
paper on Aludibond
Each 130 × 260 cm
Edition: 2
Collection of Vita Sanatio/Art &
Living – Switzerland
Collection of the artist

Weitere Versionen
Further versions:

Pigmentprint auf Fourdrinier-
Zeichenpapier
119 × 113 cm
Auflage: 5 + 2 AP

Pigment print on Fourdrinier
drawing paper
119 × 113 cm
Edition: 5 + 2 artist proofs
Photo: Nathan Murrell

Unten
Bottom:

Rauminstallation
2019
Einzelausstellung *Der müde Kasperl und die Kartografie*, Kunstmuseum Lindau
Verschiedene Arbeiten
Room installation
2019
Solo show *Der müde Kasperl und die Kartografie*, Kunstmuseum Lindau
Various works

206/207

Island II (Osterinsel)
2021
Dentalgips, Rupfen, Aluminium,
Drahtseil
Ca. 85 × 55 × 10 cm
Auflage: 3
Meine fünf Inselfavoriten – Tahiti, Osterinsel, Reichenau, Ventotene und Isola Bella – modellierte ich in zwei verschiedenen Versionen – als Wandrelief und als hängende Skulptur – und entwarf zu jeder eine Landkarte. Die Osterinsel fasziniert mich neben den künstlerisch Landart-ähnlichen, fast seriellen Monumentalskulpturen vor allem geologisch durch die abgeschliffenen Formen der alten Vulkane und einiger spektakulärer wassergefüllter Krater.
Island II (Osterinsel)
(Island II [Easter Island])
2021
Dental plaster, hessian, aluminium,
wire cable
Ca. 85 × 55 × 10 cm
Edition: 3
I modelled my five favourite islands – Tahiti, Easter Island, Reichenau, Ventotene and Isola Bella – in two different versions, as wall reliefs and as hanging sculptures, and designed a map for each. Apart from the artistic, almost serial, monumental sculptures that resemble land art, Easter Island fascinates me in particular for its geology, with the eroded forms of the

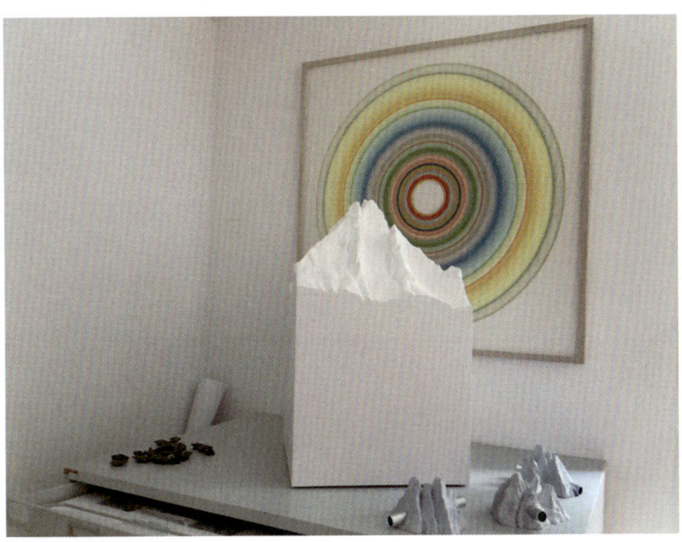

Atelier, 2023 / Studio, 2023

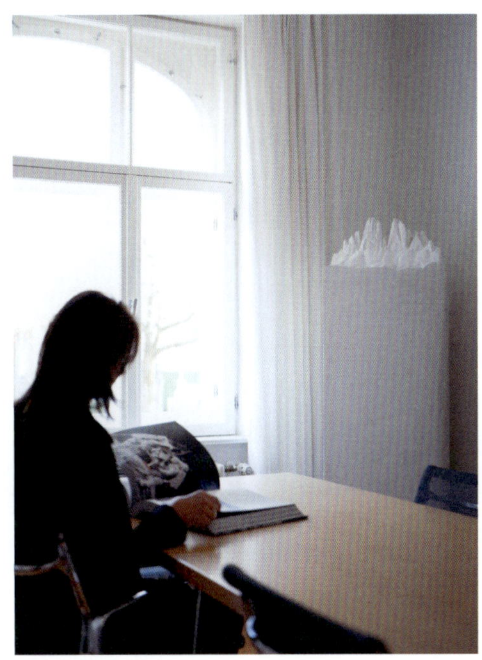

Eres-Stiftung, München, Deutschland
Eres Foundation, Munich, Germany

ancient volcanoes and several spectacular craters filled with water.

208

Rauminstallation
2021
Einzelausstellung *Stephan Huber Inseln*, Galerie Max Weber Six Friedrich, München
Verschiedene Arbeiten
Room installation
2021
Solo show *Stephan Huber Inseln*, Galerie Max Weber Six Friedrich, Munich
Various works

209

Island 1
2021
Dentalgips, Rupfen, Aluminium, Drahtseil
Ca. 80 × 60 × 10 cm
Auflage: 3
Meine Wahl fiel auf das bergige Tahiti, weil Paul Gauguin dort seine zentralen Werke, wie das von mir geliebte Bild *Woher kommen wir? Wer sind wir? Wohin gehen wir?* (1897), geschaffen hat.
Island 1
2021
Dental plaster, hessian, aluminium, wire cable
Ca. 80 × 60 × 10 cm
Edition: 3
My choice was the mountainous Tahiti, since Paul Gauguin created some of his key works there, such as a picture that I love: *Where Do We Come From? What Are We? Where Are We Going?*

210/211

Montagna sospesa/Tre Cime
2022
Einzelausstellung Stephan Huber Shining, CAS, Center for Advanced Studies der LMU, München
Dentalgips, Rupfen, Drahtseil
100 × 60 × 55 cm
Auflage: 3 + 1 AP
Montagna sospesa/Tre Cime (Suspended Mountain/Tre Cime)
2022
Solo show Stephan Huber Shining, CAS, Center for Advanced Studies of the LMU, Munich
Dental plaster, hessian, wire cable
100 × 60 × 55 cm
Edition: 3 + 1 artist proof

212

Der Weg
2023
Pigmentprint auf Fourdrinier-Zeichenpapier
71 × 48 cm
Auflage: 8 + 1 AP
Der Weg (The Route)
2023
Pigment print on Fourdrinier drawing paper
71 × 48 cm
Edition: 8 + 1 artist proof

213

Tunnel
2022
7 Variationen
Dentalgips, Pigment, Aluminiumrohr
Verschiedene Größen
Tunnel
2022
7 variations
Dental plaster, pigment, aluminium tube
Varying sizes

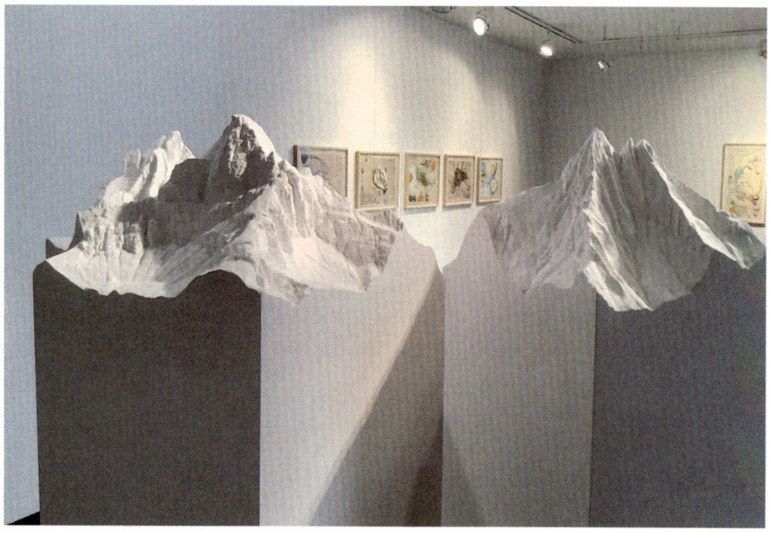

Galerie Max Weber Six Friedrich, München, Deutschland / Munich, Germany

Nachsatz / Endpaper 1

Rauminstallation
2002
Beitrag zur Gruppenausstellung
Stanze II, Museion Bozen
Room installation
2002
Contribution to the group show
Stanze II, Museion Bozen

Berge
Mountains:

Civetta
(→ 41)

Sasso Lungo
(→ 49)

Weisshorn
(→ 41)

Nachsatz / Endpaper 2

Alpenflug
1997/2018
Alle Auflagen: Pigmentprint auf
Baumwolle-Velinpapier
140 × 120 cm
Auflage: 3
87 × 72 cm
Auflage: 5
57 × 51 cm
Auflage: 5
Alpenflug (Alpine Flight)
1997/2018
All editions: pigment print on
cotton vellum paper
140 × 120 cm
Edition: 3
87 × 72 cm
Edition: 5
57 × 51 cm
Edition: 5

Nachsatz / Endpaper 3

(→ Vorsatz / Endpaper 1)

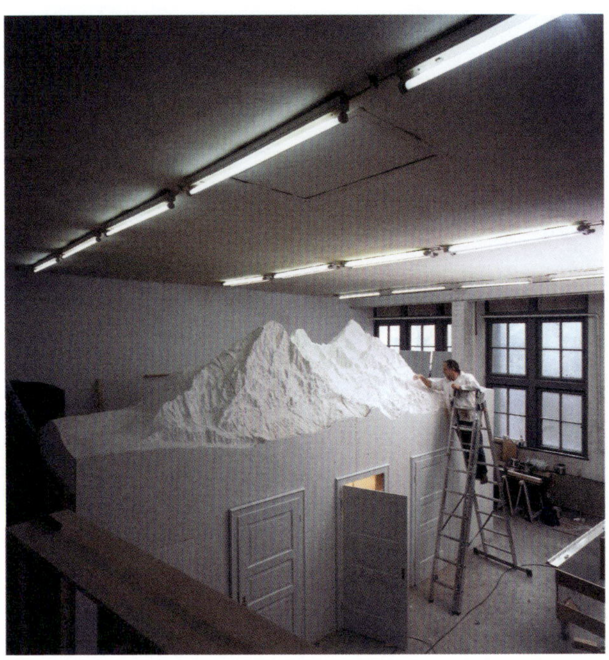

Atelier, 1999 / Studio, 1999

Biografie
Biography

Stephan Huber wurde 1952 in Lindenberg im Westallgäu geboren. Er studierte von 1972 bis 1978 an der Akademie der Bildenden Künste München und von 1974 bis 1977 Kunstgeschichte und Germanistik an der LMU in München. 1981 erhielt er das PS1-Stipendium für New York, 2006 den Bremer Rolandpreis für Kunst im öffentlichen Raum und 2008 den Kunstpreis der Stadt München. Neben zahlreichen internationalen Einzelausstellungen und Ausstellungsbeteiligungen nahm er 1987 an der documenta 8 in Kassel und 1999 an der Biennale in Venedig teil. Wichtige Kunstwerke von ihm finden sich im öffentlichen Raum, unter anderem im Maintower in Frankfurt, vor der Neuen Messe in München, vor dem Künstlerhaus in Hannover, in der U-Bahn-Station Aspern in Wien sowie in der Herzogstraße in Wuppertal.
Stephan Huber lehrte von 2004 bis 2017 als Professor für Bildhauerei an der Akademie der Bildenden Künste München. Er ist Mitglied der Bayerischen Akademie der Schönen Künste in München. Stephan Huber lebt und arbeitet in München sowie in Bidingen im Ostallgäu.
www.stephanhuberkunst.de

Stephan Huber was born in Lindenberg in the West Allgäu region of Germany in 1952. He studied art at the Akademie der Bildenden Künste in Munich from 1972 to 1978 and art history and German studies at the Ludwig Maximilians Universität in Munich from 1974 to 1977. In 1981 he was awarded a PS1 grant to New York, in 2006 the Bremen Sculpture Prize for art in public spaces, and in 2008 the Art Prize of the City of Munich. In addition to numerous international solo shows and participation in group exhibitions, he exhibited at the documenta 8 in Kassel in 1987 and at the Venice Biennale in 1999. Major artworks of his are displayed in public spaces, including the Maintower in Frankfurt, in front of the Neue Messe in Munich, at the Künstlerhaus in Hannover, in the Aspern underground station in Vienna, and in Herzogstraße in Wuppertal.
From 2004 to 2017 Stephan Huber was professor for sculpture at the Akademie der Bildenden Künste in Munich. He is a member of the Bavarian Academy of Fine Arts in Munich. Stephan Huber lives and works in Munich and in Bidingen in East Allgäu.
www.stephanhuberkunst.de

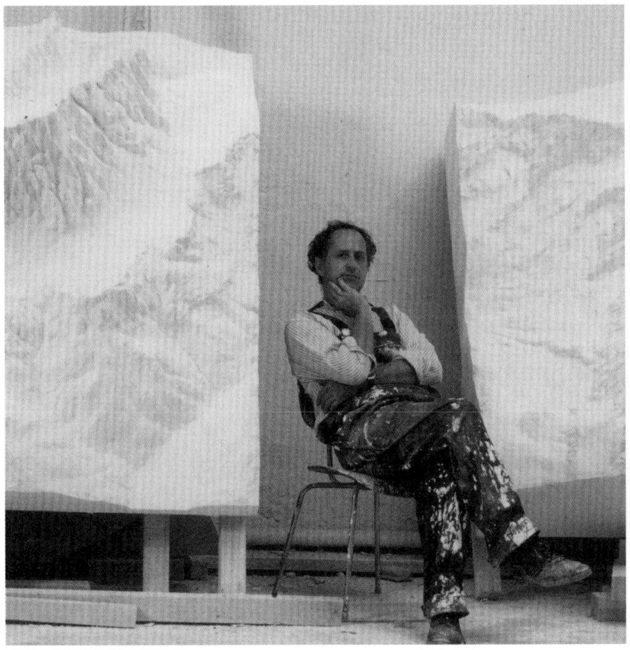

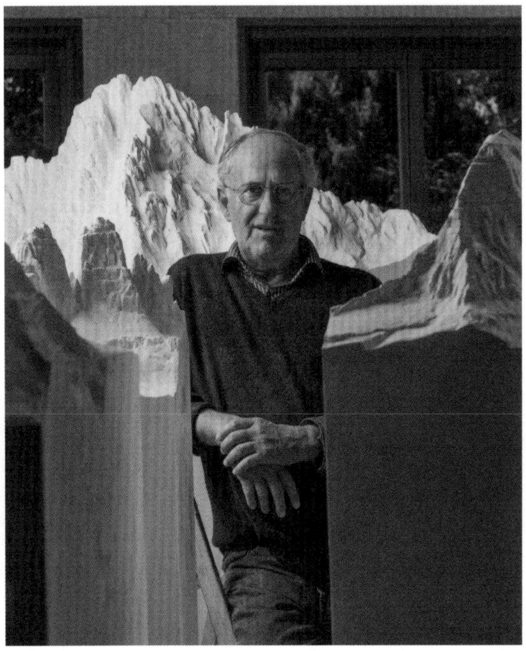

Fotonachweis
Impressum
Picture Credits
Imprint

Karo Angermann
→ 219 rechts / right

Felix Baptist
→ 187–189, 243 rechts / right

Walter Bayer
→ 66/67, 230

Leonore Braun
→ 78/79, 225 rechts / right

Malte Bruns
→ 176/177

Thomas Dashuber
→ 239 rechts / right

Bogomir Ecker
→ 216 rechts / right

Leonie Felle
→ 28, 29, 80/83, 132/133, 136–141, 182/183, 196/197, 206–211, 228 links / left, 229, 233 links / left, 237 rechts / right, 238 links / left, 240

Marianne Francke
→ 60–64

Galleria La Nuova Pesa, Rom / Rome
→ 47

Thomas Habersatter
→ 221 rechts / right

Elke Härtel
→ 226 links / left

Dieter Hinrichs
→ Vorsatz / Endpaper 3, 15–17, 19–23, 36–39, 54–57, 150, 154/155, 158/159, 228 rechts / right, 243 links / left

Elsa Hinrichs
→ 146/147

Johann Hinrichs
→ Vorsatz / Endpaper 1 , Vorsatz / Endpaper 2, 25–27, 32–35, 41–46, 59 oben / top, 71/71, 143, 145–148, 151–153, 156/157, 161–166, 178–181, 184–186, 192–195, 198–202, 205 unten / bottom, 213, 233 rechts / right, 239 links / left, Nachsatz / Endpaper 3

Stephan Huber
→ 59 unten / bottom, 218, 221, 224, 225, 226 rechts / right, 234 rechts / right, 237 links / left, 238 rechts / right

Stephan Huber / Dieter Hinrichs
→ 73–77, Nachsatz / Endpaper 2

Christoph Irrgang
→ 134/135

Pascal Jäger
→ 6, 118–123

Peter Klein
→ 215

Raimund Kummer
→ 144

Joseph Loderer
→ 30/31

MMK Frankfurt
→ 191

Nathan Murrell
→ 205 oben / top, 234 links / left

Augustin Ochsenreiter
→ Nachsatz / Endpaper 1

Alexa Rainer
→ 105–111, 113–116

Marco Rambaldi
→ 48

Sigg Collection
→ 216

Wolfgang Stehle
→ 241

Georg Tappeiner
→ 131

Lisa Ungar
→ 219 links / left

Remi Villaggi
→ 142

Elke Walford
→ 50–53

Michael Wesely
→ 49

Erschienen im / Published by
Hirmer Verlag GmbH
Bayerstraße 57–59
80335 München, Germany

Herausgegeben von / Edited by
Petra Giloy-Hirtz, Stephan Huber

Englische Übersetzung /
English translation
David Sánchez Cano, Madrid

Deutsches Lektorat und Korrektorat /
German copyediting and proofreading
Anne Funck, Munich

Englisches Lektorat und Korrektorat /
English copyediting and proofreading
Jane Michael, Munich

Projektmanagement Hirmer /
Hirmer project management
Rainer Arnold

Gestaltung und Satz /
Design and typesetting
wigel, Munich

Lithografie / Pre-press and repro
Bayermedia, Munich

Druck und Bindung /
Printing and binding
Druckerei Vogl, Zorneding

Papier / Paper
LonaOffset 120 g

Printed in Germany

Bibliografische Information der Deutschen Nationalbibliothek
Die Deutsche Nationalbibliothek verzeichnet diese Publikation in der Deutschen Nationalbibliografie; detaillierte bibliografische Daten sind im Internet über http://www.dnb.de abrufbar. /
Bibliographic information published by the Deutsche Nationalbibliothek
The Deutsche Nationalbibliothek lists this publication in the Deutsche Nationalbibliografie; detailed bibliographic data is available on the Internet at http://www.dnb.de

www.hirmerverlag.de
www.hirmerpublishers.com

ISBN 978-3-7774-4234-1

Ich danke der Herausgeberin und Autorin Petra Giloy-Hirtz sowie Stephan Berg und Uschi Demeter für ihre Beiträge in diesem Buch, meinem Gesprächspartner Reinhold Messner, der Grafikerin Petra Lüer und Rainer Arnold, meinem Projektleiter im Hirmer Verlag.
Mein weiterer Dank gilt allen jetzigen und ehemaligen Mitarbeitern, die mir bei meinen „Bergarbeiten" geholfen haben: Max Biek, Gabi Blum, Andi Fässler, Ossi Fink, Elke Härtel, Pascal Jäger, Wolfgang Kaiser, Martin Lehmer, Frank Meyer, Diego Perathoner, Anna Pfannzelt, David Regehr, Bob Schmidt, Verena Seibt, Gisbert Stach, Wolfgang Stehle und Bettina Wieler.
Für ihre Hilfe und Unterstützung sei ebenso gedankt:
Caro Angermann, Charlie Bayer, Charim Galerie, Agathe Fischnaller, Galerie Max Weber Six Friedrich, Elsa Hinrichs, Eugenie Hinrichs, Philippa Hinrichs, Raimund Kummer, Tilman von Mengershausen, Diane Messner, Roland Taferner, Lisa Ungar und Mathias Wähner.

I should like to thank the editor and author Petra Giloy-Hirtz as well as Stephan Berg and Uschi Demeter for their contributions to this book, my conversation partner Reinhold Messner, the graphic designer Petra Lüer, and Rainer Arnold, project manager at Hirmer Verlag.
I am also grateful to all current and former assistants who helped me with my 'mountain works':
Max Biek, Gabi Blum, Andi Fässler, Ossi Fink, Elke Härtel, Pascal Jäger, Wolfgang Kaiser, Martin Lehmer, Frank Meyer, Diego Perathoner, Anna Pfannzelt, David Regehr, Bob Schmidt, Verena Seibt, Gisbert Stach, Wolfgang Stehle and Bettina Wieler.
My thanks also go to the following for their help and support:
Caro Angermann, Charlie Bayer, Charim Galerie, Agathe Fischnaller, Galerie Max Weber Six Friedrich, Elsa Hinrichs, Eugenie Hinrichs, Philippa Hinrichs, Raimund Kummer, Tilman von Mengershausen, Diane Messner, Roland Taferner, Lisa Ungar and Mathias Wähner.

Nachwort
Postface

Petra Giloy-Hirtz

Ein Künstlerbuch ist es geworden. Stephan Hubers *Gran Paradiso*, assoziativer Titel eines seiner Werke und Name des höchsten Berges auf italienischem Boden, steht für all die Berge, denen er sich in seinem künstlerischen Schaffen bis heute gewidmet hat. Von Anfang seines Künstlerlebens an war er vom „Berg" fasziniert, dem er sich in über 40 Jahren künstlerischer Praxis hartnäckig in allen Facetten und Medien genähert hat: mit Skulptur, aber auch mit Zeichnung, Siebdruck, Fotografie und Buch wie mit raumfüllenden Installationen. Wie besessen von diesem Motiv – ob im Realen oder in der Fiktion, wissenschaftlich forschend und Landkarten studierend oder hingegeben an Fiktion, Einbildungskraft, Vision. Erfundenes findet sich neben den Versuchen detailgetreuer Abbildung, gleichermaßen träumend und kritisch engagiert. Große sichtbare Werke im öffentlichen Raum bis zu kleinen, in den Archiven verborgene Arbeiten versammelt die Publikation: Stephan Huber ist in seine eigene Lebensgeschichte eingestiegen. Kein Schlusspunkt, aber eine Setzung, ein Statement ist dieses Buch, keine Retrospektive, sondern eine fantastische Übersicht.

Geholfen haben dabei viele. Der Hirmer Verlag, Thomas Zuhr und Rainer Arnold insbesondere mit ihrer Faszination für das Thema, die Gestalterin des Buches, Petra Lüer, die Sammler und die Institutionen, die Bildmaterial beigesteuert haben. Und natürlich die Autor*innen mit ihren aufschlussreichen Beiträgen. Großartig, wie sich der legendäre Bezwinger der höchsten Berge der Erde und der Schöpfer von Miniatur-Berg-Skulpturen unterhalten. Reinhold Messner, der studierte Vermessungstechniker, der Extrembergsteiger und Abenteurer, der als erster Mensch die Gipfel aller 14 Achttausender bestieg, Autor, Forscher und Politiker, als der er für die Grünen fünf Jahre im Europäischen Parlament saß, versteht sich als „Bewahrer der letzten nicht urbanisierten Räume dieser Erde". Zur Sammlung des von ihm initiierten Messner Mountain Museum, sechs Häuser an sechs Orten, die mit ihren interdisziplinären Ausstellungen die

It has become an artist's book. Stephan Huber's *Gran Paradiso*, the associative title of one of his works and the name of the highest mountain in Italy, stands for all the mountains he has devoted himself to in his oeuvre. He has been fascinated by 'mountains' from the very beginning of his over forty years of artistic practice, doggedly approaching them in all their facets and in a variety of media: in sculpture, but also in drawings, silk prints, photographs, books and room-sized installations. As though obsessed by this motif, Huber explores it in reality and in the imagination, not only conducting scientific research and studying maps but also immersed in fiction, fantasy and vision. The purely invented stands next to attempts at detailed reproduction, in works that are engaged both in a sort of daydream and in a critical way. From huge sculptures visible in the public space to small works hidden in the archives, these works are featured in this publication: Stephan Huber has embarked on his own biography. This book is not a conclusion, but a continuation, a statement, not a retrospective but a fantastic overview.

Many people have helped bring it about. Hirmer Verlag, Thomas Zuhr and Rainer Arnold in particular with their fascination for the subject; the graphic designer of the book, Petra Lüer; the collectors and institutions that have contributed visual material; and, of course, the authors and their insightful essays. There is a magnificent conversation between the legendary conqueror of the highest mountains in the world and the creator of miniature mountain sculptures. Reinhold Messner, the trained surveyor, extreme mountain climber and adventurer, the first person to climb all fourteen of the world's eight-thousanders, the author, researcher and politician who sat for the Green Party in the European parliament for five years, sees himself as the 'protector of the last spaces on this earth that are not urbanised'. He founded the Messner Mountain Museum, six buildings in six different locations presenting the encounter between humans and mountains in interdisciplinary exhibitions. Their collection includes an entire group of 'mountains' by Stephan Huber.

Begegnung zwischen Mensch und Berg thematisieren, gehört eine ganze Gruppe von „Bergen" des Stephan Huber.

Stephan Berg, der Anglistik, Germanistik und Geschichte studierte, ist Kurator und seit 2008 Intendant des Kunstmuseums Bonn. Zuvor hatte er den Kunstverein Freiburg und Hannover geleitet, in dessen Räumlichkeiten er 2001 eine Einzelausstellung von Stephan Huber zeigte. In seinem Textbeitrag über das „skulpturale Gipfeltreffen" stellt er die „Berge" des Künstlers in den Kontext des Diskurses in Philosophie, Literatur und Kunst und deutet sie in seiner Analyse als „Synthese der Widersprüchlichkeit".

Uschi Demeter, freie Journalistin und Autorin, war künstlerische Projektleiterin des ersten Messner Museums Dolomites am Monte Rite. Stephan Hubers Berge sah sie zum ersten Mal auf der von Harald Szeemann kuratierten Biennale von Venedig *aAPERTutto* im Arsenale im Jahr 2001. In ihrem Beitrag erzählt sie vom aufregenden Projekt des „Museum in den Wolken", dem MMM Dolomites, und wie sie den Künstler bei seiner Installation *In die Berge schreien* im MMM Sigmundskron in Bozen unterstützt hat.

Stephan Huber hat Auswahl und Ordnung der Bilder selbst bestimmt, und hin und wieder gibt er in den Anmerkungen Kommentare zu den Hintergründen der jeweiligen Werke. Dank von allen an ihn für dieses große Unterfangen und Gratulation.

Stephan Berg, who studied history and English and German literature, has been curator and, since 2008, director of the Kunstmuseum Bonn. Previously he directed the Kunstverein Freiburg und the Kunstverein Hannover, where he mounted a solo show of Stephan Huber's work in 2001. In his essay, 'The Sculptural Summit', he situates the artist's 'mountains' within the discourse of philosophy, literature and art, analysing them as a 'synthesis of contradictions'.

Uschi Demeter, journalist and author, was the artistic project manager of the first Messner Museums Dolomites on Monte Rite. She first encountered Stephan Huber's mountains at the Venice Biennale curated by Harald Szeemann, *aAPERTutto*, at the Arsenale in 2001. In her essay she recounts the exciting project of the 'museum in the clouds', the MMM Dolomites, and how she supported the artist in his installation *In die Berge schreien* (Screaming in the Mountains) at the MMM Sigmundskron in Bolzano.

Stephan Huber has himself chosen the selection and order of the images, occasionally providing commentary on the background to the works. My thanks, and my congratulations, go above all to him for this great undertaking.

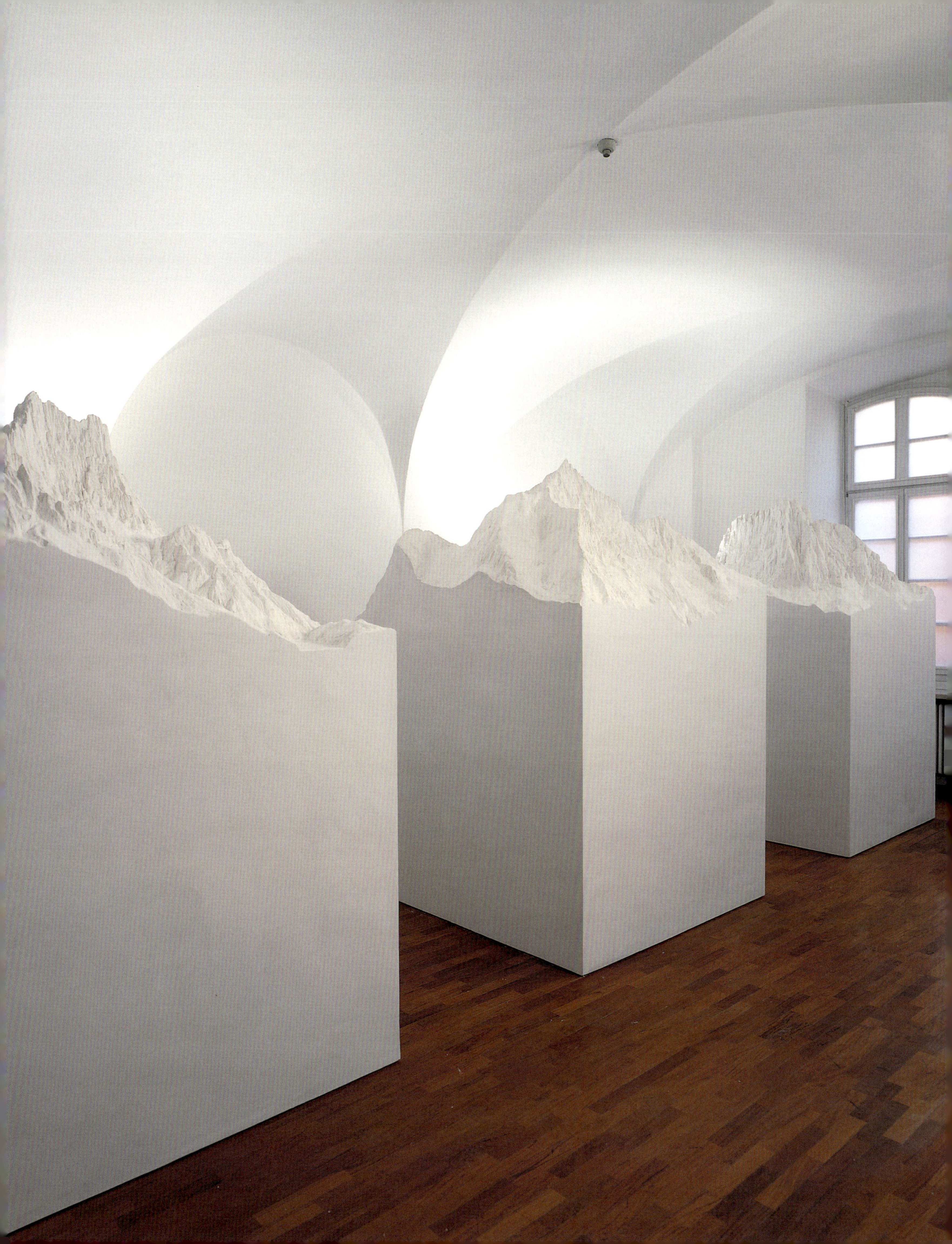

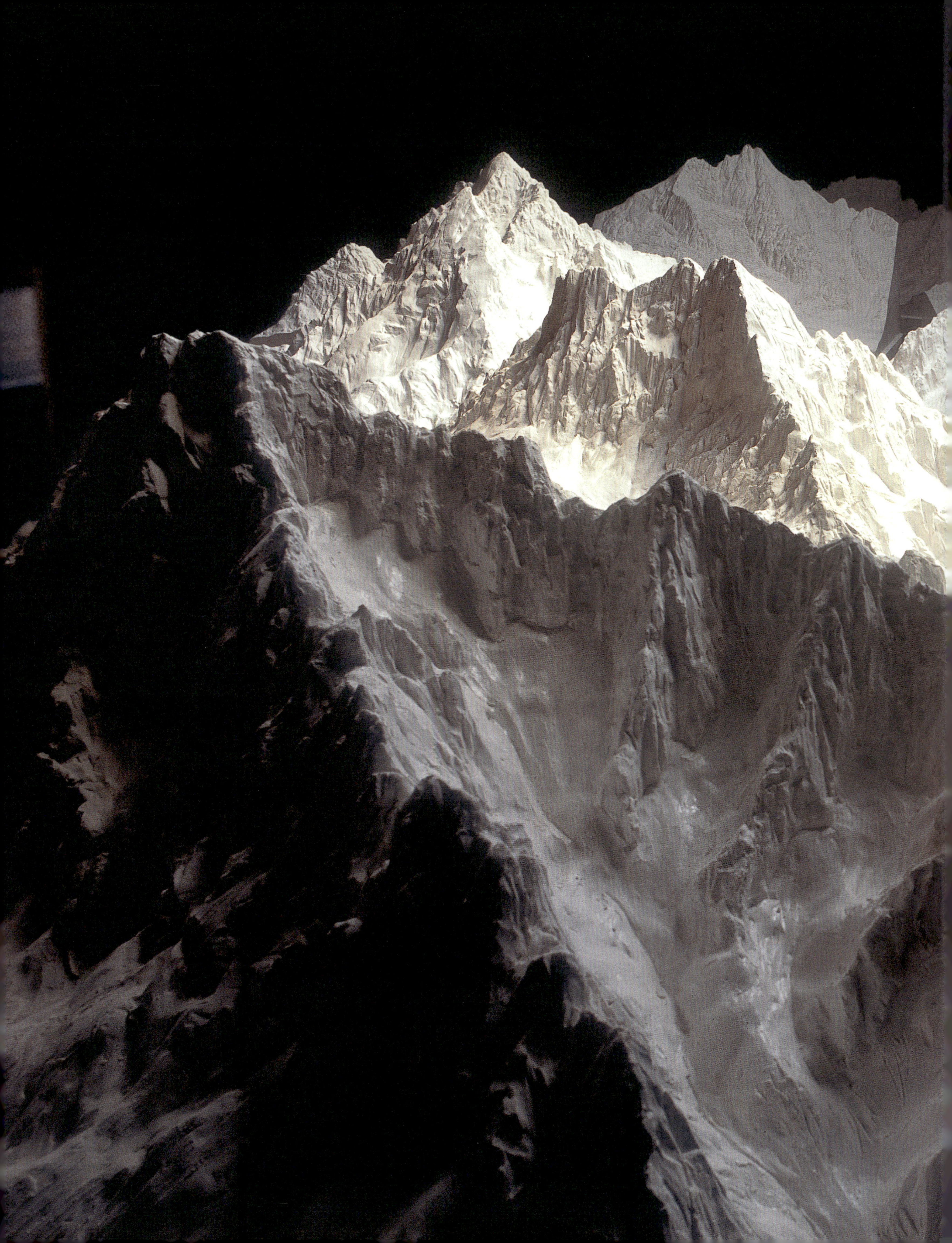

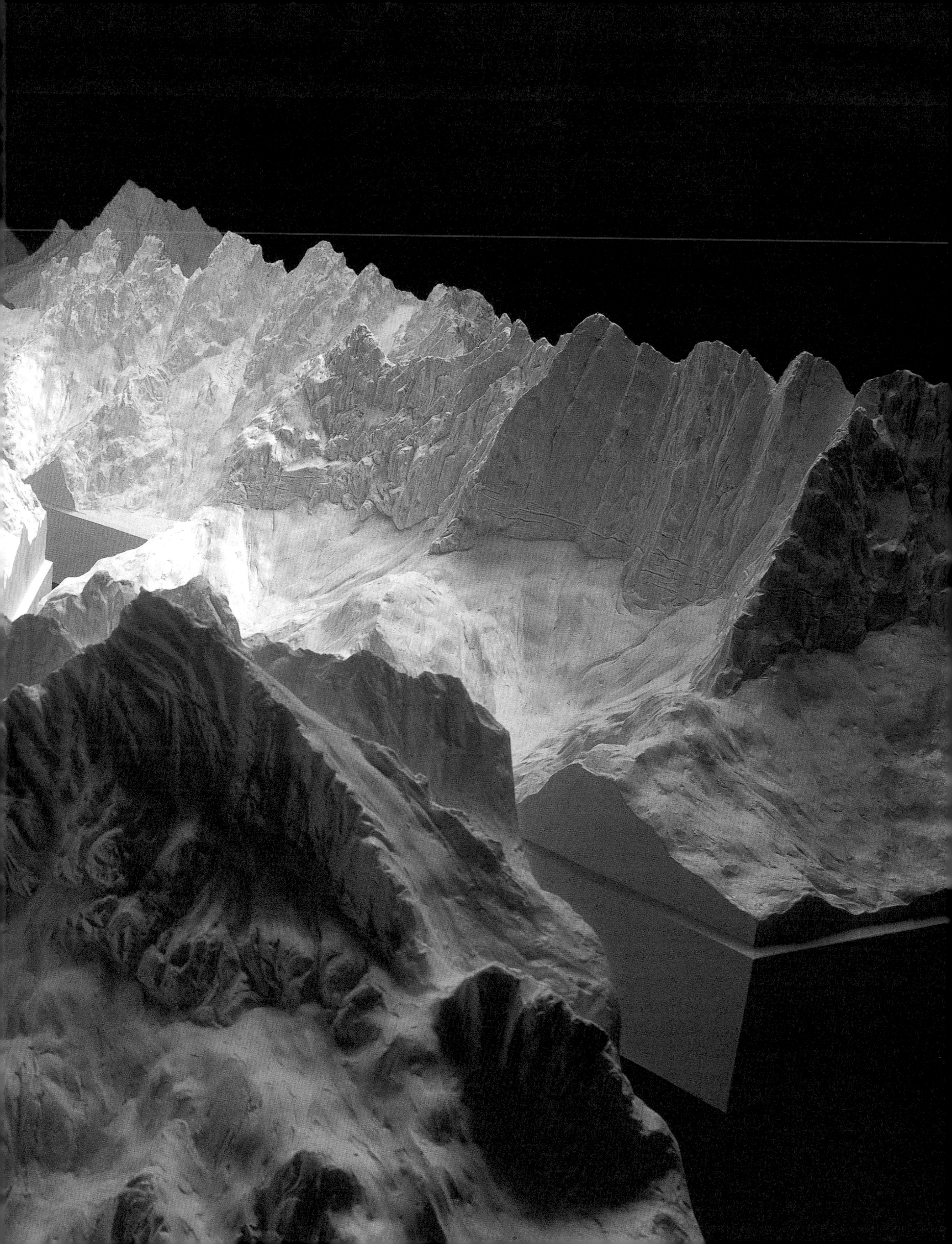

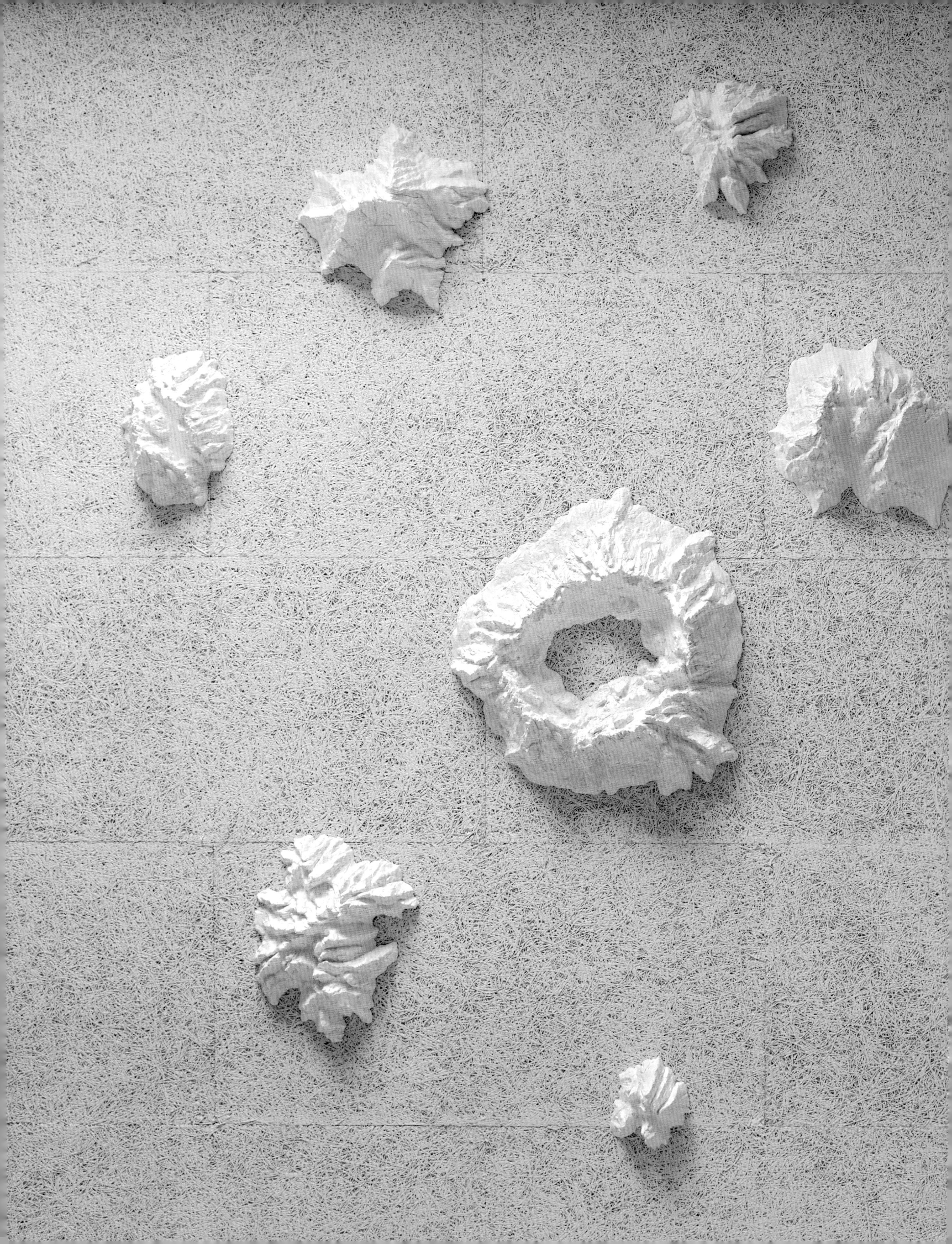